EAGLE ADRIFT

EAGLE ADRIFT

American Foreign Policy at the End of the Century

Edited by

ROBERT J. LIEBER

Georgetown University

 LONGMAN

An imprint of Addison Wesley Longman, Inc.

New York • Reading, Massachusetts • Menlo Park, California • Harlow, England
Don Mills, Ontario • Sydney • Mexico City • Madrid • Amsterdam

Acquisitions Editor: Leo A. W. Wiegman
Project Coordination and Text Design: Ruttle, Shaw & Wetherill, Inc.
Cover Designer: Scott Russo
Cover Photograph: DiMAR Interactive Corp.
Electronic Production Manager: Christine Pearson
Manufacturing Manager: Helene G. Landers
Electronic Page Makeup: Ruttle, Shaw & Wetherill, Inc.
Printer and Binder: R. R. Donnelley & Sons Company
Cover Printer: Phoenix Color Corp.

Library of Congress Cataloging-in-Publication Data

Eagle adrift: American foreign policy at the end of the century/edited
   by Robert J. Lieber.
        p.   cm.
     Includes index.
     ISBN 0-673-98269-6
     1. United States–Foreign relations–1989-   I. Lieber, Robert J.,
   1941-   .
   E840.E23   1997
   327.73—dc20   96-14445
                                                               CIP

0–673–98269–6

345678910—DOC—999897

CONTENTS
········

Preface   vii

PART I INTRODUCTION: THE DOMESTIC CONTEXT

PART II FUNCTIONAL PROBLEMS

PART III REGIONAL PROBLEMS

PREFACE

· · · · · · · · · · · · ·

Eagle Adrift is the fifth "Eagle" volume on American foreign policy over the past 18 years. The original study began in the spring of 1978 with a meeting at the Institute of International Studies at the University of California, Berkeley, and led to the publication of *Eagle Entangled* (1979)[1]. Kenneth A. Oye, Donald Rothchild, and I, along with our contributors, situated our work at the intersection between traditional U.S. foreign policy studies and more abstract international relations theory. In our writing, we aimed to assess the impact of structural change in the international system on U.S. foreign policy. Beginning with Oye's introductory essay, we identified the diffusion of power that was taking place in the post-Vietnam international environment, along with the growing importance of economic interdependence, and we analyzed the problems and strategies of adaptation adopted successively by the Nixon, Ford, and Carter administrations.

In our subsequent volumes, *Eagle Defiant* (1983) and *Eagle Resurgent?* (1987), we addressed the attempt of the Reagan administration to reassert U.S. preeminence through strategies of Reaganomics at home and the Reagan Doctrine abroad. In these studies we shared a coherent conceptual framework concerning the parameters in which foreign policy was made, the implications of a changing international environment, and the assessment of policies actually adopted.

More recently in *Eagle in a New World* (1992), published just prior to the December 1991 breakup of the U.S.S.R., we began to address the implications of fundamental structural change in the international environment confronted by the Bush administration. With the bipolar postwar order collapsing and the outlines of a new post–Cold War world only just beginning to emerge, the relative consensus among *Eagle* authors also dissipated. For example, Kenneth Oye saw more parallelism than I did regarding the costs of the Cold War for the Soviet Union and the United States, and a greater impact of the approaching end of the Cold War on reducing conflict. My own assessment of the Gulf War differed from that of Stephen Van Evera on military intervention. And Oye and Benjamin J. Cohen held divergent views over the likelihood of an emerging tripolar world economy and the costs of defections from economic multilateralism.

---

[1]The previous four *Eagle* books and their contents are listed in the Appendix to this volume.

Now, as the authors of this fifth *Eagle* volume contemplate the transformed post–Cold War and post-bipolar international system, we do so with the benefit of a longer time in which to have weighed our assessments. In this new study we incorporate the significantly increased role of domestic constraints in shaping foreign policy. More than half a decade after the end of the Cold War, it has become apparent that the disappearance of the Soviet threat has had a far more profound influence on the making of U.S. foreign policy than could have been imagined just five years ago. This has made much more difficult the formation of coherent U.S. policy across a wide range of issues.

For the first time in six decades, the United States does not face a grave international threat to its security. Fascism, World War II, and the Cold War presented a long and deadly series of external challenges, which dominated in the calculation of U.S. national interests and foreign policy. These perils, and the domestic consensus—or near consensus—on grand strategy (though not always on specific policies), fostered an unprecedented expansion of the power and scope of the federal government.

The particular domestic consequences of this diminished threat are striking. They include an erosion of presidential and executive power, and a reassertion of the Madisonian elements of the U.S. political system. These features stem from the founding of the United States in reaction against monarchical absolutism, and the preference of the framers for a constitutional system that would limit centralized executive authority. The elements are familiar to students of American Government: separation of powers, checks and balances, federalism, the restraints on executive authority embodied in the role of congress and the judiciary, and the robust interplay of domestic factions and interest groups.

The absence of threat, with its concomitant reduction in the priority for foreign affairs, makes it significantly more difficult to gain agreement with the Congress and even within the executive branch itself on coherent foreign policy measures. These changed external circumstances also result in added scope for the more personal and idiosyncratic characteristics of an administration. At the same time, countries with which the United States has had long-standing relationships are also affected. As Benjamin J. Cohen notes, the end of the Cold War has "removed the 'security imperative' to contain international commercial or financial conflicts for the sake of preserving the Western anti-Communist alliance." Although the domestic circumstances within each of these countries differ, they too tend to find that domestic priorities have taken on greater weight as they calculate international relationships in economic and security arenas.

In recognition of these changed circumstances, Part I of *Eagle Adrift* addresses "The Domestic Context." The introductory chapter analyzes the overall problem of making foreign policy without the

Soviet threat. Subsequent chapters by William Schneider and Bruce W. Jentleson evaluate public and elite opinion concerning the international role of the United States and policies toward military intervention. In Part II, "Functional Problems," Benjamin J. Cohen deals with global economic policy and challenges to America's economic security, Barry R. Posen and Andrew L. Ross analyze alternative U.S. grand strategies, and Robert Paarlberg examines the interplay between domestic and international priorities in explaining the weakness of U.S. international environmental policy. Part III, "Regional Problems," assesses the interplay of domestic and foreign determinants of policy. Chapters here deal with Russia (Stephen Sestanovich), Western Europe (Stanley Hoffmann), Japan (Steven K. Vogel), China (Edward Friedman), Latin America (Robert A. Pastor), Africa (Donald Rothchild and Timothy Sisk), and the Middle East (Steven L. Spiegel). Each of the chapters has been written specifically for this work.

Although Kenneth Oye is not an author in this volume, his important role in the four previous *Eagles* is acknowledged with gratitude, as are his comments on this project and several of its chapters. We also appreciate the opportunity afforded by the American Foreign Policy seminar at the Harvard University Center for International Affairs, chaired by Robert Paarlberg and Stanley Hoffman. A number of our chapters benefitted from presentation and discussion in that lively and valuable forum. The ornithologically inclined title for the original *Eagle Entangled* was suggested by Robert Keohane and Joseph Nye. There are multiple claims to hatching the new title and defending it against predatory competitors. However among the more convincing advocates of *Eagle Adrift* were Benjamin J. Cohen, Stanley Hoffmann, and Keir Lieber. Finally, we appreciate the role of Gerard McCauley, as well as the support and commitment of Leo Wiegman, who was our editor during the time this book was conceived and written.

Robert J. Lieber

EAGLE ADRIFT

Part

I

Introduction: The Domestic Context

1

EAGLE WITHOUT A CAUSE:
MAKING FOREIGN POLICY WITHOUT THE SOVIET THREAT
Robert J. Lieber

2

THE NEW ISOLATIONISM
William Schneider

3

WHO, WHY, WHAT, AND HOW:
DEBATES OVER POST–COLD WAR MILITARY INTERVENTION
Bruce W. Jentleson

Eagle Without a Cause: Making Foreign Policy Without the Soviet Threat

Robert J. Lieber

The end of the Cold War and the disappearance of the Soviet threat have had profound consequences, not only internationally but domestically.[1] For the first time in six decades, the United States does not face a grave international challenge to its security. Fascism, World War II, and the Cold War presented a long and deadly series of external threats that dominated in the calculation of American national interests and foreign policy.[2] These perils, and the domestic consensus—or near consensus—on grand strategy (though not always on specific policies), fostered an unprecedented expansion of the power and scope of the federal government and what Arthur Schlesinger once termed, "The Imperial Presidency."[3]

In recent years, however, the disappearance of the Soviet threat has been conducive to an erosion of presidential and executive power, and a reassertion of the Madisonian features of the American political system. These features, familiar to students of American government, include separation of powers, checks and balances, federalism, and the restraints on executive authority embodied in the role of Congress and the judiciary.[4] Their origins lie in the late eighteenth century founding of the United States, with its reaction against monarchical absolutism, and the preference of the constitutional framers for a political system that would limit centralized executive authority.

Robert J. Lieber is Professor of Government at Georgetown University and has previously taught at Harvard, Oxford, and the University of California at Davis. He is the author of six books, including Theory and World Politics *(1972),* The Oil Decade *(1986), and* No Common Power: Understanding International Relations *(3rd ed., HarperCollins, 1995). With Kenneth A. Oye and Donald Rothchild, he was co-editor and contributing author of the four previous volumes in the* Eagle *series. His current writing examines the domestic face of American foreign policy.*

Much of American constitutional history involves the tension between competing conceptions of executive power. During the past century and a half, the presidency and the executive branch have expanded their powers in response to profound domestic crises and foreign threats (the Civil War, World War I, the Depression, World War II, and the Cold War). However, postwar eras, particularly those following the Civil War and World War I, have seen at least a temporary reduction in executive power. With the disappearance of the Soviet threat and the end of the Cold War, we presently appear to be experiencing a comparable cycle.[5]

The American political system has shown itself capable of reacting forcefully to crises and external threats. The mobilization of military capacity and international leadership in the 1990–1991 case of Operations Desert Shield and Desert Storm is the most recent major example. However, in noncrisis situations, and absent the galvanizing effects of a significant external threat, the system becomes unwieldy and it is often difficult to undertake coherent policy initiatives. The absence of a threat reduces the priority and urgency of foreign affairs for most Americans and makes it significantly more onerous for the administration to gain agreement with the Congress and even within the executive branch itself on coherent foreign policy measures.

These changed external circumstances also result in more scope for the personal and idiosyncratic characteristics of an administration. Bruce Jentleson has drawn a similar distinction between *structural* and *behavioral* characteristics affecting the making of American foreign policy.[6] In the case of Clinton foreign policy, the fact that external, structural imperatives no longer dominate American grand strategy as they did during the Cold War results in increased latitude for the impact of generational change and individual behavior. For the president and most of his foreign policy team the more salient foreign policy reference points are not the role of the United States in using force to defeat Nazi Germany and Japan in World War II, nor the postwar success in containing Soviet power and rebuilding Europe and Japan, but instead the trauma of Vietnam. Indeed, a number of the administration's leading officials have been ambivalent about the Cold War itself,[7] and others—including President Clinton—were by no means unambiguous supporters of American (and United Nations Security Council) policies leading up to the Gulf War.

Absent the structural necessities imposed by the Cold War and the need to counterbalance Soviet power, these experiences and political socialization tended to leave the President and many of his closest advisors hesitant and uncertain about the use of military power, even as a companion to successful diplomacy. In the early part of the Clinton administration, the same factors helped to explain a strong preference for multilateralism even at the expense of inaction. Initially, the result was evident in areas as diverse as Somalia, Haiti, Rwanda, and Bosnia.[8]

The End of the Cold War—International Implications

Even during the height of the Cold War, American foreign policy was never made without some reference to domestic concerns. There were sometimes bitter differences over policy in the early years of the Cold War (1946–1949), the Korean War (1950–1953), Vietnam (1965–1973), and in the contrasting approaches of the Carter and Reagan administrations during the last decade of the Cold War (1977–1988). Although the president and executive branch continued to predominate in the foreign policy realm, their role came under increasing challenge from the early 1970s onward, as a result of Vietnam, Watergate, and the increased importance of international economic issues. These events tended to enhance the role of Congress and afford more access for domestic interest groups.

However, in the post–Cold War era and in the absence of an overarching foreign threat, policy across a broad array of regional and functional issues is much more heavily affected by domestic factors. Many of these make it harder to shape coherent policies and to achieve cooperation with allies or even former adversaries.

At the same time, countries with which the United States has had long-standing relationships are also affected. As Benjamin Cohen notes, the end of the Cold War has "removed the 'security imperative' to contain international commercial or financial conflicts for the sake of preserving the Western anti-Communist alliance."[9] Although the internal circumstances of America's allies and trading partners often differ, they tend to find domestic priorities taking on greater weight as they calculate international relationships in economic and security arenas. Here too, the end of the Cold War may well prove to make the extension of cooperation more difficult than originally imagined.

Half a decade after the end of the Cold War it has become apparent not only that a fundamental change has taken place in the structure of international politics, but that aspirations for a new and far more benign world order were wildly optimistic.[10] Many of those expressing such hopes attributed much of world conflict to the Cold War confrontation between the United States and the USSR and its tendency to exacerbate local struggles. Others concluded that conflict had been largely a product of Soviet actions and thus anticipated the demise of the USSR as presaging a more peaceful era. Still others blamed the United States but hoped that its less interventionist post–Cold War role would be a source of reduced conflict. From all these perspectives, however, the end of four decades of global confrontation and the demise of the bipolar structure of world politics was expected to usher in a more peaceful and orderly world system.

In practice, although conflict and war in some regions has been mitigated (for example in Central America, parts of the Middle East, and Southern Africa), other areas have experienced new or continuing hostilities (e.g., the former Yugoslavia, the Caucasus, Afghanistan, Rwanda, Somalia, Liberia). Moreover, despite a major expansion in multilateral conflict management efforts by the United Nations,[11] the results have been modest at best. Indeed, the single greatest success at multilateral cooperation to maintain international order was the conduct of a war: Operation Desert Storm, authorized by UN Security Council Resolutions and led by the United States.

And it is here that examination of the post–Cold War role of the United States becomes particularly relevant. As a series of post–Cold War crises have shown, no other single country has the ability to act so effectively on its own or to organize others in doing so. Moreover, despite the limited number of successes, existing international and regional institutions (United Nations, European Union, NATO [North Atlantic Treaty Organization], Organization for Security and Cooperation in Europe, Arab League, Organization of African Unity) have been too weak, ill-suited, or cumbersome to make a significant impact in most cases.

While the United States thus finds itself in a unique position, it has nonetheless encountered increasing problems in maintaining order or providing leadership. There exist a number of causes for this, each of them contributing to a pattern of constraints on the American role in the post–Cold War international environment. These begin with the disappearance of the Soviet threat and include the increasing weight of domestic considerations and the particular acculturation and policy choices of individual American leaders. In addition to these domestic factors, a number of international elements also create difficulties, among them problems of collective action, continuing diffusion of power and in some cases enhanced capabilities of regional actors, and the intractability of conflicts involving the modernization process and ethnic strife. Assessment of these constraints becomes important, both in understanding U.S. foreign policy behavior and because prospects for a more peaceful and stable world order are closely connected to the ability of the United States to play an effective international role.

The Cold War, for all its intensity and the dangers of superpower nuclear confrontation, produced a bipolar system with a considerable degree of stability and predictability. The stability of the bipolar world and of superpower strategic nuclear deterrence has been widely discussed elsewhere and does not require extensive elaboration here.[12] It is, however, well to recall the observation of Kenneth Waltz that, "The longest peace yet known rested on two pillars: bipolarity and nuclear weapons."[13]

In the aftermath of the Cold War, there was speculation about the likely consequences for international stability. Although Western Europe can be expected to maintain a relatively robust degree of order,[14] conditions elsewhere vary more widely and some regions face greater instability. Pierre Hassner, for example, has noted the political decomposition and anarchy that have emerged as a dominating feature in important parts of the post–Cold War world:

> The bipolar era severely limited the sovereignty and the freedom of states (particularly within the Soviet sphere). . . . Thus it was natural that communism's decline would encourage the rebirth of nations and increase their openness to external influences. What was unclear was whether the future would feature a new bipolar cleavage (this time based on a North South confrontation), a new multipolar equilibrium or global cooperation. . . . The surprise is that, although indications in the direction of each model have emerged, their course has been troubled, distorted and, in some respects, dominated by another more powerful development—political decomposition and anarchy.[15]

Moreover, as Robert Jervis has observed, areas without a recent history of stable cooperation are likely, in the aftermath of the end of bipolarity, to witness increased conflict.[16] In essence, the Cold War and nuclear deterrence not only prevented war between East and West, but the bipolar system and extended nuclear deterrence also fostered a degree of regional stability. In this regard, Erich Weede has cautioned that general nuclear deterrence prevented war between East and West, but that stability is likely to be more precarious elsewhere:

> The end of the Soviet Union and her bloc implies the abolition of extended deterrence without its replacement by another pacifying condition. Moreover, some nuclear proliferation to developing countries is to be expected. Unfortunately, the combination of precarious balances of terror with domestic instability among poor countries seems unlikely to make nuclear deterrence work as well in future as it did in the Cold War past.[17]

Immediately following the end of the Cold War, there were indications that a more stable, American-led but multilateral basis for order might emerge. With the support of the USSR, then still ruled by Secretary Mikhail Gorbachev and Foreign Minister Eduard Shevardnadze, as well as with the acquiescence of China and the active support of its allies, the United States organized and led the international response to Saddam Hussein's August 1990 invasion of Kuwait. The ousting of Iraq from Kuwait and the rout of Saddam's armed forces made abundantly clear America's preponderance of conventional forces and its unique capacity to project power. Indeed, along with the end of the Cold War and the retreat of the Soviets, these events contributed importantly to the Arab-Israeli peace process.

In retrospect, it is the uniqueness and the special circumstances of the Gulf crisis and war that stand out, rather than its place as a forerunner of the post–Cold War era.[18] Saddam Hussein was an almost uniquely brutal and unambiguous aggressor, Soviet leaders were willing to cooperate with the United States rather than use their veto in the UN Security Council, the American armed forces were at their peak after the 1980s buildup, and the administration was led by President George Bush, whose formative experiences and outlook led him to take a forceful position. However, while Bush's popularity peaked at 89 percent in the immediate aftermath of the Gulf War, public interest in foreign policy quickly dissipated with the end of the crisis and the subsequent dissolution of the USSR in December 1991. Despite a series of important foreign policy accomplishments, including successfully managing the end of the Cold War and the unification of Germany within NATO, the Bush administration met electoral defeat over domestic issues in the 1992 election.[19] In essence, with the rapid disappearance of major external threats, whether in the form of the long-standing Cold War or the military challenge from Saddam, and even before the onset of the Clinton administration, the domestic and international environment for American foreign policy had been radically recast.

The Concept of Threat in International Relations

Politics among nation-states differs intrinsically from politics *within* most states because of the absence in the international system of any formal, binding authority with the power to resolve inevitable disputes. As a consequence, the system is "anarchic." The term does not connote chaos, but instead designates the absence of government.[20] Moreover, because of this formal anarchy and the lack of any real common power with the ability to ensure security for states in the international environment, states find themselves living in what is termed a self-help system. As a result they face the necessity to prepare to defend their national interests by military or other means, or they must find ways of achieving the same objective through alliances or by obtaining the support of stronger powers.

The structure of the international system thus creates propensities shaping state behavior. While individual countries and their leaders retain considerable latitude in matters of diplomacy, international politics, and security, the nature of this system influences their behavior and constrains their choices. A particular consequence of the system involves what has become widely known as the security dilemma. As a consequence of anarchy, as well as because the relative gains of other states may jeopardize their own security,[21] states have a propensity to arm to protect themselves. However, this action creates incentives for others to act similarly, resulting in potentially greater insecurity to all. The problem is depicted concisely by Glenn Snyder:

> Even when no state has any desire to attack others, none can be sure that others' intentions are peaceful, or will remain so; hence each must accumulate power for defense. Since no state can know that the

power accumulation of others is defensively motivated only, each must assume that it might be intended for attack. Consequently, each party's power increments are matched by the others, and all wind up with no more security than when the vicious cycle began, along with the costs incurred in having acquired and having to maintain their power.[22]

Despite these conditions of formal anarchy, the self-help system and the security dilemma, countries do nonetheless find it possible to cooperate with one another. As a consequence, a substantial body of literature has developed in which the problem of "cooperation under anarchy" is addressed.[23] In some circumstances, cooperation may be the product of deliberate strategies by leaders and governments, as well as result from democratization or modernization. Cooperation can also be a response to the demands of existence in an open international economy in which the means for satisfying national needs are no longer primarily to be found within the borders of the state, but require instead joint action with other states as well as active involvement in international regimes and institutions.

A number of studies of alliance behavior have suggested that states are particularly motivated to cooperate to balance a powerful threat, rather than merely to do so in response to power per se.[24] This is consistent with the logic of Kenneth Waltz and others, who find that the threat posed by a strong and aggressive state tends to motivate others to form coalitions against it. In this sense, there is evidence that balancing dominates bandwagoning.[25] This was not only the case for countries threatened by the Soviet Union, but a similar tendency can be observed in response to the threats posed in the past by Louis XIV, Napoleon, Kaiser Wilhelm, and Hitler.

An external threat shapes state behavior in two ways. Internationally, other things being equal, it makes the threatened states more receptive to cooperation with one another to provide for their common security. When set against a greater threat posed by a major outside power, the importance of lesser, pre-existing disputes among them tends to recede in contrast. Moreover, with national security perceived to be at risk as a consequence of external threat, there are also domestic consequences. In essence, major foreign threats can affect the choices of policy elites as well as public opinion more broadly. These changes make it easier for states to enter into cooperation and alliances without the degree of domestic criticism for costs incurred (political as well as financial) that would otherwise exist.

The nature of the Soviet Union and the threat that it posed made the United States willing to bear the military and economic costs of cooperation with the European allies. The same security concerns kept the Europeans involved, despite differences with the United States and a series of recurring disputes with the Americans and each other. It is thus not surprising that, with the end of the Cold War, American leaders sometimes expressed nostalgia for the more "stable and predictable" pattern of that time, as in the widely cited remarks by Deputy Secretary of State Lawrence Eagleburger in September 1989.[26] Comparable sentiments have continued to be expressed by policymakers. Thus, commenting in June 1993, Secretary of State Warren Christopher could connect the inability of the United States to achieve allied cooperation in Bosnia to the disappearance of the Soviet threat, and contrast this with an earlier era:

> I think in a bipolar situation where it was life and death, and there was a question as to whether or not they survived in a struggle—possible struggle—with Russia, then the United States could simply let its views be known, and the allies in Europe had little choice but to go along.[27]

Even President Clinton, reacting to the October 1993 debacle in Mogadishu, could exclaim, "Gosh, I miss the Cold War."[28]

Indeed, as Daniel Deudney and John Ikenberry observe, the pervasiveness of international conflict beginning in the 1940s (i.e., including World War II and the start of the Cold War) enabled the United States not only to build a strong state, but to foster domestic social cohesion and reduce social inequalities. In their view, the end of the Cold War not only has implications for the international role of the United States, but poses serious internal dangers as well:

> The end of the Cold War threatens to unravel those accomplishments and return the United States to the impasses of the 1920s and 1930s. If modernization and democratization at home were accidental side effects of the global struggle, then sustaining the institutional legacy of the process may well be beyond the capacity of the American political system."[29]

In any case, the end of the Cold War also affects the ability of the United States to cooperate with its allies. In the past, the Soviet threat and the existence of an American-led bloc to contain it placed limits on the degree of friction that could develop among the Western partners and Japan. The need to cooperate in the face of the Soviets meant that disagreements in economic and other realms were prevented from escalating beyond a certain point because of the perception that too bitter an intra-allied confrontation could only benefit their adversary and thus weaken common security.[30]

In the aftermath of the Cold War, Europe, Germany, and Japan are better off in security terms, but the disappearance of the common threat as well as domestic economic problems, make it more difficult for them to agree with the United States or each other on matters of shared interest. This has been evident in disagreements over the Balkans, responses to terrorism, trade policy, and measures to combat proliferation.

The problem American policymakers face in gaining cooperation among former allies is more acute in dealing with former adversaries. During the Cold War, though the clash over basic values and interests was severe, there was little doubt that any agreement reached between Moscow and Washington would not only effectively bind the two parties but their blocs as well. In the post–Cold War era, however, not only does the weakness and chaos of the truncated Russian state make it harder to reach or implement agreements between Washington and Moscow, but the prospect that erstwhile members of the two blocs will follow can never be taken for granted. Moreover, the specific problems of Russia, Ukraine, and other former republics of the USSR and ex-members of the Warsaw Pact make it more difficult for the United States to ensure that agreements, for example in nonproliferation, will be implemented.

Finally, the United States faces new potential obstacles affecting its ability to intervene militarily. In the Middle East, for example, the presence of missiles and chemical and biological weapons could raise the cost of military intervention in the event of a crisis that would otherwise call for the dispatch of troops.[31] Nuclear weapons in the hands of regional actors would increase this peril by orders of magnitude. Indeed, had Saddam Hussein delayed invading Kuwait until his nuclear weapons program had come to fruition, the United States would have found it far more difficult to organize the UN coalition against him or to achieve the defeat of Iraqi forces with miraculously light U.S. and Allied casualties.

Problems of Coherent Foreign Policymaking

American public opinion after the Cold War has not become isolationist. However, it does accord a far lower priority to foreign policy than at any time in the past half-century. Only 9 percent of voters in the 1992 presidential election listed foreign policy as among the top two issues influencing their vote.[32]

The quadrennial poll taken in October 1994 by the Chicago Council on Foreign Relations showed foreign policy comprising the lowest number of overall problems since 1978 for the public and the lowest among leaders since the Council began its polling in 1974. While the same survey found 65 percent of the public and 98 percent of the leaders in favor of the United States taking an "active part in world affairs," no threat had emerged comparable to that of the former Soviet Union,[33] and the priority accorded to foreign affairs declined greatly.

Opinion polls during 1995 indicated that as few as 2 to 4 percent of Americans identified foreign policy as the most important issue facing the country. An August 1995 poll found only 4 percent identifying foreign policy as the biggest problem facing the country,[34] and a Gallup poll late in the year produced a mere 2 percent, as contrasted with responses of 20 to 27 percent during the mid-1980s.[35] Coupled with the factors cited above, this has made it more difficult for any administration to implement coherent and timely foreign policies.

The difficulty is not confined to the use of force, but encompasses a wide range of economic and environmental issues as well. As Benjamin Cohen notes, the domestic political system has become increasingly fragmented with the ebb of authority from the executive branch toward the Congress. This has given greater scope for the influence of particularist, regional, and sectional interests in decision-making.[36]

For example, as Robert Paarlberg observes, the Clinton administration was unable to deliver on international environmental commitments made during the 1992 presidential campaign. Despite the strong, unambiguous nature of the Clinton-Gore election pledges and solid Democratic majorities in both houses of Congress during the administration's first two years in office, it could not implement proposals to meet carbon-dioxide emission standards under the Rio Treaty, nor gain Senate ratification of the Biodiversity Convention.[37] Environmental measures lacked the urgency and consensus that might have enabled the administration to win congressional agreement on a proposed energy tax or overcome the problem of gaining a two-thirds majority for Senate ratification.

Indeed, domestic priorities have tended to overshadow foreign policy across a wide array of issues. This has been evident, for example, in policymaking toward China (business interests predominated over human rights and proliferation concerns when most favored nation status was being decided), debt relief for Jordan as an accompaniment to its peacemaking with Israel (Congress was slow to authorize the amounts requested by the administration), Haiti (the role of human rights groups and the Congressional Black Caucus proved influential), Africa (domestic groups and interests have sometimes shaped policy),[38] and international environmental issues (as Paarlberg has shown).

The Clinton presidency in foreign policy has become emblematic of these changed domestic circumstances. Clinton himself campaigned for office by emphasizing domestic issues, particularly the economy, and his priorities in office reflected that fact. In addition, commitment of additional time and political capital to the foreign policy realm did not offer evident political advantages. Not only were a number of the most pressing problems without self-evident solutions, but those Americans for whom foreign policy was a priority tended to favor Republicans in any case. As evidence of this, among those for whom foreign policy was a priority in the 1992 elections, 87 percent supported George Bush.[39]

The absence of an external threat, with its concomitant reduced priority for foreign affairs, thus makes it significantly more difficult to gain agreement with the Congress, and even within the executive branch itself, on coherent foreign policy measures. These changed external circumstances also result in more latitude for the personal and idiosyncratic characteristics of an administration.[40]

In the case of Clinton foreign policy, this includes a highly personalistic and sometimes indecisive decision-making style, described by Fred Greenstein:

> Related to Clinton's energy, enthusiasm, intelligence, and devotion to policy is a cluster of more problematic traits—absence of self-discipline; hubristic confidence in his own views and abilities; and difficulty in narrowing his goals, ordering his efforts, and devising strategies for advancing and communicating the ends he seeks to achieve.[41]

The effect of personality on foreign policy was initially exacerbated by the policy machinery the administration put in place. As Arnold Kantor has noted, this process incorporated a broader concept of foreign policy priorities beyond national security, but it left "primarily to the president himself the task of managing the strong centrifugal forces it generates."[42]

Upon taking office as President, Clinton was at first reluctant to devote sustained and regular attention to foreign affairs. Indeed, in October-November 1993, Secretary of State Warren Christopher, Secretary of Defense Les Aspin, and National Security advisor Anthony Lake sent memoranda to the president urging him to give them one hour a week (sic) for the discussion of foreign affairs. Clinton finally agreed, but to his "yes" added the words, "When possible."[43] His relative disinterest in foreign policy also was evident in a long interview that the president gave to Haynes Johnson who had been preparing a book on the first year of his presidency. In the author's account of it, there was not a word on foreign policy, not even on NAFTA (North American Free Trade Agreement).[44]

Not only was there limited domestic incentive for the Clinton administration to give higher priority to foreign policy, but the experience of the president and those around him tended to pull them in the opposite direction. As noted earlier, whereas George Bush's generation saw America's world role as marked by the failure of isolationism in the 1930s, and by successes in defeating Nazi Germany and Japan in World War II and subsequently containing the Soviet Union, the Clinton generation's formative experiences included the Vietnam debacle, the destruction of the Lyndon Johnson presidency that became entrapped in it, and aversion to the use of force.

Foreign policy could not be entirely de-emphasized, however, since public opinion polls showed that perceived weaknesses in Clinton foreign policy contributed to disapproval not only of presidential performance in that area, but of the administration itself.[45] This sentiment was particularly pronounced among white male voters, expressed in terms of, "I don't want my president to feel my pain, I want him to get tough with North Korea."[46]

As the post–Cold War era lengthens, the choices for the United States become more varied and often less self-evident. The uncertainties to which this gives rise have been visible in a number of ways, for example in the initial tendency of both the Bush and Clinton administrations to defer to the Europeans over Bosnia and the former Yugoslavia.[47] President Clinton, referring to the conflict less than 100 days into his administration observed that "The United States should lead. . .," but added, "I do not think we should act alone, unilaterally. . . ."[48] Nor was this view unique to the administration. Senator Robert Dole, then the Republican minority leader in the Senate, was more explicit. Although favoring the use of force in Bosnia, Dole cautioned, "I don't think we just act unilaterally, even if we are the only superpower left."[49]

Within the American foreign policy bureaucracy, officials expressed even stronger reservations. Although President Clinton and Secretary of State Christopher continued to speak of the American commitment to a "strong leadership role abroad,"[50] Undersecretary of State Peter Tarnoff caused a controversy by telling journalists that the Clinton administration expected to withdraw from many foreign policy leadership roles customarily assumed by the United States. His remarks, later partially disavowed by the secretary of state, included a pessimistic assessment of American capabilities: "We simply don't have the leverage, we don't have the influence, the inclination to use military force. We don't have the money to bring positive results anytime soon."[51]

In a concerted effort to define administration foreign policy, the president, Secretary of State Christopher, and National Security Advisor Anthony Lake delivered a series of addresses in September 1993. As expressed in Lake's words, the successor to the doctrine of containment "must be a strategy of enlargement . . . of the world's free community of market democracies." This strategy entailed four components: (1) "strengthen the community of major market democracies," (2) "foster and consolidate new democracies and market economies where possible," (3) "counter the aggression and support the liberalization of states hostile to democracy," and (4) "help democracy and market economies take root in regions of greatest humanitarian concern."[52]

While the values expressed in these speeches seemed admirable, the connection to actual policies was not self-evident, and the administration found itself on the defensive over a series of early policy failures and abortive interventions. These included inability to gain allied agreement to lift the arms embargo against the Bosnian Muslims and to bomb the Serbs in Bosnia in May 1993; the loss of 18 Army Rangers in Mogadishu, Somalia on October 3, 1993; and the decision to recall a ship, the *Harlan County*, carrying U.S. military personnel to Haiti after demonstrations in Haiti on October 12, 1993.[53]

Frustrations over the inability to achieve a coherent and effective policy, however, became particularly evident as the Bosnian situation worsened. Thus, in lamenting what he termed, "the greatest collective failure of the West since the 1930s," the Clinton administration's chief policy official for Europe, Assistant Secretary of State Richard Holbrooke, complained that he was flailing against "a gigantic stalemate machine" that produces "watered-down policy," a decision-making apparatus run by people incapable of making decisions.[54] The consequences of this policy failure, however, were appalling. As Stanley Hoffmann has written, drawing a comparison with a seemingly bygone era, "Those of us who grew up in the 1930s and were later told about the lessons of Munich believed that appeasement of aggression would not be repeated. We were wrong."[55]

The Clinton propensity for talking about policy without necessarily arriving at specific policy decisions was evident as the ongoing Bosnian crisis worsened and threatened to impact on his campaign for re-election. In the midst of his third full year as president, Clinton could say to his aides, "The status quo is not acceptable. We've got to really dig in and think (sic) about this."[56]

Although the United States had played an active role as part of the Contact Group of major powers (with Russia, Britain, Germany, and France), and had brokered a March 1994 federation agreement ending the war between Croats and Muslims, the administration had preferred to leave matters within the United Nations context. However, by the spring of 1995, and with intensified fighting in the region, pressure to act had become compelling. On March 20, 1995, the Bosnian Army, which had slowly been gaining strength, launched a major offensive against Serb positions in Northeast Bosnia. On May 1, the increasingly well-armed and trained Croatian army captured the Croatian Serb enclave of Western Slavonia. In late May, after the Serbs had bombarded Sarajevo, NATO began limited air strikes. These were immediately halted, however, after the Bosnian Serbs seized some 350 UN peacekeepers as hostages.

The impotence of the UN effort was now palpable, and the inaction of the administration was becoming untenable. Yet, in reaction to the Serbs' hostage taking and killing of civilians, President Clinton told a reporter, "I would ask [Boris Yeltsin] to call the Serbs and tell them to quit it, and tell them to behave themselves."[57] By this time, in frustration with administration policies and events in the region, both houses of Congress (including a majority of House Democrats) voted to lift the arms embargo against Bosnia and thus repudiate the administration's long-standing policy.[58] Frustration among the European allies was also mounting. In an unusually undiplomatic remark, the newly elected French president, Jacques Chirac, declared on Bastille Day that the position of leader of the free world was now "vacant."[59]

On July 11, 1995, Bosnian Serbs overran the besieged Muslim town of Srebrenica while hundreds of Dutch UN troops stood by. A similar enclave at Zepa was taken two weeks later, amid reports that the Serbs had carried out massacres of some 8,000 Bosnian men and boys from the two towns. It now appeared that U.S. forces might have to be used in potentially dangerous missions to evacuate beleaguered UN peace-keepers, who had failed to stop the fighting or protect civilians.

At this point, a change in the region and in U.S. policy began to crystallize. On August 4, 1995, the Croatian Army successfully launched a massive offensive, quickly retaking the Krajina region and precipitating the flight of tens of thousands of Croatian Serbs. A week later, President Clinton sent Assistant Secretary of State Richard Holbrooke to the region on a new peace mission and with enhanced authority to act. When Serb shelling on August 28, 1995 killed 37 civilians at the market in Sarajevo, the U.S. and NATO, with strong support from President Chirac, finally launched massive and sustained air stikes against Bosnian Serb positions.

Bosnian Serb leaders, under air attack from NATO, ground assault from Croat and Bosnian forces, and pressured by Serbian President Milosevic, agreed to a ceasefire and the movement of heavy weapons away from Sarajevo. Subsequent peace talks in Dayton, Ohio, orchestrated by Holbrooke and Secretary Christopher, produced a peace agreement among the Presidents of Bosnia, Croatia, and Serbia. The document was initialed on November 21, 1995 and subsequently signed by the parties in Paris.

Despite strong reservations in Congress and a divided public opinion, the administration pledged to dispatch 20,000 U.S. troops as part of a 60,000 member NATO peacekeeping force. The president was determined to send the troops for a one-year period, based on traditional understandings of his constitutional authority, but the administration only narrowly prevailed against efforts to cut off funds for this purpose. The measure failed by a margin of just 218 to 210 in the House of Representatives, though by a wider margin of 77 to 21 in the Senate.[60] Meanwhile, public opinion polls showed 58 percent of Americans preferring that U.S. troops be kept out of the Balkans, as against 36 percent who found it the right thing to do.[61]

In essence, with its domestic and international credibility at stake, and in response to changes on the ground, the administration had at last acted decisively. Only the United States possessed the capacity to provide this kind of international leadership, though the unique circumstances and long-delays, as well as the considerable perils in Bosnia itself, made this case far from one that foreshadowed a transformed American role.

Moreover, beyond the policies of any one administration, the ability of the United States to lead effectively in Bosnia, as in other multilateral security efforts, was constrained by an exceptional national sensitivity to casualties. In the post–Cold War environment of reduced threat, evidence of this sensitivity can be found in the horrified domestic reaction to the body of an American soldier being dragged through the streets of Mogadishu in October 1993.

The rubric for American intervention since Vietnam has been bluntly described, in the words of William Schneider, as "Win quickly or get out."[62] Interventions in Panama and Grenada during the 1980s succeeded at a domestic level because the Reagan administration could indeed win quickly and at little cost. The more costly Reagan era intervention, in Lebanon in 1983–1984, did not prove to be a domestic political liability because the administration opted to extract the Marines rather than remain in a potential quagmire. From this standpoint, the Bush-led intervention against Iraq's takeover of Kuwait also succeeded because of a clear goal, light U.S. casualties, and the rapid withdrawal of forces after the 100-hours war. Had the conflict proved to be of longer duration, however, and the casualties significantly higher, the ability of the administration to maintain public and congressional support might well have been called into question. Indeed, it is worth remembering that congressional resolutions authorizing President Bush to use force against Iraq, in support of the UN Security Council mandate, only passed the Senate by the narrow margin of 52 to 47.

These attitudes do not by any means rule out the use of force. Overall, as Bruce Jentleson has observed, the public has been more prudent than gun-shy. Public support for military intervention has been greater when the main objective has been to coerce foreign policy restraint by an aggressor state, when there has been a clear military strategy, and when the policy has been made a priority by the president and Congress.[63]

Domestic constraints on the ability of the United States to act effectively abroad have, however, increased significantly in the years since the end of the Cold War. Just as the disappearance of the Soviet threat has made it significantly harder to gain agreement among allies, so it has also made it more difficult to gather sufficient public and congressional support for ambitious foreign policy measures, whether these involve the possible commitment of troops abroad, funds for foreign assistance and UN peacekeeping, or even an active and assertive foreign policy posture. Whereas the perceived peril of the Cold War made it possible for American presidents to mobilize national and governmental resources, the reduced sense of urgency permitted the strong reassertion of domestic priorities and a concentration on efforts to address previously neglected problems at home.

In the case of Congress, this emphasis on domestic concerns has been further reinforced by the influx of new members for whom the Cold War was not part of their national political experience. Indeed, as a result of the 1990, 1992, and especially the 1994 elections, more than half the members of the U.S. House of Representatives had been elected after the opening of the Berlin Wall.

The budgetary impact has been particularly acute. The Clinton administration's own initial efforts to reduce the federal budget deficit were subsequently overshadowed by more sweeping spending cuts proposed by the Republicans in Congress after they captured both houses in the November 1994 elections. Although the defense budget was actually given a slight increase above levels proposed by the administration, the effect elsewhere was to increasingly constrain the foreign affairs budget. Long-standing pressure to reduce foreign aid was intensified, even though U.S. spending in 1994 amounted to only 0.15 percent of Gross Domestic Product (GDP) and was already the lowest among the 25 member countries of the Organization for Economic Cooperation and Development (OECD).[64] The impact extended well beyond traditional foreign aid, however. For example, debt relief for Jordan, as an accompaniment to King Hussein's signing of a peace treaty with Israel, was delayed and then forthcoming at levels below what had been initially anticipated. Similarly, contemplating the unlikelihood of major assistance to Syria if it were to make peace with Israel, in contrast to the aid Egypt and Israel received after their 1979 peace treaty, the Chairman of the House Appropriations Subcommittee on Foreign Operations, Representative Sonny Callahan (R-Alabama) observed flatly, "There is no money."[65]

Beyond budget issues, Congress also proved an increasing obstacle to the execution of foreign policy. With Republicans having gained a Senate majority in the November 1994 elections, Senator Jesse Helms became Chairman of the Foreign Relations Committee. In disputes with the administration, he withheld action on dozens of ambassadorial appointments and blocked Senate action on such major international agreements as the Chemical Weapons Convention and the START II strategic arms reduction treaty. While far from uniform in their foreign policy views, congressional Republicans were united in what one experienced journalist termed an "intense dislike of and lack of respect for Clinton."[66] This sentiment was reflected in the opposition of all 73 House Republican freshmen to the initial proposal for a financial bailout of Mexico in January 1995, even though the idea was supported by Speaker Newt Gingrich.[67]

Conclusion: Eagle Without a Cause

Characteristics of the international system and its structure, including the security dilemma and external threats, create propensities for states and their policymakers to act in certain ways, but these represent influences rather than iron laws of human behavior.[68] Hence the policies of individual American leaders do come into play. The international environment of 1945–1947 created conditions favoring a particular course of action, but ultimately it was the Truman administration that had to make specific choices, as for example in the Truman Doctrine, the Marshall Plan, containment, and the decision to intervene in Korea. More than four decades later, in the first major crisis of the post–Cold War era, considerable latitude was available for the Bush administration. In determining American policies after Saddam Hussein invaded

Kuwait in August 1990, Bush opted to lead an allied and United Nations coalition against Iraq, but the ultimate policy choices were by no means obvious at the start of the crisis.[69]

With the end of the Cold War, the reassertion of domestic priorities, the weakening of executive authority, and the problem of achieving international cooperation in the absence of a common threat make the shaping of foreign policy more difficult and constrained for any American administration. In addition, the absence of an unambiguous external threat makes it harder to mobilize elite and public support for implementing foreign policy measures and for paying the costs which these can entail.

Indeed, one area in which American foreign policy has tended to be coherent and effective, the Middle East, has been so in large part because of the continued relevance of potential threats to U.S. vital interests. Based on the three criteria identified by the Secretary of Defense for determining whether a threat affects U.S. vital interests (a threat to the survival of the United States or its key allies, a threat to critical U.S. economic interests, or the danger of a future nuclear threat), both the Arab-Israeli arena and the Persian Gulf provide a close fit.[70] Indeed, continuity was evident not only in structural terms (external threat) but also in the behavioral realm (where there was extensive stability of policies and personnel from the Bush to the Clinton administrations).

In other areas, however, American leadership also remains fundamental and there does exist some degree of latitude for policy choice. At the same time, there is little evidence of any effective substitute for American leadership in organizing collective action. In its absence, the more likely alternative is not that other countries or institutions will do so, but that there will instead be inaction and a greater degree of international instability and conflict.[71] For example, in the post–Cold War environment, cooperation on the part of major powers in seeking to limit proliferation, maintain a liberal international trade regime, or bring peace to Bosnia is unlikely to be sustained without an active, ongoing American role. Though nonhegemonic regime maintenance may be possible under some circumstances (as in the case of the European Union), ad hoc efforts, understandings, and weak organizational bodies are unlikely to be effective in the absence of American leadership.

The risks are not only those of political instability and military conflict. As Benjamin Cohen points out, for half a century, noncommunist governments maintained and extended a postwar liberal economic order despite forces of parochial nationalism. Economic conflict was kept manageable because of a shared security concern and the memory of economic breakdown in the 1930s. But the benefits of commercial and financial interdependence seem increasingly jeopardized due to the end of the Cold War and the risk that state actors will be tempted to want a "free ride" in their economic relations. Moreover, the redistribution of economic power among states has reduced the will and ability of the United States to bear as large a share of the costs of economic leadership as it did in the past.[72] As Paarlberg notes, "There is no longer a cold war security imperative to inspire generous economic policy leadership from the United States or to ensure that rival market economies will follow the U.S. lead."[73]

Whether the United States will be able and willing to sustain its political, military, and economic role remains at issue. There is little evident alternative to American leadership, yet even with this leadership the prospects for effective peacekeeping, conflict resolution, and economic order are by no means assured. In the emerging post–Cold War international system, however, unless there emerges (or re-emerges) some clear unambiguous threat, or there appears a set of policymakers unusually determined to give priority to foreign policy even within existing post–Cold War constraints, the ability of the United States to act effectively in this realm—under a Clinton administration or its successors—remains uncertain.

Endnotes

1. An earlier version of this chapter was presented as a paper, "Domestic Constraints on American Foreign Policy in the Post–Cold War World," at the 91st Annual Meeting of the American Political Science Association, August 30–September 3, 1995, Chicago, Illinois; in the American Foreign Policy seminar at the Harvard Center for International Affairs; and in the Government Department "brown bag" seminar at Georgetown University. For comments I wish to thank Robert Art, Robert Paarlberg, Stanley Hoffmann, Karl Kaiser, Celeste Wallander, Tony Smith, Kenneth Oye, Benjamin Cohen, Michael Mandelbaum, Fouad Ajami, Keir Lieber, Bruce Jentleson, Thomas Banchoff, Joseph Lepgold, Barry Posen, Aharon Klieman, William Schneider, Victor Cha, Chester Crocker, David Newsom, and Michael Pinto-Duschinsky.

2. *See, for example,* Henry A. Kissinger, *Diplomacy* (New York: Simon & Schuster, 1994), pp. 832–835; also Robert Tucker, "The Prior Question," *The National Interest,* No. 40 (Summer 1995): 108–112.

3. Arthur M. Schlesinger, Jr., *The Imperial Presidency* (New York: Houghton Mifflin, 1973).

4. Clinton Rossiter discusses James Madison as an exponent of limited government, in Alexander Hamilton, James Madison, John Jay, with an Introduction by Clinton Rossiter, *The Federalist Papers* (New York: Mentor/New American Library, 1961), p. xv. *See especially Federalist No. 10. Also see* George W. Carey, *The Federalist: Design for a Constitutional Republic* (Urbana, IL: University of Illinois Press, 1989).

5. This includes a struggle between what Bruce W. Jentleson has referred to as presidentialists and congressionalists. *See* "Who, Why, What, and How: Debates Over Post–Cold War Military Intervention," Chapter 3 in this text, pp. 41–42."

6. Jentleson has drawn a similar distinction between "structural" and "behavioral" characteristics affecting the making of American foreign policy. "Who, Why, What and How: Debates Over Post–Cold War Military Intervention," p. 41.

7. Henry Kissinger has criticized Deputy Secretary of State Strobe Talbott for writing in *Time* magazine in 1990 that the Cold War had been unnecessary and that a more

conciliatory Western policy would have ended it decades earlier. *See* Henry Kissinger, "It's an Alliance, Not a Relic," *Washington Post*, August 16, 1994, p. A19; also Kissinger, "For U.S. Leadership, a Moment Missed," *Washington Post*, May 12, 1995, p. A25.

8. Elsewhere, Michael Mandelbaum has described events in Somalia, Bosnia, and Haiti during the first nine months of the Clinton administration as "failed military interventions" that "set the tone and established much of the agenda of the foreign policy of the United States from 1993 through 1995." See "Foreign Policy as Social Work," *Foreign Affairs*, Vol. 75, No. 1 (January/February 1996): 26–33, at 26.

9. "'Return to Normalcy?': Global Economic Policy at the End of the Century," Chapter 4 in this text, p. 74.

10. Portions of this and subsequent sections incorporate material from Robert J. Lieber, "Constraints on American Foreign Policy in the Post–Cold War Era," International Political Science Association XVI World Congress, Berlin, August 21–25, 1994; "American Hegemony, Regional Security and Proliferation in the Post–Cold War International System," Conference on The National Security of Small States, Bar-Ilan Center for Strategic Studies, Bar-Ilan University, and The Leonard Davis Institute for International Studies, Hebrew University of Jerusalem, April 5–7, 1994; and "The Sources of Western Cooperation in the Cold War—and After and the Role of the Soviet Threat, Conference on East-West Relations: Confrontation and Detente, Ruhr-Universitat Bochum, September 22–25, 1993.

11. For a listing of UN peacekeeping operations, *see* Lieber, *No Common Power: Understanding International Relations* (New York: HarperCollins, 3rd ed., 1995), pp. 275–282.

12. Among others, *see* Kenneth N. Waltz, "The Stability of a Bipolar World," *Daedalus*, Vol. 93, No. 3 (Summer 1964), and "The Emerging Structure of International Politics," *International Security*, Vol. 18, No. 2 (Fall 1993): 44–79; John Gaddis, "The Long Peace," *International Security*, Vol. 10, No. 4 (Spring 1986); Robert J. Lieber, "The United States and Western Europe in the Post–Cold War World," in Kenneth Oye, R. Lieber, and D. Rothchild (eds.), *Eagle in a New World: American Grand Strategy in the Post–Cold War Era* (New York: HarperCollins, 1992), pp. 315–334.

13. Waltz, "The Emerging Structure of International Politics," p. 44.

14. For a less sanguine view, *see* John J. Mearsheimer, "Back to the Future: Instability in Europe After the Cold War," *International Security*, Vol. 15, No. 1 (Summer 1990). Much of the literature on this subject also incorporates Central and Eastern Europe. *See, for example,* Stephen Van Evera, "Primed for Peace: Europe After the Cold War," *International Security*, Vol. 15, No. 3 (Winter 1990–1991); Charles A. Kupchan and Clifford A. Kupchan, "Concerts, Collective Security, and the Future of Europe," *International Security*, Vol. 16, No. 1 (Summer 1991); and Richard K. Betts, "Systems for Peace or Causes of War? Collective Security, Arms Control, and the New Europe," *International Security*, Vol. 17, No. 1 (Summer 1992.)

15. Pierre Hassner, "Beyond Nationalism and Internationalism: Ethnicity and World Order," *Survival*, Vol. 35, No. 2 (Summer 1993): 49–65, at 50.

16. Robert Jervis, "The Future of World Politics: Will it Resemble the Past?" *International Security*, Vol. 16, No. 3 (Winter 1991/1992): 39–73.

17. Erich Weede, "Conflict Patterns During the Cold War Period and Thereafter," paper presented at Conference on The Impact of Global Political Change on the Middle East, Haifa University, May 4–6, 1993), p. 1. Also *see* Weede, *Economic Development, Social Order, and World Politics* (Boulder: Lynne Rienner, 1996), p. 145; and Benjamin Frankel, "The Brooding Shadow: Systemic Incentives and Nuclear Weapons Proliferation," *Security Studies*, Vol. 2, No. 3/4 (Spring/Summer 1992).

18. Michael Mandelbaum argues that the successful role played by the United States in the Gulf crisis was not the model for the new post–Cold War era, but instead, "the

last gasp of a morally and politically clearer age." *See,* "The Reluctance to Intervene," *Foreign Policy,* No. 95 (Summer 1994): 3–18, at 3.

19. As early as January 1992, 11 months prior to the election, a Gallup/*USA Today* poll found national defense ranked as number 14 of 15 issues for discussion and debate in the 1992 presidential campaign. Daniel Yankelovich and John Immerwahr, "The Rules of Public Engagement," in Yankelovich and I. M. Destler (eds.), *Beyond the Beltway: Engaging the Public in U.S. Foreign Policy* (New York: Norton, 1994), pp. 44–45.

20. *See, for example,* Kenneth N. Waltz, "Because some states may at any time use force, all states must be prepared to do so. . . . Among states, the state of nature is a state of war." Also, "A national system is not one of self-help. The international system is." *Theory of International Politics* (New York: Random House, 1979), pp. 102 and 104. In addition, Hans J. Morgenthau, "there can be no permanent peace without a world state. . . ." *Politics Among Nations* (New York: Knopf, 5th ed., 1978), p. 560. *And see* the discussion of anarchy in Lieber, *No Common Power* (3rd ed., 1995), pp. 5–6.

21. On the importance of relative versus absolute gains, *see, in particular,* Joseph Grieco, "Anarchy and the Limits of Cooperation: A Realist Critique of the Newest Liberal Institutionalism," *International Organization,* Vol. 42, No. 3 (Summer 1988): 485–508; Robert Jervis, "International Primacy," pp. 54–56; Robert Powell, "Absolute and Relative Gains in International Relations Theory," *American Political Science Review,* Vol. 85, No. 4 (December 1991): 1303–1320; Waltz, *Theory of International Politics,* pp. 105–106.

22. Glenn H. Snyder, "The Security Dilemma in Alliance Politics," *World Politics,* Vol. 36 (July 1984): 461. The original use of the term, "security dilemma" was by John H. Herz, *Political Realism and Political Idealism* (Chicago: University of Chicago Press, 1951.) Also see Robert Jervis, "Cooperation Under the Security Dilemma," *World Politics* (January 1978): 167–214.

23. *See, in particular,* Kenneth A. Oye, (ed.), *Cooperation Under Anarchy* (Princeton: Princeton University Press, 1986), especially Oye's contribution, "Explaining Cooperation Under Anarchy: Hypotheses and Strategies," pp. 1–24.

24. *See* the argument of Stephen M. Walt, *The Origins of Alliances* (Ithaca, NY: Cornell University Press, 1987). *In addition, see* Walt, "Alliances in Theory and Practice: What Lies Ahead?," *Journal of International Affairs* (Summer/Fall 1989), Vol. 43, No. 1: 1–17.

25. As a concept, "bandwagoning" originates with Stephen Van Evera. Kenneth Oye discusses and applies the concepts in "Constrained Confidence and the Evolution of Reagan Foreign Policy," in Oye, Lieber, and Donald Rothchild (eds.), *Eagle Resurgent? The Reagan Era in American Foreign Policy* (Boston: Little, Brown, 1987), p. 21. *Also see* Waltz, *Theory of International Politics,* pp. 125–126. However, Christopher Layne puts more emphasis on the existence of power itself, rather than on an explicit threat, in stimulating the rise of competing power. *See* "The Unipolar Illusion: Why New Great Powers Will Rise," *International Security,* Vol. 17, No. 4 (Spring 1993): 9–15.

26. Speaking at Georgetown University on September 13, 1989, Eagleburger observed that, "For all its risks and uncertainties, the Cold War was characterized by a remarkably stable and predictable set of relationships among the great powers." Quoted in Michael R. Beschloss and Strobe Talbott, *At the Highest Levels: The Inside Story of the End of the Cold War* (Boston: Little, Brown, 1993), p. 106.

27. Quoted in Steven A. Holmes, "Backing Away Again, Christopher Says Bosnia is Not a Vital Interest," *New York Times,* June 4, 1993, p. A12.

28. Quoted in Jentleson, "Who, Why, What, and How," p. 65.

29. Daniel Deudney and G. John Ikenberry, "After the Long War," *Foreign Policy,* No. 94 (Spring 1994): 21–36 at 23. Also, Deudney and Ikenberry, "America After the Long War," *Current History,* Vol. 94, No. 595 (November 1995): 364–369, at 364.

30. Kenneth Oye elaborates on this point in, "Beyond Postwar Order and the New World Order," in Oye, Lieber, and Rothchild, *Eagle in a New World: American Grand Strategy in the Post–Cold War Era* (New York: HarperCollins, 1992), pp. 3–33. Note too the argument of Stephen Walt that states balance against threats rather than versus power per se. *See The Origins of Alliances* (Ithaca: Cornell University Press, 1987), p. 5. By implication, the disintegration of the threat represented by the Soviet Union removes the basic impetus for NATO's existence. On the other hand, Russia does remain the most powerful state on the European continent and concerns about its future policies provide sufficient motivation for the Western countries to retain their alliance rather than abandon it altogether. *Also see* Gunther Hellman and Reinhard Wolf, "Neorealism, Neoliberal Institutionalism, and the Future of NATO." *Security Studies*, Vol. 3, No. 1 (Autumn 1993): 2–43.

31. Lewis A. Dunn, "Rethinking the Nuclear Equation: The United States and the New Nuclear Powers," *The Washington Quarterly*, Vol. 17, No. 1 (Winter 1994): 5–25, at 5; and Brad Roberts, "From Proliferation to Antiproliferation," *The Washington Quarterly*, Vol. 16, No. 3 (Summer 1993): 139–173, at 155.

32. Source: Voter Research and Surveys. Election day poll conducted by a consortium of CBS, NBC, ABC, and CNN.

33. Chicago Council on Foreign Relations, *American Public Opinion and U.S. Foreign Policy 1995* (Chicago, 1995), pp. 6 and 21. Concern about unfriendly countries becoming nuclear powers led the list of "critical threats" (cited by 72 percent of the public and 61 percent of leaders), followed by immigration (public 72 percent, leaders 31 percent), and international terrorism (public 69 percent, leaders 33 percent).

34. *New York Times*/CBS poll, cited in *New York Times*, October 1, 1995.

35. Steven Kull, "What the Public Knows that Washington Doesn't," *Foreign Policy*, No. 101 (Winter 1995–1996), 124.

36. Benjamin J. Cohen, "'Return to Normalcy?'", p. 74.

37. The Convention was signed by a U.S. representative on June 4, 1993 and sent to the Senate five months later. It was never submitted to a floor vote because 35 Republican Senators, one more than needed to defeat the Treaty, had decided to oppose it. Robert Paarlberg, "Earth in Abeyance: Explaining Weak Leadership in U.S. International Environmental Policy," Chapter 6 in this text, p. 139. The case also illustrates Putnam's observation that the requirement to secure domestic approval is "a crucial theoretical link" between the two levels of international and domestic bargaining. *See* Robert D. Putnam, "Diplomacy and Domestic Politics: The Logic of Two-Level Games," *International Organization*, Vol. 42, No. 3 (Summer 1988): 427–460, at 436.

38. Donald Rothchild and Timothy Sisk elaborate on this in, "U.S.-Africa Policy: Promoting Conflict Management in Uncertain Times," Chapter 13 in this text, p. 276.

39. Voter Research and Surveys, November 3, 1992.

40. Bruce Jentleson has drawn a similar distinction between "structural" and "behavioral" characteristics affecting the making of American foreign policy. "Who, Why, What, and How," p. 40.

41. Fred I. Greenstein, "The Presidential Leadership Style of Bill Clinton: An Early Appraisal," *Miller Center Journal*, Vol. 1 (Spring 94): 13–23, at 16.

42. Arnold Kantor, "Adapting the Executive Branch to the Post–Cold War World," in Yankelovich and Destler, p. 152.

43. Richard Reeves, "Why Clinton Wishes He Were JFK," *Washington Monthly*, Vol. 27, No. 9 (September 1995): 16–20, at 19.

44. Stephen E. Ambrose, *Foreign Affairs*, Vol. 73, No. 4 (July/August 1994): 168–169, reviewing Haynes Johnson, *Divided We Fall: Gambling with History in the Nineties* (New York: Norton, 1994).

45. A lack of public confidence in President Clinton's handling of foreign policy has been reported as undermining the public's belief in the president's ability to make

sound decisions. A May 1994 poll indicated that a majority of Americans disapproved of Clinton's handling of foreign policy. Of those interviewed, 53 percent disapproved and only 40 percent approved. *See* Dan Balz and Richard Morin, "Public Losing Confidence in Clinton Foreign Policy," *Washington Post*, May 17, 1994, p. A1.

46. Thomas B. Edsall, "Pollsters View Gender Gap as Political Fixture," *Washington Post*, August 15, 1995, pp. A1, A11.
47. Critics of the Clinton administration argued that it had failed to provide sufficiently forceful leadership in making the case to the Europeans for air strikes and a lifting of the arms embargo. Secretary of State Christopher's May 1993 visit to Europe was described as having given the appearance of inviting a negative reaction by allied leaders, and President Clinton was faulted as "taking cover behind the veil of the United Nations," in complaining he could not adopt the policy he wanted in Bosnia because the United Nations and America's allies would not let him. *See* Thomas L. Friedman, *New York Times*, June 20, 1993, p. E1.
48. Excerpts from Clinton's news conference, April 23, 1993, text as published in *The New York Times*, April 24, 1993, p. A7.
49. Quoted, *New York Times*, April 24, 1993, p. A6.
50. *Washington Post*, May 25, 1993, pp. A1 and A24.
51. Remarks by a "senior official," later identified as Peter Tarnoff, quoted in *Washington Post*, May 26, 1993.
52. *See* "National Security Advisor Anthony Lake's Speech at Johns Hopkins University, September 21, 1993," in *Foreign Policy Bulletin*, Vol. 4, No. 3 (November/December 1993): 39–46. For President Clinton's address to the UN General Assembly, September 27, 1995, and Secretary Christopher's speech at Columbia University, September 20, 1993, *see* Ibid., pp. 49–53 and 36–39.
53. Michael Mandelbaum emphasizes the importance of these three "failed military interventions." *See* "Foreign Policy as Social Work," especially pp. 16–26.
54. *New York Times*, August 12, 1995, p. 5.
55. Stanley Hoffmann, "What Will Satisfy Serbia's Nationalists?" *New York Times*, December 4, 1994, p. E19.
56. Stephen Engelberg, "How Events Drew U.S. Into Balkans," *New York Times*, August 19, 1995, p. A1.
57. Quoted, *The New Republic*, June 19, 1995, p. 8.
58. The House vote was 318 to 99. *See Washington Post*, June 9, 1995.
59. Chirac's comment was made on July 14, 1995, and is quoted in *The Washington Post*, December 3, 1995, p. A34.
60. *See*, Katherine Q. Seelye, "Senate and House Won't Stop Funds for Bosnia Force," *New York Times*, December 14, 1995, p. A1.
61. Data cited in R. W. Apple, "Flimsy Bosnia Mandate," *New York Times*, December 14, 1995, p. A1.
62. Schneider finds that "If a vital national interest is at stake, Americans want to take action that is swift, decisive, and relatively cost-free. " 'Rambo' and Reality: Having it Both Ways," in Kenneth A. Oye, R. Lieber, and D. Rothchild (eds.), *Eagle Resurgent? The Reagan Era in American Foreign Policy* (Boston: Little, Brown, 1987), p. 59.
63. Jentleson, "Who, Why, What, and How"; *also see* Jentleson, "The Pretty Prudent Public: Post-Vietnam American Opinion on the Use of Military Force," *International Studies Quarterly*, Vol. 36, No. 1 (March 1992): 49–73.
64. The figures were from an OECD report. *New York Times*, April 8, 1995, p.4.
65. *Washington Post*, March 16, 1995, p. A30.
66. Robert S. Greenberger, "Dateline Capitol Hill: The New Majority's Foreign Policy," *Foreign Policy*, No. 101 (Winter 1995–1996): 166.
67. Ibid.

68. On the concept of propensities that result from the structure of the international system in shaping state behavior, see Lieber, "Existential Realism After the Cold War," *The Washington Quarterly*, Vol. 16, No. 3 (Winter 1991–1992): 156–157.

69. For example, Chairman of the Joint Chiefs of Staff, Colin Powell, initially opposed efforts to liberate Kuwait and was cautious about the use of military force, preferring to concentrate on defending Saudi Arabia and relying on sanctions to pressure Iraq. Michael R. Gordon and Bernard E. Trainor, *The Generals' War: The Inside Story of the Conflict in the Gulf* (Boston: Little, Brown, 1995), pp. 33, 36, 130.

70. The three criteria are set out in a Department of Defense report defining U.S. interests and commitments in the region. The report adds, "Nowhere are these criteria met more clearly than in the Middle East." *See, United States Security Strategy for the Middle East* (Washington, DC: Office of International Security Affairs, Department of Defense, May 1995), p. 5.

71. Samuel Huntington makes a similar point: "A world without U.S. primacy will be a world with more violence and disorder and less democracy and economic growth than a world where the United States continues to have more influence than any other country in shaping global affairs." "Why International Primacy Matters," *International Security*, Vol. 17, No. 4 (Spring 1993): 68–83, at 83.

72. Cohen, "Return to Normalcy," p. 77. Elsewhere, however, Cohen has noted that a reversion to severe mercantilism is inhibited by three countervailing forces: the existence of international regimes, domestic constituencies, and cognitive changes (i.e., the understanding that economic closure is less viable as an option).

73. Robert Paarlberg, *Leadership Abroad Begins at Home: U.S. Foreign Economic Policy After the Cold War* (Washington, DC: The Brookings Institution, 1995), p. 2.

Chapter 2

The New Isolationism

William Schneider

These days, no one much argues with the view that the United States must be active in the world to protect its own economic and security interests. "Pearl Harbor ended isolationism for any realist," Senator Arthur Vandenberg said during World War II.

He was right. The Chicago Council on Foreign Relations has been surveying the U.S. public's views on foreign policy since 1974. In the latest survey, taken in October 1994, two thirds of Americans said the United States should take an active part in world affairs. Less than one in three said we should "stay out."[1]

The number of Americans who believe the United States plays a more important role as a world leader today compared to ten years ago is at its highest level ever. And almost three-quarters believe the United States will play a greater role as a world leader in the next ten years.

Nevertheless, the charge of isolationism is still heard in the land. "There is a struggle now going on," President Clinton said to a foreign affairs conference in March 1995, "between those of us who want to carry on the tradition of American leadership and those who would advocate a new form of American isolationism."

"Who, us?" the Republicans reply. "No siree." House Speaker Newt Gingrich told the same conference, "The United States must lead. There's no replacement. I didn't say dictate. I didn't say dominate. I said lead." Senate majority leader Bob Dole echoed the same theme. "You pay a price for leadership. But in my view, it's a price worth paying."

So where's the isolationist challenge coming from? Democrats argue that because Republicans reject multilateralism, they are becoming de facto isolationists. As the President put it, the new isolationists

William Schneider is political analyst for Cable News Network and a resident fellow at the American Enterprise Institute. He writes a syndicated column for National Journal *and the* Los Angeles Times *Syndicate.*

"trumpet the rhetoric of American strength" and then "eliminate any meaningful role for the United Nations," "deny resources to our peace-keepers" and "refuse aid to the fledgling democracies and to all those fighting poverty and environmental problems that can literally destroy hopes for a more democratic, more prosperous, safer world."

Indeed, Republicans proposed cutting foreign aid, reducing U.S. funding of UN peacekeeping operations, requiring congressional approval for U.S. troops to participate in peacekeeping missions and banning the deployment of U.S. soldiers under foreign command. President Clinton threatened to veto those measures.

Republicans insist that unilateralism is not isolationism. They argue that the United States must determine its own purposes in the world and act on its own interests. We cannot derive them from other countries or from international organizations. *We*, not the United Nations, must decide whether it is in our national interest to bring democracy to Haiti or relief to Somalia. *We*, not NATO, must decide whether it is in our national interest to stop the slaughter in Bosnia.

If this were simply an argument about multilateralism, Republicans would lose. In the Chicago Council survey, support for strengthening the United Nations as "a very important foreign policy goal of the United States" was 51 percent, its highest level in 20 years. A majority supported U.S. participation in international peacekeeping forces. Fewer than 1 in 5 said we should not take part. The public was split over whether we should accept a commander appointed by the United Nations or insist that a U.S. commander be put in charge of peacekeeping operations.

Public support for NATO also remained high. Indeed, a plurality of Americans believed NATO should be expanded to include Poland, Hungary, and the Czech Republic, "thereby committing the United States to defend them against attack in the same way as we are committed to defending Western Europe."

When it comes to U.S. purposes in the world that are not clearly self-serving, however, internationalists have a problem. Since the end of the Cold War, support for a *nonself-interested* American foreign policy has dropped sharply.

- Support for "protecting weaker nations against foreign aggression" as a very important U.S. foreign policy goal fell 33 points from 1990 to 1994, to its lowest level in 20 years.
- "Protecting and defending human rights in other countries" fell 24 points, to its lowest level since 1978.
- "Defending our allies' security" was down 20 points.
- "Helping to improve the standard of living of less developed nations" fell 19 points. In 1994, only 22 percent of Americans called that a very important foreign policy goal. The previous low, 35 percent, was recorded during the economic crisis of the mid-1970s.

- "Helping to bring a democratic form of government to other nations"—never a widely supported goal—declined to its lowest level of public support since 1974.

At the same time, *self-regarding* foreign policy goals such as protecting American jobs, securing energy supplies, preventing the spread of nuclear weapons, and even promoting free trade all gained public support.

A Times Mirror survey taken in June 1995 confirms the Chicago Council's findings. On three separate tests, internationalism prevailed over isolationism. But all three tests showed isolationist sentiment growing.

Almost three-quarters of the public agreed that in its foreign policy decisions, the United States "should take into account the views of its major allies." Just 18 percent disagreed. But agreement was at its lowest level since 1976, just after the Vietnam war.

By almost two to one, Americans rejected the view that the United States "should go our own way in international matters, not worrying too much about whether other nations agree with us or not." But the 34 percent who endorsed that view represented the highest figure recorded in over 20 years.

Should the United States "mind its own business internationally and let other countries get along the best they can on their own?" "No," the public responded, but only barely—51 percent answered in the negative and 41 percent answered in the positive. Again, that's the highest level of agreement since the survey's inception in 1974, tying the 41 percent affirmative response measured in 1976.

How can political leaders deal with this growing isolationism? They can evade it. They can defy it. Or they can exploit it. One can find examples of each response in the foreign policy experiences of the Clinton era, starting with the 1992 campaign itself.

Foreign Policy in the 1992 Campaign

Foreign policy was conspicuously missing from the 1992 campaign. It was partly because the election was, famously, about little more than "the economy, stupid." But it was also because the Establishment candidates, George Bush and Bill Clinton, didn't really want to hear what the voters had to say. It wasn't a good year for Establishment candidates to defend their internationalist values. So they evaded the issue.

Remember that Bush and Clinton were both challenged by protest candidates in the 1992 primaries. Jerry Brown and Pat Buchanan positioned themselves as anti-Establishment populists. Isolationism is a theme with powerful populist appeal, and both Brown and Buchanan used it. Bush and Clinton tried their best to avoid a debate on the topic because they were afraid they might lose.

By refusing to engage Buchanan in a full-scale foreign policy debate, Bush protected himself, as evidenced by the network exit poll[2] of Republican primary voters in Illinois and Michigan on March 17, 1992. Republican voters who endorsed the view that "the United States should stop worrying about other countries and put America first" voted for Bush over Buchanan by better than 2 to 1 in Michigan and by better than 3 to 1 in Illinois. Bush was fortunate that they did, because over 70 percent of Republicans in both states agreed with the statement.

Both Brown and Buchanan opposed the Persian Gulf War. Both attacked the free trade agreement with Mexico. Both wanted to cut American troop strength in Europe (Brown to a token 1000 troops). Both opposed foreign aid. Brown said he "wouldn't give a penny" to foreign aid "until every small farmer, businessman, and family" in the United States is taken care of. While Bush condemned Buchanan's isolationism, he did not try to engage his opponent on the issue. Instead, he ran an ad in Michigan attacking Buchanan for driving a Mercedes-Benz.

Clinton, too, is an internationalist. He called for a "strategy of American engagement" abroad. But he was careful to defend aid to Russia in terms of America's self-interest. Clinton said it would "save us billions in lower defense costs forever" and "increase trade opportunities dramatically." He also tried to sound tough on trade. Clinton said in Michigan that he would not approve a free-trade agreement with Mexico without "the elevation of labor and environmental standards on the other side of the Rio Grande."

The outlines of the difference between Bush's internationalism and Clinton's internationalism began to become clear during the campaign. Both reflected the political reality of growing isolationism. Bush favored a hegemonic role for the United States, along the lines of the Persian Gulf War. The United States would be the ultimate guarantor of world order and stability. Our aim, according to a Pentagon document, would be "to discourage [other countries] from challenging our leadership or seeking to overturn the established political and economic order." We'll supply the muscle. They'll supply the money. It was hegemony on the cheap.

Clinton's internationalism was more multilateral. He envisioned a "United Nations rapid-deployment force" to deal with threats to the peace. He was also more concerned with economic development, environmental protection, and human rights. But his ideas for a "Democracy Corps" and "America Houses" would involve spending very little money. It was democracy on the cheap.

In the end, when it came to foreign policy, Clinton never laid a glove on Bush. On election day, according to the network exit poll, the 8 percent of voters who said foreign policy was the issue that determined their vote selected Bush over Clinton at a ratio of 11 to 1.[3]

The Western Alliance

President Clinton's triumphant European tour in January 1994 seemed to defy the new isolationism. But on closer examination, the policy of evasion was still apparent.

In Brussels, President Clinton told the NATO allies what they needed to hear. Despite the collapse of the Soviet Union, the President said, "The core of our security remains with Europe." Clinton told the NATO secretary-general what he needed to hear about Bosnia. "We'll see if our resolve is there," the President said of the allies. "My resolve is there, I can tell you."

Next Clinton went to Prague and told the nervous Eastern Europeans what they needed to hear. "The question is no longer whether NATO will take on new members," the President said, "but when and how." Then Clinton traveled to Russia and told Boris Yeltsin what he needed to hear. He called for "a genuine equal partnership with a strong and free Russia."

One group was left out, however. The president did not tell the American people what they needed to hear. According to the White House, President Clinton went to Europe to offer a defining vision of American foreign policy in the post–Cold War era. The trip was billed as an historic moment, comparable to the announcement in 1947 of the Truman Doctrine committing the United States to the containment of communism.

President Truman, however, made a dramatic appearance before a joint session of Congress. But President Clinton kept foreign policy on the back burner.

What was Clinton's new vision? Here is how the president described it in Brussels: "The old security was based on the defense of our bloc against another bloc. The new security must be found in Europe's integration—an integration of security forces, of market economies, of national democracies."

President Clinton wanted to expand the U.S. commitment to Europe, both geographically and strategically. Geographically, he wanted to commit the United States to the security of *all* of Europe, including Russia. Strategically, our mission in Europe would become both offensive and defensive.

Our offensive mission would be to do everything possible to ensure the success of reform in Russia and Eastern Europe. As Clinton put it, "Our security in this generation will be shaped by whether reform in these nations succeeds."

Our defensive mission would be to hold back the rising tide of nationalism in the East. That's *nationalism*, not communism. We still need NATO, the president said, because "the dream of empire still burns in the minds of some who look longingly toward a brutal past." The new NATO doctrine was to be one of "pre-containment": work for reform, prepare for aggression.

The problem was that without a communist threat, Americans were in a mood to disengage. The new Clinton Doctrine, however, went in the opposite direction. It enlarged the U.S. commitment beyond Western Europe and beyond containment. Could President Clinton lead America into this brave new world?

The president's speeches in Europe may not have been intended to sell at home. More likely, their purpose was to reassure the Europeans and the Russians—and keep foreign policy off the domestic political agenda. After all, the president did not commit the United States to a major new economic aid package to Russia. He offered the Eastern Europeans only a junior partnership with NATO. He did threaten air strikes in Bosnia, but only after elaborate procedures were followed to obtain agreement with the allies and the United Nations.

Were Americans ready to make a stronger commitment to Europe? In principle, yes. But not if the costs were spelled out.

A CNN-*USA TODAY* Gallup poll taken in January 1994 asked whether various Eastern European countries should be allowed to join NATO: Poland, Hungary, Lithuania, the Czech Republic, Romania, Bulgaria, and Albania. In every case, the answer was yes. In fact, 54 percent felt Russia should be allowed to join. But did the public understand the implications? Were they willing to put American lives at risk to protect Bulgaria or Bosnia?

The poll asked Americans what they thought the United States and its NATO allies should do if Russia sought to regain control of Eastern Europe by force. Only 27 percent said send troops. That's exactly what we would be obliged to do if Eastern Europe were part of NATO. In the case of Bosnia, two-thirds opposed sending U.S. troops there, even as part of a NATO operation.

How far would Americans go to ensure the success of economic reform in Russia? Economists have long contended that Russian reformers can not succeed without substantial foreign assistance. Once again, the Truman administration provided a model. The Marshall Plan subsidized the postwar reconstruction of Western Europe. In 1947, however, American ties to Europe were written in blood. And the communist threat was real and menacing.

In 1994, most Americans said Russia was not a military threat to the United States. In fact, two-thirds described Yeltsin as an ally. But were Americans willing to send money to Russia to reduce their deficit, or to take care of their jobless? The answer was no. Almost 60 percent of Americans opposed sending more aid to Russia.

President Clinton set a high standard for himself. He said in Brussels, "History will judge us, as it judged with scorn those who preached isolationism between the World Wars, and as it has judged with praise the bold architects of the trans-Atlantic community after World War II."

But the internationalism of the Truman Doctrine did not come naturally to the American people. The population had to be mobilized. And that could only be done by the president. Truman did it after World War II. Bush did it during the Persian Gulf crisis. But Clinton never made the effort to mobilize American public sentiment behind his doctrine of engagement in Europe. It would have been a difficult and costly political fight.

Trade

At about the same time, President Clinton exploited the priority of U.S. self-interest in the area of trade. He said in his 1994 budget message,"We have put our economic competitiveness at the heart of our foreign policy." Then he backed it up with a full-court press on trade relations with Japan.

After trade talks between the United States and Japan broke down in February 1994, the president saw an opportunity to get tough with Japan. United States Trade Representative Mickey Kantor threatened Japan with trade sanctions for violating a 1989 agreement to open its market to American cellular phones. The message was, "no more Mr. Nice Guy."

It was a smart political play. Clinton had made many political enemies over the ratification of NAFTA in 1993. His critics said he wasn't tough enough on trade, that he was selling out the interests of American workers.

But former President Jimmy Carter warned the administration that "counterproductive sanctions" could have "extremely serious consequences." Writing in *The New York Times*, the house organ of the political Establishment, Carter recommended the ultimate establishment solution: a committee of "wise men . . . respected senior statesmen knowledgeable about life and politics in both countries," to advise the United States and Japanese governments on how to smooth over trade frictions. In the past, Carter wrote, when a committee of "wise men" made recommendations, their views "carried great weight and helped remove the stigma of politicization."

President Clinton's point was that maybe it's time to try a different approach—tough talk, threats, and maybe a little "politicization."

"America for ten years tried 30 different trade agreements," the president told a radio audience, "and nothing ever happened. The trade deficit just got bigger and bigger. So we're going to try to pursue a more aggressive policy now which will actually open markets."

President Clinton's aggressive trade policy paid off on another front. During the same month, the president announced that Saudi Arabia would buy $6 billion worth of commercial jet aircraft from American companies—and none from European companies.

The President hustled for that deal. He pitched it to the Saudi ambassador in person and King Fahd by telephone and by letter. He sent two cabinet secretaries to Riyadh. He put together an attractive financing deal through the Export-Import Bank.

And he reminded the Saudis that the United States had come to their defense in 1990 when they were threatened by Saddam Hussein. Remember when Secretary of State James Baker said that what the United States was fighting for in the Persian Gulf was "jobs, jobs, jobs"? Well, the payoff did come. Only too late to save George Bush's presidency.

No president had ever been that aggressive about promoting U.S. business interests abroad. And business leaders were suitably appreciative. Boeing chairman Frank Shrontz told a rally in Seattle, "Never before in my memory have we had such pro-active support from our federal government in helping level the international playing field for American industry."

The President's critics cried that there was government interference and managed trade. President Clinton appeared to them like a small-state governor hustling business for his state. So what? The president had an answer for his critics—a $6 billion aerospace contract.

The Mexican Loan Guarantee

In the case of the 1995 Mexican loan guarantee, President Clinton followed precisely the opposite strategy. He defied public opinion. But that situation, too, demonstrates the power of populist isolationism. The political Establishment had lost so much legitimacy that it had to govern by decree. That was the larger meaning of President Clinton's decision to issue an executive order bailing out the Mexican economy. It was a bold and desperate action, which was driven by the bleak prospect of getting Congress to approve a $40 billion loan guarantee package.

One would think the President of the United States, backed by the chairman of the Federal Reserve System and the majority leaders of both houses of Congress, would be able to get the plan through. The president told the nation's governors, "This is in the interest of America, not because there are some large financial interests at stake, but because there are thousands of jobs and billions of dollars of American exports at stake, the potential of an even more serious illegal immigration problem, the spread of financial instability to other countries in our hemisphere, and indeed to other developing countries throughout the world, and the potential of a more serious narcotics trafficking problem."

It should have been an easy sell. But Congress showed no inclination to respond. Investors got the message that the loan guarantees were doomed. The collapse of the peso accelerated. Under pressure from the financial markets, the administration was forced to go it alone. The president's decision to act unilaterally was not a sign of political strength. It was a sign of political weakness.

The Mexican loan guarantee was not a left-right issue or a Democratic-Republican issue. It was a *populist* issue, one that divided the Establishment from the people. Washington and Wall Street supported it. They knew it had to be done. The people were against it, by margins of better than 4 to 1. No matter how the issue was explained to people, their response was, "Why should we co-sign a note for Mexico? Why doesn't the federal government bail out Orange County, California? Or Washington, DC?"

The combined forces of President Clinton, Federal Reserve chairman Alan Greenspan and GOP leaders Bob Dole and Newt Gingrich couldn't sell the deal to Congress. That's partly the result of the 1994 midterm election. The Republican freshmen in Congress were not just conservative. They were also anti-Establishment—anti-Washington and suspicious of Wall Street. That was a big shift from the old GOP, which used to be the party of big business.

From Goldwater to Reagan to Gingrich, the Republican Party has been taken over by a more muscular and populist conservative movement. Young conservatives in Congress don't respond to what the Establishment says "has to be done." When a reporter asked a Republican freshman whether he would support the loan guarantees, the congressman replied, "Of course not. It's not in my contract."

The populist conversion applies to Democrats as well. Liberals have been an anti-Establishment force in the Democratic Party for decades. Their formative political experiences were the civil rights struggle and the anti-Vietnam war movement. In 1993, President Clinton failed to get a majority of his own party to vote for NAFTA. It was the Republicans who saved him on the NAFTA vote.

Not on the loan guarantees, however. Bob Dole said the president would have to show he could carry a majority of Democrats before he would come up with the Republican votes. The president couldn't do it on NAFTA, and he couldn't do it on the Mexican loan bail-out. That was a shrewd move on Dole's part. He probably couldn't have come up with the GOP votes either.

The president's executive order let Congress off the hook. That's why it was greeted with a huge sigh of relief. "This is great!" Gingrich exclaimed when he heard the news. Dole said the best thing about the President's action was that Congress would not have to vote on the matter.

Like the Mexican loan guarantees, NAFTA was supported by the leadership of both political parties. It was opposed by populist forces of the left, such as Jesse Jackson and Ralph Nader; of the right, such as Pat Buchanan; and of the center, such as Ross Perot. Nevertheless, NAFTA passed. That was before the 1994 election, when President Clinton could offer his supporters more political cover. And before the populist insurgency transformed the GOP.

The Panama Canal treaties of 1978 were another issue that pitted the Establishment against the people. The Establishment said, "It has to be done. The consequences of rejecting the treaties would be unthinkable."

The public's response was, "Sez who?" Americans opposed giving away the Panama Canal when the treaties were first announced, when the issue was being debated in the Senate, and when the treaties were ratified. As Senator S. I. Hayakawa (R-Calif.) put it at the time, "It's our canal. We stole it fair and square." Nevertheless, the Establishment maintained a solid front, and the treaties were ratified.

In 1994, the General Agreement on Tariffs and Trade (GATT) was another "must do" Establishment issue. But Congress was unwilling to take up GATT before the midterm election. Legislators had to come back for a special session when the political pressure would be off. In the end, GATT was ratified by a Democratic Congress that had just been overthrown by the voters. It looked like the dying gesture of the old political order.

Measures like the Panama Canal treaties, NAFTA, and GATT probably could not get through Congress today. Popular distrust of the nation's leaders, which has been building for 30 years, has turned into open revolt—a revolt captured by Perot in 1992, Gingrich in 1994, and Buchanan in 1996. As the Republicans have moved to the right and the Democrats to the left, anti-Establishment populism has become the norm for politicians of both parties.

The symbol of the Mexican bailout wasn't Clinton. It was Greenspan, who lobbied Congress for weeks. Greenspan is the ultimate Establishment figure: Washington and Wall Street. In January 1995, Greenspan gave a private, unsolicited briefing to conservative talk-show host Rush Limbaugh on the peso crisis. That neatly captures the triumph of populism. Rush Limbaugh may have more influence in Congress today than the chairman of the Federal Reserve Board.

Bosnia

Sending American troops to Bosnia in 1995 was the biggest political risk President Clinton has ever taken. He did so in defiance of public opinion.

Clinton knows two great political truths about foreign policy. One is that foreign policy cannot save you. He learned that from George Bush. In 1991, after his military triumph in the Persian Gulf, President Bush stood astride the world like a colossus. In 1992, he was toast. And if he were to want more evidence, Clinton might consider how much good the Camp David peace accords did President Carter in 1980.

The other truth is that foreign policy can destroy you. Clinton learned that lesson in his youth from Lyndon Johnson. The Vietnam War soured all of Johnson's domestic achievements, especially for young antiwar protesters like Bill Clinton.

So why did President Clinton take the risk?

There was a strong moral argument. Bosnia proves the great rule in world affairs: unless the United States acts, nothing will happen. We could enforce the peace and stop the killing, President Clinton argued. So we had to act.

There was also a strategic argument. It would confirm our leadership of the Western alliance and, once again, rescue our feckless European allies from a problem they couldn't resolve.

President Clinton was convinced that one way or another, he would have ended up sending troops to Bosnia during the 1996 campaign. Without a peace agreement, he would have had to send them on a dangerous mission to rescue UN peacekeeping forces. So he decided to send troops on his own terms. And only after a peace agreement was in place. He reassured the nation, saying "America's role will not be about fighting a war. It will be about helping the people of Bosnia to secure their own peace."

Clinton tried to be very careful about Bosnia. He had to address questions about the military risks and the command U.S. forces would serve under. "The risks to our troops will be minimized," he told the country. "American troops will take their orders from the American general who commands NATO."

Would the Americans be sitting ducks, as they were in Lebanon? He considered that, too. "We will fight fire with fire—and then some."

And what about consulting Congress? Done. "If the NATO plan meets with my approval, I will immediately send it to Congress and request its support." He did, and he received it—grudgingly.

President Clinton had his critics boxed in. They couldn't defeat his policy without undermining a U.S. commitment. As Senator John McCain (R-Ariz.) put it, "The credibility of the word of the United States President is of enormous strategic value to the American people and essential to our security."

For years, President Clinton had been widely criticized for letting his policies be determined by public opinion. He didn't follow the polls on Bosnia, however. In a CBS News poll taken immediately after the President's speech to the nation, 58 to 33 percent of the public continued to oppose sending U.S. troops to Bosnia. The public remained opposed during the following weeks. Oddly, however, President Clinton's foreign policy ratings began to go up, from 37 percent approval in the June 1995 Gallup poll to 46 percent in December, after he proposed the Bosnia intervention. It was as if he was earning points in public opinion for defying public opinion.

Clinton scored a key political victory when Bob Dole said he would support the Bosnian mission—reluctantly. Dole said, "We have one President at a time. He is the commander-in-chief. He's made his decision. I don't agree with it. I think it's a mistake. We had a better option. But now it's high noon, the troops are on the way and they're looking to us for support." Dole acted in order to preserve what he regards as the valuable tradition of bipartisanship in foreign policy—a tradition he has an interest in preserving.

The fact is, Bosnia splits the GOP. Senator Phil Gramm, one of Dole's leading rivals, was against him on the issue. But Senator McCain, a Gramm supporter, agreed with Dole. And one of Dole's leading supporters, Senator Alfonse D'Amato (R-N.Y.), said of Clinton's policy, "It is unnecessary, it is wrong, and I will oppose it with every fiber in my body."

What if President Clinton's policy in Bosnia succeeds? Dole may remember that in 1991, when a majority of Democrats in Congress opposed the Persian Gulf War, Arkansas Governor Bill Clinton supported it. And it didn't do Clinton a bit of harm.

President Clinton and Senator Dole both made bold moves and took big political risks. The president tried to lead a nervous and skeptical country in a direction he believes is right. The senator tried to lead a nervous and skeptical Republican Party to uphold the principle of bipartisanship in world affairs. In an era of growing isolationism, those are clear cases of leadership.

Ideological Realignment

Political leaders today like to believe they are all internationalists, arguing about the proper framework for conducting foreign policy, unilateral or multilateral. From the public's point of view, however, the issue is more basic. "It has now become a truism to blame the current isolationism on the end of the Cold War because there is no longer a mainframe threat in this PC world," President Clinton said in 1995. With the fall of communism, does the United States have any purpose in the world beyond promoting its own interests?

Republicans are inclined to say "no" and accuse the Democrats of multilateralism. Democrats are inclined to say "yes" and accuse the Republicans of isolationism. As Anthony Lake, the president's national security adviser, put it, "Whether the U.S. becomes isolationist or not turns on the issue of UN peacekeeping."

It's interesting that unilateralism is now being called a smoke screen for isolationism. In Speaker Gingrich's version, "We have the Roman rule that we don't come unless we're really pushed, and if we're really pushed, we're unstoppable." We must be pushed into engagement abroad.

Only a few years ago, multilateralism was considered a smoke screen for isolationism. Liberals who were critical of United States intervention abroad argued that we should act only if there is a clear international consensus behind us. Unlike, say, the approach taken in Vietnam.

The conservative model of U.S. intervention is the Persian Gulf War. We were pushed, we rallied the rest of the world to our cause, and we responded with unstoppable force. The Chicago Council poll indicates that George Bush is still given high marks for his foreign policy.

The liberal model of U.S. intervention is Haiti. We acted with restraint, and with authorization from the United Nations (though not from Congress). Most Chicago Council respondents gave the Clinton administration low marks for its handling of the situation in Haiti.

With the end of the Cold War, the ideological alignment has shifted in American politics. That's because the world agenda has shifted from containment of communism to economic development, human rights, and democracy, that is, from an East-West to a North-South agenda.

Liberals are now the most ardent internationalists. They took the lead in pressuring the Clinton administration to stand firm in Bosnia, China, North Korea, and Haiti. That signifies two things. One, there is a Democrat in the White House. Two, the Cold War is over, and the United States is once again free to become the leader of progressive forces in the world. As President Clinton said during the campaign, "I believe it is time for America to lead a global alliance for democracy as united and steadfast as the global alliance that defeated communism."

But the polling data indicate that liberals have so far failed to convince the American public. Until they do, conservatives are likely to prevail with their argument for a foreign policy driven by American self-interest. And the president will be forced to evade, defy, or exploit the public's growing isolationism.

The last time the United States was at this kind of turning point was in 1947, when President Truman articulated a rationale for the United States to assume the burden of leading the free world. That was the Truman Doctrine. So far, there has been no Clinton Doctrine.

Endnotes

1. Chicago Council on Foreign Relations, *American Public Opinion and U.S. Foreign Policy 1995* (Chicago, 1995), p. 13. Unless otherwise noted, opinion data cited in this chapter are from the Chicago Council studies.
2. Source: Voter Research & Surveys. Primary election day poll conducted by a consortium of CBS, NBC, ABC and CNN.
3. Source: Voter Research & Surveys. Election day poll conducted by a consortium of CBS, NBC, ABC and CNN, November 3, 1992.

Chapter 3

Who, Why, What, and How: Debates Over Post–Cold War Military Intervention

Bruce W. Jentleson

In his final year at West Point [1987], just as the Cold War was winding down, a classmate asked the superintendent if he thought they would ever be deployed in an operation. In the seven years since, [Captain Ed] Rowe has been to Panama as part of an invasion force, to the Middle East for the war against Iraq, to Somalia and now here [Haiti]. "These days," he said, "it's just a matter of where the next one's going to be."[1]

Two empirical facts serve as our points of departure: First, the end of the Cold War has not meant the end of war. Bosnia, Croatia, Somalia, Chechnya, Haiti, Rwanda, Iraq, Chiapas, Peru-Ecuador, Angola, Liberia, Georgia, Tajikistan, Nagorno-Karabakh, Lebanon, Algeria, Colombia—the list goes on to encompass some 90 armed conflicts, in what has been less a new era of peace than "a new season of war."[2]

Second, U.S. military forces have been actively deployed more

Bruce W. Jentleson is professor of political science at the University of California, Davis and Director of the University of California, Davis Washington Center. In 1993–1994 he served as special assistant to the director of the State Department Policy Planning Staff. He is the author of, among other works, With Friends Like These: Reagan, Bush and Saddam, 1982–1990 *(W. W. Norton, 1994) and* New Era, New Century: American Foreign Policy After the Cold War *(W. W. Norton, forthcoming), and a senior editor of the four-volume* Encyclopedia of U.S. Foreign Relations *(Oxford University Press and Council on Foreign Relations, 1997)*

The author thanks Barry Blechman, Alexander George, Stanley Hoffmann, Joe Lepgold, Bob Lieber, Ken Oye, Rob Paarlberg, Donald Rothchild, and Celeste Wallander for helpful comments. Versions of this paper were presented at the 1995 Annual Meeting of the American Political Science Association, Harvard University's Center for International Affairs, and the "Engagement and Disengagement" Conference co-sponsored by the ISA Foreign Policy Analysis Section and the Harrison Program of the University of Maryland; thanks also to the participants in these sessions.

times to more places thus far in the 1990s than in any comparable length of time during the Cold War. The Somalia intervention involved 27,000 troops at its height. In the Haiti intervention about 20,000 troops were called up. During just a few days in October 1994 another 38,000 U.S. and allied troops were ordered deployed, accompanied by naval warships and attack aircraft, in Operation Vigilant Warrior against Iraq, as Saddam Hussein threatened to re-invade Kuwait. These were in addition to the thousands of forces that were already part of Operation Provide Comfort who were stationed since 1991 in the Kurdistan area of northern Iraq. During the crisis with North Korea, Patriot missile batteries already had been put in place and contingency plans for the deployment of 10,000 additional troops to South Korea were on the verge of being approved when the crisis-defusing deal was announced. Small numbers of U.S. soldiers also have been part of UN peacekeeping forces in Macedonia, Rwanda, ex-Soviet Georgia, the Western Sahara, and the Middle East. And even prior to the deployment of an estimated 20,000 U.S. troops for peacekeeping in Bosnia, U.S. pilots attached to NATO patrolled the no fly zones and carried out air strikes, including heavy bombing raids in August-September 1995.

Consequently, while much has changed with the end of the Cold War, questions regarding the use of military force remain at the core of both U.S. foreign policy strategy and foreign policy politics. Yet much of the debate over U.S. policy has failed to progress beyond the espousal of glib slogans and the search for easy answers. We make the claim of being the sole surviving superpower, we contend that we don't want to renounce the unilateralist option, and we excoriate "multilateralism" when it appears to impose restrictions on our freedom of action—but we also want there to be enough multilateralism so that others carry their share of the global peace burden. Even as we are tempted to turn ever further inward, we keep finding our interests threatened by spreading aggression, the threat of nuclear weapons proliferating, boat people fleeing repression, drug cartels penetrating our borders, and other international crises. We say never again to nation-building, but then are confronted with the threat to the values and ideals to which we pay allegiance when another democracy is toppled by a coup, or another humanitarian disaster or genocidal "ethnic cleansing" fills the screens of CNN.

This chapter reviews and analyzes the debates on four fundamental questions as they have played out thus far during the Clinton administration:

- *Who* among the president, Congress, and public opinion should have what voice in deciding whether the United States should use military force?
- *Why* should the United States even consider such action? What are the vital interests and values that warrant it?

- *What* strategies are needed to make military force effective when it is used?
- *How* should such strategies be carried out in terms of the respective roles of the United States, other major powers, the United Nations, and regional multilateral organizations?

In considering these questions it is important to make a distinction between the *structural* and *behavioral* dimensions of the problems. By structural I mean the dilemmas that are inherent in each of these questions (i.e., structured into them), which would be there for any administration in this post–Cold War era, and which in some respects, notwithstanding the nature and extent of the changes that the end of the Cold War has wrought both internationally and domestically, have been there in previous eras as well. By behavioral I mean aspects more directly attributable to the policies of this particular administration, be they policy successes or failures. The intent in making this distinction is to provide a conceptual context as well as a critique, a broadly systemic sense of how fundamental these debates over the who, why, what, and how of the use of military force are, as well as an analytic focus on the ways in which the Clinton administration has and has not moved us closer to at least some resolution of these questions.

Who Decides?

In both its relations with Congress and its handling of public opinion, the Clinton administration has exacerbated the structural constraints inherent to post–Cold War transition era domestic politics, making an already difficult situation worse.

Clinton and Congress

The oft-cited characterization of the foreign policy provisions of the Constitution as "an invitation to struggle" between the president and Congress could be dismissed by now as hackneyed if it didn't continue to be so accurate and graphic.[3] No domain fits it better than war powers. The president is designated "commander-in-chief," the Congress is given the power to "declare war" and "provide for the common defence"—not even separate powers, but a classic example of Richard Neustadt's conceptual refinement of "separate institutions sharing powers."[4]

Nor is much resolution gained from combing *The Federalist Papers* and other sources of original intent. "Presidentialists" invoke the logic developed by Alexander Hamilton that the need for an effective foreign policy was one of the main reasons the young nation needed an "energetic government" (*Federalist No. 23*); that "energy in the executive" was "a leading character in the definition of good government" (*Federalist No. 70*); and that "in the conduct of war . . . the energy of the executive is the bulwark of national security" (*Federalist No. 75*). "Congressionalists," on the other hand, go back to the proceedings of the Constitutional Convention, during which, at James Madison's initiative, the original wording that would have given Congress the power to "make war" was changed to "declare war." They explain that this was intended to recognize that how to use military force ("make war") was appropriately a power for the commander-in-chief, while whether or not to use military force ("declare war") was for the Congress. And they also cite Hamilton, offering a very different interpretation of *Federalist No. 75* based on passages in which he calls the war power a "joint possession."

Nor is the weight of historical precedents strictly on one side or the other. One of the favorite statistics of presidentialists is that of the more than 200 times that the United States has used military force, only five have been through congressional declarations of war (War of 1812, Mexican War, Spanish-American War, World War I, World War II). About another 85 to 90 have been with at least some other legislative authorization or expression of support (e.g., the 1991 Persian Gulf War). All the others have been presidents acting on their own, which is taken as evidence of both the need for and legitimacy of presidents having such freedom of action.

This statistic, though, is somewhat deceptive. Many of the cases of presidents acting on their own involved minor incidents and brief skirmishes generally regarded as the business of a commander-in-chief. Others generally were accepted as falling within the emergency prerogative to act expeditiously to meet direct threats to the nation, which is both inherent in the powers given to any head of state and implicit in the overarching "executive power" clause of the Constitution. And in others Congress chose not to get involved, sometimes because it agreed, sometimes just to avoid responsibility. Moreover, congressionalists put less emphasis on the overall numbers than on key cases such as Vietnam, in which undeclared war had devastating consequences for all concerned.

When the War Powers Resolution (WPR) was passed in 1973, overriding a veto by President Richard M. Nixon, it was regarded by many as the salvation of the American political system. It has, however, had two fundamental problems. One is that while it was supposed to be a way of what Robert Katzmann calls "affirmatively defining the congressional role" in any decision to use military force, it has tended to be seen much more as a mechanism for trying to keep the United States out of war, for ensuring that military force is not used.[5] Constitutional issues aside, the argument that the 60-day clock weakens the credibility of threats or actual uses of military force has strategic merit. This has been the main reason why every president (Jimmy Carter no less than Ronald Reagan) has opposed the WPR, almost instinctively, and refused to invoke it. Consequently, when situations involving the use of force have arisen, our political system still has lacked accepted procedures for interbranch cooperation.[6]

The other fundamental problem has been the belief that there could be a statutory solution to what in essence is a political problem. One doesn't have to be a linguist or lawyer to see the problems in provisions such as the WPR's statement of purpose as dealing with situations in which "imminent involvement in hostilities is clearly indicated." We have spent the last 20 some years debating what hostilities are (e.g., the 1987–1988 Persian Gulf tanker war?), what the threshold for involvement in them is (e.g., having the 400,000 troops of Desert Shield in Saudi Arabia?), and when are there clear indications of their imminence. Disagreement also surrounds the provision for consultation with Congress "in every possible instance . . . before introducing U.S. armed forces into hostilities or into situations where imminent involvement in such is clearly indicated." When is consultation possible (e.g., Panama in 1989? Haiti in 1994?)? When is it "before" (e.g., once the planes are on their way, but before they have dropped their bombs, as in Libya 1986?)? To be sure, there were those who pushed for tighter and more precise language. One could, for example, define "hostilities" as the firing of any first shot at an American, or "imminent involvement" as an American soldier being within range of an enemy's weapon—say 50 feet for a gun, 10 miles for a bomb, 100 miles for a missile. Clearly, though, such language tightening presents its own problems of straight-jacketing strategy and taking too much discretion away from a president.

These are the structural problems inherited by the Clinton administration. The Clinton administration made them worse in a number of ways. One was the general tone set along the two ends of Pennsylvania Avenue by the administration's spurring of early entreaties from congressional leaders to build closer consultative relations. A task force had been set up during the pre-inaugural transition period to work with congressional leaders and staffs of both parties. "Congress and the president will always interact as both adversaries and partners," House Foreign Affairs Committee Chairman Lee Hamilton wrote in a memo to the president-elect during the transition period, "and congressional activism will continue irrespective of who is in the White House." The key therefore, Hamilton stressed, was "better consultation . . . carried out in an atmosphere of mutual respect . . . with a recognition by the President of Congress's legitimate role in policy formulation." The same message came from then-Minority Leader Robert Dole. "Consult," was his number one response to a Clinton transition team questionnaire. "This exercise was very useful, even if you throw the papers away."[7] But once in office, Clinton and his administration failed even to seriously test the sincerity of these overtures from the Hill. To be sure, a portion of the you-don't-consult-enough crossfire comes with the territory, rooted both in partisan differences and in attachments to institutional prerogatives of many congressional Democrats no less than Republicans. But there also was substance to the charges, and relations with key foreign and defense policy committee chairs became even more frayed and more quickly so than on the domestic policy side.

More specifically, the administration balked at taking up a promising WPR reform proposal backed by a prominent bipartisan group, which would have essentially traded away the 60-day clock in return for a presidential commitment to more serious and more regular consultation.[8] The Clinton administration paid some lip service, issuing a presidential review directive (PRD-28) establishing an interagency working group on the issue, but used this less to drive than to tie up the policy process.

The main reasons for the stalling on PRD-28 are quite telling. One was that the interagency group was heavily staffed by lawyers, whose view of the issue was almost exclusively as a statutory problem. They spent most of their time deliberating over "language fixes," and worrying about the ostensibly dangerous precedents being set or procedural wedges being driven by this or that formulation, missing the essence of Lee Hamilton's point about the relationship being fundamentally a political one, destined to work or not based on actions, attitudes, and relationships more than on precise statutory formulations.

Another was the worry among some White House political operatives about Bill Clinton looking "soft" if he were perceived as any less assertive of presidential prerogatives than his predecessors. "The guy who wanted to let gays into the military," was the essence of the concern, "couldn't now be seen as also letting the wimps in Congress into decisions about war and peace." To the extent that there was some truth to this, it was a problem the president had created for himself.

There also was a manifestation of classic bureaucratic inertia, the sense of why act if there was no absolute need to do so. Of course, this is what had kept happening to earlier efforts to reform the WPR. Either there was a crisis at hand and a felt need to deal directly and only with that rather than more general policy procedural issues, or without a crisis why bother today. It was only in October 1994 in a speech at Harvard by National Security Advisor Anthony Lake that the offer came to work on WPR reform with the new Congress after the upcoming November elections. Finally, as a reporter for *The Washington Post* noted, the White House had accepted "an invitation that House Foreign Affairs Committee Chairman Lee H. Hamilton and other prominent members of Congress extended in the early months of the administration."[9] But when you wait too long to go through the opening, the window may close—as it did the next month when the Republicans seized control of Congress in the midterm elections.

Nor did the administration handle well its first major war powers cases of Somalia and Haiti. Even before the political firestorm set off by the disastrous Mogadishu firefight in October 1993, Senate Appropriations Committee Chairman Robert C. Byrd (D-W. Va.) had been leading efforts to cut off funding for U.S. participation in the UN peacekeeping mission. Then amidst the political hemorrhaging following the 18 Americans killed and one ignominiously dragged through the streets of Mogadishu, Secretary of State Warren Christopher and Defense Secretary Les Aspin were hastily dispatched to Capitol Hill. But the meeting went extremely badly. The members thought they were going to be briefed, to be presented with at least the best policy rationale the administration could muster. Yet the tack Aspin and Christopher took was a "'what do you guys think' approach . . . 'I'm up here to get your ideas about what we should do.'" The reaction "was virtually catcalls," according to Elizabeth Drew; "a combination of dumbfoundedness and anger," according to Sidney Blumenthal.[10]

The Haiti intervention amounted to a close call. Had the Carter-Nunn-Powell mission not succeeded in negotiating a peaceful landing, the outcry on the Hill likely would have been deafening. Other than the Congressional Black Caucus and some other liberal Democrats who had been pushing for military action, most others on the Hill were non-supportive if not outright opposed. The usual presidentialist claim of the exigencies of a crisis situation as impeding consultation with Congress was not a very convincing rationale in this situation, given that the administration had gone to the UN Security Council almost two months earlier for the "all necessary means" authorizing resolution. National Security Advisor Lake's offer on the WPR the following month likely was prompted by a mixed realization of the political risks in coming this close to a major war powers clash yet again, and some sense of being in more of a position of strength with things apparently going well in Haiti.

But with the new Republican Congress, "Pennsylvania Avenue diplomacy" came close to a breakdown in relations.[11] In June 1995 House Republicans actually tried a clever ploy, proposing a repeal of the WPR, apparently unafraid that this president would make much use of the power and with an eye to an unfettered Republican president in 1996. One can envision other presidents who would have jumped at such an offer from Congress; indeed its congressional sponsors had letters of endorsement from Ford, Carter, and Bush. But not Clinton; he didn't oppose it, but he didn't offer any support. Consequently, the proposal was defeated as Republicans sufficiently worried by the then-immediate crisis in Bosnia (the UN peacekeepers taken hostage by the Bosnian Serbs) and the President's own mixed messages of maybe/maybe not escalation joined with Democrats who favored WPR reform but not repeal.

The Republican Congress took even sharper aim at tying the President's hands on multilateral peacekeeping.[12] United Nations peacekeeping was one of the only foreign policy items in the original "Contract with America," and the clear intent was both to rack up some politically easy budget cuts and to exploit the emotional "wedge issue" aspects of the concept of U.S. troops serving under foreign command. The Senate tempered these proposals, but even the compromise versions posed policy problems for the Clinton administration and kept it on the political defensive.

Yet even more significant than any one specific issue was the general sense that the who-decides-foreign-policy pendulum had swung more towards Congress than ever before in the contemporary era. Senate Majority Leader and presidential candidate Robert Dole set out for Europe in January 1995 to conduct his own talks on Bosnia directly with British and French leaders. Foreign leaders who came to Washington didn't just stop on the Hill for courtesy calls but did a large share of their business there. In June 1995, French President Jacques Chirac found himself "pleading with Congress" to support an agreement he and President Clinton had reached for increased funding of the UN Peacekeeping Force, (UNPROFOR) in Bosnia. "It is up to the U.S. Congress to give the green light to the initiative," the French President said while the American president stood at his side in a striking scene.[13]

There needs to be a line separating even the most contentious battles over legislation from the direct diplomacy practiced by members of Congress who meet with foreign leaders to push their own diplomatic initiatives that are not coordinated with and often are in opposition to official administration policy. We saw some of this in the 1980s, with Senator Jesse Helms' efforts to provide his own reassurances of support to counter the Reagan administration's policy shift in 1985 away from Chilean dictator General Augusto Pinochet, and with House Speaker Jim Wright's 1987 initiation of negotiations in his office in the Capitol with Nicaraguan Sandinista President Daniel Ortega. The ends being pursued by Gingrich and Dole no more justified their means than did Helms' or Wright's.[14] It is never a good practice for a member of Congress—*any* member of Congress—to set himself or herself up as an alternative track of diplomacy circumventing the president. Battles over who decides what U.S. policy should be through our own constitutional processes are one thing; raising questions about who's in charge of the actual carrying out of U.S. diplomacy are quite another. The immediate effects and the precedents thus set when that line is crossed cannot be healthy ones for American foreign policy.

The politics of the deployment of U.S. troops to Bosnia as part of NATO's Implementation Force (IFOR) following the signing of the Dayton agreement were telling in a number of respects. On the one hand the president was not stopped from deploying the troops. But on the other he was not exactly supported in doing so. In late October, only two days before the Dayton conference was to convene, the House overwhelmingly passed a resolution opposing deployment. While it was a non-binding resolution, the 315 to 103 margin sent a strong message. Gingrich then sent a letter to the White House posing so many questions and concerns that the President's "Dear Mr. Speaker" response ran nine pages, single spaced.[15] Then in December, even once the Dayton conference had succeeded and the President had publicly committed the United States to send troops as part of IFOR, the House came very close to passing a funds cutoff measure (210–218 vote) and did pass a resolution that was at best a mixed message in that it stated support for the troops themselves but "disowned the deployment decision."[16] The Senate resolution was more supportive, but it too contained far more caveats, criticisms and reservations than presidents usually get from the senior body when putting American troops on the ground. Moreover, when it has come to approving funds for the civic, political and economic assistance programs needed to help rebuild the Bosnian state, Congress has had more leverage and has been less than forthcoming.

Public Opinion: More Prudent than Gun-Shy

There's little doubt that the American public is not very eager to use military force. The only one of 11 general scenarios posed in a February 1994 Roper poll for which a majority of respondents definitely supported using force was "if the U.S. itself is attacked" (80 percent). The Clinton campaign slogan "it's the economy, stupid" is well-ensconced in political folklore. Now that the Cold War is over, the domestic agenda has priority. Moreover, no one wants another quagmire, nor more scenes like Mogadishu.

But while all this is conventional wisdom, two tempering observations are important. First, taken in a longer historical perspective, and not just compared to the ostensible paragon of the Cold War consensus, we see that the American public has rarely gone to war readily. This is not just a post–Vietnam or post–Cold War trend. We entered both World Wars over two years after they had started. When Woodrow Wilson ran for re-election in 1916, his slogan was "He kept us out of war." It was only after the decoding of the "Zimmerman telegram," a message from the German foreign minister to his minister in Mexico suggesting an alliance in which they would together "reconquer the lost [Mexican] territory in Texas, New Mexico, and Arizona," and then the sinking by German U-boats of three U.S. merchant ships that the threat to U.S. security was sufficiently direct both to convince Wilson that war was the only recourse and enable him to make the case to the American public.

Even more to the point, President Franklin Roosevelt, who earlier had tried to convince the country that it couldn't ignore Hitler, ran for re-election in 1940 on the promise that "your President says this country is not going to war."[17] A poll taken the week after Hitler invaded Poland in September 1939 showed 94 percent of Americans opposed to the United States declaring war. As late as October 1941 over 75 percent were still opposed to going to war. It was only after "the day of infamy" of the Japanese surprise attack on Pearl Harbor that the American public finally became willing to recognize that geography no longer made security in isolation possible. Some historians, noting that the initial declaration of war passed by Congress was only against Japan, still wonder whether even then the United States would have gone to war against Germany had Hitler not declared war against us a few days later.

The Cold War consensus with its much greater readiness to support the use of force to contain communism was much more the historical exception than the rule. The Korean War showed that public support could wither as casualties mounted and military stalemate set in. But whatever the disillusionment with the Korean War, it did not shake the general readiness to use military force against communism. Polls about intervening to stop communism in Latin America, to defend West Berlin, to defend the Philippines, and other such containment scenarios elicited strong public support. Even then there was a touch of pragmatism to public opinion, as "rollback" scenarios such as intervening to overthrow communist governments in Eastern Europe did not get the same high support as containment ones. But the 60 to 70 percent initial levels of support for sending U.S. troops to Vietnam, a little country halfway around the globe, stands in sharp contrast to the persistent opposition to getting involved in either World War I or World War II until the threats hit us right here at home. By the 1970s not only had the public become disillusioned with the Vietnam War, but it had doubts about using military force just about anywhere. For example, the 1974 Chicago Council on Foreign Relations survey found a bare plurality of 40 to 39 percent in favor of defending even Western Europe against a Soviet invasion. As for the Third World, the same survey found 64 percent agreeing that the lesson of Vietnam was not to commit troops to other civil wars.[18]

A second tempering observation is that the post–Cold War public's reluctance to use force should not be exaggerated to the point of imputing chronic gun-shyness. To go back to the Roper poll, if we include those who said they "probably" would support the use of force, we get strong majorities for eight of the eleven scenarios, including some that have close domestic links (combat the flow of illegal drugs into the U.S., police the flow of illegal aliens) but also others such as "if close allies of the U.S. are attacked" and even "provide humanitarian relief" and "be part of a United Nations peacekeeping force." What doesn't get support are purposes such as "intervene in a civil war" and "overthrow another government." This fits with the trend that began in the 1980s toward a more "prudent" set of attitudes in which support has been greater for the use of force when the principal policy objective was to coerce *foreign policy restraint by an aggressor state*—as, for example, against Iraq in the 1990–1991 Gulf War, which overall received strong public support—than when it was to impose *internal political change* within another state—e.g., against the Nicaraguan Sandinistas, a policy for which even Ronald Reagan with his "great communicator" skills could never muster significant public support.[19] Even in the case of the 1989 invasion of Panama, the 82.5 percent post–invasion support was less revealing, reflecting as it did the "halo effect" of success, than the only 32 percent support in polls just two months earlier. On the other hand the 1987–1988 Persian Gulf reflagging naval operation, very much a foreign policy restraint mission, got average support of 55 percent despite the significant risks it ran.

Looking at the polls on recent specific cases, we find similar patterns.[20] Sixty-one percent supported the October 1994 mobilization against Saddam's attempt to re-invade Kuwait. During the spring 1994 crisis with North Korea, and despite the apparent risks involved, polls showed support close to 50 percent for taking military action in what clearly was another case of seeking to restrain a potential aggressor. On the other hand, polls on Haiti, very much an internal politics case, showed average levels of support no higher than about 35 percent, and not even that much higher after the quick and easy success was achieved.

The Somalia polls provide a variation on this basic pattern. Early polls show very high levels of support, averaging 74 percent, for what was considered a genuinely humanitarian mission. But as events recast the mission in more internal politics terms, support dropped—an average of 47 percent in polls done June through September 1993, and 35 percent in the months immediately following the Mogadishu debacle (October–December 1993). Even then, though, while less naively embracing humanitarian intervention the public still wasn't ready to just give up on such purposes. A Times Mirror poll the same month as Mogadishu still showed 56 percent in favor of "sending U.S. military forces to Asian or African countries to prevent famines and mass starvation."[21] The following year in the Rwanda crisis, one poll found 61 percent willing to support U.S. troops as part of a UN peacekeeping operation to "occupy [Rwanda] and stop the killing."[22] Such a high level of support likely was more a reflection of the horrific intensity of the moment and not sustainable, but it does indicate the ambivalence Americans still feel about the moral imperatives on the one hand and the risks on the other of humanitarian crises.

This ambivalence has been especially evident on Bosnia. Of all the post–Cold War cases, Bosnia is the most mixed both in terms of having elements of inter-state aggression, intra-state civil war, and humanitarian crisis, and in terms of fears of quagmire on the one hand and moral outrage on the other. For the most part the polls averaged in the 40–45 percent support range There were moments when there was support for tougher action; e.g., 62 percent at the beginning of the Clinton administration favoring "sending UN troops including some U.S. troops to help the Bosnians defend themselves against the Serbs." But even with IFOR deployed and doing well, polls in early 1996 showed the public pretty evenly divided. And, again, consistent with the other cases, those who saw the principal objectives of the mission as humanitarian and/or restraining aggression to safeguard regional security were most likely to be supportive, while those who saw it more as yet another effort to remake a government were much less supportive.

Another way of analyzing these dynamics is through a typology like the one presented by Andrew Kohut and Robert Toth of Times Mirror, differentiating the public according to general attitudes toward the use of military force.[23] While the specific categorizations may not be precisely how I would draw the lines, the key point is that 30 percent fall into their "interventionist" category, 48 percent into their middle categories, and only 21 percent into "noninterventionists." This too evidences a pattern of less blanket opposition to the use of force than is often presumed.

Thus in this aspect of domestic politics as well, there is a difference between the structural problem of political constraints and the behavioral one of constraints becoming straight-jacketing prohibitions on the use of military force. The Clinton record in this regard is mixed. From the outset there was the unfavorable contrast between the tough talk on Bosnia during the presidential campaign when that seemed the way to rouse the public, and the indecisiveness when it came to taking action that risked mixed public reviews. The events of October 1993, notably the announced withdrawal from Somalia and the *USS Harlan County* incident in the harbor of Port-au-Prince, Haiti, left strong impressions of a President letting his foreign policy sway with the public opinion polls. While at one level the eventual decision to send the military into Haiti often has been hailed as demonstrating Clinton's willingness to go against the grain of public opinion, it's worth remembering how backed into a corner the President had gotten himself and how much more he seemed to have to lose from not carrying through on his commitments. There was a similar sense with Bosnia. Moreover, as is discussed later, both of these cases were less matters of forcefully imposed military interventions than of the carrying out of negotiated military occupations. The questions still outstanding were whether Clinton would and could mobilize a reluctant public to support the use of military force in a genuinely more forceful and potentially more immediate manner.

Why Intervene? The Vital Interests Conundrum

The Clinton administration has been criticized for lacking a guiding conception of what the vital interests of the United States are. While some of this is deserved, there is an important distinction that is often missed between not being able to formulate a fixed and generalizable set of criteria as to what vital interests are, a conceptual problem never as readily resolved as pundits like to purport (another structural problem, in the terms of this analysis), and this particular administration's halting and shifting efforts to do so (behavioral).

"To establish a hierarchical order, an order of priorities, among all possible objectives of a nation's foreign policy," wrote Hans Morgenthau, "must be the first step in framing a rational foreign policy."[24] In fact, though, when the effort is made to actually conceptualize and identify vital interests, the task is revealed as quite the conundrum. Even in Morgenthau's own work, he was torn between whether interest *is* defined as power, or that it *should be*. His 1951 book, *In Defense of the National Interest*, was subtitled *A Critical Examination of American Foreign Policy*, and reads as an attempt to convince American statesmen who were not thinking and acting in this manner that they ought to do so.[25] Moreover, bearing in mind both the exclusion problem of the interpretation of Acheson's definition of vital interests as a defense perimeter without South Korea, and the inclusion problem of Vietnam as a vital interest (of which Morgenthau was among the earliest and intellectually severest critics), the Cold-War-as-golden-age myth is to be avoided on this count as well.

The Gulf war case is the exception that proves the rule. This was a case of naked aggression, in a region that every American who had ever stood in a gasoline line considered to be of genuine pocketbook relevance to his or her daily life, perpetrated by a demonic leader, who was on the verge of acquiring nuclear weapons. Even then the consensus on the interests at stake being sufficiently vital to go to war over had to be skillfully cultivated by the Bush administration. Yet, when President Bush attempted in his January 1993 farewell address at West Point to go further and articulate a broad conception of when the United States should use military force, his criteria weren't any more specific or operational than

> where the stakes warrant, where and when force can be effective, where no other policies are likely to prove effective, where its application can be limited in scope and time, and where the potential benefits justify the potential costs and sacrifice.

Anything more specific than that, Bush stated, just was not possible. "There can be no single or simple set of fixed rules for using force . . . Each and every case is unique."[26] Joint Chiefs of Staff Chairman Colin Powell took a stab at it in an article in *Foreign Affairs*, identifying key questions to be answered—for example, are the political objectives important, clearly defined, and understood; what are the likely risks and costs? However, he also agreed to there being "no fixed set of rules" and that it was impossible to make little more in the way of a general statement than that "the use of force should be restricted to occasions where it can do some good and where the good will outweigh the loss of lives and other costs."[27]

Thus the conundrum: We need to be able to establish which interests are vital and which are not, but there is no fixed formula for doing so.[28] The inherent problem is well-stated by Alexander George and Robert Keohane:

> In principle, the criterion of national interest . . . should assist decisionmakers to cut through much of this value complexity and improve judgements regarding the proper ends and goals of foreign policy. In practice, however, national interest has become so elastic and ambiguous a concept that its role as a guide to foreign policy is problematic and controversial.[29]

Indeed, realistically, it may well be that we can do no better than Supreme Court Justice Potter Stewart's approach to pornography, "I know it when I see it." Some cases will be very clear: a film that is blatantly pornographic, an attack on our own borders or against a major ally. But beyond that, in the same way that the Court felt that it could not do any more than affirm a set of general principles and criteria to be applied to individual cases, foreign policy strategists also need to establish a core set of principles and criteria but are unlikely to be able to achieve much greater formulaicness.

This is especially true for the post–Cold War world. Mikhail Gorbachev was only being partially facetious when during his last visit to Washington as Soviet leader he quipped, "We're going to do a terrible thing to you . . . We're going to take away The Enemy." We still can point to enemies, but no single overarching Enemy. Saddam Hussein, for example, still fits the "little e" bill, and the Clinton administration has been consistent and persuasive in establishing the why for the continued efforts to deter and contain Iraq. And in other instances such as the North Korean nuclear threat in 1993–1994 and China's provocations against Taiwan in March 1996, the administration effectively focused on the vital interests that were at stake while avoiding demonization and blending credible shows of force with negotiating strategies. Indeed one could discern opposition to inter-state aggression that endangered U.S. allies and international stability more generally as a core principle and criterion running through these cases.

The greater difficulty has come with those cases which are not just classical inter-state aggression but while possibly having this dimension also involve ethnic and other intra-state conflicts which, as the U.S. ambassador to Somalia put it about that country, are "not a critical piece of real estate for anybody in the post–Cold War world."[30] The vitalness of the interests at stake in such conflicts is far from a given. But we also find it difficult to completely relegate them to insignificant status. Amidst the genocides, the repressions of human rights, the spread of lawlessness and other fundamental violations of our most basic values, we find ourselves wrestling particularly with the interrelationship of interests and ideals. Is it being too much like Mother Theresa and making foreign policy into "social work," as Michael Mandelbaum has argued, to give national interest weight to humanitarian concerns? Or is the very distinction between interests and values "largely fallacious," as Stanley Hoffmann stresses, in that "a great power has an 'interest' that goes beyond strict national security concerns and its definition of world order is largely shaped by its values?"[31]

All of these considerations are inherent, part of the structural problem. One gets some perspective on this by looking back historically at other periods of strategic uncertainty, to see how inherently problematic it always has been under such conditions for any major power to achieve clarity and consistency about its vital interests.[32] Still, though, many of the Clinton administration's wounds on this question of the national interest have been self-inflicted, most searingly in Somalia. One finds two main assessments of the lessons of Somalia, and neither is very complimentary. One was that we never should have stayed longer than the original 90 day relief mission, and that this administration was too soft in its view of what constituted a vital interest. The other was that a U.S. administration that would be forced to cut and run by a warlord in a small country couldn't be trusted to be tough enough to stand by our interests when truly vital ones were threatened.

The fallout from Somalia was especially evident in efforts to formulate a broader policy for U.S. participation in multilateral peace operations. This is discussed further in a later section; the point here is how much of a retreat was evident from the initial broad conception of the interests warranting an active U.S. military role to the approach that comes across as one of delimiting the conception of vital interests to establish when and why we *will not* intervene militarily. This, for example, was a strong message to be discerned from the July 1994 *National Security Strategy* document.[33] The section "Deciding When and How to Employ U.S. Forces" begins with a statement of the "key dangers" against which U.S. military forces are intended to respond: "those posed by weapons of mass destruction, regional aggression and threats to the stability of states." We also get some definition of our "vital or survival interests—those of broad overriding importance to the survival, security and vitality of our national entity." And of still important but not quite vital interests—"areas where we have a sizable economic stake or commitments to allies, and areas where there is a potential to generate substantial refugee flows into our nation or our allies'." But none of this gets us past the problem of being so general as to be potentially all encompassing. Worse, though, is that the rendition of caveats and conditionalities in both their strictures and tone go well beyond narrowing the range of what we will do to convey a sense of focus on what we will not do:

> Although there may be many demands for U.S. involvement, the need to husband scarce resources suggests that we must carefully select the means and levels of our participation in particular military operations . . .

> In all cases, the costs and risks of U.S. military involvement must be judged to be commensurate with the stakes involved . . .

> In every case, we will consider several critical questions before committing military force. Have we considered nonmilitary means that offer a reasonable chance of success? . . . Do we have reasonable assurance of support from the American people and their elected representatives? . . . Do we have an exit strategy? Our engagement must meet reasonable cost and feasibility thresholds.

When the administration did finally intervene in Haiti and Bosnia, it pointed to these cases as evidence that it now did have a guiding conception of the national interest. But even if one concurs with the administration's conception as manifested in these cases (and takes the Hoffmann view over the Mandelbaum one on the "Mother Theresa debate"), one still is left with the fact that these were more negotiated occupations than coercive interventions. What could one conclude about a future scenario in which defending the interests at stake might require a more coercive use of military force? It wasn't clear that we yet had much more insight into what the Clinton administration's answer would be. The most one could conclude was that there was a partly pragmatic and partly political calculation of casualties avoidance at work. This is not an insignificant consideration, but given too much emphasis it reverses the calculus so as to make the definition of which interests are vital too contingent on potential casualties, rather than determining the risks of casualties we are willing to take based on the vitalness of the interests at stake. Moreover, it allows adversaries to play on this calculus with their own strategies of either attrition or terrorist-type "big bang."

What Strategies? A Nobel Prize and a Great Victory, But Their Limits as Models

Toward the end of the Cold War there emerged what appeared to be two models for successful military and diplomatic efforts to end or prevent war. One was the United Nations in its peacekeeping capacity. The record of UN peacekeeping successes included key roles in ending the Iran-Iraq war, the Soviet invasion of Afghanistan, independence for Namibia, and the civil wars in El Salvador, Cambodia, and Mozambique. The UN record was so impressive as to garner the 1988 Nobel Peace Prize. United Nations peacekeeping forces "represent the manifest will of the community of nations," read the Nobel Committee's citation. Through and because of them, the United Nations "has come to play a more central role in world affairs and has been invested with increasing trust."[34]

The other was the 1990–1991 Gulf War against Iraq. The 27-nation coalition assembled and led by the United States under UN Security Council auspices was equally impressive as a diplomatic achievement and as a military operation. All sorts of hopeful precedents were set: U.S.-Soviet cooperation against a common enemy, highly effective U.S.-European "out of area" military collaboration, the re-affirmation to moderate Arab allies of the credibility of U.S. commitments to their security, and a demonstration of the validity of the U.S. military's post–Vietnam doctrine of "decisive force."

Neither of these, however, has held up very well as a more general strategy.

The United Nations vastly increased its peace operations from 5 in 1988 to 17 in 1994, and with a concomitant eight-fold increase in the number of blue-helmeted troops from 9,570 to 73,393, and an exponential soaring in the peace operations budget from $230 million to $3.6 billion. But the recent record, to say the least, has hardly won any prizes. United Nations-bashing aside, the key point is analytic recognition of the fundamental differences in the nature of the conflicts and the point in their cycle at which UN forces are intervening between the 1980s and the 1990s cases. Virtually all of the successes of the 1980s genuinely fit the definition of peace*keeping*, in that the UN forces were brought in after the parties had agreed to the terms of peace and with the mission of ensuring and facilitating the keeping of that peace. But in the 1990s in cases like the former Yugoslavia (UNPROFOR), Somalia (UNOSOM II) and Rwanda (UNAMIR), the mandates have been defined as peacekeeping but in actuality the conflicts still have been raging and the reality of the missions has been the need for peace*making*. To the extent that the parties had reached any agreements, they principally were but partial ones, holding actions, gambits, even outright deceptions. Where the missions genuinely have been peacekeeping ones, as along Arab-Israeli truce lines (UNTSO, UNDOF, and UNIFIL) and in Cyprus (UNFICYP), they have continued to be relatively successful. But even a Nobel laureate method will not succeed when applied to purposes as fundamentally different as is peacemaking from peacekeeping.

The Desert Shield-Desert Storm model has shown some greater relevance and validity. Defense Secretary Les Aspin's 1993 "Bottom-Up Review" (BUR) and associated efforts to develop post–Cold War strategic doctrine have been based on the capacity to fight simultaneously two major regional wars each on the scale of the Gulf War. And while no warfare or even mobilization on this scale has been repeated as yet, the October 1994 Vigilant Warrior redeployment against Iraq, and the mid-1994 deployments against North Korea did largely follow classical conceptions of conventional deterrence and coercive diplomacy. "In both cases, deterrence worked," as Aspin's successor Defense Secretary William J. Perry concluded, "because the United States had a ready force and was prepared to use it."[35] The same could be said for the strategy used in February–March 1996 in response to China's provocations against Taiwan.

The problem, though, is precisely the discrepancy between the doctrinal and force planning centrality of the regional deterrence model, and the greater frequency of occurrence of ethnic and other such conflicts. A year after the BUR, Defense Secretary Perry acknowledged that it was problems associated with ethnicity that were driving "much of the need for military forces in the world today."[36] Indeed, as of late 1995 there were 47 serious ethnic conflicts, at least one in every major region.[37]

Here too it is important to distinguish the inherent structural problems from the policy-behavioral ones. Ethnic conflicts have *never* been easy to resolve or even limit. As John Chipman puts it, "when national or ethnic feelings can be expressed as interests, they tend to be subject to negotiations; when they are seen to be little more than the exercise of pride, they become uncompromising in their essence." It is striking, as Chipman quotes the observation by the French intellectual Julian Benda in the 1920s, "how commonly men let themselves be lulled on account of some wound to their pride, and how infrequently for some infraction of their interest." David Rapaport makes the corroborating point that ethno-religious struggles in the twentieth century have lasted six times longer on average than inter-state wars. Donald Rothchild presents striking data on the death tolls of African wars with an ethnic or nationality component, most of which ended only through the elimination or capitulation of one side, neither of which has tended to come before many years of protracted conflict.[38]

However, again, to acknowledge such inherent difficulties as structural problems must not be taken as any sort of resignation to inevitability or rationalization for failed policies. Within the limits of counterfactual reasoning, and without presuming to claim that some policy X or Y definitely would have worked, a number of recent analyses do build strong cases for policies that could have worked better even in places like Somalia and the former Yugoslavia.[39] Drawing both on these and more general critiques, as well as by comparison to some of the Clinton administration's successes, we can identify five principal flaws in its basic strategies: (1) more rhetoric than action on preventive diplomacy; (2) loose and inaccurate characterizations of what constitutes a "humanitarian" intervention; (3) a misguided belief in both the possibility and efficacy of impartiality in peacemaking situations; (4) yet another administration that has adopted limited war doctrine; and (5) uneven use of threats and a consequent careless husbanding of U.S. credibility.

1. First, for all the preaching about "preventive diplomacy," there has been too little practice of it.[40] Warren Christopher spoke in his con-

firmation hearings as secretary of state of "a new diplomacy that can anticipate and prevent crises . . . rather than simply manage them." Tony Lake spoke of the "greater emphasis on tools such as mediation and preventive diplomacy" so that "in addition to helping solve disputes, we also help prevent them." United Nations Secretary General Boutros Boutros-Ghali's 1992 *Agenda for Peace* devoted a full chapter to preventive diplomacy. The Conference (now Organization) on Security and Cooperation in Europe (CSCE/OSCE) committed in its 1990 Charter of Paris for a New Europe to "seek new forms of cooperation . . . (for) ways of preventing, through political means, conflicts which may emerge." But opportunities to act early have been missed in Yugoslavia, in Somalia, in Rwanda, and in Haiti.

Some analysts have questioned whether the whole concept of preventive diplomacy is yet another false and misleading "alchemy for a new world order."[41] While the case can be made that it has been "oversold" and its risks undervalued, to therefore simply write it off is to commit the mirror-image mistake of those too eager and too uncritical in their embrace. The logic of acting early to prevent disputes from escalating is unassailable, as I have argued more extensively elsewhere. Indeed the very preventive successes achieved by the Clinton administration when it has pursued preventive diplomacy, as in Macedonia where U.S. troops were deployed in mid-1993 as part of a UN peacekeeping force, demonstrate what is possible. In those cases like Bosnia and Rwanda in which there was no prevention, the case evidence strongly supports the view that the United States and others in the international community *did* have specific and identifiable opportunities to have some impact to limit if not prevent these conflicts, but its statecraft was flawed, inadequate or even absent. Moreover, as more theoretical and conceptual bases for the argument, there are numerous studies that demonstrate both that the sources of ethnic conflict are less "primordialist" than "purposive," and thus susceptible to actions by international actors which could alter the cost-benefit calculus of resorting to mass violence; and that the onset of mass violence amounts to the crossing of a Rubicon after which however tense the conflicts already are, they become that much more difficult to resolve, until they reach what Bill Zartman calls a "hurting stalemate" . . . but which of course only comes after tens of thousands of deaths.

2. The characterization of many of the interventions undertaken as humanitarian accurately describes the consequences of the conflicts but disguises their fundamentally political causes. Back in April 1991, when a deadly cyclone hit Bangladesh, killing 139,000 people and doing $2 billion worth of damage to this already impoverished country, and American military forces were sent to help provide relief and reconstruction, this genuinely was a humanitarian intervention. But the starvation in Somalia, the outbreak of plague in Rwanda, the fears of annihilation of the Kurds in Iraq and the Muslims in Bosnia, all were politically precipitated humanitarian crises. In Somalia, for example,

the idea that U.S. troops ever could have just alleviated the immediate starvation in Somalia and then left, as the Bush administration initially portrayed the mission, was a mistake at best and misleading at worst. What really would have been the reaction had Clinton pulled the U.S. troops out totally in March 1993 and a few weeks later chaos resumed, mass starvation again boded, and the accomplishments of the UN peacekeeping force in Somalia, UNITAF, started to come undone? The real problem was the failure both by Bush initially and by Clinton thereafter to recognize that anything beyond short-term alleviation required a strategy that *had* to be political. There is no question that it is very hard to cross the line from immediate rescue to "nation-building." But that was the choice. And to the extent that it was made, it was made poorly, with a strategy that was full of blunders but not necessarily unworkable. Can anyone really believe that to have simply acquiesced to Aideed in Somalia would have worked, either for the Somali people or for its message about the will and preferences of the international community? The United States and the United Nations "were right to focus on Aideed," Steven David argues, "but efforts should have been carried out earlier and more decisively." Others have made similar critiques.[42]

Similarly, in Rwanda, which President Clinton called "the world's worst humanitarian crisis in a generation," there actually was quite a bit of early warning about the intensification of the political conflict and its potential for mass violence. There even was a 2,500 member UN observer force already in the country when the mass killings began in April 1994, but it lacked both sufficient mandate and the command and firepower capabilities to intercede. Even after the violence had ebbed, the humanitarian crisis was so fundamentally political, leaving virtually no ground on which to stand impartially, that faced with refugee camps taken over by the same Hutus who had led the genocidal attacks, the head of Doctors Without Borders felt compelled to question "how can physicians continue to assist Rwandan refugees when by doing so they are also supporting killers."[43]

3. These also are manifestations of what Richard Betts terms the "delusion of impartiality."[44] Impartiality is easy in a Bangladesh cyclone-type rescue mission. And it is fundamental to peacekeeping, when both sides need to be confident that the international party will not take sides, and that each can feel assured that it will not be disadvantaged so long as it abides by the terms of the peace. The terms of the peace also provide an objective basis for defining the terms of impartiality, and establishing procedures for handling accusations of violations. But when the parties are still in conflict, what does it mean to be impartial? To apply the same strictures to both sides, even if these leave one side with major military advantages over the other? To not coerce either side, irrespective of which one is doing more killing, seizing more territory, committing more war crimes?

This all along was a key fallacy in the Bosnian arms embargo. It may have had lawyerly logic and it may have struck a political balance among the positions of the major powers, but in real terms there was nothing impartial about the imbalance of military power thus ensconced between the already well-armed Bosnian Serbs and the limited military assets of the newly independent Bosnian government. Even worse, the whole UNPROFOR strategy was based on impartiality very much defined as equally noncoercive treatment, even when the one side (the Bosnian Serbs) was the far greater perpetrator of continued warfare and ghastly atrocities. "Such lofty evenhandedness," as Betts has put it, "may make sense for a judge in a court that can enforce its writ, but hardly for a general wielding a small stick in a bitter war."[45] All this reached heights of absurdity in the spring and summer of 1995, when the Bosnian Serbs took UN peacekeepers hostage on the grounds that the NATO air strikes violated impartiality; UNPROFOR then still opted for the least tough response possible in the name of impartiality; the Bosnian Muslims then threatened that they too would take UN peacekeepers hostage if UNPROFOR did not show its impartiality by resuming the air strikes to stop the continuing Serb attacks; the Serbs then expanded their attacks and ethnically cleansed ostensibly UNPROFOR-guarded Muslim "safe havens"; and UNPROFOR still stuck to its do-nothing-equally definition of impartiality. It was only with the August 1995 NATO air strikes targeting the Bosnian Serbs and the "non-red light" given to the Croatian military in the Krajina, which amounted to breaking out of the limits of impartiality, that things began to change.

4. The essence of the problem with the *limited war doctrine* is that its central term substitutes a description of the hoped-for scope of the conflict for an analysis of its nature. Debate over limited war doctrine goes back to the post–Korean War critique of the "Never-Again" school, through the 1960s–1970s lesson-drawing from Vietnam, to the Shultz versus Weinberger debate of the 1980s, and most recently the "decisive force" doctrine most closely associated with General Colin Powell and manifested in the 1989 Panama intervention and especially the 1991 Gulf War.[46] This lineage and context was acknowledged by Joint Chiefs of Staff Chairman John Shalikashvili as a basic tension between those (most often diplomats) who seek "to apply just enough force to gain a negotiated agreement" and those (most often generals) who prefer "to apply so much force that he gains acquiescence."[47]

Part of the problem inherent in the limited war doctrine has been the frequent underestimation of the willingness of parties for which the conflict is very much total to bear the costs of continued warfare.[48] Part also has been the overestimation with such parties of appeals to reason, as in the views expressed by a senior Clinton State official in mid-1994 that if they could just draw up the right map for partitioning Bosnia the Serbs would see "that this is a reasonable settlement and that they ought to opt for this rather than war."[49] Instead it was only when the diplomatic heat was turned up through the more assertive approach to negotiations led by Assistant Secretary of State Richard Holbrooke, and when some of the limits on the military side were dropped through the combined effects of the NATO air strikes and the Croatian offensive, that the Serbs changed their calculation of what was "reasonable."

Both the scope and the limits of the progress made in the ensuing months of the Bosnian peace negotiations are quite telling. To the extent that a stable peace is achieved, we are likely to continue to look back to the shift away from limited war strategy as a key factor. If progress does not continue, the reasons will be important, for to the extent that even a shift in use of force strategy proves inadequate, one of the implications arguably will be that limited war not only is ineffective but "net negative" in allowing and even contributing to conflicts becoming more protracted and thus that much harder to resolve at a later point in time than they were at earlier stages.

In this respect and others, the whole logic of using force only as a last resort is open to question. While there's no doubt that the usual preference should be to avoid having to use military force, it is extremely unrealistic to believe that leaders like Aideed, Milosevic, and Karadzic will agree to peaceful methods of conflict resolution as long as they think they can achieve their goals through their own military means at costs they deem acceptable. Different situations have to be analyzed to assess whether and how preventive military action or the threat thereof is likely to be more deterrent than exacerbant, but as Jane Holl argues, "preserving force as a last resort implies a lockstep sequencing of the means to achieve foreign policy objectives that is unduly inflexible and relegates the use of force to in extremis efforts to salvage a faltering foreign policy."[50]

5. Experience and analysis show two factors to be key in the coercive use of threats: the nature and scope of the demands being made, with threats tending to be more effective for limited rather than extensive demands, and the credibility of whatever threats are made as perceived by the target.[51] When the Clinton administration has abided by these tenets, its threats have had impact; when it hasn't, they have not.

Iraq is the case where the Clinton administration most backed up the threats with action, and it proves the point. The response in October 1994 to Saddam's remobilization and threat to re-invade Kuwait was quick, firm, and active. President Clinton was clear and unequivocal in his statements. He backed them by immediately beginning to move what was projected to reach 70,000 American and allied ground, air, and sea forces into the region, to reinforce the substantial forces already there. And Saddam backed down.[52]

In contrast, in Haiti, where one threat after another had been diluted or postponed, especially the embarrassing incident in October

1993 of the *U.S.S. Harlan County* steaming into the harbor of Port-au-Prince but being turned back to sea by demonstrators on the docks, it took the troop carriers actually and confirmably being in the air for General Cedras to take the administration's invasion threat seriously.

On Bosnia it's been a mixed message. No doubt that the fulfillment of the pledge to deploy the 20,000 U.S. troops recouped some of the credibility that had been lost by the gap between the administration's rhetoric and its action up until then. But the very need to recoup was part of the problem. The message that only when finally forced to do so, when most if not all other options have been exhausted and only when an aggressor's defiance and disregard for the West had reached the brazen extremes that the Serbs' did in May–June 1995, will the United States commit its military forces, is not all that credibility-enhancing in the long run. Moreover, it remains to be seen what will happen with the one year "sunset" provision self-imposed on the U.S. deployment. If the situation is shaky yet U.S. troops are withdrawn anyway, or if the situation deteriorates soon after a troop withdrawal, the position that these were the terms of the original commitment might have political resonance and even legalistic validity, but it would risk forfeiting whatever credibility had been recouped.

Here too, not just on Bosnia and not just for the Clinton administration, part of the problem is the structural one of the greater difficulties inherent to the post–Cold War era of the projection of credibility being even less of a unilateral matter than before. The Europeans were not exactly a paragon of consistency or robustness at any point during the break-up of Yugoslavia. The Russians asserted their own interests. The United Nations was way too reluctant to turn the key. But the point nevertheless remains that it is the United States that risks paying the steepest price in terms of damaged credibility. It therefore is incumbent on any administration either to take such constraints into consideration before making threats or to commit itself sufficiently to the strategy to ensure that support necessary to carry it out can be built.

How to Constitute Uses of Military Force?
The Dilemmas of Multilateralism

It was quite the swing of the political pendulum from candidate Clinton's ardent support for creating a standing UN military to the berating of the world body in President Clinton's first speech to the UN General Assembly on the need to "know when to say no."

Article 43 of the UN Charter had called on "All Members . . . to make available to the Security Council, on its call and in accordance with a special agreement or agreements . . . [to be] negotiated as soon as possible . . . armed forces, assistance and facilities . . . necessary for the purpose of maintaining international peace and security." This standing force was to be directed by a Military Staff Committee (Articles

45–47), consisting of the chiefs of staff of the armed forces of the permanent members of the Security Council, which would directly advise the
Security Council and would be in operational charge of the military
forces. None of this ever happened, in part because of the Cold War rivalries and in part because of deep-seated American domestic opposition to such sovereignty-encroaching measures. Thus when candidate
Clinton endorsed dusting off these UN Charter provisions, it was going
much further than just supporting the traditional UN peacekeeping
mode of financial and troop contributions mission-by-mission, for
stated purposes and on a temporary basis.

The interagency task force set up to develop a policy plan along
these lines was one of the first of all the foreign policy task forces (its
presidential review directive, or "PRD," was number 13, among approximately 30 such directives set out in the first six months). It was a
"top priority," UN Ambassador Madeleine Albright stated in May 1993
congressional testimony, "to ensure that the UN is equipped with a robust capacity to plan, organize, lead and service peacekeeping activities."[53] Initial reports on PRD–13 leaked to the press in June and July
included draft recommendations for a number of far-reaching proposals
("forward-leaning," in State Department parlance) including increased
U.S. funding and troop commitments, and a willingness to put American troops "under the 'operational control' of UN commanders 'on a
regular basis.'"[54]

The timing could not have been worse, as this was also the moment in which the Somalia operation was coming asunder. Mats Berdal
makes the point that it was "not only disingenuous but also factually
inaccurate to assert, as was done in Congress, that Americans had died
in Somalia because they were operating under UN command. . . . The
decision to use units of the Special Forces against a suspected Aideed
stronghold was made at the headquarters of the Special Operations
Command in Florida and relayed directly to the Special Operations
Command deployed in Mogadishu . . . the Special Representative of the
Secretary General was not informed . . . and the [UN] Force Commander was only told about the operation just before it was launched."[55]
None of that mattered, though, in the virtual reality of American politics. The conservative populist opposition to things UN, already set off
by reports of how far PRD-13 was going as a matter of general policy,
was now fueled by the outrage over the Mogadishu incident.

In the ensuing months, the Clinton administration not only got out
of Somalia, but by the time PRD-13 had become Presidential Decision
Directive (PDD)-25 it was toned down and scaled back. Among its provisions and policy guidance:

> The U.S. does not support a standing UN army, nor will we earmark
> specific U.S. military units for participation in UN operations. . . .

It is not U.S. policy to seek to expand either the number of UN peace operations or U.S. involvement in such operations. . . .
The U.S. assessment rate should be reduced to 25 percent [from 31.7 percent]. . . .

The criteria delineated for whether to vote for UN peace operations, whether to agree to finance them, and whether to commit U.S. forces to them were increasingly restrictive with the level of commitment and with a distinct overall tone of no-until-proven-yes.[56]

"Multilateralism" had become a dirty word. Administration opponents railed against any and all ideas and policies that could be tarred with this new measure of ostensibly being soft and naive. They scored many political points, but it wasn't very constructive in terms of answering the "how" question of constituting effective post–Cold War strategies. Casting the basic strategic options as unilateralism versus multilateralism presented a flawed dichotomy and a false choice. It simply is the nature of many of the threats and problems the United States faces in the post–Cold War world that multilateral strategies inherently work better than unilateral ones. The real issue is how to overcome the problems inherent to acting multilaterally so that these strategies can reach their potential. American leadership is key for that, and the administration could be criticized for failing to exert sufficient leadership—but that has less to do with the rhetoric about maintaining versus abandoning American leadership than about redefining the U.S. leadership role consistent with the nature of the threats, the structure of the system, and the distribution of power that characterize this new era.

From this perspective, politics aside, there still has been ample basis for criticizing the United Nations. Secretary General Boutros-Ghali has come under criticism for over-reaching in his own role, particularly in Somalia and Bosnia. The system suffers from enormous overload: of the total of 34 peace operations conducted by the UN since its inception, 21 had been initiated since 1988. That is an enormous agenda for any institution, especially for one with so little institutional capacity for such operational requisites as command and control, communications, intelligence, training, supply and logistics, and the like. Moreover, the structure of decision-making authority for conducting such operations would be the envy of Rube Goldberg. The lines of authority go this way and that, cross over, get jagged, and generally add up to a bottom line of decision-making too slow and indecisive to either carry out complex and speedy military operations or to convey credibility to an aggressor.[57] The "dual-key" arrangement in Bosnia by which the United States and NATO could not take military action without prior UN approval undermined credibility and complicated operations. The whole setup was "insane," Assistant Secretary of State Holbrooke lamented in July 1995 when UN authorities wouldn't let NATO retaliate for the UN peacekeepers taken hostage.[58] Indeed by October 1995 Boutros-Ghali was acknowledging that "enforcement is beyond the power of the UN. . . . In the future, if peace enforcement is needed it should be conducted by countries with the will to do it."[59]

The approach taken in both the Gulf War and in Bosnia with IFOR of combining UN political authority with U.S.-led diplomatic coalition-building and military command can serve as at least a partial model. The Security Council has unique political legitimacy with which to authorize the use of military force. This is especially important in those conflicts that are at least partially intra-state and thus raise issues of sovereignty and its rights and limits.[60] But other than conventional peacekeeping, when hostilities are actual or imminent, the conduct of combat needs to be left with national military authorities in coalitions (ad hoc or formal alliance) of varying sizes and forms.

Regional multilaterals such as the OSCE also have important roles to play. The 1994 CSCE-to-OSCE name change was intended to reflect a shift, as a former U.S. ambassador put it, from "a set of principles" as embodied in the 1975 Helsinki Final Act to "an operational organization." The organization's November 1990 Charter of Paris for a New Europe sought to build on Helsinki and anticipate the post–Cold War greater salience of intra-state instability by legitimizing "mandatory third-party involvement" in disputes involving threats to democracy and human rights, on the grounds that "in order to strengthen peace and security among our states, the advancement of democracy, and respect for and effective exercise of human rights, are indispensable." Such OSCE third party interventions, as Abram and Antonia Chandler Chayes conclude in their recent study, have had the most success "in relatively low-level situations."[61] Yet the significance of these is not to be underestimated, as with the successful efforts to reduce tensions and manage the conflicts in such recent cases as Russia-Estonia, Moldova and Hungary-Romania.

The prospects for other regional multilaterals need to be assessed even more cautiously, although not totally dismissed. The Organization of American States (OAS) did play a role in the Haiti crisis, drawing legitimacy from its recently passed Santiago resolution (June 1991) delineating as grounds for intervention "the sudden interruption of the democratic political institutional process." The Organization of African Unity (OAU) created in June 1993 its "Mechanism for Conflict Prevention, Management and Resolution," which has been implemented in the Western Sahara and Burundi, albeit cautiously and with mixed results, and with doubts persisting as to whether it can overcome its own internal rivalries and institutional weaknesses. In Asia the ASEAN (Association of Southeast Asian Nations) Regional Forum (ARF) is still in its formative stages, as are the Middle East Arms Control and Regional Security (ACRS) and other multilateral "working groups."[62]

Of course, unilateralist options always remain for the United States. The July 1993 attack on Baghdad in retaliation for the attempted assassination of former President Bush was a unilateral act, and appropriately so. Virtually every speech and congressional testimony and policy document includes the unilateralist caveat. But this is mostly a truism, and at that one that is unlikely to have many applications in the post–Cold War era. The challenging and crucial questions on strategy are those that address the structural, procedural, political, operational, and other problems of acting multilaterally, and do so for the many forms that multilateral action can take.

Conclusion

"Gosh, I miss the Cold War," President Clinton went so far as to remark in the days after the October 1993 Mogadishu debacle.[63] Such nostalgic lamentations, however, reflect classic selective history. Were we really that adept in the wars we fought in Korea and Vietnam? In the 1982–1984 Lebanon intervention? In the controversies and indeed constitutional crisis over aiding the Nicaraguan contras? There was no golden age when it comes to the use of military force. Even the best answers the American political system has devised to the questions of who should make the decisions, why force should be used, what strategies such uses should take, and how they are to be carried out have not been without limits, temporality or downsides. My emphasis on the structural dimension of these policy challenges is intended to bring out the ways in which these questions have some aspects that have a history to them, and some that are inherent to the complexities and uncertainties of post–Cold War international relations and domestic politics with which any administration would have to wrestle. Indeed the splits today are not just between but within the political parties, each of which has internationalist and isolationist factions.

The point of the structural/behavioral distinction has been to be able to acknowledge such inherent constraints and dilemmas and from there to make the central analytic issue whether the policies and performance of the Clinton administration have moved us at least closer to working answers to the who, why, what, and how questions about the use of U.S. military force in the post–Cold War era. The record in this regard is a mixed one.

First, the question of who decides between the President and Congress has been more avoided than addressed, and even that with some close calls. The immediate political costs and constraints have been contained, but only by deferring the central issue—indeed, the most central issue any democracy must grapple with—for yet another day. And, paradoxically, the public may be more ready to support the use of military force at least for certain policy objectives than leaders realize.

Second, the administration has made a consistent and effective case about the "why" question with respect to threats of inter-state aggression (e.g., North Korea 1994, Iraq 1994, China-Taiwan 1996). But it first overreached and then overly compensated on issues involving the interrelationship of interests and values. A more coherent conception did begin to emerge through its Haiti and Bosnia interventions, although since both were more negotiated occupations than coercive interventions the question still remained about what interests would be deemed sufficiently vital to take riskier and more assertive military action.

Third, with respect to strategy ("what"), the inter-state/intra-state distinction again is evident. Force and diplomacy were effectively integrated against the threat of North Korean nuclear proliferation, against Iraqi efforts to break out of UN-mandated containment, against Chinese provocations against Taiwan. The threats made were credible, both in terms of the judgment displayed and the resolve conveyed. But a comparably effective mix of political and military strategies for ethnic and other conflicts with significant intra-state dimensions has yet to be found. Preventive diplomacy has to be taken from rhetoric to action. Interventions should not be called humanitarian, and especially should not be carried out on these terms, unless the designation fits the causes and not just the consequences of the conflicts. When that is not the case, traditional notions of peacemaking and doctrines of limited war need to be recognized as not fitting.

Finally, the debate over multilateralism needs to get beyond both espousal of the term as a cure-all and decrying of it as a dirty word. The real issue is not if nations should act multilaterally but how we can effectively do so, and not just about the United Nations but also about regional multilateral organizations and other international institutions, as well as nations coordinating and acting collectively on more informal and de facto bases. Given that the United States is likely to continue to need to play a leadership role in almost every multilateral configuration, it's all the more essential that our own political debate get ahead of the curve. To be sure, other political forces bear a lot more of the blame than the Clinton administration for the "straw-manning" of this debate. But its initial over-reaching and then overcompensating contributed to the problem.

There's no question that the second part of the Clinton first term went much better than the first part. The key to continuing that pattern, should there be a second Clinton term, is to learn from both the successes and the failures. The latter requires avoiding the rationalizing notions either that no other policies were possible than the ones followed, or that to the extent that a successful policy eventually was found that's all that really matters. To do this is of course inherently difficult, psychologically no less than politically; it also is strategically wise.

Endnotes

1. John F. Harris, "Troops Who Have Served in Both Find Haiti A Cut Above Somalia," *Washington Post*, October 6, 1994, p. A26.
2. SIPRI, *Yearbook: World Armaments and Disarmament, 1987–1993*, (New York: Oxford University Press, annual volumes); Edward Luttwak, "Toward Post-Heroic Warfare," *Foreign Affairs*, Vol. 3, 74 (May/June 1995): 109.
3. Edward S. Corwin, *The President: Office and Powers, 1787–1957* (New York: New York University Press, 1957).
4. Richard E. Neustadt, *Presidential Power: The Politics of Leadership*, 2nd ed. (New York: John Wiley & Sons, 1980).
5. Robert A. Katzmann, "War Powers: Toward a New Accommodation," in Thomas E. Mann (ed.), *A Question of Balance: The President, the Congress and Foreign Policy* (Washington, D.C.: Brookings Institution, 1990), p. 45.
6. The Supreme Court's 1983 *Chadha* decision striking down the legislative veto took at least some of the potential bite out of the War Powers Resolution, but remains untested in this regard and thus also not the answer.
7. From memoranda prepared for the Clinton Administration's National Security Transition Group, December 1992–January 1993.
8. Among the supporters were Senators Sam Nunn, John Warner, George Mitchell, David Boren, William Cohen, and John Danforth, as well as Lee Hamilton. The key trade was a reversal of the presumption built into the 60-day clock, from requiring troop withdrawal unless Congress passed a resolution of approval or declaration of war during that period to allow continued deployment unless a resolution of disapproval was passed (and, because of *Chadha* a vetoable joint resolution rather than a nonvetoable concurrent one), in return for a presidential commitment to more serious and more regular consultation with the congressional leadership (primarily a "group of six" of the leadership of both the House and Senate, to be expanded under certain circumstances to a "group of eighteen," also including the chairs and ranking members of the intelligence, armed services, and foreign relations/foreign affairs committees).
9. Thomas W. Lippman, "White House Seeks Talks on War Powers," *Washington Post*, October 25, 1994, p. A12.
10. "To make matters worse, the room wasn't large enough for the some two hundred fifty members who turned up . . . there was no sound system, so people began to shout . . . even before the meeting was over, officials at the White House got calls reporting a 'disaster' on Capitol Hill." Elizabeth Drew, *On the Edge: The Clinton Presidency* (New York: Simon & Schuster, 1994), pp. 327–328; Sidney Blumenthal, "Why Are We in Somalia?" *The New Yorker* (October 25, 1993): 51.
11. The term is from my earlier article, "American Diplomacy: Around the World and Along Pennsylvania Avenue," in Mann, *A Question of Balance*, pp. 146-200.
12. Jeremy D. Rosner, *The New Tug-of-War: Congress, the Executive Branch and National Security* (Washington, DC: Carnegie Endowment, 1995): especially Chapter 3.
13. Michael Dobbs and John F. Harris, "French President Chirac Asks Congress to Fund More Peacekeeping in Bosnia," *Washington Post*, June 15, 1995, p. A34.
14. For a comparable critique, *see* Jentleson, "American Diplomacy," pp. 155–156, 175–176; *see also* James M. Lindsay, *Congress and the Politics of U.S. Foreign Policy* (Baltimore: Johns Hopkins University Press, 1994), pp. 120–126.

15. Letter dated November 13, 1995, from President Bill Clinton to Speaker of the House Newt Gingrich.

16. Pat Towell and Donna Cassata, "Congress Takes Symbolic Stand on Troop Deployment," *Congressional Quarterly Weekly Report*, December 16, 1995, p. 3817.

17. Richard J. Barnet, *The Rocket's Red Glare: When America Goes to War, The Presidents and the People* (New York: Simon & Schuster, 1990), p. 211.

18. John E. Rielly, *American Public Opinion and U.S. Foreign Policy, 1975* (Chicago: Chicago Council on Foreign Relations, 1975).

19. Bruce W. Jentleson, "The Pretty Prudent Public: Post Post-Vietnam American Opinion on the Use of Military Force," *International Studies Quarterly*, 36 (March 1992): 49–74.

20. Bruce W. Jentleson and Rebecca Britton, "Still Pretty Prudent: Post–Cold War American Public Opinion on the Use of Military Force," paper presented at the 1996 Meeting of the International Studies Association, San Diego, California, April 1996.

21. Andrew Kohut and Robert Toth, "Arms and the People," *Foreign Affairs*, Vol. 73 (November/December 1994): 60.

22. University of Maryland, Program on International Policy Attitudes, polls conducted June 13–18 and July 7–13, 1994.

23. Kohut and Toth, "Arms and the People," p. 57.

24. Cited in Richard N. Haass, *Intervention: The Use of American Military Force in the last-Cold War World* (Washington, DC: Carnegie Endowment, 1994), p. 69.

25. Hans A. Morgenthau, *In Defense of the National Interest: A Critical Examination of American Foreign Policy* (New York: Alfred A. Knopf, 1951).

26. President George Bush, "Remarks at the United States Military Academy," January 5, 1993, in Haass, *Intervention*, Appendix F, pp. 199–204.

27. Colin L. Powell, "U.S. Forces: Challenges Ahead," *Foreign Affairs*, Vol. 71 (Winter 1992/1993): 32–46.

28. Donald Neuchterlein, a former diplomat, offers another definitional effort. He delineates eight "value factors" as his key criteria: proximity of the danger, nature of the threat, economic stake, sentimental attachment, type of government aided, effect on balance of power, national prestige at stake, support of key allies. This list, however, is even longer than the Bush and Powell ones, and no more clear, objective, or operational. *See* Donald E. Neuchterlein, *America Recommitted: United States National Interest in a Restructured World* (Lexington: University of Kentucky Press, 1993), p. 28.

29. Alexander L. George and Robert O. Keohane, "The Concept of National Interest: Uses and Limitations," in Alexander L. George (ed.), *Presidential Decisionmaking on Foreign Policy: The Effective Use of Information and Advice* (Boulder, Colo: Westview Press, 1980), p. 217.

30. *Washington Post*, September 4, 1995, p. A43.

31. Michael Mandelbaum, "Foreign Policy as Social Work," *Foreign Affairs*, 75 (January/February 1996), pp. 16–32; Stanley Hoffmann, "In Defense of Mother Theresa: Morality in Foreign Policy," *Foreign Affairs*, 75 (March/April 1996), pp. 172–175.

32. *See, for example*, Emily O. Goldman, "Thinking About Strategy Absent the Enemy," *Security Studies*, 4 (Autumn 1994).

33. President of the United States, *A National Security Strategy of Engagement and Enlargement* (Washington, DC: Government Printing Office, July 1994).

34. Sheila Rule, "UN Peacekeeping Forces Named Winner of the Nobel Peace Prize," *New York Times*, September 30, 1988, pp. A1, A10; also *Los Angeles Times*, September 30, 1988, p. 10.

35. "What Readiness to Fight Two Wars Means," letter to the Editor, *New York Times*, February 16, 1995.

36. Defense Department Report (News Clips), "Ethnicity Problems Are Driving Military Requirements," Speech by Defense Secretary William Perry, May 5, 1994.

37. Paper delivered by Professor Ted Robert Gurr, "The Ethnic Challenge to International Security," Panel on New Security Issues, Conference on Engagement and Disengagement: New Directions in U.S. Foreign Policy, November 2–4, 1995, University of Maryland. *See also* Gurr's book, *Minorities at Risk: A Global View of Ethnopolitical Conflicts* (Washington, DC: U.S. Institute of Peace Press, 1993).

38. John Chipman, "Managing the Politics of Parochialism," *Survival*, 35 (Spring 1993): 146; David C. Rapaport, "Interventions and Ethno-Religious Violence; Self-Determination and Space," Working Paper #8, UCLA Center for International Relations, November 1994, p. 9; Donald Rothchild, "Pressures and Incentives for Cooperation: The Management of Ethnic and Regional Conflicts in Africa." *See also* Roy Licklider (ed.), *Stopping the Killing: How Civil Wars End* (New York: New York University Press, 1993), and I. William Zartman (ed.), *Elusive Peace: Negotiating an End to Civil Wars* (Washington, DC: Brookings Institution, 1995).

39. Mohamed Sahnoun, *Somalia: The Missed Opportunities* (Washington, DC: United States Institute of Peace Press, 1994); John L. Hirsch and Robert B. Oakley, *Somalia and Operation Restore Hope: Reflections on Peacemaking and Peacekeeping* (Washington, DC: United States Institute of Peace Press, 1995); Terence Lyons and Ahmed I. Satr, *Somalia: State Collapse, Multilateral Intervention and Strategies for Political Reconstruction*, Brookings Occasional Papers (Washington, DC: Brookings Institution, 1995); Steven R. David, "The Necessity for American Military Intervention in the Post–Cold War World," in *The United States and the Use of Force in the Post–Cold War Era*, A Report by The Aspen Strategy Group (Queenstown, MD: Aspen Institute Press, 1995), pp. 39–70; V. P. Gagnon, Jr., "Ethnic Nationalism and International Conflict: The Case of Serbia," *International Security*, 19 (Winter 1994–1995): 130–166; Warren Zimmerman, "The Last Ambassador: A Memoir of the Collapse of Yugoslavia," *Foreign Affairs*, Vol. 2, 74 (March/April 1995): 2–21; Lawrence Freedman, "Why the West Failed," *Foreign Policy*, No. 97 (Winter 1994–1995): 53–69.

40. This section draws on my paper, "Preventive Diplomacy and Ethnic Conflict: Possible, Difficult, Necessary," which is part of the University of California Institute on Global Conflict and Cooperation (IGCC) Project on "The International Spread and Management of Ethnic Conflict," forthcoming in a book edited by Donald Rothchild and David Lake.

41. Stephen John Stedman, "Alchemy for a New World Order: Overselling 'Preventive Diplomacy'," *Foreign Affairs*, Vol. 3, 74 (May/June 1995): 14–20.

42. David, "Necessity for American Military Intervention," in Aspen Strategy Group, *U.S. and the Use of Force*, p. 60; Sahnoun, *Somalia: Missed Opportunities*; Hirsch and Oakley, *Operation Restore Hope*; Walter Clarke and Jeffrey Herbst, "Somalia and the Future of Humanitarian Intervention," *Foreign Affairs*, 75, 2 (March/April 1996), pp. 70–85.

43. Douglas Jehl, "U.S. Policy: A Mistake?" *New York Times*, July 22, 1994, pp. 1 and 5; Alain Destexhe, "A Border Without Doctors," *New York Times*, February 9, 1995; see also the extraordinarily thorough and revealing study by Howard Adelman and Astri Suhrke, with Bruce Jones, *Early Warning and Conflict Management: Lessons from the Rwanda Experience*, Study 2 of the Project on International Response to Conflict and Genocide, March 1996 (xerox).

44. Richard R. Betts, "The Delusion of Impartial Intervention," *Foreign Affairs*, Vol. 6, 73 (November/December 1994): 20–33.

45. Ibid., p. 25.

46. Alexander L. George, "The Role of Force in Diplomacy: A Continuing Dilemma for U.S. Foreign Policy," in Gordon Craig and Alexander George, *Force and Statecraft*, 3rd ed. (New York: Oxford University Press, 1995), pp. 258–274; and Christopher M. Gacek, *The Logic of Force: The Dilemma of Limited War in American Foreign Policy* (New York: Columbia University Press, 1994).

47. Speech to the Georgetown Institute of Foreign Service, November 16, 1994.

48. Andrew J. R. Mack, "Why Big Nations Lose Small Wars: The Politics of Asymmetric Conflict," in Klaus Knorr (ed.), *Power, Strategy and Security: A World Politics Reader* (Princeton: Princeton University Press, 1983), pp. 126–151; Steven Rosen, "War, Power and the Willingness to Suffer," in Bruce Russett (ed.), *Peace, War and Numbers* (Beverly Hills: Sage 1972), pp. 167–184. "Unless we suffered more than 40 percent casualties," a former Viet Cong battalion commander stated, "we considered our forces were still intact"; Robert G. Kaiser, "Communist Leaders Stoutly Defend Tet Losses," *Washington Post*, May 16, 1994, p. A12.

49. William Drozdiak, "NATO Presses Bosnia's Combatants to Accept Partition," *Washington Post*, June 10, 1994, p. A24.

50. Jane E. Holl, "We the People Here Don't Want No War: Executive Branch Perspectives on the Use of Force," in Aspen Strategy Group, *U.S. and the Use of Force*, p. 124 and passim.

51. George, "The Role of Force in Diplomacy," and George and William E. Simons (eds.), *The Limits of Coercive Diplomacy*, 2nd ed. (Boulder, Colo: Westview Press, 1994).

52. On the Reagan and Bush policies in the 1980s and the lead-up to Saddam's invasion of Kuwait, *see* my book, *With Friends Like These: Reagan, Bush and Saddam, 1982–1990* (New York: W. W. Norton and Company, 1994).

53. Cited in Mats R. Berdal, "Fateful Encounter: The United States and UN Peacekeeping," *Survival*, 36 (Spring 1994): 32.

54. Cited in Ibid., p. 34.

55. Ibid., pp. 40–41; Clarke and Herbst, "Somalia and the Future of Humanitarian Intervention."

56. Department of State, *The Clinton Administration's Policy on Reforming Multilateral Peace Operations*, May 1994; *see also* the follow-up report put out by the White House, *A Time for Peace, Promoting Peace: The Policy of the United States*, February 1995.

57. *See, for example*, the charts in Jim Whitman and Ian Bartholomew, "UN Peace Support Operations: Political-Military Considerations," in Donald C. F. Daniel and Bradd C. Hayes (eds.), *Beyond Traditional Peacekeeping* (London: Macmillan, 1995), pp. 178–179.

58. *Washington Post*, July 18, 1885.

59. John M. Goshko, "Balkan Peacekeeping Exposes Limits of UN, Boutros-Ghali Says," *Washington Post*, October 10, 1995, p. A21.

60. Jentleson, "Preventive Diplomacy and Ethnic Conflict." For further discussion of this issue see a number of the excellent articles in Gene M. Lyons and Michael Mastanduno (eds.), *Beyond Westphalia? State Sovereignty and International Intervention* (Baltimore: Johns Hopkins University Press, 1995).

61. Abram and Antonia Handler Chayes, eds., *Preventive Diplomacy in the Post–Communist World: Mobilizing International and Regional Organizations* (Washington, DC: Brookings Institution, 1996), p. 10. *See also* Joseph Lepgold, "Does Europe Still Have a Place in U.S. Foreign Policy? A Domestic Politics Argument," in Douglas T. Stuart and Stephen Szabo (eds.), *Discord and Collaboration in a New Europe: Essays in Honor of Arnold Wolfers* (Washington, DC: Johns Hopkins Foreign Policy Institute Press, 1994), p. 179.

62. On the Middle East *see* Alan Makovsky, Bruce W. Jentleson, et. al., *Building a Middle East Community: The Future of the Multilateral Middle East Peace Process* (Washington, DC: Washington Institute for Near East Policy, forthcoming 1996).

63. Devroy and Smith, "Clinton Re-Examines a Foreign Policy Under Siege."

Part

II

Functional Problems

···

4

"Return to Normalcy"? Global Economic Policy at the End of the Century

Benjamin J. Cohen

Global economic policy, like all of foreign policy, ultimately is about security—the pursuit of safety in an unsafe world. But safety from what? What is the threat? In economic relations between states, physical survival or territorial integrity are not normally thought to be at question. What is really at issue is political independence—the ability to promote material well-being at home free of constraining influence from abroad. Each nation's goal is, to the extent possible, to maximize economic policy autonomy against all threat of outside interference.

In this respect, as in so many others, the United States has long been a privileged exception in the international community—a country largely free to do its own thing. Most nations are resigned to the inherent limitations of an interdependent world economy, where everyone is to some extent dependent on, and therefore vulnerable to, everyone else. Some compromise of policy autonomy is considered normal: the price to be paid for the manifold benefits of global trade and investment. But America, after World War II, was not a normal country. As acknowledged global leader, the United States enjoyed a degree of economic independence second to none. In policy terms, we were able to greatly insulate ourselves from the influence of others. Even more crucially, we could often impose our own will elsewhere, shaping policies and structures overseas to suit domestic interests and preferences. Autonomy was not absolute—but it was close. Call it the Sinatra doctrine. As in the crooner's signature song, America could truthfully boast that in most circumstances "I did it my way."

Benjamin J. Cohen is Louis G. Lancaster Professor of International Political Economy at the University of California, Santa Barbara. Educated at Columbia University, he has taught at Princeton University and the Fletcher School of Law and Diplomacy, Tufts University. He is the author of eight books, including In Whose Interest? *(New Haven: Yale University Press, 1986) and* Crossing Frontiers: Explorations in International Political Economy *(Boulder, CO: Westview Press, 1991).*

Today, however, it seems (to quote another popular ballad) "the times, they are a-changing." As the twentieth century—"the American century"[1]—draws to a close, the United States senses that its exceptionalism is becoming sharply diminished. Increasingly, we feel hemmed in by forces beyond our immediate control: less able to act unilaterally in managing economic affairs at home or abroad; more and more "normal," in effect becoming just like any other country. The decade of the 1920s, that momentous epoch when the American century began, was happily celebrated by contemporaries as a welcome "return to normalcy." Are we now, at the fin de siècle, experiencing yet another "return to normalcy"—only this time, one rather less to our liking? If so, how serious is the problem, and what can we do about it?

These are the questions addressed in this chapter. At issue is the apparent decline of America's policy autonomy in the world economy. Appearances, I shall argue, do not deceive. But our "return to normalcy," while real, is actually quite different from what most observers have in mind. Challenges to our economic security come from not one but two directions: from other states, whose income and wealth have grown relative to our own; and from the marketplace, where private actors have gained increasing influence over the conduct of public policy. The threat from other states, I suggest, is really less ominous than popularly supposed. The threat from the marketplace, on the other hand, often tends to be gravely underestimated. Future policy responses from Washington must be based on an accurate assessment of challenges from both directions.

Basic Trends

The story of America's apparent "return to normalcy" is a familiar one.[2] At the end of World War II, as the cliché goes, the United States bestrode the world like a colossus. More recently, by contrast, policy autonomy in economic affairs has been eroded by developments both at home and abroad. Domestically, our political system has grown ever more fragmented as a result of the historic ebb of authority from the executive branch toward Congress, where particularist regional or sectoral interests can more easily exercise effective influence over decision-making. Internationally, tensions and frictions have been exacerbated by the emergence of new centers of power in Europe, Japan, and elsewhere, each determined to promote its own distinct interests and preferences; as well as by the end of the Cold War, which has removed the "security imperative" to contain commercial or financial conflicts for the sake of preserving the Western anti-communist alliance. In addition, the sheer complexity of policy has risen owing to a proliferation of, and multiplying linkages among, economic issues, magnifying uncertainties about both instrumentalities and outcomes.

Cumulatively, these developments have combined to cast an increasingly long shadow over America's sense of national economic security.

The change, however, should not be exaggerated. The United States was never quite the world "hegemon" that many historical accounts would seem to suggest; nor are we yet the pitiful helpless giant that many fear we might become. A decline of autonomy should not be mistaken for a fall from grace.

It is true that in the immediate postwar years we were, as Robert Keohane wrote in the first volume of this series, a "Gulliver among the Lilliputians"[3]—the only major industrial country left untouched by the devastation of global hostilities. No swarm of foreigners could tie this giant down. America accounted for one-third of the world economy, including nearly half of all manufacturing output. United States exports dominated markets everywhere; New York was the world's financial capital; and the dollar was in universal demand as an international currency, freeing us from any need to worry about how to finance possible deficits in our external accounts. The United States was unique in its ability to act unilaterally, abroad as well as at home. Washington also enjoyed an unprecedented influence in the design of postwar economic institutions, including the General Agreement on Tariffs and Trade (GATT) and the International Monetary Fund (IMF). GATT was founded on the same two principles of reciprocity and non-discrimination that the United States had been promoting since the first Reciprocal Trade Agreements Act of 1934. The IMF was built around the linchpin of the dollar, preserving America's privileged status in monetary affairs.

Yet even at the height of its power, the United States was never wholly unconstrained. As rich as we were, we could hardly ignore the problems of economic reconstruction in Europe and Japan or development elsewhere. Prosperity at home, it quickly became clear, would be out of the question without generous programs of financial assistance and trade liberalization for our friends abroad. Nor, as influential as we were, could we have our way unreservedly in the design of the GATT and IMF. Institution-building also required accommodating the interests and disabilities of others. In GATT, special provisions were conceded on issues ranging from Britain's system of Imperial Preference to the use of trade measures for balance-of-payments purposes. In the IMF, Washington was forced to retreat from its demands for tough conditionality in the financing of external deficits. America may have dominated the postwar scene, but it was no imperial monarch. As economist William Diebold once remarked, no U.S. policymaker from that period ever published a memoir entitled "My Days as a Happy Hegemon."

Conversely, despite all the adverse developments of the last half century, the shadow over America's economic security is not as dark as many fear. For some observers, over-reacting to diminished influence, the days of the Sinatra doctrine are now truly and conclusively over.

We are not just *becoming* more "normal," it is said. We have indeed *become* "normal"—an economy no less vulnerable than others. In the words of Jeffry Frieden: "The United States is facing constraints more similar to those of relatively smaller countries."[4] In fact, this formulation is misleading. Gulliver has not metamorphasized into merely another Lilliputian. In most respects, the United States today still maintains a degree of economic independence second to none. More nuanced appraisal of recent experience, I submit, suggests that our latitude for unilateral action in the world economy remains remarkably broad.

Trends, however, have clearly not been favorable. In that more limited sense, we really have undergone a kind of "return to normalcy": a fading, if not yet an end, of the Sinatra doctrine. Gulliver we remain, but in a weakened state. The question is: Where do we go from here? Challenges to U.S. economic security have expanded, and indeed continue to intensify, across a broad range of policy issues, from the management of interest rates and fiscal policy to the regulation of trade or investment flows. As indicated, threats come from two directions: from other states and from the marketplace. Neither challenge is as well understood as it should be.

The Threat from Other States

Most obvious is the threat coming from other states. Gulliver, plainly, is not what he used to be. Our nation's share of global output has declined dramatically over the last half century, dropping by nearly half from its postwar high. Large trade surpluses have been replaced by even larger trade deficits; the dollar has shrunk in both value and attractiveness; and we have gone from being the world's richest creditor to the dubious distinction of top debtor. Erstwhile Lilliputians, meanwhile, have grown impressively in both wealth and influence, including Germany and its partners in the European Union, Japan, and the newly industrializing economies of East Asia and Latin America. It would now seem easier for others to tie the giant down than it used to be.

How serious is this threat? The answer, I suggest, is less discouraging than often thought. The challenge from other states is material. But it is neither mortal nor unmanageable.

Toward a Mosaic World Economy

In some quarters, it has become fashionable lately to take a rather despairing view of prospects for inter-state relations in the global economy. In the aftermath of World War II, the victorious Allies (including, in time, even the former enemy nations of Germany and Japan) succeeded in creating a remarkably open and prosperous international economic system. Rising volumes of trade and investment played a key role in promoting the continued growth of national economies; domestic markets, in turn, became increasingly integrated on a scale not previously seen in this century. More importantly—until now, at least—the governments of the non-communist world succeeded in maintaining and even extending the liberal postwar order despite ever-lurking forces of parochial nationalism and particularist interest. Policy conflict among nations was not absent, of course: tensions and friction are endemic to any system of economic relations among sovereign states. But the important point is that for more than 50 years conflict was kept *manageable*, as national policymakers cooperated to avert any serious threat of disintegration or breakdown in the global economy such as occurred in the 1930s. The caliber of international economic management may not have been to everyone's taste, but it did contrive, by and large, to preserve the acknowledged benefits of commercial and financial interdependence.

As the end of the century approaches, however, those benefits seem increasingly jeopardized, for two reasons. One is the end of the Cold War, which has removed one of the most important adhesives that, for over four decades, helped to hold the noncommunist world together—namely, the spectre of a military threat from the Soviet Union. With that threat now gone, many fear,[5] the perceived value of the Cold-War alliance system will in time be eroded, ultimately intensifying the narrow egoism of state actors and adding to temptations to "free ride" in economic relations. Resistance to concessions under present cooperative arrangements may grow, and possibly even unilateral defections from commitments previously made, risking greatly amplified tensions and friction across a broad range of economic issues.

The other reason is the accelerating redistribution of economic power among states, which has altered significantly both the ability and the willingness of the United States to bear its traditionally large share of the costs of economic leadership. Throughout most of the postwar period, U.S. policymakers clearly understood that with disproportionate influence must also come disproportionate responsibility. Any temptation to abuse power to suit our own policy preferences, narrowly defined, was tempered by a self-conscious commitment to preserving the cohesion and vitality of the system as a whole.[6] Hence other governments could generally rely on Washington's resolve and capacity for timely concessions or generous sacrifices, when necessary, to facilitate agreement and promote the welfare of its friends. More recently, by contrast, a weakened Gulliver has grown weary of being the main bulwark against opportunistic free-riding by others; and, indeed, has become increasingly intemperate in its own pursuit of self-interest, compounding the risk of conflict in economic affairs. The liberal order can no longer automatically count on its principal patron.

For both reasons, therefore, some erosion in the quality of collective economic management would appear likely, if not inevitable. In the words of one recent study: "There is no longer a cold war security imperative to inspire generous economic policy leadership from the United States or to ensure that rival market economies . . . will follow the U.S. lead."[7] A cautious outlook, to this extent, is not unjustified.

Some observers would go further, arguing that the very fabric of the liberal order will be increasingly threatened in coming years. It is not just that the impulse for cooperation is apt to be more or less diluted, they suggest. It is that cooperation will be supplanted altogether by a more basic and compelling instinct in state behavior—the drive to compete and, if possible, to prevail over all others. In the words of Edward Luttwak, "the very nature of states is relentlessly adversarial."[8] Hence as the exigencies of the Cold War fade and American leadership is withdrawn, traditional geo-politics will be gradually replaced by an emergent "geo-economics"—"the continuation of the ancient rivalry of the nations by new industrial means."[9] Economic warfare is just around the corner.[10]

Such fears, however, are unnecessarily alarmist. Predictions of imminent disintegration and breakdown in fact seem unwarranted. Certainly it is not implausible to argue that the postwar system—based as it was on the unusual combination of bipolar Cold War and U.S. predominance in economic relations—constituted a rather exceptional interlude in the broad sweep of history. But that hardly justifies a hopeless pessimism about what comes next, as the American century ends. Not all the gains of the last 50 years must inevitably be lost. And the reason, quite simply, as I have argued previously,[11] is that other fundamental changes have also occurred, and they will not disappear even with the ending of the Cold War and U.S. predominance. A good number of those changes act, in effect, as "countervailing forces" to help "lock in" many of the benefits of commercial and financial interdependence that have been achieved since 1945. Economic warfare is not in fact inevitable.

At the international level, for instance, a variety of global regime structures[12] have been set in place to help promote collective economic management, in many instances formally institutionalized in multilateral organizations like the IMF and GATT—recently succeeded by the new World Trade Organization (WTO)—or in regularized procedures such as the annual economic summits of the so-called Group of Seven.[13] Regimes, of course, by no means guarantee that all state behavior will be mutually cooperative. They do, however, significantly increase the probability that, geo-economics withstanding, the tensions and frictions so endemic in international economic relations can be successfully contained. Similarly, at the national level, a variety of influential constituencies have been created by the opening of domestic economies that now have an important stake in the maintenance of systemic stability—including, in particular, firms and industries that have become increasingly dependent on exports, imports, or transnational production and investments for a substantial portion of their earnings. As Helen Milner has argued: "Increased economic integration [has] altered the domestic politics of trade."[14] And finally, at the level of cognition, a variety of attitudinal changes have been bred by the achievements of the liberal postwar order that can also be expected to oppose any closure in economic relations. Nearly half a century of successful experience with growing commercial and financial interdependence has clearly altered the dominant economic culture of the times. Social values and perceptions have quite obviously shifted in favor of greater appreciation of the benefits of mutual restraint and open markets.

Precisely *how* influential any of these countervailing forces are likely to be is difficult to say. In principle, international regimes, domestic politics, and social values all matter importantly to policymakers. In practice, however, their effectiveness in determining state behavior clearly tends to vary from one issue to another and even, for any single issue, from one time to another. Prospects for inter-state relations, therefore, are also likely to vary both across issues and across time, depending on the relative strength of disintegrative and countervailing forces in each individual instance. Outcomes are likely to be not only highly idiosyncratic but also frequently mutable.

In short, no uniform or predictable pattern of change can be expected. International economic relations have always been messily ambiguous and differentiated to some extent. But now they are becoming yet more variegated and multi-layered than ever—growing closer together in some instances, splitting wider apart in others, and occasionally even reversing direction under the pressure of events. Increasingly, the system is taking on the characteristics of a colorful and complex *mosaic*—a world not easily reduced to simple aggregative analysis or broad facile generalization. Much depends on the detail, with cooperation and conflict in continuous contention over every kind of issue.

Still Primus Inter Pares

In this emerging mosaic economy, inconstant and unpredictable, Americans may be excused for feeling rather more insecure than previously. A nation accustomed to doing it "my way" can hardly be expected to remain complacent as uncertainty grows and the risk of economic conflict keeps mounting. Moreover, the emergence of new power centers elsewhere inevitably corrodes our insulation from foreign influence. The threat from other states is not imaginary.

But here too fears seem unnecessarily alarmist. Gulliver may be weakened, but only relatively. The United States still commands an impressive array of resources, based on an economy that remains the largest, most diversified, and most technologically advanced anywhere. America is the world's biggest exporter and investor, home to its most attractive financial markets and source of its most widely used currency—a colossus no longer, but still clearly *primus inter pares* among states. To repeat: "return to normalcy" does not mean that we have now become truly "normal." In policy terms, America still retains more capacity for unilateral action than any other country.

Of course, our continuing advantage could only be transitory. Present trends, after all, might persist and even accelerate, adding irreversibly to the prosperity and power of other states, as many prominent analysts—labeled "declinists" by Samuel Huntington[15]—have contended. The United States may simply be enjoying the last warm glow of the American century's twilight years. But other observers, so-called revivalists,[16] disagree, arguing to the contrary that Gulliver's apparent weakening either has been greatly exaggerated or else can be more or less easily corrected.[17] The evidence would seem to support this latter, more cautious assessment.

A glance at various economic indicators, for instance, suggests that most of America's apparent decline occurred rather early in the postwar period and was attributable largely to the remarkable rapid recovery of the ruined economies of Europe and Japan—what Joseph Nye calls the "World War II effect."[18] More recently the U.S. share of world output and exports, as well as of most leading sectors in manufacturing, has remained comparatively steady, with little sign of continuing downward trend. Gulliver's condition is not deteriorating persistently. In Nye's words:

> In general . . . the indices of economic power at various levels of aggregation are reasonably consistent. They show a relatively sharp decline during the postwar quarter century of supposed U.S. hegemony and relatively moderate change since then.[19]

More importantly, the indices suggest no new concentration of power elsewhere capable of seriously challenging America's still preeminent position in commercial and financial affairs. Insofar as influence has been redistributed among states, it has tended to diffuse rather than converge elsewhere. America faces no single rival with resources to match our own—not Japan, with gross output still less than two-thirds of ours; not Europe, still far from genuine economic union; certainly not Russia; nor, yet, China. Hence despite our "return to normalcy," our policy independence remains considerable. Even a weakened Gulliver can feel secure, to some degree, when there is no other Gulliver in sight.

In short, the threat from other states is actually a good deal less ominous than popularly perceived. True, the days of near-absolute autonomy are over. Our economy is more exposed to external influence than before; our ability to impose our will on others is noticeably reduced. Yet across a broad range of issues, the policy initiative clearly remains with the United States. Few governments are willing to pursue programs for long that openly contravene key U.S. interests or preferences. Even fewer feel that they can safely ignore pressures or demands from Washington. And none would even think to claim for itself a right to the kind of unilateralism in foreign economic affairs that Americans still casually accept as their birthright. Though diminished, U.S. exceptionalism remains real, as demonstrated by recent experience in relations with all our major trading partners.

Japan

Nowhere is America's continuing, albeit diminished, advantage more evident than in our troubled dealings with Japan, the world's second biggest national economy. Since their military defeat in World War II, the Japanese have emerged as perhaps America's most formidable commercial rival, best symbolized by their persistent surpluses in foreign trade. In finance, they have also become our single largest creditor. Yet in policy terms it is still the United States, not Japan, that sets the agenda for the bilateral relationship. We may not always get what we want, but it is we who determine what will be discussed, and it is the Japanese who are expected to do the accommodating.

Clearly the most contentious issue between the two countries is the persistent imbalance in our mutual trade. Since the early 1980s Japan's surplus with the United States has averaged over $50 billion a year, generating angry resentment and increasingly aggressive complaints from the American Government. Overwhelmingly, the tone of bilateral relations has been defined unilaterally by Washington in what one critic has labeled America's "blame-thy-neighbor policy."[20] In effect, the United States has cast itself in the role of *demandeur*, repeatedly assaulting the Japanese over allegedly "unfair" trade practices and, under threat of sanctions, pressuring Tokyo for a variety of one-way policy concessions. Could anyone imagine the tables being turned, with Japan threatening in similar fashion to punish a recalcitrant United States?

Washington's paramount objective in recent years, under Republican Presidents Ronald Reagan and George Bush as well as Democrat Bill Clinton, has been to ensure equal opportunity for U.S. firms and products in the Japanese market—the proverbial "level playing field." The goal of market penetration has been pursued through a variety of negotiating strategies, including talks about individual product-specific import barriers as well as broader approaches like the market-oriented, sector-specific (MOSS) discussions begun in 1985 and the so-called Structural Impediments Initiative (SII) initiated in 1989. Additional leverage was provided by inclusion of the infamous "Super 301" procedure, with its threat of possible retaliatory measures against nations labeled unfair traders, in the Omnibus Trade Act of 1988.[21] George Bush's Trade Representative Carla Hills called Super 301, an expanded version of Section 301 of the Trade Act of 1974, her "crowbar" to pry open the markets of Japan and other targeted countries.[22] And yet further pressure has been applied by Hills's successor, Clinton appointee Mickey Kantor, who since taking office in 1993 has vigorously promoted a more "results-oriented" approach to negotiations with Japan, stressing a need for explicit and verifiable performance targets.

Japanese reactions to Washington's "aggressive unilateralism,"[23] not surprisingly, have tended to become increasingly embittered over time. Gradually abandoning their customary deference, Japanese elites now often openly criticize U.S. attitudes, which they regard as an outdated relic of America's early postwar superiority. Today, they say, Japan is an emerging economic superpower and should stand up more firmly to Washington's persistent demands. Representative was the 1989 Japanese bestseller *The Japan That Can Say No*, by Akio Morita, co-founder of Sony Corporation, and Shintaro Ishihara, a prominent conservative politican, which strongly urged more assertive use of Japan's own growing leverage to promote Japanese interests.[24] For many in Japan, the book was an accurate expression of their rising level of irritation and impatience with what they see as outright "bullying" by the United States. Observed one U.S. expert as early as 1990: "Japanese public opinion is increasingly turning anti-American, and the mood is one of growing resentment, frustration and contempt."[25] In late 1992, an influential panel of Japanese businessmen noted "a growing amount of frustration lingering just below the surface in Japan" about what it termed America's "self-centered thinking" on trade.[26] By 1993, some 64 percent of Japanese considered U.S.-Japan relations "unfriendly," up from 36 percent in 1990 and just 21 percent in 1985.[27] Commented the *New York Times* in 1994: Repeated trade disputes "leave no doubt that the well of distrust between the world's two economic superpowers is deepening."[28]

Furthermore, the Japanese have their own grievances against America, such as discriminatory government procurement programs, restrictions on the sale of Alaskan oil, and arbitrary interpretations of existing fair-trade laws. In their view, the United States is making Japan a scapegoat for its own many inadequacies: a low savings rate, insufficient investment, poor schools, racial tensions, and the like. According to a Foreign Ministry spokesman in 1993, "two-thirds to three-quarters of the problems" between the two countries were "of American making."[29] Where once Americans were viewed with respect and even admiration, they are increasingly seen as the international equivalent of spoiled, indolent children. "The source of the problem," said the Speaker of Japan's parliament in 1992, "is the inferior quality of U.S. labor. U.S. workers are too lazy. They want high pay without working."[30] America, the Japanese say, should concentrate on getting its own house in order.

Yet for all their unhappiness, and even disdain, the Japanese still find it difficult to say No to Washington, which remains the main guarantor of Japan's military security, and continue to acquiesce to a trade agenda largely set by the United States. During George Bush's four-year presidency, no fewer than 13 new agreements were negotiated by the two countries, all involving concessions by Tokyo on matters ranging from Japanese government procurement practices and licensing procedures to market access for an array of U.S. exports.[31] In addition, several other market-opening measures were agreed upon in a separate Action Plan announced by President Bush and Prime Minister Kiichi Miyazawa at a meeting in Tokyo in January 1992. Most prominent in the Plan was a Japanese pledge to help promote sales of U.S. automobiles and automotive parts in Japan. According to President Bush, the agreement was expected to result in an increase of U.S. exports by as much as $10 billion a year by 1995.[32]

The same pattern has also continued with the Clinton administration. In July 1993, Tokyo reluctantly agreed to a new so-called Framework Agreement (formally, the United States-Japan Framework for a New Economic Partnership), which for the first time, as advocated by Trade Representative Kantor, formally committed both sides to a "results-oriented" use of objective criteria to assess outcomes of their talks.[33] For the Clinton administration, the time for a more traditional "rules-oriented" approach to negotiation was at an end. Too often, it seemed, the results of past agreements had tended to fall rather short of expectations, leading simply to further cycles of acrimonious bargaining and accommodation. Indeed, that seemed precisely why past discussions of Japanese import barriers had been forced to escalate from the product-specific to MOSS to SII. Henceforth, in the words of the Framework Agreement, "tangible progress must be achieved." And over the next two years a fair amount of "progress" could indeed be claimed by Washington as, bit by bit, the Japanese agreed to further liberalization in a variety of sensitive areas, including public-sector construction, rice, cellular telephones, insurance, glass, telecommunications, medical equipment, and finally, once again in mid-1995, automobiles and auto parts. "Economic acupuncture," one observer called it—a "speak-loudly-and-carry-a-small-needle strategy [that] seems to be producing results."[34]

Acquiescence, of course, is not the same as unconditional surrender. Even if seemingly unable to say No, the Japanese do not say Yes readily; and as America's global economic predominance has gradually receded and Cold War memories fade, the quarrels between the two countries clearly have grown in both scope and intensity. Over the years, the pattern of the relationship has become depressingly familiar—periodic eruptions followed by irate charges and countercharges, hard-nosed negotiations, and, ultimately, carefully balanced compromise accords allowing each side to save face. More recently, the accusations have become more vituperative, the bargaining more unfriendly, and the outcomes even more inconclusive. Since the Framework Agreement was signed, America and Japan have twice gone to the very brink of economic war before, at the last minute, finding some basis for backing off. In late 1994 punitive tariffs on a wide range of Japanese imports were narrowly averted, following a highly publicized confrontation earlier in the year between President Clinton and Prime Minister Morihiro Hosokawa, when Japan acceded to U.S. demands to carry through on previous liberalization pledges. And then again in 1995, the threat of 100 percent duties on Japanese luxury cars was withdrawn when Tokyo consented to a new automotive pact. In both instances the Japanese eventually gave in, but not without real struggle and certainly not on terms initially sought by Washington. As *The Economist* observed after the 1995 deal:

> So has America got what it wanted? It likes to think so. Bill Clinton hailed the deal as a "major step forward for free trade. . . ." But closer inspection suggests that America is deluding itself. . . . Previous deals have led to rancour because the two sides interpreted them differently. This one will be no exception.[35]

Even so, is there any other country capable of doing even as much? It is still the United States that can, with impunity, employ a stategy of aggressive unilateralism. It is still Japan that is expected to respond to U.S. complaints, not the reverse. The ambiguity of the auto deal or previous accords may not be exceptional. But America's continuing edge in setting the agenda for the relationship certainly is.

Others

The story is much the same in our relations with other key trading partners as well. *China*, for example, has also been the object of intense and often angry complaints from the U.S. Government. Since the start of its market reforms in the late 1970s, China has emerged as a major force in global economics—the world's third largest national economy, though still desperately poor in per-capita terms, and now in eleventh place among world exporters. Yet despite its enormous size as well as its strategic importance in the Pacific region, that country, like Japan, has been repeatedly assaulted over allegedly unfair trade practices and threatened with punitive sanctions. And like Tokyo, Beijing has been pressured into one-way concessions that meet some, if not all, of Washington's economic policy objectives. Here too the agenda has been set largely by the United States.

At the top of the agenda have been issues of market access for U.S. exporters and China's lack of enforcement of intellectual property laws. As early as the mid-1980s, Washington took the initiative in persuading Beijing to reduce the number, secrecy, and severity of administrative barriers to imports. In 1992, under threat of U.S. retaliation, the Chinese agreed to dismantle a large proportion of their existing import restrictions.[36] And in 1995, again narrowly averting sanctions, Beijing pledged at last to crack down on domestic producers of pirated foreign videos, compact disks, and computer software.[37] As in the accords with Japan, considerable ambiguity remained to obscure just how much Washington was really able to achieve with all its strong-armed tactics. Results, ultimately, would depend on the cooperation of the Chinese authorities who, as the *New York Times* drily noted after the 1995 agreement, "so far have been inconsistent" in their follow-through.[38] Moreover, for all its efforts, Washington has also had its share of failures. In 1994, attempts to link favorable U.S. tariff treatment of Chinese imports to human-rights issues in China were summarily abandoned;[39] and in 1995, a new threat of sanctions was withdrawn despite Beijing's failure to curtail controversial sales of missile technology to Iran and Pakistan.[40] Nonetheless, it is clear that the initiative still lies with the United States. Like Japan, it is China that is expected to respond to U.S. complaints, not the reverse.

The same of course has always been true for *Canada*, our largest— but also quite distinctly junior—trading partner. Economic ties between our two nations plainly bind one side far more than they do the other. While for Americans the relationship is important but hardly central, for Canadians it is absolutely pivotal. Indeed, how could it be seen otherwise, with the United States accounting for almost three-quarters of Canada's exports (almost 20 percent of Canadian GDP) and two-thirds of its imports? Canadians recognize that this structural dependence leaves them with comparatively few policy options. Hence they accept American exceptionalism as an unpleasant but unavoidable reality. On issues ranging from automobiles and beer to steel and wheat, it is Washington that makes the demands and Ottawa that is placed on the defensive. The American side does not always win its battles. In 1993, for example, bilateral arbitration panels, set up under the United States-Canada Free Trade Agreement of 1988, ruled in Canada's favor on two high-profile disputes initiated by U.S. complaints—one involving exports of live swine to the United States, the other alleging illegal subsidization of Canadian timber production.[41] In both cases, punitive tarrifs imposed by Washington had to be refunded to Canada. But in the broader context of U.S.-Canadian relations it is clear that most fights are picked by the United States and most concessions are made by Canada.

Nor is the story much different in our relations with *Europe*, that other great player in the international trade game. Together, the 15 members of the European Union (EU), led by recently unified Germany, constitute the biggest economic bloc in the world—bigger than any single national economy, even America's. Germany alone is the world's second largest exporter and ranked number two (after Japan) among international creditors. Yet in transatlantic relations too the agenda is set largely by Washington, which has always felt a need to keep a keen eye on Europe's ambitious integration efforts. Americans are not alone, of course, in worrying that while pursuing their regional project, the Europeans might attach a higher priority to local problems than to issues of concern elsewhere. Other outsiders also recognize that Europe could be tempted to ease transitional difficulties or resolve internal conflicts by deliberately discriminating against external rivals. But only America has had the capacity, as well as the will, to bring significant pressures to bear when its commercial or financial interests appear jeopardized. Repeatedly, therefore, Europe has been called upon to respond to U.S. complaints under threat of punitive sanctions.

An apt example was provided by the dispute that erupted in early 1988 over plans for merging Europe's banking markets.[42] Initially, in a draft directive, the European Commission—the central administrative body of the European Community (EC), as the EU was then known—proposed that non-EC banks be accorded the same rights of establishment throughout the Community as EC banks only if EC banks were granted identical rights in non-EC countries. Because of prevailing geographic limits on banking operations in the United States, such a strict "mirror-image" requirement would have made it impossible for American banks to qualify for the Community market. Not surprisingly, therefore, the U.S. Government objected strongly and felt obliged to threaten retaliatory action until the Commission agreed, in a revised directive, to a more relaxed requirement of "national treatment" for EC banks in the United States. The incident did not last long and, despite some remaining differences on banking regulation, was already effectively over by mid-1989. The so-called Second Banking Coordination Directive, as revised, was formally adopted by the Community in December 1989.

In 1992, another example was provided by a long-running fight over European subsidies for grain exports and oilseed production, which the EU finally pledged to reduce (over the objections of the French Government) to avert promised punitive tariffs on European white wines and other food products.[43] And in later years yet more battles have been waged over everything from aerospace subsidies and steel to shipbuilding and the procurement practices of European public utilities—always with the possibility of American retaliation dangled over the heads of negotiators.[44] Europe clearly understands that it is no more immune to aggressive unilateralism by Washington than any of America's other trading partners. In the Commission's words: "The European Commission's principal remaining concern is the United States' willingness to threaten or actually engage in unilateral trade action."[45] Thus with Europe too, America still enjoys an exceptional capacity to play the role of *demandeur*.

The Threat from the Marketplace

In state-to-state relations, therefore, it appears that U.S. economic security is not really quite so seriously threatened as many fear. Though a colossus no longer, we are still able to manage our economic diplomacy reasonably effectively. As compared with the United States, no other nation exercises anything like the same degree of policy unilateralism. As compared with other governments, Washington remains unique in its ability, most times, to get more than it gives in negotiations. We are not yet just another "normal" country—at least not as far as other countries are concerned.

But there is also a second threat to America's economic security, the challenge of the marketplace, which is both more serious and, potentially, much less easily managed. In that respect, we are indeed becoming much more like a "normal" country, effectively constrained by outside influence.

Insular No Longer

Over the course of the postwar period, world markets have, as indicated, become integrated on a scale not previously seen in this century. National economies everywhere have become increasingly open and interdependent, more and more reliant on one another for mutual trade and investment. And while few observers question the material benefits of this historic transformative process—variously labeled economic internationalization, transnationalization, or globalization—it is clear that there are costs too in terms of potential impacts on the conduct of public policy. The more a country's economy becomes entangled with the affairs of foreigners, the less are government officials free to make choices to suit purely domestic priorities and objectives.

Among the countries most prominently caught up in this globalization process is, of course, the United States—once one of the most insular of national economies, now like so many others intimately linked in all kinds of ways to the outside world. Historically, America's policy exceptionalism was firmly grounded in a high degree of self-sufficiency. Though a major world trader by virtue of our overall size, foreign exports and imports traditionally played no more than a marginal role domestically. And while we reigned for decades as the globe's biggest source of capital, as well as the supplier of its most widely circulated currency, our monetary and financial policies long remained essentially home-grown. But now we too have become more closely entangled with the affairs of others: more dependent on foreigners for vital necessities like oil or credit; less protected from the effects of commercial or financial developments elsewhere. In effect, like others, we have competed for a commensurate share of the benefits of a liberal economic order. Thus like others we have also been forced to accept a concomitant loss of autonomy for public policy.

Not all Americans would regard this as an unfavorable turn of events. Political conservatives, who distrust government authority at any level, might actually applaud a passing of power from the public to the private sector—from despised politicians to competitive market actors. As an approach to governance, however, such a transformation may be regarded as regressive and even profoundly undemocratic, insofar as it subverts the will of the general electorate. Politicans may be ineffectual or even unsavory, but in our constitutional system they can at least be held accountable for their actions. Market actors, by contrast, are neither elected nor politically accountable, and may not even be citizens. If the will of the majority, however poorly refracted through the lens of representative government, can be thwarted by the economic power of an anonymous minority, democracy itself is threatened. The stakes could not be higher.

Unlike challenges from other states, however, the challenge of the globalized marketplace is neither easy to withstand nor, typically, amenable to formal negotiation. This is not just a question of individual constituencies—firms, labor unions, consumer groups, and the like—with a self-interested axe to grind. Particularist pressures, exercised directly on government through lobbying or other "rent-seeking activities," have always been an integral part of the policy process, in Washington no less than in any other national capital. What is different today is the more indirect role that markets now play in influencing public policy—a challenge at once less tractable and more impersonal.

The key to this new role is the wider choice set that comes to privileged elements of the private sector with the globalization of economic activity. For major market actors, international integration means more degrees of freedom—more room for maneuver in response to the actual or potential decisions of government. Higher taxes or regulation may be evaded by moving production or sales offshore; formal sanctions on a trading partner may be dodged by dealing through a third country; tighter monetary policy may be circumvented by accessing foreign sources of finance. And this broader latitude, in turn, means a significant increase of leverage in relation to political authority. Recalling the language of Albert Hirschman, influence in the policy process may be thought to depend on the relative availability of the options of Exit, Voice, and Loyalty.[46] The greater the ability of market actors to evade the preferences of public officials ("exit"), the less will government be able to count on or command submissive "loyalty." The private sector gains more "voice" to promote its own priorities and objectives.

In effect, therefore, economic globalization gives market actors a kind of de facto veto power over official policy, elusive but effective. It is elusive because it is exercised indirectly, through commercial processes rather than formal lobbying. Economic security is threatened, but not from intent that is purposive or hostile. The veto is effective because it involves a menace, the risk of exit, that may never be implemented but is always present. The pressure on policymakers is neverending. The imperative for government is to avoid provoking exercise of the exit option. This means, above all, maintaining at all times the confidence and good will of the private sector. Public policy must be made to conform persistently to what the markets appear to desire, whether or not this coincides with the preferences of elected officials. Less and less can government ignore the signals of the marketplace. Today, more and more, it is the private sector that gets to do it—or gets the government to do it—"my way."

The Globalization of Finance

Nowhere is this new challenge more evident than in the realm of finance, where economic globalization has progressed perhaps most extensively over the last half century. Fifty years ago, after the ravages of the Great Depression and World War II, money and capital markets everywhere—with the notable exception of the United States—were generally weak, insular, and strictly controlled, reduced from their previously central role in the world economy to offer little more than a negligible amount of trade financing. Starting in the late 1950s, however, private lending and investment once again began to gather momentum, powered by policy liberalization and deregulation as well as by accelerating financial innovation and technological development. The result has been a phenomenal growth of cross-border capital flows and an increasingly close integration of domestic markets. Like a phoenix risen from the ashes, global finance took flight and soared to new heights of influence in the affairs of nations.[47]

The core issue posed by financial globalization, long familiar to economists, is best summarized in terms of what I have elsewhere labeled the "Unholy Trinity"—the intrinsic incompatibility of exchange-rate stability, capital mobility, and national policy autonomy.[48] Integration of financial markets facilitates the option of capital flight, thus imposing an increasingly stark trade-off on government. Autonomy of national policy can be preserved only by giving up some degree of exchange-rate stability, with all the attendant risks of currency volatility abroad; an independent exchange-rate target can be maintained only by sustaining the confidence of international investors, at the cost of reduced control over economic performance at home. The stringent logic of the Unholy Trinity has always been a factor in the thinking of other countries, with comparatively more open economies—part of what made some compromise of policy autonomy seem "normal." Now, with increasing capital mobility, the United States too is learning how to live with the constraining influence of global finance.

For many years, we were effectively shielded from "normalcy" in finance by the international popularity of the dollar, which as indicated gave us a relatively painless way to pay for external imbalances. More recently, however, the greenback's appeal has faded considerably, eroding our exceptionalism in monetary affairs—partly owing to our persistent deficits, which have added inexorably to our foreign borrowing (increasing the supply of dollars worldwide); and partly to the resurrection of global capital markets, which has expanded access to attractive alternatives such as the Deutsche mark and yen (decreasing dollar demand). Adequate payments financing, therefore, can no longer be taken for granted. Over the past quarter century, our currency has depreciated in value by some two-thirds in relation to both its German and Japanese rivals. America's creditors now have to be wooed if they are to be induced to add to—or even merely hold onto—their outstanding dollar claims. The alternative, always lurking in the background, is the risk of a dollar crisis.

America's financial vulnerability has been increasingly evident in recent years, especially since collapse of the postwar Bretton Woods system of fixed exchange rates in the early 1970s. During the Carter administration, an early attempt to promote accelerated growth at home was quickly aborted by a flight from the dollar abroad, which could be stemmed in the end only by a dramatic tightening of monetary policy, raising interest rates to their highest level in peacetime history. In the words of Paul Volcker, who as the new head of the Federal Reserve engineered the unprecedented reversal of policy:

> Five years earlier, the argument that had clinched the victory of floating exchange rates in many minds was that domestic economic priorities would not need to be sacrificed. . . . But here we were, back to "defending" an exchange rate, with a more vigorous (if quite tardy) use of monetary policy than had ever been invoked under Bretton Woods.[49]

Likewise, the defiant assertion of policy independence of the first Reagan administration, emphasizing a controversial mix of "supply-side" tax cuts and easier monetary policy, ultimately also was muffled by a resulting increase of currency volatility—first a record appreciation of the dollar from 1981 to 1985, which caused a massive deterioration of our trade balance and a concomitant rise of foreign borrowing; and then subsequent bouts of dollar depreciation, each requiring yet more accommodating measures at home to avert or ease selling pressures in exchange markets overseas. Interest-rate reductions or government spending programs that might seem desirable for domestic purposes have, more and more, been restrained by a fear of renewed flight from the dollar. To propitiate creditors and investors, higher priority has been placed on federal budget reductions than on initiatives to create jobs or promote growth. And above all, inflation has been elevated to the rank of public enemy number one, overshadowing all other policy objectives. Effectively, as the *New York Times* has commented, the "anti-inflation cause—bolstered by the growing power of traders in the free-swinging capital markets to call the tune—has taken over center stage. . . . [Policymakers] are finding their own starring roles circumscribed by legions of private investors who hold the reins in today's capital markets."[50]

The discipline on domestic policy was certainly noticeable during the foreign-affairs minded administration of George Bush, who was repeatedly accused of lacking the "vision thing" on economic matters. It has been even more manifest during the presidency of Bill Clinton, despite his celebrated campaign slogan "It's the economy, stupid." Early Clinton proposals to expand investment in job training and infrastructure were swiftly abandoned after an unfavorable reception by financial markets. Subsequently, weakness of the dollar muted administration opposition to interest-rate increases voted by the Federal Reserve, despite the consequent risk of domestic recession. "Increasingly," concludes Paul Volcker, "the United States has found itself on the defensive in managing its monetary affairs and the dollar."[51] As our overseas debts continue to grow, Washington's ability to overrule the veto of the financial marketplace has clearly, if gradually, diminished. The dilemma has been well summarized by Walter Russell Mead:

> [T]he supports of the international role of the dollar have been gradually eroding for more than a generation, and the long-term outlook for the greenback's international role is becoming bleaker. . . . This situation presents the United States with two problems. First, there is the prospect of the gradual loss of the economic and political benefits that flow from control of the world's principal money supply. Second, there is the danger of a steep decline, potentially even a crash, of the value of the dollar as demand for it shrinks.[52]

The veto is not absolute, of course. Here too it is important not to exaggerate. As Helen Milner has cautioned, "external debt can be detrimental to any economy. But the mere fact of its existence has no clear implications for a country's influence in the world. Arguments that link debt automatically to decline should be treated with skepticism."[53] Yet the seriousness of the problem can hardly be disputed. The weakness of the dollar in a world of increased capital mobility acts undeniably as a constraint; and in contrast to the challenge from other states, which does not seem unmanageable, the threat from the marketplace seems to leave much less room for unilateral action. Economic globalization, particularly in the financial realm, is the real reason for concern about America's policy autonomy today.

Policy Options for the Future

How is the United States to respond to current challenges to its economic security? In principle, three broad options may be identified, which we could call Ignore, Isolate, or Engage. In practice, only the last of these would seem to make sense in contemporary circumstances, though it is not easy to implement.

For some observers, the only safe option is to focus on economic affairs at home—in effect: *Ignore* the outside world, with all its pesky tensions and frictions. Do as the Japanese, as well as many other foreigners, advise: Concentrate on getting our own house in order. Henry

Nau, for example, has distinguished between "globalism" and "domesticism" in economic policy, arguing that first priority should be accorded to internal rather than external challenges. The globalist view, according to Nau, traces economic problems "largely to the malfunctioning of the international economic system itself. . . . The alternative approach reverses the globalist logic and places national policymaking at the foundation of the world economy."[54] In a similar vein, Robert Paarlberg contrasts policies that are either "outward-first" or "inward-first" and contends that "in today's circumstances effective U.S. leadership may have to begin at home . . . Outward-looking efforts will stand little chance of being consistent or credible abroad until unity of purpose has been achieved or restored at home."[55] An inward-first approach would not only start with domestic challenges but would also accord strict priority to internal rather than external concerns. And the theme is echoed by David Spiro as well, who writes:

> [T]he United States still has the largest economy in the world, and so what is good for the United States is still by and large good for the stability of the international political economy. If the United States can clean its own house, then international finance and international monetary stability will benefit.[56]

Unfortunately, what is good for the United States is not necessarily good for others, any more than what is good for General Motors is always good for the United States. In an interdependent world, inward-looking policies inevitably produce significant external consequences, including sizable feedbacks into the domestic economy itself. That is precisely what the challenge of economic globalization means. Externalities may reinforce domestic priorities if, for example, an expansionary fiscal policy, by pushing up interest rates, attracts a capital inflow to help underwrite investment and growth at home. But reverse ripple effects, such as a flight from the dollar, might also occur, as they have done during every recent administration. America cannot pretend that it is the same insular nation it once was, burying its head in the sand like an ostrich. That leaves too much of our economic anatomy exposed to a good swift kick in the butt.

Why not, then, do more to restore the economic insularity that was the basis of our traditional policy exceptionalism? Many Americans, nostalgic for the good old days of the Sinatra doctrine, would seek to turn back the globalization process—in effect: *Isolate* ourselves from the outside world, in order to reduce our vulnerability to foreign influence. Economic security would be promoted through a comprehensive program of "de-linkage" and separate development. On the production side, a "sophisticated neomercantilism"[57] would aim to minimize dependence on foreigners through protectionist trade and industrial policies and restrictions on inward direct investment and cross-border corporate alliances. On the monetary side, taxes or capital controls would be deployed to limit our exposure to the vagaries of external financial markets.[58] Priority for domestic concerns would be cultivated by suppressing rather than ignoring potentially disruptive externalities.

Renewed insularity, however, could not be implemented easily and would certainly not be attainable without considerable dislocation and sacrifice. In principle, any amount of de-linkage is possible. All that is needed is the will to impose new taxes or controls of sufficient severity to effectively eliminate opportunities for profitable international exchange. As Louis Pauly has suggested, "states can still defy markets" if they so desire.[59] But the costs involved, economic as well as administrative, would almost certainly be astronomical. Would Americans truly be prepared to give up most of the material benefits of commercial and financial interdependence? Could the necessary political support really be mobilized to cut our oil consumption in half? To deprive grain farmers of the bulk of their sales? To give up the foreign financing that allows us to absorb imports well above the level of our exports? To defy the most fundamental rules of the postwar order that we were so instrumental in establishing? In practice, popular assent would seem unlikely except in the most dire of circumstances, such as wartime or a national-security crisis. In more ordinary times opposition would undoubtedly be vigorous, given the many constituencies that now have such a stake in the maintenance of globalized markets.

That leaves the final option: *Engage* actively with the outside world, but on the basis of a fully accurate assessment of current threats to our economic security. Engagement means sustaining and even extending, rather than ignoring or reversing, our overseas involvements, to continue sharing in the gains of an open economic system. But it also means making the most of both our strengths and weaknesses in the world's emerging mosaic economy, to preserve as much as possible of our historic policy autonomy. The essence of the option is an enlightened use of our remaining exceptionalism in relation to other states to compensate for Washington's diminished capacity in relation to the globalized marketplace.

The objective, as always, should be to maximize the interests of the United States. In inter-state relations, despite the emergence of power centers elsewhere, we still enjoy a unique degree of policy unilateralism. That leverage can be used to defend ourselves against opportunistic behavior by other governments. It can also be used to promote cooperative responses to the constraints imposed by economic globalization. As Joseph Nye has written: "Increasingly, the issues today do not simply place one state against another; they are issues in which all states try to control nonstate transnational actors. The solutions . . . will require collective action and cooperation among states."[60] Collaboration among governments holds out the greatest promise of regaining some policy leverage in relation to the private sector; and the United States, because of its still disproportionate influence, remains best placed to exercise the needed leadership. Engagement thus requires a balancing of challenges to our economic security. Strategy, in every instance, must be tailored to our situationally specific capabilities.

Three distinct strategies are feasible: multilateralism, regionalism, and unilateralism.[61] *Multilateralism* would involve a renewed commitment to the liberal postwar order, stressing wide participation in the collective management of common problems to suppress economic conflict and promote cooperation. *Regionalism*, by contrast, would focus on the potential benefits of agreements among smaller groups of countries, emphasizing a presumed trade-off between inclusiveness and achievement in negotiating forums—the idea that more progress may be possible over a wider range of issues when cooperation is restricted to a like-minded and relatively homogeneous group of countries. *Unilateralism*, finally, would eschew collective approaches altogether in favor of a more narrowly defined policy of self-interest, promoted through an assertive and even aggressive use of national power in economic diplomacy. Though typically treated as mutually exclusive alternatives, these three approaches are not in fact necessarily competitive. In a differentiated and multi-layered economic system, they may in practice be made to function as complementary components of an effective global policy—three cards in a potentially winning hand.

Playing the hand is not easy. The separate strategies must be managed not to work at cross-purposes. Unilateralism cannot be carried to the point where it provokes noncooperation or even retaliation by others. Regionalism should not be promoted at the expense of wider structures of interdependence. The strategies must also be prioritized, with preference given to the broadest possible solutions to common problems whenever feasible, backed by the appropriate international institutions. More universal approaches have the natural advantage of maximizing the economic gains to be shared by all concerned. Regional accords thus should be designed to be flexible and nonexclusionary, so that they may, in the words of Robert Lawrence, become "building blocks" rather than "stumbling blocks" on the path to more inclusive arrangements.[62] And aggressive unilateralism should be used to open markets and economic opportunities around the world, not close them. In effect, the slogan might be: Multilateralism where feasible, regionalism where necessary, and unilateralism only as a very last resort. Policy should be implemented in *modular* form to conform to the heightened complexity of a mosaic economy.

To some extent, of course, that is what Washington does already. Elements of all three strategies have been evident in the behavior of every recent administration. Examples of unilateralism, some quite aggressive, have been cited previously. Multilateralism, however, also continues to be pursued with remarkable vigor, particularly in the area of trade policy under the auspices of GATT—now succeeded by the new World Trade Organization (WTO)—where the United States was instrumental both in the inception and finally, in late 1993, the conclusion of the Uruguay Round, the broadest and most comprehensive negotiation of commercial liberalization in history.[63] And regionalism too has been high on Washington's agenda, particularly during the Clinton presidency. Building on earlier initiatives from the Reagan and Bush years, the Clinton administration completed negotiation and ratification of the North American Free Trade Agreement (NAFTA) in 1993; and in 1994 won the agreement of other states to start building wider free trade agreements in both the Western Hemisphere (the Free Trade Area of the Americas) and the Asia-Pacific region (Asia-Pacific Economic Cooperation).[64] In 1995, there was even talk of a new free trade agreement with the European Union: a Trans-Atlantic Free Trade Area.[65]

However, something also has been missing until now in the way Washington plays its hand—specifically, a clear sense of strategic *design*, along with the tactical subtlety and finesse needed to fit existing resource means to ends. That the U.S. government is not well organized to formulate and implement coherent economic strategies is of course a well-known theme and requires no elaboration here.[66] What does require emphasis is the need for more systematic adaptation to the specific nature of contemporary challenges to America's economic security—a clearer understanding of what "return to normalcy" really means at the end of the American century. That is what enlightened engagement means. By matching strategies to remaining international capabilities, Washington can still realistically aspire, more than any other government, to doing it "my way."

Endnotes

1. The expression is attributed to Henry R. Luce. *See* his "The American Century," *Life*, February 11, 1941, pp. 61–65.
2. Benjamin J. Cohen, "An Explosion in the Kitchen? Economic Relations With Other Advanced Industrial States," in Kenneth A. Oye, Robert J. Lieber, and Donald Rothchild (eds.), *Eagle Resurgent? The Reagan Era in American Foreign Policy* (Boston: Little, Brown, 1987), Chapter 4; and "Toward A Mosaic Economy: Relations With Other Advanced Industrial Nations," in Kenneth A. Oye, Robert J. Lieber, and Donald Rothchild (eds.), *Eagle in a New World: American Grand Strategy in the Post-Cold War Era* (New York: HarperCollins, 1992), Chapter 5.
3. Robert O. Keohane, "U.S. Foreign Economic Policy Toward Other Advanced Capitalist States: The Struggle to Make Others Adjust," in Kenneth A. Oye, Donald Rothchild, and Robert J. Lieber (eds.), *Eagle Entangled: U.S. Foreign Policy in a Complex World* (New York: Longman, 1979), Chapter 3.
4. Jeffry A. Frieden, "Comments," in Robert L. Paarlberg, *Leadership Abroad Begins at Home: U.S. Foreign Economic Policy After the Cold War* (Washington: Brookings Institution, 1995), p. 98.
5. *See, for example,* C. Fred Bergsten, "The World Economy After the Cold War," *Foreign Affairs*, Vol. 69, No. 3 (Summer 1990).

6. That commitment was of course the foundation for the familiar theory of hegemonic stability, which stresses the key role of a single dominant state in the maintenance of order in international economic relations. The theory was separately developed some two decades or more ago by Charles Kindleberger, Robert Gilpin, and Stephen Krasner. *See* Charles Kindleberger, *The World in Depression, 1929–1939* (Berkeley: University of California Press, 1973); Robert Gilpin, *U.S. Power and the Multinational Corporation* (New York: Basic Books, 1975); and Stephen D. Krasner, "State Power and the Structure of International Trade," *World Politics*, Vol. 28, No. 3 (April 1976). The conventional appellation for the theory is attributed to Robert O. Keohane, "The Theory of Hegemonic Stability and Changes in International Economic Regimes," in Ole R. Holsti, Randolph M. Siverson, and Alexander L. George (eds.), *Change in the International System* (Boulder, Colo.: Westview Press, 1980), pp. 131–162. For a useful recent survey, *see* David A. Lake, "Leadership, Hegemony, and the International Economy: Naked Emperor or Tattered Monarch with Potential?" *International Studies Quarterly* (December 1993), pp. 459–489.
7. Paarlberg, *Leadership Abroad Begins at Home*, p. 2.
8. Edward N. Luttwak, *The Endangered American Dream* (New York: Simon and Schuster, 1993), p. 35. *See also* his "From Geopolitics to Geo-Economics," *The National Interest* (Summer 1990), pp. 17–23.
9. Luttwak, *The Endangered American Dream*, p. 34.
10. In addition to Luttwak, notable exponents of this view include Shafiqul Islam, "Capitalism in Conflict," *Foreign Affairs*, Vol. 69, No. 1 (1989/1990); and Lester Thurow, *Head to Head: The Coming Economic Battle Among Japan, Europe, and America* (New York: William Morrow, 1992).
11. Cohen, "Toward a Mosaic Economy."
12. The standard definition of an international regime is a set of "implicit or explicit principles, norms, rules, and decision-making procedures around which actors' expectations converge in a given area of international relations." *See* Stephen D. Krasner, *International Regimes* (Ithaca, NY: Cornell University Press, 1983), p. 2.
13. The Group of Seven comprises the United States, Britain, Canada, France, Germany, Italy, and Japan. Meetings of the finance ministers of the Group of Seven also take place on a regular basis, though for some purposes consultations are limited to the Group of Five (excluding Canada and Italy) or even smaller configurations (e.g., the United States, Germany, and Japan).
14. Helen V. Milner, *Resisting Protection: Global Industries and the Politics of International Trade* (Princeton, NJ: Princeton University Press, 1988), p. 290. *See also* I.M. Destler and John S. Odell, *Anti-Protection: Changing Forces in United States Trade Politics*, Policy Analyses in International Economics, No. 21 (Washington: Institute for International Economics, September 1987); and Frieden, "Comments," pp. 89–102. But for a less sanguine appraisal, stressing the increasing influence of more traditional protectionist interests in recent years, *see* Anne O. Krueger, *American Trade Policy: A Tragedy in the Making* (Washington: AEI Press, 1995).
15. Samuel P. Huntington, "The U.S.—Decline or Renewal?" *Foreign Affairs*, Vol. 67, No. 2 (Winter 1988/1989): 76–96. Among the authors specifically cited by Huntington are David P. Calleo, *Beyond American Hegemony* (New York: Basic Books, 1987); and, above all, Paul Kennedy, *The Rise and Fall of the Great Powers: Economic Change and Military Conflict from 1500 to 2000* (New York: Random House, 1987). The theme of America's hegemonic decline is of course a familiar one in the formal academic literature. *See especially* Robert O. Keohane, *After Hegemony: Cooperation and Discord in the World Political Economy* (Princeton, NJ: Princeton University Press, 1984); and Robert Gilpin, *The Political Economy of International Relations* (Princeton, NJ: Princeton University Press, 1987).
16. The term is from Paul Kennedy, "Fin-de-Siecle America," *The New York Review of Books*, June 28, 1990, pp. 31–40.

17. *See for example*, Henry R. Nau, *The Myth of America's Decline: Leading the World Economy into the 1990s* (New York: Oxford University Press, 1990); Joseph S. Nye, Jr., *Bound to Lead: The Changing Nature of American Power* (New York: Basic Books, 1990); and Richard Rosecrance, *America's Economic Resurgence: A Bold New Strategy* (New York: Harper and Row, 1990). Skepticism about America's presumed hegemonic decline has long been expressed in the more formal academic literature. *See for example*, Bruce Russett, "The Mysterious Case of Vanishing Hegemony, or Is Mark Twain Really Dead?" *International Organization*, Vol. 39, No. 2 (Spring 1985): 207–231; and Susan Strange, "The Persistent Myth of Lost Hegemony," *International Organization*, Vol. 41, No. 4 (Autumn 1987): 551–574.

18. Nye, *Bound to Lead*, especially Chapter 3.

19. Ibid., p. 78.

20. Islam, "Capitalism in Conflict," p. 179.

21. The toughest such measure yet legislated by Congress, the Super 301 procedure (actually set out in Section 310 of the 1988 Act) calls for identification by the Trade Representative of unfair trading countries and practices—labeled, in Washington's bureaucratic language, "priority countries" and "priority practices"—and sets out timetables for negotiation and possible retaliation. For some discussion, *see* Jagdish Bhagwati and Hugh T. Patrick (eds.), *Aggressive Unilateralism: America's 301 Trade Policy and the World Trading System* (Ann Arbor, MI: University of Michigan Press, 1990).

22. As quoted in *New York Times*, January 29, 1989, p. F4.

23. The term "aggressive unilateralism" has been popularized by economist Jagdish Bhagwati, one of the policy's most severe critics. *See, for example,* Bhagwati and Patrick, *Aggressive Unilateralism*; and Bhagwati, *The World Trade System at Risk* (Princeton, NJ: Princeton University Press, 1991).

24. Akio Morita and Shintaro Ishihara, *The Japan that Can Say "No": The Case for a New U.S.-Japan Relationship* (Tokyo: Kobunsha, 1989). Interestingly, Morita more recently has become more sympathetic to U.S. complaints, suggesting that Japan is "inviting its own economic decline" by resisting U.S. demands to open its economy. As quoted in *New York Times*, January 16, 1993.

25. Islam, "Capitalism in Conflict," p. 176.

26. As quoted in *New York Times*, December 23, 1992, p. A1.

27. *The Economist* (September 25, 1993), p. 18.

28. *New York Times*, May 2, 1994, p. C1.

29. As quoted in *New York Times*, January 16, 1993.

30. Yoshio Sakurauchi, at the time one of Japan's most powerful politicans, as quoted in *New York Times*, January 21, 1992, p. C1.

31. Merit E. Janow, "Trading with an Ally: Progress and Discontent in U.S.-Japan Trade Relations," in Gerald L. Curtis (ed.), *The United States, Japan, and Asia* (New York: Norton, 1994), Chapter 2.

32. *New York Times*, January 10, 1992, p. A1.

33. *New York Times*, July 10, 1993, p. 1. For some evaluation, *see* Council of Economic Advisers, *Annual Report, 1994* (Washington: February 1994), Chapter 6; and Janow, "Trading With an Ally."

34. Thomas L. Friedman, "U.S. Approach to Japan: 'Economic Acupuncture,'" *New York Times*, March 18, 1994, p. C1.

35. *The Economist* (July 1, 1995), p. 65.

36. Council of Economic Advisers, *Annual Report, 1995* (Washington: February 1995), Chapter 6.

37. Because of its lax enforcement of intellectual property rights laws, China had been designated a "priority country" under the 1988 Super 301 law. Had negotiations failed, the Chinese would have faced 100-percent tariffs on around $1 billion worth of their sales in the United States—the biggest trade sanctions in American history.

38. *New York Times*, February 27, 1995, p. A1.

39. At issue was the annual renewal of the most-favored-nation (MFN) status for Chinese imports—meaning entry at the same low tariff rates as members of GATT—which had first been granted in 1980. Renewal, which previously was routine, became increasingly controversial after the Tiananmen Square incident of 1989, and in 1993 was explicitly tied to broader human-rights improvements in China by the new Clinton administration. Abandonment of the link a year later was directly related to threatened counter-measures by Beijing against U.S. business interests in the burgeoning Chinese market.

40. *New York Times*, July 29, 1995, p. 3.

41. *New York Times*, May 8, 1993, p. 17.

42. *See* Douglas Croham, *Reciprocity and the Unification of the European Banking Market*, Occasional Paper No. 27 (New York: Group of Thirty, 1989).

43. *New York Times*, November 21, 1992, p. 1.

44. Michael Smith and Stephen Woolcock, "Learning to Cooperate: The Clinton Administration and the European Union," *International Affairs*, Vol. 70, No. 3 (July 1994), pp. 470–471.

45. As quoted in *New York Times*, July 7, 1995, p. C2.

46. Albert O. Hirschman, *Exit, Voice and Loyalty: Responses to Decline in Firms, Organizations, and States* (Cambridge, MA: Harvard University Press, 1970).

47. For further discussion, *see* Benjamin J. Cohen, "Phoenix Risen: The Resurrection of Global Finance," *World Politics*, Vol. 48, No. 2 (January 1996).

48. Benjamin J. Cohen, "The Triad and the Unholy Trinity: Lessons for the Pacific Region," in Richard Higgott, Richard Leaver, and John Ravenhill (eds.), *Pacific Economic Relations in the 1990s: Cooperation or Conflict?* (Boulder, Colo.: Lynne Reiner, 1993), Chapter 7. Adding free trade to the equation produces what Tommaso Padoa-Schioppa calls the "Inconsistent Quartet." *See* Tommaso Padoa-Schioppa, "The European Monetary System: A Long-term View," in Francesco Giavazzi, Stefano Micossi, and Marcus Miller (ed.), *The European Monetary System* (Cambridge, England: Cambridge University Press, 1988), Chapter 12.

49. Paul Volcker, in Paul Volcker and Toyoo Gyohten, *Changing Fortunes: The World's Money and the Threat to American Leadership*, (New York: Times Books, 1992), p. 151.

50. *New York Times*, November 15, 1994, p. C1.

51. Volcker, *Changing Fortunes*, p. xiv.

52. Walter Russell Mead, "An American Grand Strategy: The Quest for Order in a Disordered World," *World Policy Journal*, Vol. 10, No. 2 (Spring 1993), p. 14.

53. Helen V. Milner, "American Debt and World Power," *International Journal*, Vol. 46 (Summer 1993), p. 559.

54. Henry R. Nau, "Where Reaganomics Works," *Foreign Policy*, No. 57 (Winter 1984–1985): 15. *See also* Nau, *The Myth of America's Decline*. For a critical discussion, *see* C. Fred Bergsten, "Reaganomics: The Problem?" *Foreign Policy*, No. 59 (Summer, 1985), pp. 132–144.

55. Paarlberg, *Leadership Abroad Begins at Home*, pp. 3, 85. For a critical discussion, *see* Jeffry Frieden's comments in the same volume, pp. 89–102.

56. David E. Spiro, "Capital and Debt Policy," in Robert J. Art and Seyom Brown (eds.), *U.S. Foreign Policy: The Search for a New Role* (New York: Macmillan, 1993), pp. 185–186.

57. The phrase is attributable to Theodore Moran, who is otherwise a critic of the approach. *See* Theodore H. Moran, *American Economic Policy and National Security* (New York: Council on Foreign Relations Press, 1993), Chapter 4.

58. For some recent critical discussion, *see* Peter Garber and Mark P. Taylor, "Sand in the Wheels of Foreign Exchange Markets: A Sceptical Note, *Economic Journal*, Vol. 105 (January, 1995), pp. 173–180; and Peter B. Kenen, "Capital Controls, The EMS and EMU," *Economic Journal*, Vol. 105 (January, 1995), pp. 181–192.

59. Louis W. Pauly, "Capital Mobility, State Autonomy and Political Legitimacy," *Journal of International Affairs*, Vol. 48 (Winter 1995), p. 373.

60. Nye, *Bound to Lead*, pp. 186–187.
61. Cohen, "Toward a Mosaic Economy," pp. 168–173. In that earlier essay, a fourth strategy was also mentioned: minilateralism, involving an "inner club" approach to the management of common problems. But since the line between minilateralism and regionalism is tenuous at best, it actually seems best simply to combine the two under the unified term *regionalism*.
62. Robert Z. Lawrence, "Emerging Regional Arrangements: Building Blocks or Stumbling Blocks?" in Richard O'Brien (ed.), *Finance and the International Economy* (Oxford: Oxford University Press, 1991).
63. For some evaluation, *see* Susan M. Collins and Barry P. Bosworth (eds.), *The New GATT: Implications for the United States* (Washington: Brookings Institution, 1994); and Organization for Economic Cooperation and Development, *The New World Trading System: Readings* (Paris: OECD, 1994).
64. Council of Economic Advisers, *Annual Report, 1995*, pp. 217–231.
65. *The Economist*, May 27, 1995, p. 15; and *New York Times*, May 29, 1995, p. 3; June 3, 1995, p. 5.
66. *See for example*, Raymond Vernon and Debora Spar, *Beyond Globalism: Remaking American Foreign Economic Policy* (New York: Free Press, 1989).

Chapter 5

Competing U.S. Grand Strategies[1]

Barry R. Posen and Andrew L. Ross

Overview

The dissolution of the Soviet Union and the demise of the threat that it posed to U.S. interests and U.S. security requires the United States to reconsider its national security policy. What are U.S. interests; what are the threats to those interests; what are the appropriate remedies for those threats? In short, what is to be the new grand strategy of the United States? The state of the U.S. economy, national finances, and persistent social problems largely drove foreign and defense policy from the 1992 Presidential race. The first months of the Clinton administration were characterized initially by indirection, later by a near single-minded focus on economic issues. Security related foreign policy problems were dealt with sequentially, and incrementally; no obvious grand scheme emerged until the Assistant to the President for National Security Affairs, Anthony Lake, proposed in September 1993 that we make a transition "From Containment to Enlargement." Not until July 1994 were the ideas initially advanced by Lake codified in the administration's first *National Security Strategy*. During the first three years of the Clinton administration, as during the Bush administration before

Barry R. Posen is Professor of Political Science at MIT and a member of the Defense and Arms Control Studies Program. He is the author of The Sources of Military Doctrine *(1984), and* Inadvertent Escalation *(1991). He has held fellowships from the Harvard University Center for International Affairs, Council on Foreign Relations, Rockefeller Foundation, and the Woodrow Wilson Center. Dr. Posen's current activities include work on the use of military force, grand strategy, and nationalism.*

Andrew L. Ross is Professor of National Security Affairs in the Department of National Security Decision Making, U.S. Naval War College. He is editor of The Political Economy of Defense: Issues and Perspectives *(1991), co-editor of* Strategy and Force Planning *(1995), and the author of numerous articles and book chapters on strategic planning, regional security, weapons proliferation, the international arms market, defense industrialization, and security and development. Professor Ross has held research fellowships at Cornell, Princeton, and Harvard and taught in the political science departments at the University of Illinois and University of Kentucky.*

it, the "strategy debate" has been largely confined to academic writing and editorial columns. Nevertheless, five basic alternative positions have emerged; this essay will develop, refine, and critique them.

The two most imminent questions are when should the United States be prepared to consider the use of force, and what kinds of military forces should the United States try to sustain? Although it is our usual practice in the United States to address these questions in a practical, atheoretical, incremental way, we would be better served in this time of change by asking the big questions first. That is what grand strategy is all about. During the Cold War, the simple fact of great Soviet power was a sufficient, if crude, guide to our actions. No more. In a reordered and still unfolding international environment, the United States must once again, as it did in the aftermath of World War II, reconsider its role in the world, the principles that should inform that role, and what it wants to accomplish. Despite the continuing search for a new paradigm, scant progress has been made to date.[2]

Five grand strategies now compete in our public discourse. They may be termed neo-isolationism; selective engagement; collective, or cooperative, security; containment; and primacy. These five alternatives may be arrayed on a continuum or spectrum of grand strategy alternatives, with isolationism and primacy as the two bookends. At the isolationist end of the spectrum, U.S. global ambitions are modest, action is infrequent, and forces are small. At the primacy end of the spectrum, ambitions are great, action is frequent, and military forces are large and technologically very advanced. Below, we develop these strategies in their purest form; we borrow liberally from many authors, but on issues where other authors may have kept silent, or been inconsistent, we impose consistency. We do this in the interest of clarity. We attempt to distinguish these strategies in five ways: the major problem of international politics that they identify; their basic premises and assumptions; their preferred political and military instruments; their positions on a number of basic questions now on the U.S. agenda, including nuclear proliferation, regional conflict, ethnic conflict, and humanitarian intervention; and the kind of military force structure that they will require. The force structure analysis is indicative rather than comprehensive; as a heuristic device we rely substantially on the array of alternative force structures developed by the late Les Aspin during his tenure as Chairman of the House Armed Services Committee and more recently as Secretary of Defense early in the Clinton Administration.

Neo-Isolationism

Neo-isolationism, or disengagement, is at one extreme end of our grand strategy spectrum. The new isolationism subscribes to a fundamentally realist view of international politics and thus focuses on power.[3] It differs from the isolationism of the 1920s and 1930s which eschewed in-

volvement in world politics as much on the basis of a moralistic dis-
taste for great power politics as on a calculation of U.S. interests and
plausible threats to those interests.[4] Neo-isolationists ask who has the
power to threaten the sovereignty of the United States, its territorial integrity, or its safety. The answer is that nobody does.[5] The collapse of
the Soviet Union has left a rough balance of power in Eurasia. No state
has the capability to conquer the others and so agglomerate enough
economic capability and military mobilization potential to threaten
the U.S. way of life. Like traditional isolationism, it observes that the
oceans make such a threat improbable in any event. The United States
controls about one-quarter of gross world product, twice as much as its
nearest competitor Japan, and while not totally self-sufficient, is better
placed than most to "go it alone." And neo-isolationism is further
strengthened by the fact that U.S. neighbors to the north and south are
militarily weak and destined to stay that way for quite some time. The
United States is inherently a very secure country.[6] Indeed the United
States can be said to be strategically immune.[7]

The new isolationists have embraced a constricted view of U.S. national interests that renders internationalism not only unnecessary but
counterproductive. National defense—the protection of "the security,
liberty, and property of the American people"[8]—is the only vital U.S.
interest. Given the absence of threats to the U.S. homeland, national
defense will seldom justify intervention abroad. The United States is
not responsible for, and cannot afford the costs of, maintaining world
order. In addition, the pursuit of economic well-being is best left to the
private sector. And the promotion of values such as democracy and human rights inspires ill-advised crusades that serve only to generate resentment against the United States; consequently, it is a poor guide to
policy and strategy.[9]

-The new isolationism is strongly motivated by a particular understanding of nuclear weapons. It concedes that nuclear weapons have increased the sheer capacity of others to threaten the safety of the United
States. But nuclear weapons make it very hard, indeed nearly inconceivable, for any power to win a traditional military victory over the
United States. Nuclear weapons ensure the political sovereignty and
the territorial integrity of this country. The collapse of the Soviet
Union has so reduced the military resources available to its successor
states that the old, admittedly exaggerated, fear of a counterforce attack
on U.S. nuclear forces is out of the question. There can be no politically
rational motive for any country large or small to explode a nuclear
weapon on the North American continent. United States retaliation
would be devastating. Moreover, the fact that Britain, France, the People's Republic of China (PRC), and Russia have retaliatory nuclear
forces makes it quite likely that these powers will deter each other.

The new isolationism would concede, however, that our great capabilities are a magnet for trouble so long as we are involved in any way

in various political disputes around the world. Intervention in these disputes is thus a good way to attract attention to the United States.[10] The strong will try to deter the United States; the weak to seduce it; the dispossessed to blame it. Neo-isolationism would argue that those who fear terrorism, especially terrorism with nuclear, biological, or chemical weapons, can increase U.S. safety by staying out of foreign conflicts. Neo-isolationism advises the United States to preserve its freedom of action and strategic independence. Even traditional alliance relationships that obligate the United States in advance, such as NATO, ought to be dismantled.

Since neo-isolationism proposes that the United States stay out of wars abroad, its preferred political instrumentalities should be obvious. International organizations are a place to talk, perhaps to coordinate international efforts to improve the overall global quality of life, but not to make or keep peace. This would implicate the United States and draw it into conflicts.

Most of the foreign policy issues now facing the United States would disappear. Only in the area of humanitarian assistance does it seem plausible that neo-isolationism would undertake action abroad.[11] But this would be confined to disasters—famines, epidemics, earthquakes, and storms. The United States might be willing to help clean up the mess after foreign wars have sorted themselves out. But intervention of any kind during wars would be viewed as a mistake, since at least one side is likely to be disadvantaged by humanitarian assistance to the others and would thus come to view the United States as an enemy.

Neo-isolationism obviously generates a rather small force structure. It is unlikely to cost more than two percent of GDP.[12] First and foremost, the United States would need to retain a secure nuclear second strike capability to deter nuclear attacks from any quarter. Modest air and missile defenses might be put in place to deal with low-grade threats. Second, the U.S. intelligence community would have the task of watching worldwide developments of weapons of mass destruction to forestall any terrorist threats against the United States. If such threats occurred, it would be its job to find an address against which retaliation could be directed. Third, the United States would probably wish to retain a capable navy (perhaps a third to a half the current size), and diverse special operations forces. The purpose would largely be to protect U.S. commerce abroad from criminal activity—piracy, kidnapping, and extortion. The remainder of U.S. forces would be structured as a cadre to preserve skills at ground and tactical air warfare in the event that the balance of power on the Eurasian land mass seemed to be eroding, perhaps requiring the United States to return to a more activist policy. A major mission of the intelligence community would be to provide early warning of the necessity of such a shift. Given these limited missions, "Force A," in Table 5.1, is larger than necessary.

Table 5.1

Comparison of Alternative Future Force Structures and Their Costs: House Armed Services Committee, 1992 vs. Clinton Plan

	Force A	Force B	Force C	Force D	Base Force	Clinton-BUR
Army						
Active divisions	8	8	9	10	12	10
Reserve divisions	2	2	6	6	6	8
Marines*						
Active divisions	2	2	2	3	2 1/3	3
Reserve divisions	1	1	1	1	1	1
Air Force						
Active wings	6	8	10	11	15	13
Reserve wings	4	6	8	9	11	7
Navy						
Total ships	220	290	340	430	450	346
Carriers	6	8	12	15	13	12
Attack subs	20	40	40	50	80	45–55
Amphibious assault ships**	50	50	50	82	50	44

Personnel	Force A	Force B	Force C	Force D	Base Force	Clinton/BUR
Active	1,247,000	1,312,000	1,409,000	1,575,000	1,626,000	1,450,000
Reserve	666,000	691,000	904,000	933,000	920,000	905,000
1997 Budget Authority (DOD+DOE, *** billions in 1997 dollars)	231	246	270	295	291–301	253

*Marine divisions and Navy carriers each have associated air wings, respectively slightly larger and slightly smaller than their Air Force counterparts, which number 72 aircraft.

**These transport Marine units to their attack positions; 10–12 of these ships are very large, roughly half the size of a standard Nimitz class carrier, and carry Vertical and Short Take-off and Landing (VSTOL) aircraft, helicopters, and hovercraft.

Alternative Forces A,B,C,D were devised by the House Armed Services Committee under the leadership of then Chairman Les Aspin.

Force A: A "foundation" of nuclear, forward presence, special operations, and continental defense forces, and an industrial mobilization base, plus one "major regional contingency" such as the 1991 war against Iraq, and a modest humanitarian intervention capability.

Force B: The preceding plus sufficient airpower to heavily support an ally in a second major regional contingency.

Force C: The preceding plus sufficient forces in reserve to comfortably sustain a large new forward deployment for a major regional contingency, plus the capability to mount a small invasion, similar to the attack on Panama in 1989.

Force D: The preceding plus a second humanitarian intervention, plus the ground forces for a second major regional contingency.

Base Force: Proposed by President Bush and Former Chairman of the Joint Chiefs of Staff Colin Powell, "superpower lives here."

Clinton/Bottom Up Review: Two "near simultaneous regional contingencies" plus a moderate peacekeeping operation plus substantial forward presence. (Objective for the year 2000; the 1997 force structure is close but not identical; it was devised under the leadership of then Secretary of Defense Les Aspin.)

***DOD = Department of Defense; DOE = Department of Energy

Thus the United States would avoid war for the foreseeable future and save a great deal of money in its defense budget. The less pleasant side of this policy is that the disappearance of the United States from the world stage would likely precipitate a good deal of competition abroad for security. Aspiring regional hegemons would act with greater daring. Proliferation of nuclear weapons would intensify; there would likely be more intense regional arms races; there would likely be more war. Weapons of mass destruction would probably be used in some of these wars, with many unpleasant side-effects even for those not directly involved. On the one hand, all this military competition could damage international commerce, to the economic disadvantage of the United States. In some parts of the world, trade would simply become unsafe. In many other parts of the world, trade would become less "free," as states paid closer attention to their economic autonomy as a means to military autonomy. On the other hand, others would be diverting more resources to national security, and the United States would be spending less, which could enhance its relative economic competitiveness. Moreover, greater military competition in the world might increase the attractiveness of the United States as a safe haven for capital and reduce the attractiveness of foreign investment for Americans, suppressing U.S. interest rates.

Selective Engagement

The strategy of selective engagement is motivated by both power and peace. Like isolationism, it emerges from the realist tradition of international politics and its focus on large concentrations of power. Like collective security, it is interested in peace. Selective engagement is mainly concerned, however, with peace among powers that have substantial industrial and military potential—the great powers.[13] By virtue of the great military capabilities that would be brought into play, great power conflicts are much more dangerous to the United States than conflicts elsewhere. Thus Russia, the wealthier states of the European Union, the People's Republic of China, and Japan matter most. The purpose of U.S. engagement should be to affect directly the propensity of these powers to go to war with one another. These wars have the greatest chance of producing large scale resort to weapons of mass destruction—a global experiment that the United States ought to try to prevent. These are the areas of the world where the world wars have originated, wars that have managed to reach out and draw in the United States—in spite of our strong inclination to stay out. The argument then is that Eurasia sinks into warfare when the United States is absent, not when it is present; and once it does, we ultimately regret it.[14]

Advocates of selective engagement start from the premise that U.S. resources are scarce; it is simply impossible to muster sufficient power and will to enforce peace through collective security worldwide.[15] Counting on others to pull their weight is unreasonable; the allies barely spent their fair share to oppose the far more imminent Soviet threat.[16] Why will these self-interested powers allocate greater resources to the more diffuse goal of collective security? And the fact that many of our allies are liberal democracies makes them quite sensitive to risks and costs—especially casualties among their own troops. They will not be disposed to risk much. Desert Storm does not suggest a permanent overwhelming universal U.S. military superiority. Iraq was a perfect enemy; Kuwait was a perfect theater. Others may not be so easy. A collective security policy might not permit the nearly single-minded focus on one adversary that facilitated success in Desert Storm.

Advocates of selective engagement are thus doubtful that international organizations can build sufficient credibility to deter most aggressors. They believe that credibility is a function in part of clear, immediate, strategic interests, and in part a function of real military power. They focus on trying to ensure that the great powers understand that the U.S. does not wish to find out how a future Eurasian great war might progress and has sufficient military power to deny victory to the aggressor.[17]

This raises the greatest tension in the selective engagement argument. The United States must maintain military forces and threaten war largely for the purpose of preventing great wars that could either draw it in or produce the risk of grave damage to it due to the resort to weapons of mass destruction. A traditional realist position threatens and wages war to prevent aggressors from building sufficient power to challenge the United States directly. The neo-isolationist would argue that if you want to avoid war, stay out of the affairs of others. And they remind us that it is quite unlikely that the results of such a war could decisively shift the balance of power against the United States. The advocate of selective engagement resists this deductive logic, largely due to the experience of the United States having been drawn against its intentions into two costly world wars that started in Eurasia.

Selective engagement advocates are worried about nuclear proliferation, but their concern is heavily colored by political analysis.[18] Proliferation in some countries matters more than others.[19] Countries seeking nuclear weapons who have no conflict of interest with the United States or its friends are viewed more favorably than those who do. The Non-Proliferation Treaty (NPT) is viewed as an instrument to permit countries who have neither the wealth to support nuclear forces, nor the political insecurity or ambition to need or want them, to find a refuge from a race that they would rather not run. Selective engagement advocates may be willing to try to cajole India, Israel, Pakistan, or Ukraine into surrendering their nuclear capabilities and joining the NPT. But it is absurd to turn neutrals or friends into enemies on this issue alone. If these countries resist our blandishments, we should quietly accommodate them.

Proliferation really matters in politically ambitious countries that have demonstrated a certain insensitivity to risks and costs. North Korea, Iraq, and Iran fall easily into this category. What should be done about them? The answers are case specific. The most important thing is to convince them that they are being watched, and that the United States intends to stand against any ambitions they might have. Depending on the pace of their weapons programs, and the extent of their bellicosity, stronger measures may be warranted. There is no consensus on the use of force, however. Advocates of selective engagement are always sensitive to costs, risks, and limits; it may not be possible to destroy these nascent nuclear forces at reasonable cost.

Where countries have maneuvered through gaps in the NPT—signing it but violating it—every effort must be made within the framework of the treaty to bring them into compliance. Failure to do so will damage its credibility among good faith parties to the treaty, and among countries considering future adherence.

Regional competitions among small states matter to the extent that they could energize intense great power security competition. This risk preserves the Persian Gulf as a core U.S. security interest.[20] The problem is not so much U.S. dependence on Gulf oil; it is the far greater dependence on energy imports of many of the other great powers. A struggle over the control of the Gulf could draw in great powers on opposing sides, or set off competition elsewhere to expropriate energy resources. Moreover, should most of the economic potential associated with this oil fall into the hands of one ambitious actor, it could provide the underpinnings for a substantial military challenge. If Iraq could achieve the military development it did on its own oil revenues, how much more might it have achieved with the revenues of Kuwait, much less Saudi Arabia? Even if such a power would not pose a direct threat to the United States, it would certainly be in a position to pose a threat to many of its neighbors. A great war in the Persian Gulf, with the risk of large scale use of weapons of mass destruction, is the kind of experiment that the United States probably ought not to wish to run. And of course, the rivalries in the Middle East and Persian Gulf partake of religious, nationalist, and ethnic aspects that add an inflammatory passion to the security competition.

Advocates of selective engagement are concerned with ethnic conflict where it runs the risk of producing a great power war. Fortunately, there are not many places where this seems likely. Arguably, there is only one dangerous potential conflict of this type in Eurasia today—the rivalry between Russia and Ukraine. Conflicts elsewhere in Eurasia may tempt one or more great powers to intervene, and thus they merit a certain degree of judicious diplomatic management. Most of these conflicts do not engage the vital interests of any state—they are strategically uninteresting. Yugoslavia contains no military or economic resources that would add to or subtract from the security of any European great power. This is the main reason why the Europeans behaved so sluggishly. Advocates of more direct U.S. engagement raised the specter of a wider war as a major threat to U.S. interests. But the widest war they could conjure up would have matched several relatively weak military powers against each other over stakes as meager as Kosovo and Macedonia.

Advocates of selective engagement view humanitarian intervention as a question to be settled by the normal processes of U.S. domestic politics. There is no clear strategic guide to which interventions are worth doing and which not. Their perspective does suggest several critical considerations. The most important strategic question is the opportunity cost. Given one's best estimate of the plausible course of the humanitarian intervention, what will be its consequences for the U.S. material and political ability to intervene in more strategically important areas if trouble should arise during or after the humanitarian intervention? An intervention to bring order to Somalia required the equivalent of a single division of ground forces and involved the risk of relatively modest U.S. casualties. But the sheer horror of what transpired earlier proved insufficient to preserve U.S. public support through the relatively modest U.S. casualties that ensued. To preserve by force the unitary, multi-ethnic, ethnically intermingled Bosnia-Herzegovina that existed at the moment of Yugoslavia's dissolution could have required three or more U.S. divisions for the indefinite future, plus European forces.[21] Casualties could have been high. It would thus have been difficult to intervene elsewhere during an intervention to enforce peace in the former Yugoslavia. As the casualties mount in any intervention, and the bloodshed begins to make our own position more morally ambiguous to the American public, the political will to act in more important regions could erode.

A selective engagement policy probably requires a force structure similar to those proposed by the late former Secretary of Defense Les Aspin in 1992 as "Force B" or "Force C."[22] (See Table 5.1.) A strong nuclear deterrent is still needed to deter nuclear attack on the United States and to protect our freedom of action in a world of several nuclear powers. Since the United States has an interest in stability in three critical areas of the world (both ends of Eurasia and the Persian Gulf), and since simultaneous trouble in at least two cannot be ruled out, it is reasonable to retain a "two regional war" capability. Both Force structures have sufficient air and ground forces for one major contingency, and sufficient air forces to support a regional ally in a second contingency. Force C places additional emphasis on sea and air lift and on aircraft carrier task forces, perhaps more than is truly necessary, given that the United States ought to be able to identify the location of the interests over which it might be willing to threaten or wage war. Force C also assumes that the United States must maintain sufficient reserve forces to sustain with ease a new major forward deployment of indeterminate duration, and at the same time conduct a small offensive operation such as the invasion of Panama. These additions seem a conservative interpretation of the forces necessary for selective engagement. Force Structure B may be adequate.

Selective engagement does have its own problems. First, the strategy lacks a certain romance. There is little idealism or commitment to principle behind the strategy. It focuses rather narrowly on interests defined in terms of power. Can such a strategy sustain the support of a liberal democracy long addicted to viewing international relations as a struggle between good and evil?

Second, the strategy expects the United States to ignore much of the trouble that is likely to occur in the world. Great power rivalries are currently muted, and if successful, the strategy will (quietly) keep them so. It is, however, an open question as to whether a regular tendency to avoid involvement in the issues that do arise will ultimately affect the ability of the United States to pursue its more important interests. United States prestige and reputation may suffer, limiting its ability to persuade others on more important issues. Arguably, it was fear of such a result that provided one of the impulses for the ultimate U.S. involvement in trying to end the war in Bosnia.

Finally, the selective engagement strategy does not provide clear guidance on which ostensibly "minor" issues have implications for great power relations, and thus merit U.S. involvement. It posits that most will not matter, but admits that some will. Some connections are more obvious than others, but all will be the subject of debate. Since trouble in peripheral areas is likely to be more common than trouble in core areas, the selective engagement strategy gives its least precise positive guidance on matters that will most commonly figure prominently in the media, and hence in the public debate on U.S. foreign policy. The responsible practice of selective engagement will require considerable case by case analysis and public debate. It will be seductive for policymakers to make blanket assumptions that most things matter, or that few things matter. Neither would be appropriate.

Collective Security

Collective, or, increasingly, cooperative, security is the only one of our five strategic alternatives that is informed by liberalism rather than realism.[23] The major problem motivating advocates of collective security, consequently, is peace, not power.[24] It is important not to confuse means with ends in the elaboration of this strategy. Yes, advocates propose to act collectively, through international organizations as much as possible. But this is not the most important distinguishing feature of the strategy. Its most important feature is the proposition that peace is effectively indivisible, and that the United States has a huge national interest in world peace.[25]

Advocates of collective security share a number of premises.[26] These premises differ somewhat from those of past advocates of collective security. They believe that the conditions have never been better for such a policy. The motives of great powers to collaborate are presumed to be greater. The barriers to cooperation are presumed to be lower. Indeed, the "quiet cataclysm" of recent years—the relatively tranquil ending of the world as we knew it during the Cold War—is yet another indication that war itself is obsolescent.[27]

Previously, great powers could view small wars as unlikely threats to their national security. But the emergence of weapons of mass destruction means that almost any arms race and/or war can produce a world class disaster.[28] The U.S., and indeed the rest of the industrialized world, simply cannot live with these risks indefinitely.[29] Similarly, a high level of "strategic interdependence" is posited. Wars in one place will likely spread; unsavory military practices employed in one war will be employed in other wars. The use of weapons of mass destruction begets their use elsewhere; ethnic cleansing begets more ethnic cleansing. The organization of a global information system helps connect these events in fact by providing strategic intelligence to good guys and bad guys; it connects them politically by providing images of one horror after another in the living rooms of the citizens of economically advanced democracies. Now is the time to transform international politics and banish the risk of war.

Collective security advocates also believe that we now have more effective means to employ to achieve our goals. In the past, advocates of this policy relied on world public opinion, and on economic sanctions. They understood that it is difficult to get self-interested states to support military intervention on the side of peace in distant places. So they stressed the impact of these less costly measures. Collective security advocates still intend to use these mechanisms, but history has taught them to be skeptical that they will prove sufficient. Instead it is argued that real military action is cheaper than it once was. Here they reason from the experience of Desert Storm: the United States is presumed to hold decisive military-technological superiority and is thus able to wage speedy, low-casualty wars. Thus the costs of enforcement are believed to have dropped.[30]

Advocates of collective security have added the arms control mechanisms developed in the last two decades to their repertoire. With enough arms control agreements, and enough intrusive verification, states around the world will be able to avoid conflicts arising from misperception or first-strike advantages.[31] All that will be left are the true "bad guys" who can be intimidated by the threat of high technology warfare. And if not, they can be decisively defeated in short order.

Finally, advocates of collective security tend to believe that the great powers are no longer the main problem. Because most are democracies, or on the road to democracy, and democracies have historically tended not to fall into war with one another, little great power security competition is expected.[32] There seems to be an additional belief that democracies will find it easier to cooperate in collective security regimes than would states with less progressive domestic polities. One problematical aspect of democracies is often overlooked, however: their publics must be persuaded to go to war. Since the publics in modern liberal democracies seem to be quite casualty sensitive, the case for risking the lives of their troops in *distant* wars is inherently difficult to make.[33] So decisive military superiority is a necessary condition for repeated action to enforce the peace.

A collective security strategy does depend on international organizations to coordinate collective action. They are part of the complicated process of building sufficient credibility to convince all prospective aggressors that they will regularly be met with decisive countervailing power.[34] Collective security sets high goals: the banishment of military force from international politics. Prospective aggressors must be deterred. The threat of great powers to intervene—even when they have no immediate interests at stake—must be made credible. A standing international organization with substantial domestic and international legitimacy is necessary to coordinate multilateral action and to create the expectation of regular, effective intervention for peace.[35]

The task of building sufficient general multilateral credibility to deter a series of new and different potential aggressors would seem very difficult. Regular U.S. action to oppose the Soviet Union during the Cold War did not entirely dissuade that regime from new challenges. Since this was an iterative bipolar game, credibility should have accumulated; that does not seem to have happened. Instead U.S. credibility appears to have been quite high in Europe where direct interests were great and deployed military power was strong. Elsewhere, Soviet behavior was often mischievous. It is quite likely, therefore, that a true collective security strategy would involve the United Nations, and effectively the United States, in a number of wars over many years before its ability to deter the ambitious and reassure the fearful were to be fully established.[36]

Proliferation is a key issue for collective security advocates. They support very strong measures to prevent and reverse it.[37] They not only supported the renewal and indefinite extension of the NPT in 1995, they also believe that its safeguards should be strengthened. The demonstration effect of any new proliferation is presumed to be great. It is therefore reasonable to oppose any new nuclear power beyond those declared nuclear weapons states in the original nuclear NPT.[38] Moreover, the policy will be pursued equally versus friends, enemies, and neutrals. Israeli, Indian, and Ukrainian nuclear weapons are all bad, regardless of the fact that the United States has no political conflict of interest with any of these countries. Proliferation must also be headed off for another reason: the more nuclear powers there are in the world, the more dangerous it will be for international organizations to act aggressively against miscreants, the less likely they will be to act, and the more likely it is that the entire collective security edifice will collapse.[39] War to prevent new nuclear powers from emerging would be reasonable in some circumstances.[40]

Regional conflicts among states are of critical interest to collective security advocates. Cross border aggression has always been their most clear cut problem. It can never be acceptable anywhere and must be banished from world politics.

Ethnic conflict within nominal states emerges as a new problem for a collective security strategy.[41] Historically, collective security tried to establish the conditions for peace among a small number of great powers and empires. Today we have many more states, and even more groups aspiring to statehood. Politically conscious groups often span the boundaries of several territorially defined states. Thus intergroup conflict may become interstate conflict. Even when irredenta are not involved, civil wars may attract outside intervention by the greedy, and thus precipitate international wars. Finally, ethnic conflict tends to be among the fiercest. The brutal behavior that emerges on the television screens of the world sets a bad example.

Collective security advocates are willing to contemplate direct military action for humanitarian reasons.[42] Obviously the banishment of aggressive war would serve humanitarian ends. But the connection between immediate humanitarian concerns and the task of building sufficient credibility to deter future aggressors is tenuous. Indeed, the goals may conflict, as often seemed the case in Bosnia-Herzegovina. In the first phase of that war, the United States and other democratic states could have supplied arms to the Bosnian Muslims with relative ease to help them fend off the military attacks of the Serbs. They might even have flown tactical air sorties to assist the Muslims. But it is unlikely that UN humanitarian efforts to move aid into Bosnia would have survived such a policy. A full scale intervention with several hundred thousand troops might have been necessary to simultaneously stop the Serbs and sustain the UN humanitarian effort to save lives. Collective security advocates seem inclined to pursue short term humanitarianism and political principle at the same time.

What kind of U.S. force structure is required to pursue collective security? Advocates have suggested that a smaller one than that advocated by the Clinton administration would suffice.[43] But this assessment focuses on means: it assumes that others will cooperate to the maximum extent of their ability—that is, that they will maintain larger forces than they currently plan. And it ignores the necessity for a period of regular and consistent military action if there is to be any hope of building the international credibility necessary to affect the calculations of prospective aggressors everywhere.

A true collective security policy could involve the United States in several simultaneous military actions. United States forces were recently engaged in Iraq and in Somalia simultaneously, while advocates of intervention in Bosnia clamored for a third U.S. military action. United Nations forces were deployed in several other places—arguably in insufficient numbers to accomplish their missions completely. The experience in Desert Shield and Desert Storm, and in the Somali relief operation, suggests that U.S. leadership is the key ingredient needed to elicit substantial international cooperation.[44] It is not the subtle diplomacy of the United States that proves critical, but rather its military reputation, which depends on large, diverse, technologically sophisticated, and lushly supplied military forces capable of decisive operations. At least initially, the United States would have to provide disproportionate military power to launch a global collective security regime. General Colin Powell's "Base Force" or then Congressman Aspin's "Force D" (see Table 5.1) may be necessary to pursue a true collective security policy with a good chance of success.

Containment

Selective engagement seeks to ensure peace and stability by preventing conflict among the major powers. Primacy, which is discussed later, tries to discourage the emergence of a peer competitor; some believe that such a competitor has already emerged, or re-emerged. Russia, though smaller and weaker than its Soviet predecessor, is presumed to be on the move again.[45] China, too, is expected to emerge as a serious challenger in the not too distant future. The remedy that worked the last time, containment, should be resurrected. These views are most prominently identified with Zbigniew Brzezinski and Henry Kissinger, and have surfaced with the greatest clarity in the debate on whether NATO should formally expand and offer membership and protection to former eastern European members of the Warsaw Pact. The first candidates for admission would be Poland, the Czech Republic, and Hungary, and perhaps Slovakia. United States policy intimates that newly independent states that were previously part of the Soviet Union might also someday join the Alliance.

Advocates of a revived containment policy are moved by one key problem, the classical geopolitical fear of a hegemonic power that could influence, if not control, much or all of Eurasia. This would inevitably affect U.S. power, influence, and ultimately security. Thus the United States should again, as it has in the past, act to oppose the rise of specific candidate hegemons. Russia is the candidate of the moment; observers should not be lulled by the relative decline in capability precipitated by the dissolution of the Soviet Union, the collapse of the Soviet economy, and the deterioration of the Soviet, now Russian, military. Containment advocates cite a new Russian assertiveness, demonstrated in diplomatic, military, and economic interventions large and small around its periphery.[46] Russia brings three qualities to the table, and they inevitably make for trouble. First, Russia is simply a very large country territorially, centrally located in Eurasia but also spanning the continent. It thus possesses tremendous inherent strategic reach, and considerable material reserves. Second, the Russian state possesses the largest single ethnic-cultural population in Europe, broadly defined, by nearly a factor of 50 percent: 120 million Russians to roughly 80 million Germans. (Thirty million non-Russians also live in Russia.) Another 30 million Russians live outside the borders of Russia, making for potentially greater strength, but also providing an enduring pretext for Russia to intervene in the internal affairs of several of its newly independent neighbors, and a lever with which to do so. The combination of a large and reasonably well-educated population, and considerable physical resources makes Russia's current economic weaknesses appear as a transient phenomenon.[47] Finally, it is argued that Russian culture somehow contains within it the seeds of expansion.[48] (One notes here echoes of Cold War logic, which viewed communism as inherently aggressive.)

The principal instrument for implementing a new containment policy is the expansion of NATO. Indeed, to be fair, it is the debate on NATO expansion that has precipitated the elaboration of a new containment argument. And it should be noted that many favor NATO expansion because of its presumed benefits for the domestic development of eastern European states. NATO membership would somehow suppress nascent local nationalisms, discourage conflict among eastern European states, and ensure against Russian aggression. NATO would "Promote Stability" so that democracy would have an easier time taking hold.[49] Brzezinski and Kissinger see the Russian threat as somewhat more imminent. Moreover, both fear the seductive effect of a "security vacuum" in eastern (newly rechristened "central") Europe. "A Russia facing a divided Europe would find the temptation to fill the vacuum irresistible."[50] Moreover, Germany too will be tempted into this vacuum, on her own, if the NATO alliance that is meant to defend her ignores her interests in a deep security buffer that would provide a bulwark against a future assertion of Russian power. As the Russian-German competition unfolded, NATO would be more and more impotent, and the principal states of Europe would begin to cut more traditional security deals. The old "struggle for mastery in Europe" would return. NATO expansion to the Czech Republic, Hungary, Poland, and Slovakia solves all problems: the United States is anchored in Europe; the Russians are kept out; the Germans are kept happy and safe.

Supported, indeed prodded, by the Clinton administration, NATO decided in January 1994 to expand. Though the how, who, and when of NATO expansion remain unclear, attempts have been made to explain the why of expansion. According to Strobe Talbot, NATO's enlargement would ensure collective defense against any new threats; induce the countries of East and Central Europe and the former Soviet Union to embrace political and economic liberalization, civilian control of the military, and respect for human rights; and contribute to the peaceful resolution of disputes in the new Europe.[51] It is evident, however, that the administration's case for expansion incorporates the logic of containment as well as that of collective, or perhaps more accurately cooperative, security. As Talbot put it, ". . . among the contingencies for which NATO must be prepared is that Russia will abandon democracy and return to the threatening patterns of international behavior that have sometimes characterized its history. . . ."[52] Thus NATO expansion is viewed as a hedge not merely against possible new threats but against an old threat.

Advocates of NATO expansion are not utterly unmindful of the possibility that this would precipitate a reaction from Russia for wholly defensive reasons. Hence, they usually advocate a simultaneous diplomatic approach to Russia in the form of some sort of "security treaty."[53] Moreover, they concede that NATO should not move large forces forward onto the territory of new members.[54] The combination of a formal diplomatic act of reassurance and military restraint is expected to ameliorate the possibility that the eastward march of a mighty and formerly adversarial military coalition could be perceived to pose a threat to Russia.

Because the new containment policy is so closely tied to NATO expansion, advocates say little about other regions in the world. Brzezinski, however, adds a more forward U.S. policy around the Russian periphery to NATO expansion.[55] In some recent work, Brzezinski describes an "oblong of maximum danger," which extends from the Adriatic to the border of the Chinese province of Sinkiang and from the Persian Gulf to the Russian-Kazakh frontier.[56] Here he expects a stew of ethnic and nationalist conflict and proliferation of weapons of mass destruction, a "whirlpool of violence." The precise nature of U.S. interests here is not well developed. Similarly, Henry Kissinger alludes to the role of a revived NATO in the resolution of future crises that will surely attend the adjustment of Russia, China, and Japan to the changed circumstances of the post–Cold War world, though he also alluded to Korea, Indonesia, Brazil, and India.[57] The question of proliferation does not enjoy as high a priority as it does in some other strategies; Brzezinski is the most forthright in placing geo-political considerations first: ". . . Ukraine's independent existence is a matter of far greater long-range significance than whether Kiev does or does not promptly dismantle its post-Soviet nuclear arsenal."[58]

Advocates of a revived containment policy are remarkably inexplicit about its costs. Indeed, as of this writing, only one appraisal of the costs of NATO expansion to the four eastern European countries most often suggested as the initial candidates for membership has appeared in the public debate on the policy.[59] An assessment of the current threat offered by competent military analysts who generally support expansion is not particularly alarmist:

> One should avoid assuming worst-case scenarios. Even a re-armed Russia would not be the military Leviathan the Soviet Union once was. It would have an imposing military force, but probably not a great deal more than that of Iran, Iraq, or North Korea—in short, a major regional contingency-sized threat. Defending against such a threat would be very different than against the theater-wide challenge posed by the Warsaw Pact during the Cold War. Moreover, to pose that kind of threat, Russia would have to mobilize and concentrate its military forces against Europe, leaving its eastern and southern flanks vulnerable. If the United States can defend the Persian Gulf and South Korea from these threats from several thousand miles away, then NATO should be able to defend Poland and other East-Central European states from a distance of several hundred kilometers.[60]

We have quoted this statement, by declared advocates of NATO expansion, at length, to illustrate one point. According to these analysts, there is no imminent or even remote military threat to these eastern European countries that NATO cannot deal with rather comfortably with its current capabilities. Even if they are wrong, and a Russian military buildup would require some kind of countervailing NATO buildup, it is pretty clear that the Russians have a long way to go, which means NATO would have a long time to consider whether it wished to defend eastern Europe, and how to do so. This single paragraph is thus quite revealing about the true extent of the current Russian threat, which is minimal. If this is a fair assessment, then one wonders what is actually driving the advocates of the new containment policy. In our judgment, it is not the imminence of a Russian threat. It is first the desire to anchor the United States in a diplomatic enterprise that will preserve and widen its involvement in European and international affairs, simply because this is viewed as an unalloyed good in its own right. Second, it is to forestall even a hint of an independent German foreign policy in the east.[61] It is thus possible to view a revived containment policy in Europe as nothing more than the adaptation of a politically familiar vehicle to the task of preserving U.S. primacy.

Even though it is Russia that has most captured the imaginations of those who would have us cling to containment, concern has also been expressed about the People's Republic of China. Current economic trends in that country suggest that it could become a formidable economic competitor in the first quarter of the next century. Its new economic capability could easily be translated into not only regional but also perhaps global military might.[62] Indeed China's military modernization plans already have set off alarm bells in neighboring countries. The admission of Vietnam into the Association of South East Asian Nations (ASEAN) can be read in part as reflecting concerns about China's intentions. China's rapid economic growth, improving military capabilities, stridency on Taiwan, and interest in the South China Sea have led to the suggestion that it would be prudent to hedge against the failure of engagement with China with a strategy of "hidden containment." Such a strategy would include maintaining U.S. military presence in the region, the establishment of a robust diplomatic relationship with Vietnam, and perhaps even the revival of something along the lines of the South East Asia Treaty Organization (SEATO).[63] According to *The Economist*, containment ". . . should mean recognizing that China is a destabilising force and impressing upon it the need to forswear force in trying to settle its grievances." More specifically, "China should be left in no doubt that an invasion of Taiwan . . . would comprehensively wreck relations with capitalist Asia and the West. . . ."[64] Thus a strategy that "worked" during the Cold War against the Soviet Union, once thought to be the most formidable of adversaries, has not lost its salience, despite the demise of the Soviet Union and the end of the Cold War. Containment is an appropriate response not only to the behavior of the presumed successor to the Soviet threat—Russia—but also to the behavior of China, a presumed future danger.

Because current advocates of containment do not stress the immediate military threat consituted by Russia or China, or both, the military forces necessary for the strategy ought not to be overwhelming. The RAND analysts cited above (footnotes 49 and 60) view Russia as a "major regional contingency." Even if China must be contained simultaneously, this ought not to constitute more than a second "major regional contingency," if that. Given that these two states would be the focus of U.S. military efforts, some of the humanitarian and small scale intervention forces in Force C could be jettisoned, or reoriented toward Russia and China. Thus, it seems possible that this force is roughly adequate to the task of containment at the present time. As the Russian economy recovers, and as the Chinese military benefits from the fruits of China's rapid economic growth the U.S. force structure would need to grow accordingly.

Primacy

Primacy, finally, is located on the other extreme end of our continuum of grand strategies. Primacy, as selective engagement, is motivated by both power and peace. But it is power, and a particular configuration of power, that is key. According to the variant of realism that informs primacy, only a preponderance of power ensures peace. The traditional realist conception of the balance of power that underlies selective engagement is viewed as insufficient. Peace is the result not of a balance of power but of an imbalance of power. It is not enough, consequently, to be "first among equals." Even the most clever Bismarckian orchestrator of the balance of power will ultimately fall short. One must simply be "first." In NATO, for instance, the United States should not be satis-

fied with a mere seat at the table. The United States must sit at the
head of the table. Both world order, therefore, and national security require that the United States maintain the primacy with which it
emerged from the Cold War.

Primacy is most concerned with the trajectories of present and possible future great powers. As for selective engagement, Russia, the most
significant members of the European Union (essentially Germany,
France, and Britain), China, and Japan matter most. But primacy goes
beyond the logic of selective engagement in its focus on present and potential future great powers. War among the powers with the greatest industrial and military capability poses the greatest threat to world order
and U.S. security for the advocates of selective engagement. For the advocates of primacy, the greatest threat to order and security is the rise
of a peer competitor from the midst of the great powers. The objective
for primacy, therefore, is not merely preserving peace among the great
powers, but preserving U.S. supremacy by politically, economically,
and militarily outdistancing any global challenger on the order of the
former Soviet Union.

Certainly the most serious threat would be posed by an across-the-
board political, economic, and military challenger. Yet even a power
that rivaled the United States in only one or two of these three dimensions of national power could erode U.S. preponderance. That the Soviet Union during the Cold War was able to issue a credible challenge
in the political and military realms but not in the economic did little to
allay U.S. fears.

It is generally the one-dimensional challenge that is seen as providing the near term threat to continued U.S. primacy. The realm in which
the United States is alleged to be most vulnerable is the economic; the
power most often accused of attempting to exploit that vulnerability is
Japan; and Europe is expected to be the next economic contender. For
some the U.S.-Soviet Cold War of old has given way to a U.S.-Japanese
economic Cold War that the United States is in danger of losing.[65]
These fears of Japanese economic aggrandizement rest on the impressive economic performance of Japan during recent decades. Japanese
economic growth, productivity, savings, investment, research and development, and exports are thought to fuel not only Japan's economic
competitiveness but its economic power, which translates into "increased control of capital, facilities, markets and technology."[66] In the
zero-sum world of primacy, an increase in Japanese economic power
portends a decline in U.S. power and influence that directly "threatens
American economic well-being."[67] The recommended antidote to
American economic vulnerability and counter to the Japanese challenge lies not in protectionism and Japan-bashing but in long-term domestic economic renewal. Courageous economic decisions at home—a
reduced federal budget deficit, improvements in the national infrastructure, increased savings and investment rates, increased commercial (as

opposed to military) research and development, improved education and training—and cooperation rather than confrontation abroad are needed if America's economic ills are to be redressed and its economic primacy restored.[68] A sound domestic economy is the foundation of both international economic competitiveness and political and military power and serves as a crucial underpinning of primacy.

The most likely candidate for future peer competitor, and therefore long-term threat, is China.[69] Russia will continue to struggle with its political and economic transitions. Europe's unification will remain economically and, especially, politically incomplete. Separately, none of Europe's powers will be terribly noteworthy contenders. In particular, Germany will remain preoccupied with the political and economic costs of reunification. And Japan will continue as little more than a one-dimensional power. China, on the other hand, has the world's most rapidly growing economy. Already the third largest in the world, the Chinese economy is poised to overtake Japan's. Soon after the turn of the century, its economy may well be as large as that of the United States. Meanwhile, the Chinese military is pursuing a modernization program that features the development of power projection capabilities. Though there is considerable uncertainty surrounding its political future, China could well tip the international scales of power in the first half of the next century.[70] The foremost long-term problem for architects of a strategy of primacy, therefore, involves preventing the emergence of a Chinese hegemon that is able to dominate Eurasia.

Though not directed solely or even specifically at China, the draft Defense Planning Guidance (DPG) leaked to the press in March of 1992 provides the most fully developed blueprint for "precluding" the rise of such a peer competitor. The authors of the draft DPG were unyielding in their insistence that the United States maintain its status as the world's sole superpower:

> Our strategy must now refocus on precluding the emergence of any potential future global competitor.
>
> Our first objective is to prevent the reemergence of a new rival, either on the territory of the former Soviet Union or elsewhere, that poses a threat on the order of that posed formerly by the Soviet Union. This is a dominant consideration . . . and requires that we endeavor to prevent any hostile power from dominating a region whose resources would, under consolidated control, be sufficient to generate global power.[71]

Those parts of the world thought most likely to harbor potential peer competitors were Western Europe, East Asia, the territories of the former Soviet Union, and Southwest Asia.

The Department of Defense's strategic planners seem to have rather quaintly envisioned the United States as a benevolent, or at least benign, hegemon that would be able to maintain its global dominance by ruling with the interests of others in mind. Thus:

> The U.S. must show the leadership necessary to establish and protect a new order that holds the promise of convincing potential competitors that they need not aspire to a greater role or pursue a more aggressive posture to protect their legitimate interests. . . . [I]n the non-defense areas, we must account sufficiently for the interests of the advanced industrial nations to discourage them from challenging our leadership or seeking to overturn the established political and economic order. . . . [W]e will retain the pre-eminent responsibility for addressing selectively those wrongs which threaten not only our interests, but those of our allies or friends, or which could seriously unsettle international relations.[72]

Present and aspiring major powers were to be persuaded, it seems, that they could rest easy, that they need not bother investing in the political, economic, and military means they might otherwise require to safeguard their interests. Indeed, any assertion of strategic independence by the likes of Germany and Japan would only erode the global and regional stability sought by all. A benevolent big brother, they and others were to be convinced, could be trusted to provide that stability. Who could possibly object to the United States so selflessly volunteering to shoulder—and all on its own!—the burden of maintaining world order?

In addition to maintaining U.S. primacy by reassuring others of the purity of its intentions, the draft DPG envisioned the United States seeking to preclude the rise of challengers by promoting international law, democracy, and free market economies and precluding the emergence of regional hegemons. Particularly in the territories of the former Soviet Union, support for political and economic transformation was seen as the best way to ensure that Russia would not revert to the authoritarian, expansionist habits of old, though the United States was to hedge against the failure of political and economic reform. In Europe, the United States would work against any erosion of NATO's preeminent role in European security and the development of any security arrangements that would undermine the role of NATO, and therefore the role of the United States, in European security affairs. The countries of East and Central Europe were to be integrated into the political, economic, and even security institutions of Western Europe. In East Asia, the United States was to maintain a military presence sufficient to ensure regional stability and prevent the emergence of a power vacuum or a regional hegemon. The same approach applied to the Middle East and Southwest Asia, where the United States intended to remain the preeminent extra-regional power. The United States would also endeavor to discourage India's hegemonic ambitions in South Asia.

The regional dimension of the strategy outlined in the draft DPG therefore tracks with the global dimension. The aspirations of regional as well as global hegemons are to be thwarted.[73]

Despite its ambitious objectives, the resources required to support a strategy of primacy are not considered to be beyond the realm of the possible, particularly since the strategy does not place an inordinate emphasis on military means. Advocates of primacy, as those of selective engagement, do recognize that U.S. resources are scarce. But for them, U.S. resources are not as scarce as proponents of selective engagement would have us believe. Scarcity, after all, is a relative concept. Indeed, the United States is a wealthy country that all too often acts as if it were poor. That need not be the case. The problem is not a lack of resources, they would have us believe, but a lack of public will and support. In addition, proponents of primacy seem to presume that hegemonic states have access not only to their own resources but also to those of others. The U.S. solicitation of financial contributions during the Gulf War was an instance not of a beggar nation passing the hat but of a superpower "persuading" noncombatants who would benefit from the liberation of Kuwait and defeat of Iraq to pay for military action the United States was bound to pursue with or without them. Only a hegemonic power can exercise such compelling persuasion.

Advocates of primacy share with the new isolationists and selective engagers a healthy skepticism of international organizations. International organizations have little if any power and therefore can do little to maintain or, particularly, restore peace. Yet international organizations should not be entirely rejected either because of fears that they may draw the United States into conflicts or worries that they cannot credibly deter aggression. They do have utility, even if it is severely (and properly) circumscribed. Even a hegemonic power will, from time to time, find it useful to exploit the diplomatic cover provided by international organizations such as the United Nations and the various regional organizations that litter the world. If the facade of multilateralism renders the rule of an extraordinary power more palatable to ordinary powers, as it did during the Gulf War, international organizations are a strategic asset.

Proponents of primacy view proliferation, regional conflict, ethnic conflict, and humanitarian intervention in much the same light as the advocates of selective engagement. Proliferation is as much a concern for primacy as it is for cooperative security and selective engagement. The threat to U.S. interests posed by the proliferation of nuclear and other weapons of mass destruction and their means of delivery was highlighted in the draft DPG. Denial must remain the first line of defense in combating proliferation. Ultimately, however, a more enlightened and differentiated stance may be required. Some proliferators matter more than others.

Regional conflict matters most when it impinges on major power relations and the rise of potential peer competitors and regional hegemons. Outside of the Persian Gulf, most conflicts in what was once referred to as the Third World will be of little concern. Much the same can be said for ethnic conflict, however reprehensible it may be, and humanitarian disasters.

The forces needed to support a grand strategy of primacy should inspire a sense of *déjà vu*. A Cold War force, in particular the Bush administration's Base Force, would do just fine. The draft DPG, after all, was intended to provide the classified rationale for a 1.62 million person Base Force. (See Table 5.1).[74] General Colin Powell apparently saw this force as the "bottom line" if U.S. primacy was to be preserved.[75] The Base Force is larger than that identified earlier as sufficient to support the less ambitious grand strategy of selective engagement and would cost more. But in the absence of a near term threat on the order of a peer competitor, the force structure required to support primacy need not necessarily be tremendously larger than the Clinton administration's Bottom-Up Review force.[76] It must, however, continue to be modernized. Indeed, if the objective is actually to deter any state from considering a challenge to U.S. preeminence, then it is logical for the U.S. military to pursue a level of qualitative superiority over potential challengers that would discourage them from entering the competition. Thus the U.S. must dominate what has come to be called the revolution in military affairs. The force must also be capable of what the Bush administration termed reconstitution: the ability to expand U.S. military capabilities to deter, and if necessary respond to, the rise of a global challenger. Any post–Cold War downsizing of U.S. military capabilities must, therefore, be done in a manner that facilitates the reconstitution of those capabilities. Thus the level of defense spending required to support a grand strategy of primacy would likely be greater in the future than it would be now, as a consequence of both modernization and expansion.[77]

One of the foremost advocates of primacy has argued that "it matters which state exercises the most power in the international system," that U.S. primacy is to be preferred to that of another power and is superior to a world in which no one is able to exercise primacy (the balance of power world implicitly embraced by selective engagement), and that primacy enables a state to achieve its objectives without resorting to war.[78] It would seem, however, that the quest for primacy is a preordained failure. It is inevitable that new great powers will rise in the future. Their rise may be delayed, but not prevented. Attempting to prevent their rise will only sap America's strength. Declaring the prevention of their rise the objective of U.S. strategy is a virtual invitation to struggle. States also, as the advocates of selective engagement recognize, coalesce against hegemons rather than rally around them. The pursuit of primacy poses as well the constant risk of imperial over-stretch. Primacy is notoriously open ended. One can never have enough. A little bit more will always seem better. An imperial appetite can never be satiated; attempting to do so only drains the national trea-sury. Ultimately, primacy is unsustainable and self-defeating. By at-tempting to preserve the U.S. primacy that was such a prominent fea-ture of our Cold War strategy,[79] its advocates are looking to the past rather than the future.[80] Primacy is a rationale for the continued pur-suit of Cold War policy and strategy in the absence of an enemy.[81]

Conclusions

This brief overview cannot do justice to the full range of argumenta-tion about which the advocates of these five alternative grand strate-gies disagree. But it is a start. By way of conclusion three general points are in order.

First, although the five alternatives are not entirely mutually exclu-sive, for the most part one cannot indiscriminately mix and match across strategies, as both post–Cold War administrations have at-tempted to do, without running into trouble. There are serious, even fundamental, disagreements about strategic objectives and priorities, the extent to which the United States should be engaged in interna-tional affairs, the form that engagement should assume, the means that should be employed, the degree of autonomy that must be maintained, and when and under what conditions military force should be em-ployed. Some combinations just do not go together. One cannot be iso-lationist, except when it comes to friends such as Israel. One cannot wage war in the name of collective security in Bosnia-Herzegovina and then fail to do the same if Russia helps destabilize the Georgian Repub-lic and still expect to establish a well-founded fear of international reac-tion on the part of aggressors everywhere. Selective engagement may ultimately draw the United States into strategically unimportant con-flicts if the United States consistently tries to wrap its actions in the rhetoric and institutions of collective security. Primacy wrapped in the mantel of multilateralism may gradually erode international institu-tions. And the rhetoric and diplomacy of a new containment strategy probably does not permit, as the advocates would claim, particularly friendly relations with the objects of the policy.

One can imagine an attempt to mix and match selectively across the five grand strategies and to build a consensus upon a core set of pre-cepts, particularly upon the four of the five strategies that are interna-tionalist. Yet any attempt to do so in a coherent and internally consistent manner must acknowledge the formidable and profound differences among our five alternatives. These differences cannot easily be reconciled.

Second, these alternative strategies generate different force structures, two of which may prove attractive because of the money they save. But leaders should understand that these force structures constrain future political leaders—or ought to constrain them. An isolationist force structure cannot quickly be recast for collective security or humanitarian intervention. A force structure designed for selective engagement may prove inadequate for the full range of collective security missions. A true collective security force structure may include more intervention capabilities than needed for strategic weight in great power wars, perhaps at some cost to the ability of the United States to wage heavy combined arms warfare. A force structure tailored for primacy permits most kinds of military operations but may be so impressive that it causes some states to compete more rather than less with the United States. A containment force structure will specialize to take on one or more "designated' adversaries, at some cost to the flexibility needed for other missions.

Finally, it should be clear that these five strategies produce different advice about U.S. use of force abroad. Isolationism suggests "almost never." Collective security could imply "almost always." Selective engagement advises "it all depends," but suggests some rough criteria for judgment. Containment speaks for itself and allows one's adversaries to point the way. Primacy implies whenever the employment of force is necessary to secure or improve the U.S. relative power position. The longing for clear decision rules on when to use force should not, however, outweigh the more fundamental concerns that ought to drive the U.S. choice of strategy. What factors beyond its borders do the citizens of the United States, and their leaders, believe most affect the safety, sovereignty, and territorial integrity of the country, and why? What should the United States do about them, and why do we think our preferred remedies will work?

Endnotes

1. The first version of this essay was submitted by Barry R. Posen as written testimony for the House Armed Services Committee on March 3, 1993. An earlier version of this chapter appeared in Strategy and Force Planning Faculty (eds.), *Strategy and Force Planning* (Newport: Naval War College Press, 1995), pp. 115–134. The discussion below is our interpretation of the major positions in the current US grand strategy debate. We have borrowed liberally from the work and the ideas of many authors and have caricatured some positions for the sake of analytic clarity. Posen bears primary responsibility for the sections on isolationism, collective security, and selective engagement; Ross for the section on primacy.

2. Richard N. Haass, "Paradigm Lost," *Foreign Affairs*, Vol. 74, No. 1 (January/February 1995): 43–58.
3. The new isolationists seldom refer to themselves as isolationists. Indeed, they often vociferously deny isolationist tendencies. Earl Ravenal, "The Case for Adjustment," *Foreign Policy*, No. 81 (Winter 1990–1991): 3–19, offers a diagnosis of international politics and a prescription for U.S. foreign and defense policy that are quite close to what we dub "neo-isolationism." He seems to want to call his policy "disengagement." Doug Bandow, "Keeping the Troops and the Money at Home," *Current History*, Vol. 93, No. 579 (January 1994): 8–13, prefers "benign detachment." For a revealing example of the application of this new isolationism, *see* Ted Galen Carpenter, "South Korea: A Vital or Peripheral U.S. Security Interest?" in Doug Bandow and Ted Galen Carpenter (eds.), *The U.S.-South Korean Alliance: Time for a Change* (New Brunswick, N.J.: Transaction Publishers, 1992), pp. 1–15.
4. The most sophisticated, and perhaps least conventional, version of the new isolationism is offered by Eric A. Nordlinger, *Isolationism Reconfigured: American Foreign Policy for a New Century* (Princeton: Princeton University Press, 1995). Unlike other variants, Nordlinger's national strategy of isolationism and its concurrent foreign policy appears to be informed more by liberalism than realism.
5. Alan Tonelson, "Superpower Without a Sword," *Foreign Affairs*, Vol. 72, No. 3 (Summer 1993): 179, observes that ". . . few international conflicts will directly threaten the nation's territorial integrity, political independence or material welfare." The article is largely an attack on the ability of the developing Clinton defense budget to support an ambitious collective security foreign policy.
6. Christopher Layne, "The Unipolar Illusion: Why Great Powers Will Rise," *International Security*, Vol. 17, No. 4 (Spring 1993): 48, makes this point. He uses it to support an argument for a grand strategy that he calls "strategic independence." It bears some similarity to the selective engagement strategy outlined below, albeit a rather inactive version of the strategy.
7. According to Nordlinger, *Isolationism Reconsidered*, p. 6, "The United States is strategically immune in being insulated, invulnerable, impermeable, and impervious and thus has few security reasons to become engaged politically and militarily."
8. Bandow, "Keeping the Troops and the Money at Home," p. 10.
9. Bandow, "Keeping the Troops and Money at Home," pp. 8–13, expands on these points.
10. "Indeed, U.S. intervention in other regional antagonisms and conflicts—whether unilaterally or collectively—is the only way that such violence can reach America's shores and heartland or impair the core values and true interests of American society." Ravenal, "The Case for Adjustment," p. 8.
11. Robert W. Tucker and David C. Hendrickson, *The Imperial Temptation: The New World Order and America's Purpose* (New York: Council on Foreign Relations, 1992), prefer a strategy, which, like Layne's, amounts to a very conservative version of selective engagement. They do not offer a particularly elaborate argument *for* such a strategy, rather they argue *against* the strategy we term "collective security." They suggest that in the context of "selective engagement" the United States should spend more money on foreign economic assistance and less on military power. *See* p. 206.
12. Ravenal, "The Case for Adjustment," pp. 15–19, develops a force structure and defense budget within these parameters that is explicitly geared to support a grand strategy quite similar to what we label isolationism. He suggests an active force of 1.1 million people, with six army and two marine divisions, 11 tactical air wings, six carriers with five air wings, and a strategic dyad of submarines and bombers, which could be funded for about $150 billion in constant 1991 dollars, perhaps 175 billion 1997 dollars, or roughly 2.5 percent of GDP. *See* Force A in Table 5.1,

which is roughly the same size, but which then Congressman Aspin estimated would cost considerably more, $231 billion 1997 dollars, roughly 3 percent of GDP. *See also* Tonelson, pp. 179–180, who argues for a similar force structure, but who seems to subscribe to a conservative version of selective engagement. The Center for Defense Information (CDI) has proposed that an even smaller force structure would be sufficient to support a strategy of disengagement. For $104 billion in constant 1993 dollars, CDI proposes to field an active force of only 500,000 people, three Army and one Marine divisions, four Air Force tactical wings, two carriers and 221 other combat vessels, and a nuclear force of 16 submarines. *See* "Defending America: CDI Options for Military Spending," *The Defense Monitor*, Vol. 21, No. 4 (1992).

13. Robert Art, "A Defensible Defense: America's Grand Strategy After the Cold War," *International Security*, Vol. 15, No. 4 (Spring 1991): 5–53; and Stephen Van Evera, "Why Europe Matters, Why the Third World Doesn't: American Grand Strategy After the Cold War," *Journal of Strategic Studies*, Vol. 13, No. 2 (June 1990): 1–51, are the two most complete expositions of selective engagement type strategies. *See also* Andrew C. Goldberg, "Selective Engagement: U.S. National Security Policy in the 1990s," *The Washington Quarterly*, Vol. 15, No. 3 (Summer 1992): 15–24. Josef Joffe, "'Bismarck' or 'Britain'? Toward an American Grand Strategy after Bipolarity," *International Security*, Vol. 19, No. 4 (Spring 1995): 94–117, recommends a policy obliquely similar to selective engagement.

14. The Heritage Foundation argues for a somewhat similar strategy in the ironically mistitled *Making the World Safe for America: A U.S. Foreign Policy Blueprint* (April 1992), and employs the term "Selective Engagement," as the heading of its summary discussion, p. 31. The approach is a bit more classical, however. They focus on threats to interests and are less concerned about peace among great powers. *See also* Kim R. Holmes (ed.), *A Safe and Prosperous America: A U.S. Foreign and Defense Policy Blueprint*, (Washington, DC: The Heritage Foundation, June 1994).

15. Art, "Defensible Defense," p. 45.

16. Joffe, "Collective Security," op. cit.

17. On the value of U.S. engagement as a means to help secure great power peace, and the priority of this mission over others, *see* Van Evera, "Why Europe Matters," pp. 8–10; Art, "Defensible Defense," pp. 45–50.

18. Art, "Defensible Defense," pp. 23–30, offers a nuanced discussion of the risks of nuclear spread, and concludes that the U.S. ought to try to discourage it by reassuring possible great power proliferators like Germany and Japan. Both Art and Van Evera are silent on the question of whether conventional war should be waged to prevent some states from getting nuclear weapons.

19. Heritage Foundation, *Making the World Safe*, p. 12 is explicit, "America should not shrink from discriminating against states it considers potentially most hostile, for example Iran, Libya, and North Korea; viewed through the lens of America's interests, all states are not equal. . . . Anti-proliferation measures should include . . . military action to prevent the proliferation of mass destruction weapons."

20. Art, "Defensible Defense," p. 47; Heritage Foundation, *Making the World Safe*, pp. 17–19; Stephen Van Evera, "The United States and the Third World: When to Intervene?" in Kenneth A. Oye, Robert J. Lieber, and Donald Rothchild (eds.), *Eagle in a New World* (New York: HarperCollins, 1992): 127–131, makes a comprehensive case for U.S. intervention in the Persian Gulf in 1990, Operation Desert Shield, but expresses skepticism about the necessity for Operation Desert Storm.

21. Barry R. Posen, "A Balkan Vietnam Awaits 'Peacekeepers'," *Los Angeles Times*, February 4, 1993, p. B7. The article assesses the force requirements to police the "Vance Owen Plan," which intended to preserve a unitary Bosnia Herzegovina. The three principle ethnic and religious groups in Bosnia would have remained intermingled, as they were at the outset of the war. Thus the police problem would have

been quite complex and demanding, similar to the British problem in Northern Ireland. Supervision of the agreed separation of combatant forces in the far less ambitious Dayton Accord, which formally divides Bosnia Herzegovina into a weak confederation of three self governing entities, and which many believe virtually ensures the partition of the country, nevertheless required the equivalent of three NATO divisions.

22. Representative Les Aspin, Chairman, House Armed Services Committee, "An Approach to Sizing American Conventional Forces for the Post–Soviet Era: Four Illustrative Options," February 25, 1992. Then Congressman Aspin argued that this force could comfortably handle two major and one minor regional military contingencies simultaneously.

23. On the differences between realism and liberalism *see* Charles W. Kegley, Jr. (ed.), *Controversies in International Relations Theory: Realism and the Neoliberal Challenge* (New York: St. Martin's Press, 1995); and Paul R. Viotti and Mark V. Kauppi, *International Relations Theory: Realism, Pluralism, Globalism*, 2nd ed. (New York: Macmillan, 1993). Viotti and Kauppi refer to liberalism as "pluralism."

24. Inis L. Claude, *Swords into Plowshares: The Problems and Progress of International Organization*, 4th ed. (New York: Random House, 1971), p. 247; Arnold Wolfers, *Discord and Collaboration* (Baltimore: Johns Hopkins, 1962), pp. 183–184, ". . .'any aggressor anywhere' is in fact the national enemy of every country because in violating the peace and law of the community of nations it endangers, if indirectly, the peace and security of every nation."

25. The question immediately arises as to how we would characterize the "grand strategy" of the Clinton administration. For the most complete statement of its grand strategy *see A National Security Strategy of Engagement and Enlargement* (The White House, February 1995). As stated at the outset, we have striven to outline alternative strategies with the greatest possible clarity. Policy papers are inevitably more nuanced. It is our judgment that the Clinton administration leans strongly in the direction of a "collective security" strategy. Nevertheless, a reader of their recent policy papers might come away with the impression that "selective engagement" is the strategy. Alternatively, one might hypothesize that "collective security" would be the Clinton strategy if the administration were free to follow the instincts of its principal foreign and defense policy officials but that harsh experience, competing priorities, and domestic constraints have pulled the administration in the direction of a more "selective" approach. So the document in question asserts the U.S. interest in "promoting cooperative security measures" (p. 3) but also notes that "our engagement must be selective, focusing on the challenges that are most relevant to our interests and focusing our resources where we can make the most difference" (p. 7). A careful reading of the entire document reveals a curiously dialectical quality, featuring a near debate between collective security rhetoric and selective engagement rhetoric.

26. Many collective security advocates have adopted the term "cooperative security" for their preferred strategy. The main thing that distinguishes the two is that "cooperative security" encompasses *both* the traditional methods and objectives of collective security plus elaborate and intensive arms control schemes that aim through quantitative and qualitative restrictions to remove the capability for offensive action from as many countries as possible. Offensive capabilities would reside only in the combined forces of a coalition of peace loving states and would be used only to reverse aggression by the small number of miscreants who fail to shed their offensive capabilities and obey the rules. It is suggested that the combination of the two somehow renders both more achievable. *See* Ashton B. Carter, William J. Perry, and John D. Steinbruner, *A New Concept of Cooperative Security*, Occasional Paper, (Washington, DC: Brookings Institution, 1992); Janne E. Nolan (ed.), *Global Engagement: Cooperation and Security in the 21st Century* (Washington,

DC: Brookings Institution, 1994); Paul B. Stares and John D. Steinbruner, "Cooperative Security and the New Europe," in Stares (ed.), *The New Germany and the New Europe* (Washington, D.C.: Brookings Institution, 1992), pp. 218–248. For a shorter exposition *see* Randall Forsberg, "Creating a Cooperative Security System," in *After the Cold War: A Debate on Cooperative Security*, Institute for Defense and Disarmament Studies Reprint, first published in *Boston Review*, Vol. 18, No. 6 (November/December 1992).

27. John Mueller, *Quiet Cataclysm: Reflections on the Recent Transformation of World Politics* (New York: HarperCollins, 1995). For Mueller, the quiet cataclysm ". . . suggests that big problems are often merely reflections of differences of ideas, and thus can change without big means, and particularly without war" (p. 2).

28. "Proliferation of destructive technology casts a shadow over future U.S. security in a way that cannot be directly addressed through superior force or readiness. Serious economic and environmental problems point to an inescapable interdependence of U.S. interests with the interests of other nations." Carter, Perry, and Steinbruner, *A New Concept of Cooperative Security*, p. 4.

29. Charles Krauthammer, "The Unipolar Moment," *Foreign Affairs*, Vol. 70, No. 1 (1990/1991): 31–32. "The post–Cold War era is thus perhaps better called the era of weapons of mass destruction. The proliferation of weapons of mass destruction and their means of delivery will constitute the greatest single threat to world security for the rest of our lives. That is what makes a new international order not an imperial dream or a Wilsonian fantasy but a matter of the sheerest prudence." Unlike many collective security programs, this one stresses results over process; it counts on a dominant role by the United States as the world's dominant power. And the objectives, though large, are still limited. The plan does not seem to call for the banishment of conventional weapons and conventional war, merely all other types.

30. *See* Carter, Perry, and Steinbruner, *A New Concept of Cooperative Security*, pp. 24–30. ". . . the special military capability of the United States would be used to give coalition forces an advantage that not only insured a military victory, but one that could be achieved with minimal losses to coalition forces. Therefore it should provide maximum deterrent to any potential aggressor" (p. 25).

31. Ibid., pp. 20–24. *See also* Forsberg, "Creating a Cooperative Security System," pp. 2–3; Stares and Steinbruner, "Cooperative Security and the New Europe," pp. 222–226.

32. Charles A. Kupchan and Clifford A. Kupchan, "Concerts, Collective Security, and the Future of Europe," *International Security*, Vol. 16, No. 1 (Summer 1991): 149–150. *See also* Richard Ullman, *Securing Europe* (Princeton: Princeton University Press, 1991), p. 76: "Only democratic polities would have the openness that is the precondition of confidence. Only democracies share a commitment both domestically and internationally to the rule of law and to the peaceful settlement of disputes." The argument is largely about the feasibility of establishing an elaborate collective security regime in Europe. *See also* Forsberg, p. 2.

33. Harvey Sapolsky and Sharon K. Weiner, "War Without Killing," *Breakthroughs*, Vol. 2, No. 2 (Winter 1992–1993): 1–5.

34. Claude, *Swords into Plowshares*, p. 247.

35. Carter, Perry, and Steinbruner, *A New Concept of Cooperative Security*, pp. 24–25: ". . . an integral part of any cooperative security regime must be the capability to organize multinational forces to defeat aggression should it occur. This capacity would provide a background deterrent effect as well as physical protection. The United Nations Security Council can authorize multinational military forces for this purpose." *See also* Kupchan and Kupchan, "Concerts," pp.125–127.

36. Speaking of Europe as a laboratory for "cooperative security," Jonathan Dean observes, "Ultimately, however, the existence of an effective multilateral peacemaking system depends on the willingness of its member states to use military force to

contain organized violence, even at the cost of placing their citizen soldiers in harm's way. If its member governments do not have this determination now, these costs may be much greater later. The new European system may go the way of the League of Nations." Dean, "Moving Toward a Less Violent World—Test Case, Europe," in *After the Cold War*, p. 7. Tucker and Hendrickson, *Imperial Temptation*, p. 202, fear that a collective security policy will lead inevitably to an excessive U.S. emphasis on the maintenance and employment of military power.

37. Commission on America and the New World, *Changing Our Ways, America and the New World* (Washington DC: Carnegie Endowment for International Peace, 1992), suffers from vagueness but seems to recommend a collective security strategy, while maintaining a U.S. capability for unilateral action. *See* pp. 73–75 for a discussion of nuclear proliferation.

38. Dean, "Moving Toward a Less Violent World," pp. 6–7, seems to view the discouragement of nuclear proliferation as one of the primary purposes of a collective security regime.

39. Advocates seldom make this point explicitly, but a similar point is made by Carter, Perry, and Steinbruner, *A New Concept of Cooperative Security*, p. 51: ". . . many countries that feel threatened by an intrusive reconnaissance strike capability they cannot match can aspire to chemical agents as a strategic counterweight."

40. "The Commission believes that the use of military force to prevent nuclear proliferation must be retained as an option of last resort." Commission on America and the New World, *Changing Our Ways*, p. 75; ". . .those states that acquire such weapons anyway will have to submit to strict outside control or risk being physically disarmed." Krauthammer, "Unipolar Moment," p. 32; Tucker and Hendrickson, *Imperial Temptation*, infer an inclination among collective security advocates to wage war to prevent nuclear proliferation.

41. Comments by collective security advocates on the war in Yugoslavia reveal a strong desire for some collective security organization to intervene militarily. *See* Forsberg, "Creating a Cooperative Security System," p. 3; Dean, "Moving Toward a Less Violent World," p. 7; Adam Roberts notes, without offering a general explanation, that much of the UN's recent military activity is in conflicts of this kind. *See* Adam Roberts, "The United Nations and International Security," *Survival*, Vol. 35, No. 2 (Summer 1993): 8–11. *See also* Lori Fisler Damrosh (ed.), *Enforcing Restraint: Collective Intervention in Internal Conflicts* (New York: Council on Foreign Relations Press, 1993); and Gareth Evans, "Cooperative Security and Intrastate Conflict," *Foreign Policy*, No. 96 (Fall 1994), pp. 3–20.

42. Commission on America and the New World, *Changing Our Ways*, p. 51, "The United States should be more actively engaged in strengthening the collective machinery to carry out humanitarian actions. In this way we can reduce the likelihood of having to choose between unilateral military intervention and standing idle in the face of human tragedy."

43. *See* William W. Kaufmann and John Steinbruner, *Decisions for Defense* (Washington DC: Brookings, 1991), pp. 67–76 which offers a "cooperative security" force structure that would cost roughly $150 billion (1992 dollars, excluding DOE expenses on nuclear weaponry) annually by the end of the century. Their recommended force structure is quite similar to Aspin's Force A, in Table 5.1. The authors seem to argue that the adequacy of such a force structure would depend on a series of prior diplomatic developments in the world that would, for all intents and purposes, put a functioning cooperative security regime in place. They are silent on the precise force structure necessary to move international politics to this happy state. Jerome B. Wiesner, Philip Morrison, and Kosta Tsipis, "Ending Overkill," *Bulletin of the Atomic Scientists* (March 1993), pp. 12–23, offer a force structure costing $115 billion per year, which they seem to believe is consistent with a collective security strategy. Though small, the air and naval forces they recommend are quite capable; the army they recommend, with a total active personnel strength

of 180,000 would barely be adequate for a repetition of Operation Desert Shield. It is difficult to see how it could support a collective security strategy.

44. Roberts, "The United Nations and Collective Security," pp. 16–17. Laying out the realist theoretical argument for why coalitions need leaders, and leaders are defined by great power, is Joseph Joffe, "Collective Security and the Future of Europe," *Survival*, Vol. 34, No. 1 (Spring 1992): 40–43.

45. "If not openly imperial, the current objectives of Russian policy are at the very least proto-imperial. That policy may not yet be aiming explicitly at a formal imperial restoration, but it does little to restrain the strong imperial impulse that continues to motivate large segments of the state bureaucracy, especially the military, as well as the public. The underlying and increasingly openly stated consensus behind the policy appears to be that the economic and military integration of the once-Soviet states under Moscow's political direction would prompt the re-emergence of Russia as a mighty supranational state and a truly global power." Zbigniew Brzezinski, "The Premature Partnership," *Foreign Affairs*, Vol. 73, No. 2 (March/April 1994): 76. Oddly, though he presents many of the same arguments for NATO expansion in a subsequent article, he is somewhat less alarmist about the extent of the current danger emanating from Russia. *See* Zbigniew Brzezinski, "A Plan for Europe," *Foreign Affairs*, Vol. 74, No. 1 (January/February 1995): 26–42. "In expanding NATO, one should note that neither the alliance nor its prospective new members are facing any imminent threat. Talk of a 'new Yalta' or of a Russian military threat is not justified, either by actual circumstances or even by worst-case scenarios for the near future. The expansion of NATO should, therefore, not be driven by whipping up anti-Russian hysteria that could eventually become a self-fulfilling prophecy. NATO's expansion should not be seen as directed against any particular state, but as part of a historically constructive process of shaping a secure, stable, and more truly European Europe" (p. 34).

46. This includes low level military interventions in Moldova, Georgia, and probably Armenia and Azerbaijan, the introduction of at least one division into the civil war in Tadjikistan, and the violent repression of secessionism in Chechnya. It also includes some economic coercion, for example manipulation of energy exports to Ukraine to affect its policy on Crimea, the Black Sea Fleet, and nuclear disarmament. Russia's somewhat truculent opposition to NATO expansion, and its utter unwillingness to settle a half-century old dispute over the Kurile islands claimed by Japan is viewed as unsettling diplomacy. The Russian military has also asserted a duty to protect Russians living as minorities abroad. *See* Brzezinski, pp. 72–73. A disturbing account of many of these Russian actions is found in Fiona Hill and Pamela Jewett, *Back in the USSR: Russia's Intervention in the Internal Affairs of the Former Soviet Republics and the Implications of United States Policy Toward Russia*, Strengthening Democratic Institutions Project (Cambridge, Mass.: John F. Kennedy School of Government, January 1994).

47. Brzezinski, "The Premature Partnership," is actually ambiguous on the question of Russia's possible economic revival. At one point he suggests that efforts to restore the empire ". . . would condemn Russia not only to dictatorship but to poverty." p. 72. In the same article, however, he suggests that the long term consequences of the Clinton Administration's tendency to treat Russia more as a diplomatic partner than as a rival would or could dilute ". . . the Euro-Atlantic alliance while permitting a regionally hegemonic Russia, eventually revitalized under the umbrella of the American-Russian partnership, to become again the strongest power in Eurasia." p. 77. It is difficult to reconcile the prediction of impoverishment with the prediction of revitalization and hegemony.

48. Brzezinski calls this "the imperial impulse." pp. 71–75. *See also* his *Out of Control, Global Turmoil on the Eve of the Twenty-First Century* (New York: Collier, 1993), pp. 173–181. "The Russian people have always had a special quasi-religious and quasi-philosophical sense of their historical destiny" (p. 174).

49. Ronald Asmus, Richard Kugler, and Stephen Larrabee, "NATO Expansion: The Next Steps," *Survival*, Vol. 37, No. 1 (Spring 1995): 9; *See also* the systematic critique offered by Michael E. Brown, "The Flawed Logic of NATO Expansion," *Survival*, Vol. 37, No. 1 (Spring 1995): 38–39.

50. Henry Kissinger, "Expand NATO Now," *Washington Post*, December 19, 1994.

51. Strobe Talbot, "Why NATO Should Grow," *The New York Review of Books*, August 10, 1995, p. 27.

52. Furthermore, ". . . the rationale for NATO's continued existence must include what Secretary of Defense William Perry has called 'a hedge against pessimistic outcomes. . . ,'" Talbot, "Why NATO Should Grow," p. 29.

53. Brzezinski, "Premature Partnership," pp. 81–82; Kissinger, "Expand NATO Now," *Washington Post*, December 19, 1994.

54. Ibid., and Zbigniew Brzezinski, "A Bigger-and Safer-Europe," *New York Times*, December 1, 1993, p. A23.

55. Brzezinski, pp. 79–82. He urges ". . . political assurances for Ukraine's independence and territorial integrity. . . ," ". . . a more visible American show of interest in the independence of the Central Asian states, as well as of the three states in the Caucasus. . . ," and ". . . some quiet American-Chinese political consultations regarding the area. . . ."

56. Brzezinski, *Out of Control*, pp. 163–166.

57. Kissinger, "Expand NATO Now."

58. Brzezinski, "Premature Partnership," p. 80.

59. The non-partisan Congressional Budget Office estimates that the expansion of NATO to include the Czech Republic, Hungary, Poland, and Slovakia could cost between $21.2 billion and $124.7 billion (1997 dollars) over the next fifteen years. The low figure would connect the new members' military forces to existing NATO forces, but only modestly improve their combat capability. The high figure would improve the military power both of existing NATO forces and of the new members to resist a hypothetical attack by some two dozen effective heavy divisions–a revived, but not expanded, version of the Russian military force currently stationed west of the Urals. *See* CBO, *The Costs of Expanding the Nato Alliance* (Washington DC: US Congress, Congressional Budget Office, 1996), pp. xiv, 13-18, 28, 40.

60. Asmus, Kugler, and Larrabee, ". . . The Next Steps," p. 32.

61. Ronald Asmus, Richard Kugler, and Stephen Larrabee, "Building a New NATO," *Foreign Affairs*, Vol. 72, No. 4 (September/October 1993): 34, "While Germany remains preoccupied with the staggering challenge of the political and economic reconstruction of its Eastern half, the need to stabilize its eastern flank is Bonn's number one security concern." *See also* Brzezinski, "A Plan for Europe," p. 42, "Most important, a united and powerful Germany can be more firmly anchored within this larger Europe if the European security system fully coincides with America's."

62. Karen Elliott House, "The Second Cold War" *Wall Street Journal*, February 17, 1994. She alludes to ". . . the looming threat of a militarizing, autocratic China," and observes that ". . . a resurgent China flexes its muscles at increasingly fearful neighbors." The editorial speaks of Russia in similar terms, and thus is aptly titled. *See also* International Institute for Strategic Studies, *Strategic Survey 1994–95* (London: Oxford University Press, 1995), pp. 160–168 for a concise survey of China's current internal problems and external relations. The section notes ". . . a notable shift in the U.S. to more explicit concern about Chinese military power" (p. 165). John Caldwell, *China's Conventional Military Capabilities, 1994–2004: An Assessment*, (Washington, DC: The Center for Strategic & International Studies, 1994); Chong-Pin Lin, "Chinese Military Modernization: Perceptions, Progress, and Prospects," *Security Studies*, Vol. 3, No. 4 (Summer 1994): 718–753; and Steven Mufson, "Measuring the Muscle in China's Military Future," *Washington Post Na-*

tional Weekly Edition, July 31–August 6, 1995, pp. 16–17.

63. Thomas L. Friedman, "Dust Off the SEATO Charter," *New York Times*, June 28, 1995, p. A19.

64. "Containing China," *The Economist* (July 29, 1995): 11 and 12.

65. Samuel P. Huntington, "America's Changing Strategic Interests," *Survival*, Vol. 33, No. 1 (January/February 1991): 10; and Samuel P. Huntington, "The Economic Renewal of America," *The National Interest*, No. 27 (Spring 1992): 15. Huntington here is, characteristically, quite explicit: "The one area of U.S. weakness is economics and the challenge in that area comes from Japan. In a world where economic power and economic issues are increasingly important, that challenge is a real one . . . the United States is obsessed with Japan for the same reasons that it was once obsessed with the Soviet Union. It sees that country as a major threat to its primacy in a crucial arena of power." "America's Changing Strategic Interests," p. 8. *See also* Samuel P. Huntington, "Why International Primacy Matters," *International Security*, Vol. 17, No. 4 (Spring 1993): 71–81.

66. Huntington, "America's Changing Strategic Interests," p. 9.

67. Huntington, "America's Changing Strategic Interests," p. 10.

68. Huntington, "America's Changing Strategic Interests," p. 11; and Huntington, "The Economic Renewal of America," p. 17.

69. One proponent of primacy, Zalmay Khalilzad, has written that China ". . . is the most likely candidate for global rival." Khalilzad, *From Containment to Global Leadership? America and the World After the Cold War* (Santa Monica, Calif.: RAND, 1995), p. 30.

70. On the ascendance of China, *see* Nicholas D. Kristof, "The Rise of China," *Foreign Affairs*, Vol. 72, No. 5 (November/December 1993): 59–74.

71. "Excerpts from Pentagon's Plan: 'Prevent the Emergence of a New Rival,'" *New York Times*, March 8, 1992, p. 14. For reportage *see* Patrick E. Tyler, "U.S. Strategy Plan Calls for Insuring No Rivals Develop," *New York Times*, March 8, 1992, pp. 1 and 14; and Barton Gellman, "The U.S. Aims to Remain First Among Equals," *Washington Post National Weekly Edition*, March 16–22, 1992, p. 19. For examples of contemporary commentary *see* Leslie Gelb, "They're Kidding," *New York Times*, March 9, 1992, p. A17; James Chace, "The Pentagon's Superpower Fantasy," *New York Times*, March 16, 1992; and Charles Krauthammer, "What's Wrong With the 'Pentagon Paper'?" *Washington Post*, March 13, 1992, p. A25. Relatively extensive quotations from the draft DPG appear here because we feared that we would not be believed if we put all of this in our own words.

72. "Excerpts from Pentagon's Plan: 'Prevent the Emergence of a New Rival,'" p. 14.

73. The Bush administration's support for the basic thrust if not the precise wording of the draft DPG is evident in Dick Cheney, "Active Leadership? You Better Believe It," *New York Times*, March 15, 1992, Section 4, p. 17. The draft DPG is placed in the larger contexts of the Bush administration's national security policy and strategy and a discussion of primacy in U.S. policy and strategy by David Callahan, *Between Two Worlds: Realism, Idealism, and American Foreign Policy After the Cold War* (New York: HarperCollins, 1994).

74. General Colin L. Powell, Chairman, Joint Chiefs of Staff, *National Military Strategy of the United States* (Washington, DC: U.S. Government Printing Office, January 1992), p. 19.

75. Callahan, *Between Two Worlds*, p. 135.

76. Les Aspin, *Report on the Bottom-Up Review*, October 1993. The Bottom-Up Review called for a force of 10 active and 5 reserve Army divisions, 11 active and 1 reserve/training carriers, 45–55 attack submarines, 346 ships, 13 active and 7 reserve Air Force fighter wings, and 3 active and 1 reserve Marine divisions.

77. For example, the Congressional Budget Office (CBO) estimates that the modernization of the entire Bottom-Up Review Force Structure with new technology

weapons currently in development or production would require between $7 and $31 billion more per year than the current budget plans for the year 1999, which is little different from the 1997 plan. *See* CBO, *An Analysis of the Administration's Future Years Defense Program for 1995–1999* (January 1995), p. 50.

78. Huntington, "Why International Primacy Matters," p. 70. Huntington more specifically argues that "Power enables an actor to shape his environment so as to reflect his interests. In particular it enables a state to protect its security and prevent, deflect, or defeat threats to that security. It also enables a state to promote its values among other peoples and to shape the international environment so as to reflect its values" (pp. 69–70).

79. *See* Christopher Layne and Benjamin Schwarz, "American Hegemony—Without an Enemy," *Foreign Policy*, No. 92 (Fall 1993): 5–23.

80. More extended critiques of primacy are provided by Callahan, *Between Two Worlds*; Robert Jervis, "International Primacy: Is the Game Worth the Candle?" *International Security*, Vol. 17, No. 4 (Spring 1993): 52–67; and Layne, "The Unipolar Illusion."

81. Perhaps the Committee on the Present Danger should be recast as the Committee on the Remote Danger!

Chapter 6

Earth in Abeyance: Explaining Weak Leadership in U.S. International Environmental Policy

Robert Paarlberg

When Bill Clinton and Al Gore were inaugurated in January 1993, the international environmental policy community expected an immediate invigoration of U.S. global leadership. Vice President Gore, just before joining the Clinton ticket, had written a best selling book entitled *Earth in the Balance*, which particularly stressed the importance of stronger U.S. environmental leadership in the areas of climate change and biodiversity. "[T]he rest of the world," Gore wrote, "quite naturally expects the United States to offer leadership." He proposed that the United States lead in mobilizing the expenditure of perhaps $100 billion—a modern day "Global Marshall Plan"—to protect future generations against global environmental calamities. To help launch such an international effort, U.S. leaders would begin convening annual environmental summit meetings, among the heads of state of both rich and poor countries.[1]

Gore's bold vision of U.S. global environmental leadership found its way into the official manifesto of the 1992 Clinton-Gore campaign. In their campaign book, *Putting People First*, Clinton and Gore wrote, "The world faces a crisis because of global climate change, ozone depletion, and unsustainable population growth. These developments threaten our fundamental interests—and we must fight them at a global level. America must lead the world, not follow."[2] Clinton and Gore went on to criticize the laggard posture that George Bush had assumed at the time of the 1992 United Nations "Earth Summit" conference in Rio de Janeiro. In Gore's words, "The Earth Summit was a suc-

Robert Paarlberg is a professor of political science at Wellesley College and an associate at the Harvard University Center for International Affairs. His recent publications in-clude Leadership Abroad Begins at Home: U.S. Foreign Economic Policy After the Cold War *(Brookings Institution, 1995), and* Countrysides at Risk: The Political Geography of Sustainable Agriculture *(Overseas Development Council, 1994).*

cess for the world as a whole, but it was a serious setback for our nation. At a crucial moment in history, when the rest of the world was requesting and eagerly expecting American leadership—not to mention vision—our nation found itself embarrassed and isolated at Rio."[3]

In Rio, Bush had stood virtually alone among most industrial country leaders by refusing to undertake firm international commitments in two key areas: climate change and biodiversity. He held back despite intense criticism from U.S. environmental activists and Democratic leaders in Congress, including then Senator Gore, and an extraordinary plea during the Summit from his own EPA Administrator, William K. Reilly, the nominal leader of the U.S. delegation in Rio. Bush had earlier promised to be "the environmental president," and had initially lived up to this promise by promoting a strong new 1990 Clean Air Act, but by 1992—partly in response to the onset of an economic recession—he was abandoning his environmental policy agenda, both at home and abroad, and yielding to the anti-regulatory preferences of his so-called Competitiveness Council, a cabinet-level agency headed by Vice President Dan Quayle. This Council weakened U.S. environmental policymaking during the final years of the Bush administration by giving private companies a direct political channel through which they could seek relief from regulations of all kinds.

The election of Bill Clinton and Al Gore, just five months after the Earth Summit, seemed to presage a return of environmental policy leadership and activism. One of President Clinton's first actions was to abolish the Bush-Quayle Competitiveness Council and replace it with a White House Office of Environmental Policy, to ensure that environmental activists would now have a direct political channel to the White House. Bruce Babbitt, a committed environmentalist, became Secretary of the Interior, and high level positions throughout the executive branch—including the Department of State—were given to former environmental activists from organizations such as the World Resources Institute, the Wilderness Society, the National Audubon Society, and the Sierra Club. Al Gore's former chief legislative aide in the Senate, Carol Browner, became administrator of the Environmental Protection Agency (EPA).

This strong executive branch environmental policy team set about quickly, especially in the areas of biodiversity and climate change, to make amends for Bush's Earth Summit performance. On Earth Day in April 1993, President Clinton confirmed his intent to sign the biodiversity convention and went on to accept quantitative targets for reducing U.S. greenhouse gas emissions, promising a detailed plan for meeting those targets by the end of the summer. This allowed Clinton's newly designated Under Secretary of State for Global Affairs, Timothy Wirth, to announce to the United Nations, in June 1993, that U.S. environmental policies had "sharply changed" since the Bush era. The U.S. would now "publicly resume the leadership that the world expects," said Wirth.[4]

This claim proved to be premature. Before 1993 had ended, U.S. environmental policy leadership had once more begun to falter. President Clinton did fulfill his pledge to sign the international treaty on biodiversity in June 1993, but he then failed to secure a timely Senate ratification of the treaty, which meant that in November 1994 the U.S. government had to participate formally in the first conference of Convention parties as an "observer." In the area of climate change policy, President Clinton also encountered difficulties. He formally committed the United States to reducing its greenhouse gas emissions to 1990 levels by the year 2000, but he failed to secure from Congress the broad based energy tax critical to meeting that goal, so by the time of the 1995 Berlin climate change conference, U.S. officials had to admit that the President's pledge would not be fulfilled. The Clinton administration was forced to rely on a climate change policy that was largely voluntary, one that would cost only $1.9 billion over six years—not much of a contribution to Gore's original vision of a $100 billion global Marshall Plan.[5]

Why did the Clinton administration, which came into office with such an ambitious international environmental policy vision, revert so quickly to the lagging performance of its predecessor? Here we shall argue that executive branch intentions in the area of environmental policy matter less than legislative branch preferences and support. Presidents cannot be environmental policy leaders abroad until they have first built an adequate policy consensus at home, especially within Congress, where the powers of the U.S. government to tax, spend, and regulate ultimately reside. This lesson takes on special force in the post–Cold War era, which has seen a power shift away from the executive branch of the federal government, both toward Congress and toward state and local government.

In this chapter, we first review in detail the frustrations encountered by the Clinton-Gore administration in biodiversity and climate change policy to learn what blocked more forceful action. We discover that U.S. environmental policy leadership was blocked in each case by a lack of political consensus at home, particularly within the U.S. Congress, rather than by a lack of willing followers abroad. This discovery should force both policy advocates and environmental policy analysts to reconsider some basic assumptions. Policy analysts, specifically, need to reconsider the priority they habitually assign to international cooperation problems abroad. Cooperation abroad is important, but it isn't always the most important starting point. For the United States at least, the task of international environmental policy leadership must now first be addressed at home.

The Collapse of the Clinton-Gore Vision: 1993–1995

The Clinton-Gore 1992 campaign stressed two areas in which the Bush-Quayle administration had failed to provide international environmental policy leadership: the protection of biodiversity and a response to human-induced climate change. Why did the Clinton-Gore administration, so quickly after it came into office in 1993, find its own leadership efforts faltering in these same two areas?

Biodiversity

The Convention on Biodiversity (officially, the United Nations Framework Convention on Biological Diversity) was written into final form just prior to the 1992 Earth Summit, following four years of international discussions and negotiations. The Convention has as its goal the conservation and sustainable use of the earth's biological diversity, particularly in the species-rich but currently threatened forest ecologies of the tropics. It is an agreement that assumes a continued commercial use of tropical country genestocks (mostly by private biotechnology and pharmaceutical companies headquartered in rich countries), but it calls for a fair international sharing of the resulting commercial gains. Signatories to the Convention are obliged to develop national plans for protecting habitat and species, either on site, or "ex-situ" in gene banks, zoos, and botanic gardens. If they are rich countries they must provide funds and technology to help developing countries in this effort; they must pursue biotechnology development safely; and they must agree to share fairly, with source countries, the revenues of such development. If they are "source" countries, they must ensure commercial access to their biological resources.

The drafting of this Convention was heavily promoted by tropical countries within the United Nations Environmental Programme (UNEP), partly with pure biodiversity concerns in mind, and partly as a means to secure financial advantages and technological assistance from industrial countries. The required financial transfers to developing countries that were specified by the Convention (initially set at $200 million), together with the risk of diminished patent protection associated with technology sharing, bothered a number of rich countries other than the United States, including Japan, England, and France. Yet most judged this a price worth paying to facilitate north-south cooperation at Rio, and to gain from developing countries some new guarantees of commercial access plus assurances of improved species and habitat protection. A total of 153 nations, rich and poor, officially accepted the Convention at the Rio Earth Summit. Only the United States, at the direction of President Bush, formally refused to sign.[6]

President Clinton had come into office promising to reverse this policy; accordingly, his United Nations Ambassador signed the Convention on June 4, 1993, and five months later he submitted it to the U.S. Senate for ratification. Why was a prompt ratification not forthcoming?

Clinton thought he had prepared the way for a successful two-thirds ratification vote by gaining formal endorsement for the Convention from the same U.S. biotechnology and pharmaceutical firms that had earlier been in opposition. In the spring of 1993 he had gained this endorsement by negotiating, with representatives of these firms, a side agreement in which he promised to add some unilateral "interpretations" to the Convention during the ratification process to ensure that it would not in practice jeopardize essential patent protections or compromise opportunities for the industry to pursue research and innovation. Clinton unilaterally incorporated language to this effect into the formal Letter of Submittal sent by the State Department to the Senate in November 1993.[7] Activists in the U.S. environmental community conspicuously criticized this side agreement with industry as a compromise, one that could undercut the implementation of the Convention, yet Clinton knew the importance of securing private industry cooperation. No international agreement on biodiversity could hope to be effective, even if ratified, without support from U.S. international biotechnology and pharmaceutical firms.[8]

By the time the Convention was submitted for ratification, it was thus strongly endorsed by the executive branch and officially supported by a broadly based coalition of U.S. biotechnology and pharmaceutical companies, agricultural associations, environmental and developmental nongovernment organizations (NGOs), scientific groups, and academic associations.[9] Initially, the Senate Foreign Relations Committee also strongly recommended ratification. Yet a floor vote on ratification was never quite taken during the 1993–1994 (103rd) Congress, because a significant minority of Republican Senators (35 in all, one more than needed to defeat a treaty in the Senate) had decided—for a mix of principled and partisan reasons—to oppose the Convention.

This opposing minority group, which included Jesse Helms (R-N.C.), who was then the ranking Republican member of the Foreign Relations Committee, and Bob Dole (R-Kan.), who was then the Minority Leader, objected to the modest foreign assistance obligations required by the Convention, warned against any treaty that might undercut U.S. sovereignty by enlarging the authority of international institutions designed within the United Nations, and dismissed Clinton's unilateral "interpretations" as not binding on the Convention's other signatories. The purely Republican cast to this minority coalition indicated that one of its goals was also simply to embarrass the president.

Clinton's Majority Leader, Senator George Mitchell (D-Me.), originally intended to achieve ratification by the end of the 1993–1994 congressional session, but when it became clear the votes were not there, Senate action was deferred.[10] This meant that in November 1994 Undersecretary Wirth had to attend the first international meeting of all parties to the Convention in Nassau, as only an observer. By that time, all of the other major industrial countries (and 92 countries in all) had ratified the signed Convention; only the United States had not. Wirth asserted in Nassau that President Clinton would resubmit the Convention to the newly elected (and Republican-controlled) 104th Congress, but he conceded that the new Senate Foreign Relations Committee—now chaired by Senator Helms—would be an even more difficult group to work with (Wirth characterized Helms as "not a great fan of treaties").[11]

This Senate blockage of ratification did not prevent the U.S. executive branch from participating in some international biological diversity initiatives under the framework of the Convention.[12] In December 1994, for example, Wirth helped to launch a new International Coral Reef Initiative—together with six other nations—to protect the biodiverse ecosystems of coral reefs, mangrove forests, and sea grass beds.[13] Still, key developing countries were unhappy with the U.S. posture. In April 1995 (by which time 120 nations had ratified the Convention, but the United States still had not), the government of India, speaking also for Brazil, Indonesia, and Malaysia, warned that U.S. access to medicinal plants and other biological material from these source countries might be blocked if the United States did not ratify the Convention soon. Under Secretary Wirth replied with a weak lesson in U.S. constitutional realities: "The President proposes, but Congress disposes."[14]

Climate Change

The Clinton administration's performance also fell well short of its original promises in the area of climate change policy. During the 1992 campaign, Clinton and Gore harshly criticized President Bush for failing to embrace the quantified climate change policy objective proposed by the European Community at the Rio Earth Summit: a limiting of carbon-dioxide emissions to 1990 levels by the year 2000. Clinton and Gore had promised, during the 1992 campaign, to strengthen the UN Framework Convention on Climate Change that came out of Rio by embracing such an emissions limitation goal as U.S. national policy, and Clinton formally did so in April 1993.[15] He was momentarily hailed as having restored the United States to a position of international leadership on climate change policy.[16] Almost immediately, however, he failed to secure from Congress the broadly based tax on energy that he knew might be needed to meet his new emissions limitation commitment, and was forced to fall back upon a weak set of mostly voluntary measures. These measures quickly fell short, and U.S. negotiators consequently had to attend the 1995 Berlin climate change conference acknowledging that the president's new greenhouse gas limitation pledge would not be fulfilled.

The quantified emissions limitation objective Clinton had embraced was actually quite a modest one. His 1990 U.S. emissions level goal (1.46 billion carbon-equivalent tons) was only about 7 percent below the emissions level (1.57 billion tons) that would have been expected for the year 2000 without new emissions restraints.[17] Technically, this modest degree of limitation would have been easy to achieve by 2000 (Clinton carefully stopped short of promising stabilization after 2000), at little or no cost to the U.S. economy. Energy waste in the U.S. economy is so high that greenhouse gas emissions can be limited substantially in the short run simply by taking steps such as switching to energy-conscious building codes, or discouraging employer-subsidized automobile parking, which would make economic sense anyway. In terms of greenhouse gas emissions per capita, and also in terms of emissions per unit of GNP, the United States is currently the worst performer among all of the leading industrial powers.[18] Consequently, the United States has a great deal of room to cut emissions at little or no overall economic cost, an advantage which should have made Clinton's modest limitation goal for the year 2000 relatively easy to attain.

Clinton's goal was certainly a modest one relative to the larger problem of human-induced global climate change. If attained by the United States in the year 2000, it would reduce the world's total industrial carbon emissions by just 1.4 percent.[19] Committed environmentalists found this goal far too modest, because it did not promise any continued stabilization of U.S. emissions after 2000, because it said nothing about eventually reducing emissions below 1990 levels, and because it did not address the looming issue of increased emissions from large and coal-dependent industrializing nations in Asia, especially China and India.

The parameters of the climate change challenge are sobering in this regard. If the purpose is to halt a buildup of human-induced greenhouse gases in the earth's atmosphere, and thus guarantee against a human-induced global warming, even a permanent and worldwide stabilization of emissions at 1990 levels would not be adequate. After all, the annual emissions levels of 1990 were high enough to create the problem in the first place. The practical difference (for human-induced global warming) between an emissions stabilization scenario and a no-controls strategy would be trivial at least in the short term, less than three-tenths of one degree Celsius.[20]

To halt human-induced warming a sharp and costly reduction of greenhouse gas emissions would be required, perhaps to a level 75 percent below 1990 levels, and Yale University economist William Nordhaus has estimated that the investments required to halt human-induced warming in this fashion might cost as much as $30 trillion (if estimated in terms of discounted income lost over the period 1985–2105).[21]

Because the link between measured greenhouse gas accumulations and measured global warming has so far been hard for science to establish (human-induced warming is hard to disentangle from the earth's natural warming and cooling trends), and because the localized effects of warming on actual climate change or on sea level rise are even more difficult to project with confidence, governments have naturally shied away from these huge economic costs of trying to halt human-induced global warming entirely.[22] The boldest emissions reduction goal recently under actual political discussion has been a mere 20 percent carbon dioxide emissions reduction goal (from global 1990 levels by the year 2005), promoted since 1994 by an Alliance of Small Island States (AOSIS), the countries most worried about sea-level rise. This AOSIS goal is in keeping with a 20 percent reduction goal provisionally endorsed by technicians at a Toronto climate change conference in 1988, yet in 1995 it was rejected by most participants in the first UN Framework Convention on Climate Change (FCCC) Conference in Berlin, where the setting of any concrete reduction goals was deferred for at least two years.[23]

The position taken by the United States at the 1995 Berlin climate change conference was telling. The United States not only favored deferring all concrete post–2000 reduction goals; it even favored deferring pledges of post–2000 stabilization.[24] Clinton was forced to take this weak post–2000 posture at the Berlin conference because of difficulties he had already encountered in fulfilling his modest pre–2000 greenhouse gas limitation pledge.

Clinton's climate change difficulties—his retreat from international leadership—stemmed principally from his failure in 1993 to secure congressional support for a broad based energy tax, which he had requested as one part of his first year deficit reduction plan. This energy tax proposal was presented primarily as a deficit reduction measure, and only secondarily as a climate change policy. During the congressional debate, in fact, Clinton and Gore were practically silent on the advantages the tax might provide in reducing U.S. greenhouse gas emissions.

One reason for this odd silence was the peculiar form of the tax. It was proposed as a tax on all energy production—including nuclear power, hydro power, and even windmills—whether greenhouse gases such as carbon dioxide were being produced or not. Committed environmentalists had hoped for a more narrow "carbon" tax on the burning of fossil fuels, especially coal and petroleum. A modest $6 per ton carbon tax would have been enough to stabilize U.S. carbon dioxide emissions at 1990 levels by the year 2000.[25] Al Gore, as a U.S. Senator, had been an advocate of the carbon tax approach,[26] but Clinton decided that a pure carbon tax would never be enacted by Congress, because it would hit coal producing and coal using states, especially in the Midwest, too hard.[27] He thus decided to propose his more broadly based tax on all energy sources (a so-called BTU tax), while adding some environmental content at the margin by placing surcharges on energy generated from fossil fuel sources such as coal and petroleum.

It did not take Congress long to reject this compromise. Clinton's broad based energy tax proposal offended the middle class (which had been promised a tax cut, not a tax increase, by Clinton in the 1992 campaign) without fully mollifying fossil fuels industries. Coal state and coal industry representatives—led by Senator Robert C. Byrd (D-W.

Va.)—argued that the coal industry was already being burdened by the terms of the 1990 Clean Air Act, and should be excused from the surcharge.[28] When Clinton gave in to the coal industry but left the proposed surcharge in place for petroleum, he angered oil producing and home heating oil using state representatives.[29] Debate over the proposal degenerated into a divisive contest over which industries would get exemptions and which would not. In the end, Clinton had to agree to withdraw the broad based energy tax proposal altogether, and replace it with a far more modest (and environmentally insignificant) 4.3 cent per gallon increase in the 14.1 cent per gallon federal tax on gasoline.

Clinton's failed effort to secure a broadly based energy tax in 1993, despite Democratic control of both houses of Congress, undercut the power reputation of administration environmentalists such as Gore, and reduced the President's subsequent inclination to consider strong actions on climate change. When he finally produced his official composite climate change policy in October 1993, it included no revived energy tax proposal, no new international negotiations initiatives, and not even a tightening of Corporate Average Fuel Efficiency (CAFE) standards for automobiles, despite Clinton's 1992 campaign pledge to seek such a tightening. The thrust of Clinton's Climate Change Action Plan (CCAP) was almost purely voluntary. The CCAP consisted largely of two new government-industry partnership schemes, to be known as Climate Challenge and Climate Wise Companies (run by the Department of Energy and EPA). These were voluntary programs designed to entice utilities and other U.S. companies into negotiating domestic emissions reduction agreements with the government in return for a mix of technical assistance and public recognition, at a total cost to taxpayers of $1.9 billion over six years.[30] The administration tried to claim that this approach alone would be enough to limit U.S. greenhouse gas emissions to 1990 levels by the year 2000.

Environmental groups were immediately suspicious of the voluntary approach, and of the administration's optimistic projections. In April 1994, the Natural Resources Defense Council charged that the Clinton plan would achieve only about one-third of the emissions reductions it promised, and within a year even the administration was backing away from its original projections, as emissions remained high partly because of unexpectedly strong U.S. economic growth rates and unexpectedly low energy prices. In the spring of 1995, on the eve of the Berlin climate change conference, Under Secretary Wirth, who headed the U.S. delegation to the conference, admitted that the United States would probably miss its own stabilization goal by a wide margin.[31]

The United States was not the only industrial country that went to the 1995 Berlin conference reporting a lagging performance on emissions stabilization. Among the major European Union (EU) countries, only Germany and Britain were safely on track toward meeting their stabilization targets.[32] Still, the Clinton administration's inability to set in place a credible climate change policy at home badly undercut its reputation and capacity for environmental policy leadership abroad. It was Germany, not the United States, that took the lead prior to the Berlin conference in proposing language for a new international protocol that would go beyond mere stabilization to seek ambitious carbon dioxide emissions reductions after the year 2000. To back up this international proposal, Germany even made a unilateral commitment to reduce its own emissions 25 percent by 2005, from 1990 levels.[33] The United States joined other heavy emitters (such as Japan) and oil exporting countries (such as Saudi Arabia) in opposing this more ambitious approach.[34]

By 1995, having earlier criticized the Bush administration for foot-dragging on climate change policy, the Clinton-Gore administration thus found itself stuck in a remarkably similar international role.

Explaining the Collapse of the Clinton-Gore Vision

Why was the bold international leadership vision of the Clinton-Gore administration reduced so quickly, down toward the more timid standard set earlier by Bush-Quayle? In the biodiversity and climate change cases there is a clear answer: it is Congress, not the executive branch or the president, that has final say over U.S. environmental policy, both at home and abroad. The environmental policy preferences of the executive branch might have been moving toward greater boldness when the Clinton-Gore team arrived on the scene in 1993, but the preferences of Congress were already by then moving toward greater timidity, and tactical efforts to appease congressional preferences through compromise were insufficient to secure administration goals.

While the tone of U.S. environmental policy can at times be set by the executive branch, the content still tends to be set by Congress, which has final say over the raising and spending of money, and also over the regulation of U.S. private industry. President Ronald Reagan's executive branch discovered this truth during the early 1980s, when his efforts to dismantle regulations (through the appointment of anti-environmental officials such as Interior Secretary James G. Watt and EPA Administrator Anne Gorsuch Burford) met frustration at the hands of a Democratic House of Representatives that was still strongly pro-environment. Congressional objections blocked many of Reagan's deregulatory efforts, and in the end it was his executive branch that had to retreat—but not before his assistant EPA administrator, Rita Lavelle, was sentenced to six months in prison for lying to Congress, and more than 20 of his political appointees within EPA had resigned in disgrace.[35]

It was largely because of congressional sentiments that the regulatory strictness of U.S. environmental policy tightened during the Bush administration (the efforts of Vice President Quayle's Competitiveness Council to weaken regulations notwithstanding). During the

1989–1992 Bush administration the 1990 Clean Air Act was enacted, the Superfund cleanup was accelerated, an international agreement was reached to move toward a complete phase out of chlorofluorocarbons (CFCs), ocean disposal of sludge was ended, bans on driftnet fishing were imposed, offshore oil exploration was halted, new drinking water standards were set, international agreements on hazardous waste export were negotiated, and hundreds of old landfills were closed.[36] The key to this strong environmental record, during the Bush years, was strong pressure from a Democratic Congress (including a Democratic Senate once again, after the 1986 midterm election). Where Bush was willing to work with this Democratic Congress to tighten environmental regulations (as in the case of the 1990 Clean Air Act) he met striking success.[37] He was defeated whenever he tried to defy the Democratic Congress (as when he attempted not to enforce a congressional ban on the import of tuna from Mexico, which were caught with purse seine nets that endangered porpoises). He was defeated by Congress in this case even though the congressional law in question, the Marine Mammal Protection Act, had been found by an international panel in 1991 to be in violation of existing international trade rules under the General Agreement on Tariffs and Trade (GATT).[38]

The strong push that Congress gave to U.S. environmental policy during most of the Bush administration reflected, in part, unprecedented concern for environmental issues among voters and campaign contributors following a series of spectacular and well publicized calamities: in 1984, the lethal industrial accident at Bhopal; in 1985, the discovery of the Antarctic ozone hole; in 1986, the nuclear plant disaster at Chernobyl; in 1988, the U.S. summer heat wave and global warming fears; and finally in 1989, the *Exxon Valdez* oil spill. Growing U.S. popular concern for environmental issues came to be reflected in the growing membership lists and financial assets of prominent national environmental advocacy and action organizations, such as the Natural Resources Defense Council, the National Audubon Society, the Sierra Club, the Wilderness Society, and the Nature Conservancy. The enlarged power assets of these groups were, for a time, brought to bear on Congress with significant effect.

When did U.S. popular concern for environmental issues peak? Measured in terms of media attention, concern peaked in 1989, the year of the *Exxon Valdez* oil spill. By 1990, the year of the Clean Air Act, total network news minutes devoted to environmental coverage in the United States had begun to decline, so much so that by 1993, the first year of the Clinton presidency, network news coverage of environmental issues was 60 percent below its 1989 peak.[39] As media attention declined, support for activist environmental organizations did also. Dues-paying membership in the five activist environmental groups mentioned above peaked in 1990, at 2.4 million, and thereafter began a decline down to 2.1 million members by 1995. The financial income of

U.S. environmental groups reached its highest point as well in 1990, and the groups subsequently hit hardest by falling popular support were precisely those that had been calling for the most aggressive policy actions. Greenpeace, for example, lost nearly a million members in just three years.[40]

One purely temporary event helps explain this fall off in public support for U.S. environmental activism: the painful 1990–1992 economic recession, which heightened a popular fear that tight environmental regulations in the U.S. economy might be responsible for job loss.[41] President Bush (following the advice of his Office of Management and Budget director, Richard Darman) made a clumsy attempt to exploit this shift in popular mood during his last year in office, by going to the 1992 Rio Earth Summit conference in the defiant posture of an anti-regulator.[42] When Gore and Clinton criticized this Bush posture during the 1992 presidential campaign, and then (just barely) won the election, environmentalists concluded—somewhat erroneously—that a new mandate to push their agenda had been conferred.

Clinton and Gore took over the executive branch in 1993 preaching environmental activism, but by then the U.S. Congress—although still under Democratic control—was beginning to listen to the country's more cautious mood. When Interior Secretary Babbitt proposed higher grazing fees early in 1993, to help prevent abuse of federal lands, a coalition of western Senators—Democrats as well as Republicans—forced him to withdraw the plan within three months. Clinton's proposal for a broadly based energy tax failed shortly thereafter, forcing his administration (as noted above) into its weak and mostly voluntary posture on climate change.

To make things worse, the environmental community weakened itself in Congress in 1993 by failing to take a unified position on ratification of the North American Free Trade Agreement (NAFTA). Most of the large New York and Washington-based environmental groups that were accustomed to working within the political system (the Environmental Defense Fund, National Audubon Society, National Wildlife Federation, Natural Resources Defense Council, and World Wildlife Fund) did not object to free trade in principle, and were willing to support NAFTA, providing some specific environmental policy conditions were attached. They negotiated successfully for most of what they wanted, including a specific provision against downward harmonization of environmental standards, plus creation of a North American Commission for Environmental Cooperation that would be empowered to monitor and pressure for enforcement of environmental laws on both sides of the border.[43] This "work from the inside" approach was rejected, however, by a number of powerful U.S. environmental groups—such as Friends of the Earth, Greenpeace, and the Sierra Club—that mistrusted free trade, and that joined with organized labor to oppose NAFTA ratification. NAFTA was eventually approved by

Congress in 1993, but not before these divisions within the environmental community over trade issues had undercut the strength of the movement in other policy areas.

Then in 1994, the mood in Congress turned decisively against governmental regulations of all kinds, not only dooming Clinton's (highly bureaucratic) health care reform proposal, but also spelling trouble for environmental regulations. In February 1994, Congress defeated a long-standing plan to elevate the EPA to cabinet rank, stipulating that EPA first had to demonstrate, with cost-benefit analysis, that its regulations were worth the social price.[44] The *New York Times* editorial page concluded, following this defeat, that "The era of automatic congressional acceptance of laws that promise cleaner air or cleaner anything is pretty much over."[45] The 1994 failure on the part of the Senate to ratify the biodiversity convention was thus not an isolated event. In all, ten out of eleven environmental bills failed to pass the U.S. Congress in 1994.[46] Even the indirect tactic used successfully by moderate environmentalists during the NAFTA debate—the tactic of linking environmental conditions to trade agreements—became harder to use in 1994, when Congress refused to extend the president's authority to seek approval of trade agreements with strict environmental conditions on a "fast track."

The ambitious environmental policy agenda of the Clinton-Gore executive branch was thus blocked in 1993–1994 by a switch in popular and congressional preferences to a deregulatory and anti-governmental direction. Ominously for environmental activists, this blockage came at a time when the U.S. economy was in a strong recovery mode, and when both houses of Congress were still under Democratic control.

Any remaining congressional inclination to follow Clinton's environmental policy lead was ended following the stunning Republican victory in the November 1994 midterm election. Republican hostility to environmental regulation, which had long been held in check as a minority party view in Congress (especially in the House), suddenly became the majority party view. One way to measure the magnitude of this change is to examine the numerical ratings on environmental and regulatory policy preferences that have been given, by interested advocacy groups, to senior Democratic and Republican members of the 103rd Congress (1993–1994). Table 6.1 provides a comparison of ratings given by two groups: the League of Conservation Voters (LCV) and the Competitive Enterprise Institute (CEI). LCV ratings reflect support for environmental policy, on a scale from 0–100, and senior Democrats in the 103rd Congress (committee chairs), in both the House and Senate, were given average LCV ratings three times as high as senior Republicans (ranking minority members). CEI ratings reflect support for fewer governmental regulations on industry, and here senior Republicans were given average ratings, in both the House and Senate, four times higher than senior Democrats.

Table 6-1

Average Environmental and De-regulatory Ratings for Senior Members, 103rd Congress (1993–1994)

	House		Senate	
	Senior Democrats (N=24)	Senior Republicans (N=23)	Senior Democrats (N=20)	Senior Republicans (N=20)
Average LCV Rating (0–100)	73.3	21.6	72.1	23.8
Average CEI Rating (0–100)	13.2	74.6	16.6	76.1

Source: League of Conservation Voters (LCV) and Competitive Enterprise Institute (CEI) ratings of members of 103rd Congress.

Most of these senior members simply changed places (committee chairs became ranking minority members, and vice versa) following the Republican victory in November 1994, meaning that dozens of pro-environmental Democrats were suddenly replaced as Congressional leaders and committee chairs by anti-regulation Republicans.

The Republican capture of Congress in 1995 did more than simply constrain new environmental policy leadership options. It raised the prospect of a U.S. retreat from some existing environmental commitments and obligations, and left the Clinton administration fighting hard simply to hold on to existing gains. In February 1995, in partial fulfillment of their "Contract With America," the new House Republican majority (joined by 60 Democrats) gave strong approval to a measure that would compensate land owners when regulations reduced their property values; impose elaborate scientific review of health, safety, and environmental protection rules; and require complicated cost/benefit and risk assessments for all new environmental regulations, even those proposed under existing laws such as the Clean Air Act and Clean Water Act. EPA Administrator Browner called this legislation "a full frontal assault on protecting public health and the environment," and it required a Democratic filibuster to block its passage in the Senate.[47] In September, however, the House and Senate both agreed on a new spending bill for the Department of Interior that placed a moratorium on the listing of new species for protection under the Endangered Species Act, restored the right of mining companies to gain access to mineral deposits on federal lands for a fraction of the real worth of those deposits, cut the National Park Service role in managing a vast section of the Mojave Desert, opened national forests to increased logging, cut the budget of the National Biological Service, and limited options for new grazing regulations. And the House, in drafting its spending bill for the EPA, voted to cut the EPA program budget by nearly one-third, to just $4.9 billion. Republicans in Congress also sought to reduce, by 40 percent, the funds being spent by the Clinton administration to promote voluntary (and thus far inadequate) greenhouse gas emissions reductions.[48] Even as the U.N. Intergovernmental Panel on Climate Change was issuing a new draft report in 1995 (its first in five years), which strengthened the scientific consensus that at least some of the earth's recent warming had been human-induced, Republicans in Congress rejected the need for any action. Representative Dana Rohrabacher (R-Calif.), the new head of an energy and environment subcommittee in the House, derided the climate change hypothesis as "unproven at best and liberal claptrap at worst," and as "soon to go out of style in our Newt Congress."[49]

The original Clinton-Gore vision of U.S. environmental policy leadership abroad thus failed due to a loss of political support at home—and especially in Congress—for any kind of aggressive environmental policy action. Without a consensus in Congress to support environmental activism at home, it was impossible to offer effective environmental policy leadership abroad. Both at home and abroad it was Congress, not the president or the executive branch, that determined the final content of U.S. federal environmental policy by writing (or unwriting) environmental legislation, by appropriating (or failing to appropriate) tax dollars for environmental purposes, and by ratifying (or failing to ratify) international environmental agreements. President Clinton and his executive branch may have come into office intending to restore U.S. environmental policy leadership, but an opposing preference among many leaders at home, a preference to spend less time and less money on all kinds of environmental activism, put increasingly severe limits on what Clinton could actually achieve.

Lessons for International Relations Theory

The cases reviewed here carry lessons for the study and conduct of U.S. foreign policy, but they also challenge some of the larger assumptions built into contemporary international relations theory. Most international relations scholars have depicted global environmental policymaking as an "international cooperation" problem.[50] The greatest barriers to successful policymaking are presumed to be differences between governments abroad, not differences within governments at home.[51] The analysis presented above calls this approach into question.

International relations theorists understand that some governments will be more eager than others to make international environmental commitments, or more eager at some times than at others, but they like to attribute differences in eagerness more to system-level differences (in *relative* vulnerability to the threat, or in anticipated *relative* share of the collective abatement cost) than to absolute interests or to political dynamics or institutions within states, at the unit level.[52] They assume that willingness to act will depend heavily upon a difficult strategic interaction among states at the system level, designed to allocate relative gains and losses. In this system-level cooperation game, the laggards will constantly try to take a "free ride" on the unilateral commitments of the leaders, thereby making the leadership that is needed to secure cooperation more difficult to secure.[53]

According to one dominant variant of this system-level approach, a faltering of one state's leadership (e.g., a faltering of U.S. leadership) is likely to reflect a loss of that state's "hegemony" within the international system, rather than some intra-national dynamic or peculiarity (such as an internal business cycle downturn, or a change of party control in Congress). The best substitute for U.S. leadership after hegemony, according to this approach, will be a spread of international institutions or "regimes," capable of facilitating cooperation among states even in the absence of a dominant leading power.[54] A slightly different school of thought holds that environmental policy cooperation problems among states can also be solved if political leaders are able to defer to well-established transnational networks of knowledge-based experts, known as "epistemic communities."[55]

These various "international cooperation" approaches do not provide a satisfying diagnosis for the recent weakness we have documented here in U.S. environmental policy leadership abroad. When a minority of the U.S. Senate blocked ratification of the International Biodiversity Convention, it was not because of uncertainty over international cooperation. The danger that other states would fail to follow the U.S. lead (or take a "free ride" on that lead) was not in play here, since 120 other states had already signed and ratified the convention. And the solution to this decline in U.S. leadership, caused by Senate blockage, was not to create stronger international institutions. Jesse Helms, the leading Senate critic of the Convention, objected partly because of his view that the international institutions that had helped create the treaty (such as UNEP) were already too strong. Nor can we blame, in this case, an absence of technical consensus within the "epistemic community" that studies international species protection. There was enough technical consensus behind the convention to secure prompt ratification from 120 independent governments around the world, and eventually to gain broad based support within the United States (once Clinton's unilateral understandings had been attached) from the private industries that were most directly affected, as well as from scholars and environmentalists. International cooperation was being paralyzed in this case by minority partisanship within the U.S. Congress, made influential through a unique, 200-year-old feature of the U.S. political system, the constitutional requirement that international treaties be ratified by a (hard to attain) two-thirds vote in the Senate.[56]

Standard international cooperation approaches also fail to provide a strong diagnosis for U.S. leadership failure in the area of climate change policy. It was not a fear of "free riding" by other industrial nations abroad that blocked congressional support for Clinton's broad-based energy tax proposal in 1993. The EU by then had officially gone farther than the United States in the direction of energy taxes; it had proposed a carbon tax geared toward greenhouse gas emissions control at the Rio Earth Summit in 1992. It was partly because of inaction in the United States that the EU subsequently downgraded this proposal to an energy tax with some exemptions for energy-intensive industries and major exporters, conditional on comparable actions by major competitors such as the United States.[57] In the end, the EU as a whole did not go beyond specifying community-wide parameters for "voluntary" carbon taxes, but as of 1996 five individual member states—Finland, Sweden, Denmark, Norway and the Netherlands—nonetheless had such taxes in place.[58] Considering gasoline taxes specifically, it is the United States that has been taking the free policy ride. Combined state and federal gasoline taxes in the United States have averaged only about one-eighth as high, per gallon, as gasoline taxes in the rest of the industrial world.[59]

Stronger international institutions also seem an unlikely remedy for the failure of the United States and other industrial countries to embrace more committed climate change policies. It may be true that nonindustrial countries are waiting for stronger international institutions. Countries such as India, China, and Brazil have been demanding stronger international institutional guarantees of financial and technical assistance, as their condition for accepting any restriction on energy-intensive development activities, and pending such guarantees they may insist that the climate change policy burden be left with the already wealthy nations of the industrial world. Such inadequacies in global governance institutions did not, however, play a major role in the U.S. congressional decision to reject broad-based energy taxes in 1993.

Nor can we blame this U.S. rejection of a stronger climate change policy on lack of a transnational scientific or technical consensus, regarding the greenhouse gas threat. The current scientific and technical consensus on climate change is not strong enough to support short term actions that would impose steep costs on industrial societies (e.g., carbon taxes large enough to reduce greenhouse gas emissions quickly, by 20 percent or more from current levels). Yet the current technical consensus certainly is strong enough to support a low-cost "no regrets" greenhouse gas policy, one based on energy conservation measures that would be of benefit to society even if there were no greenhouse gas threat. A modest carbon or energy tax, of the kind that would ensure meeting the Rio goal of limiting emissions in the year 2000 to 1990 levels, would clearly qualify as a "no regrets" policy for the United States.[60] It was not so much a rejection of the current international technical consensus on climate change that prevented Congress from enacting Clinton's energy tax in 1993; it was, instead, a more fundamental and more visceral opposition in the U.S. Congress to any new taxes on the middle class (an opposition for which the president deserves some blame, given the tone of his 1992 election campaign).

The biodiversity and climate change cases examined here show that a lack of policy consensus within governments can be as serious an impediment to international cooperation as divergent preferences and strategic interactions among governments. The U.S. government is particularly susceptible to having divergent internal environmental policy preferences, because power is shared across three separate branches (executive, legislative, and judicial) at the federal level, and below that level enormous power remains in the hands of autonomous state and local authorities. Only after executive branch leaders in Washington have developed a sufficiently unified and supportive domestic policy consensus—across all these branches and levels of government at home—will they be well positioned to offer effective environmental policy leadership abroad.[61]

United States executive branch policymakers, eager to provide leadership abroad, have looked for ways to escape this fundamental domestic constraint. They have considered using preemptive international agreements to finesse their domestic opposition. This is an approach seemingly endorsed by a more sophisticated set of international relations scholars, those who (following the work of Robert D. Putnam) describe the international cooperation problem as a "two level game." These scholars accept the fact that governments are frequently divided at home, and they concede that international agreements cannot be pursued successfully abroad unless they can be successfully ratified at home.[62] Yet these scholars tend to view the domestic ratification hurdle as one that can be more easily cleared *after* the right kind of preemptive international agreement has been struck. If executive branch negotiators are cunning enough to strike agreements that promise gains for just the right domestic constituencies, those groups at home opposed to policy change will find themselves isolated and weakened. Outward-looking executive branch leaders might in this fashion escape their domestic constraints, creating political space for policy change at home by first entering into agreements abroad.[63]

This approach must be endorsed with great caution. Starting with an international negotiation can just as easily make the subsequent process of domestic policy change more difficult. Opponents of change at home will then be able to slur the new negotiated initiative as a "concession to foreigners," or they will be able to raise the difficult issue of international burden sharing and perhaps argue that "foreigners are not doing their share." It is politically unhealthy for the government of one nation to start debating the "fair share" of another nation, since an important political value—accountability—will be lost. Opportunistic politicians, always tempted to mask their own failings by shifting blame onto foreigners (since foreigners do not vote in their district), will find more room to be opportunistic once a domestic policy debate becomes explicitly internationalized.

Options for executive branch leaders to escape domestic constraints by entering into preemptive negotiations or agreements abroad will vary issue by issue. In the area of U.S. foreign trade policy, protectionist demands at home can at times be deflected and weakened through the preemptive negotiation of agreements abroad, particularly when Congress grants in advance that such agreements will be ratified on a special "fast track" (as a package, in a single deadline-driven vote, with no committee or floor amendments allowed). In the area of environmental policy, however, where no equivalent of fast track authority has ever been granted by Congress, where treaty ratification requirements in the Senate are difficult to satisfy, where separate state and local governments frequently have primary jurisdiction, and where displeased property owners or industries can easily paralyze policy at any time with real or threatened lawsuits, the domestic ratification of strong international agreements (those that go beyond the terms of existing domestic legislation) will be much harder for U.S. executive branch leaders to finesse after the fact. The unratified state of the Biodiversity Convention is a case in point.

The United States has enjoyed great success at times as an international environmental policy leader, but not always through the "cooperation theory" or "two level game" tactic of sending executive branch officials abroad to negotiate a preemptive international agreement. The United States has enjoyed greater success when it has been able to start the process within the domestic policy arena, first tightening policy unilaterally at home, and only then seeking to extend tighter policy standards abroad.

The U.S. leadership that helped in creating the 1987 Montreal Protocol, an international agreement to protect stratospheric ozone from the threat of human-induced chlorofluorocarbon emissions, is a case in point. The United States originally helped pave the way for CFC disciplines by acting unilaterally at home. In 1977, pressures from domestic environmental groups forced Congress to amend the Clean Air Act to place a ban on CFCs in aerosol sprays. The benefits of this unilateral domestic policy step were considerable. In addition to reduced CFC production (U.S. production fell by half, which at the time implied a 25 percent fall in world production), private U.S. companies such as DuPont began to invest in the development of ozone-safe CFC substitutes. By March 1986, DuPont was able to announce that substitutes for CFCs could be available within five years, if market conditions and policies warranted the development effort, and in September 1986 a coalition of U.S. industries issued a policy statement supporting international regulation of CFCs.[64] This energized international negotiations and helped lead to the Montreal Protocol, an agreement that generalized to the rest of the world (and especially to Europe) the regulatory policy which U.S. industry had already said it was willing to accept. In the United States at least, this was not really a case of using an international agreement to preempt domestic political or industry opposition in "two-level game" fashion; by 1986, significant domestic U.S. opposition to the agreement had already been overcome.

Richard Benedick, the principal U.S. negotiator of the Montreal Protocol, subsequently concluded that "it may be desirable for a leading country or group of countries to take preemptive environmental protection measures in advance of a global agreement." Benedick endorsed this approach because he had seen that unilateral actions could serve as examples that help to legitimate change elsewhere, stimulate research into technical solutions, slow adverse trends (thus buying time for the development of technical solutions, or for the conduct of multilateral negotiations), and make moral suasion by leading countries more credible.[65]

Unilateral domestic policy steps can have powerful and valuable international policy consequences even when not followed up by an international agreement. After environmental impact assessments were introduced unilaterally into U.S. domestic law in 1969, U.S. officials tried repeatedly to spread this innovation abroad by negotiating a formal treaty. The United States had no success promoting a formal treaty, but the example of U.S. policy was strong enough by itself to convince some 30 other countries by 1990 to adopt similar legislation without any treaty obligation.[66]

Conclusion: Environmental Policy Leadership Begins at Home

There is no escaping the need for U.S. international environmental policy leadership, and no escaping the need to build that leadership on a strong and broadly based domestic foundation. Executive branch zeal is not enough. Policy strength may ultimately depend more upon support and coalition building in Congress than upon decisions taken by the president, the vice president, the secretary of state, or the EPA administrator.

What can be done when the domestic foundation weakens? Executive branch leaders might try to finesse their domestic opponents with "two-level game" initiatives, stratagems abroad designed to create more room for action at home. We have seen, however, that internationalizing the policy debate before a domestic consensus has formed can give domestic policy opponents additional arguments for resisting change, incurring risks of diminished accountability both at home and abroad.[67]

Arguments for stronger U.S. environmental policies abroad must therefore be made persuasive on their own terms, to a wide domestic political audience at home. This will not be an easy task, since environmental circumstances within much of the United States have recently been improving, masking the fact that environmental circumstances in much of the rest of the world, and in the global commons, remain in such peril. Over the past several decades, partly because of strict and costly environmental policies, air and water quality in the United States have been markedly improved; environmental circumstances in most of the developing world and the states of the former Soviet Union have meanwhile continued to worsen.[68] The citizens in rich countries such as the United States, who have long enjoyed isolation from the poverty of the developing world, are now starting to enjoy a dangerous kind of isolation from developing world environmental degradation as well.[69] Having successfully moved toward a clean up of their own air and water at home, citizens of rich countries—including the United States—have become less inclined to care about polluted air and water abroad.

What will it take, in the post–Cold War era, to reconnect domestic society and domestic political leaders in the U.S. Congress to international environmental problems? If even those international environmental problems that can affect U.S. citizens directly, such as climate change and species loss, are no longer considered urgent within the U.S. Congress, then what are the chances that concern can be raised for more distant issues, such as polluted air and water in the cities of Asia and Latin America, or soil nutrient depletion in Africa? A timely and adequate official response is hard, at this point, to envision. United States citizens legitimately concerned with these severe environmental problems abroad may feel it necessary in the years ahead to make more of their individual efforts outside of their own government, through unofficial institutional channels, such as private and unaffiliated environmental nongovernmental organizations (NGOs).

A stronger official response from the U.S. government may only come in cases where human welfare within the United States itself is demonstrably threatened, as it was (and still is) in the case of stratospheric ozone loss. Yet even here the U.S. Congress, in its new mood of ecocomplacency, has considered retreating. Late in 1995, a group of prominent Republicans in the House introduced legislation that would have postponed the ban on CFC production (scheduled for January 1, 1996) earlier negotiated by the Bush administration and ratified by the Senate in 1993. Representative Tom DeLay (R-Tex.), the Republican whip in the House, actually suggested repealing the CFC ban, arguing that the link between CFCs and human health risks was debatable ("Is the cost worth it? I don't think so," said DeLay).[70]

Perhaps one reason for this backsliding has been a reluctance on the part of environmental activists to reward politicians for taking modest steps. Enjoying their role as uncompromising activists in search of high-cost international policy initiatives, environmental groups have failed to reward those elected officials who have been willing to take more modest "no regrets" steps. In doing so, they have left open the field to politicians who are now advocating no steps at all, or worse, to politicians (amply rewarded by anti-environmental industry and citizens' groups) who are advocating steps backward. Environmental activists seeking more ambitious U.S. policy steps abroad may have to abandon some of their own earlier absolutism, and find new ways to reward those politicians still willing to take the small steps with which every journey must begin.

Endnotes

1. Vice President Al Gore, *Earth in the Balance: Ecology and the Human Spirit* (New York: Plume, 1993), pp. xvi, 297, 302.
2. Governor Bill Clinton and Senator Al Gore, *Putting People First: How We Can All Change America* (New York: Times Books, 1992), p. 94.
3. Gore, *Earth in the Balance*, p. xiii.
4. William K. Stevens, "Gore Promises U.S. Leadership on Sustainable Development Path," *New York Times*, June 15, 1993, p. C4.
5. President William J. Clinton and Vice President Albert Gore, Jr., "The Climate Change Action Plan," Executive Office of the President, October 1993. The U.S. continued to spend roughly $130 billion on environmental efforts at home every year during the first years of the Clinton administration, but it formally spent only one-two hundredth as much ($600 million through the Agency for International Development) on direct environmental policy efforts abroad. Roughly 60 percent of domestic environmental policy costs were paid by private firms and consumers, the rest by state, local, and federal government. Frances Cairncross, "Environmental Pragmatism," *Foreign Policy*, No. 95 (Summer 1994): 52. *See also* Patti L. Petesch, *North-South Environmental Strategies, Costs, and Bargains* (Washington, DC: Overseas Development Council, 1992), p. 80.
6. Edward A. Parson, Peter M. Haas, and Marc A. Levy, "A Summary of the Major Documents Signed at the Earth Summit and the Global Forum," *Environment*, Vol. 34, No. 8 (October 1992): 14.
7. This side agreement did not alter the Convention itself but gave political reassurance to the private trade. *See* Richard N. Cooper, *Environmental and Resource Policies for the World Economy* (Washington, DC: Brookings Institution, 1994), p. 8.
8. Robert L. Paarlberg, *Leadership Abroad Begins at Home: U.S. Foreign Economic Policy After the Cold War* (Washington, DC: Brookings Institution, 1995), p. 80.
9. "Congress Fails to Ratify Treaty to Protect World's Biological Diversity," *International Environment Reporter*, October 19, 1994, p. 845.
10. "Congress Fails to Ratify Treaty to Protect the World's Biological Diversity," *International Environment Reporter*, October 19, 1994, p. 845.
11. "Dowdeswell Calls on Nations to Set Clear Policies, Priorities Under Treaty," *International Environment Reporter*, December 14, 1994, p. 1021.
12. There are precedents in U.S. arms control policy for executive branch adherence to unratified treaties.
13. "Nations Join Together to Protect, Manage Coral Reefs, Related Ecosystems," *International Environment Reporter*, December 14, 1994, pp. 1022–1023.

14. According to India's Environment Minister Kamal Nath, "We cannot wait forever, and we do not want to be pushed into any corner. But if the ratification does not take place in the next three months, then obviously we must prevent other countries from taking advantage of the benefits accruing from our genetic material." Sanjoy Hazarika, "India Presses U.S. to Pass Biotic Treaty," *New York Times*, April 23, 1995, p. A13.

15. Clinton and Gore, *Putting People First*, p.97.

16. *See, for example,* Gregg Easterbrook, "From Uncle Smoke to Mr. Clean," *New York Times*, op-ed, August 13, 1993, p. A27.

17. Joel Darmstadter, "The U.S. Climate Change Action Plan: Challenges and Prospects," *Resources*, No. 118 (Winter 1995): 21.

18. In November 1994, the Organization of Economic Cooperation and Development (OECD) reported that U.S. emissions, by these two measures, were worse than those of any other member of the Group of Seven (G-7) major industrialized countries. *See* "U.S. Tops G-7 Nations for Emissions of Greenhouse Gases, OECD Report Says," *International Environment Reporter*, Current Reports, November 30, 1994, p. 980.

19. The gain would be even smaller if measured against the larger backdrop of the earth's naturally occurring carbon emissions, which still outpace human-induced emissions roughly 29 to 1, and smaller still if measured against all greenhouse effects, including natural noncarbon effects such as water vapor. *See* Gregg Easterbrook, *A Moment on the Earth* (New York: Viking, 1995), p. 312.

20. Henry Lee, "Introduction," in Henry Lee (ed.), *Shaping National Responses to Climate Change: A Post-Rio Guide* (Washington, DC: Island Press, 1995), p. 5.

21. *See* Nordhaus, "An Optimal Transition Path for Controlling Greenhouse Gases," *Science* 258, No. 5086 (November 20, 1992): 1317.

22. Richard N. Cooper, *Environmental Resource Policies for the World Economy* (Washington, DC: Brookings Institution, 1994).

23. "Concrete Action on Protocol Deferred; Two-Year Negotiation Process Established," *International Environment Reporter*, Current Report, April 19, 1995, p. 283.

24. If the United States were to continue limiting its emissions to 1990 levels beyond the year 2000, the cumulative constraint on U.S. economic growth could eventually become noticeable, but it would still be quite small in relative terms. Between 1990 and 2020, this "stabilization" policy might reduce annual real GNP growth in the United States by 0.02 percentage points. By way of comparison, the oil price increases of 1974 and 1979 reduced annual U.S. GNP growth by 0.2 percentage points between 1975–1985, or roughly ten times as much. Dale W. Jorgenson and Peter J. Wilcoxen, "The Economic Effects of a Carbon Tax," in Lee (ed.), *Shaping National Responses to Climate Change: A Post-Rio Guide* (Washington, DC: Island Press, 1995), pp. 238, 245.

25. Dale W. Jorgenson and Peter J. Wilcoxen, "The Economic Effects of a Carbon Tax," p. 239. The economic burden of such a tax on users of coal would have been significant (it might cause roughly a 17 percent increase in coal prices), but users of petroleum and natural gas would see less than a 4 percent increase in prices, and a portion of the substantial revenues collected could hypothetically be used to soften the pain felt by affected industries.

26. Writing in *Earth in the Balance*, he advocated replacing a portion of the existing tax burden with a carbon-dioxide tax, with the tax proceeds to be used in an "Environmental Security Trust Fund" that would finance a national switch-over to environmentally benign technologies. *See* Gore, p. 349.

27. Almost 90 percent of electricity used in Ohio comes from coal. *See* Matthew L. Wald, "Pondering an Energy Tax That Can't Please All People," *New York Times*, January 31, 1993, p. F10.

28. Peter Passell, "Economic Scene," *New York Times*, May 13, 1993, p. D2.

29. Bruce N. Stram, "A Carbon Tax Strategy for Global Climate Change," in Lee (ed.), *Shaping National Responses to Climate Change*, p. 233.

30. President William J. Clinton and Vice President Albert Gore, Jr., "The Climate Change Action Plan," Executive Office of the President, October 1993.

31. Steven Greenhouse "Officials Say U.S. Is Unlikely to Meet Clean-Air Goal for 2000," *New York Times*, March 30, 1995, p. A6.

32. Germany and Britain find it relatively easy to stay within 1990 emissions levels in the short run by shutting down antiquated coal burning industries (especially in East Germany), steps that would probably be taken anyway, in the absence of a climate change scare. *See* "Global Warming and Cooling Enthusiasm," *The Economist*, (April 1, 1995): 33.

33. "Concrete Action on Protocol Deferred; Two-Year Negotiation Process Established," *International Environment Reporter*, Current Report, April 19, 1995, p. 283.

34. "Concrete Action on Protocol Deferred; Two-Year Negotiation Process Established," *International Environment Reporter*, Current Report, April 19, 1995, p. 283.

35. Kevin Carmody, "It's a Jungle Out There: Environmental Journalism in an Age of Backlash," *Columbia Journalism Review* (May/June 1995): 41.

36. Gregg Easterbrook, *A Moment on the Earth: The Coming Age of Environmental Optimism* (New York: Viking, 1995), p. 456.

37. Bush's EPA Administrator, William Reilly, worked effectively with liberal congressional Democrats, such as Senate Majority Leader George Mitchell and Representative Henry Waxman of California, to pass the Clean Air Act in 1990.

38. Paarlberg, *Leadership Abroad Begins at Home*, pp. 43–44.

39. Kevin Carmody, "It's a Jungle Out There," p. 45.

40. Keith Schneider, "Big Environment Hits A Recession," *New York Times*, January 1, 1995, p. F4; Scott Allen, "Murky Times for Environmentalism," *Boston Globe*, November 12, 1994, p. 1.

41. According to Ben Beach, chief spokesman of the Wilderness Society in Washington, "The No. 1 cause of our problems has been the economy . . . When the economy went down, so did our membership." Quoted in Schneider, ""Big Environment Hits a Recession," p. F4.

42. Easterbrook, *A Moment on the Earth*, pp. 461–462.

43. Daniel Magraw, "NAFTA's Repercussions: Is Green Trade Possible?" *Environment*, Vol. 36, No. 2 (March 1994): 14–20, 39–45.

44. When this amendment was attached, even some environmental lobbyists stopped supporting the cabinet-elevation measure, and it failed by a 227–191 vote. *New York Times*, February 7, 1994, p. 1A.

45. *New York Times*, February 13, 1994, Section 4, p. 14.

46. Carmody, "It's a Jungle Out There," p. 42.

47. John H. Cushman, Jr., "House Approves a New Standard for Regulations," *New York Times*, March 1, 1995, p. 1; Timothy Noah, "Regulatory Overhaul Headed for Defeat," *Wall Street Journal*, July 19, 1995, p. A2.

48. John Cushman, Jr., "Spending Bill Would Reverse Nation's Environment Policy," *New York Times*, September 22, 1995, p. 1; David Rogers, "Waivers to House's EPA Funding Bill Are Dropped in Rebuff to GOP Leaders," *Wall Street Journal*, November 3, 1995, p. A16; William K. Stevens, "U.N. Warns Against Delay in Cutting Carbon Dioxide Emissions," *New York Times*, October 25, 1995, p. A13.

49. William K. Stevens, "Scientists Say Earth's Warming Could Set Off Wide Disruptions," *New York Times*, September 18, 1995, p. 1A; William K. Stevens, "In Energy Tug of War, U.S. Misses its Goal on Emissions," *New York Times*, November 28, 1995, p. B8.

50. Oran R. Young's important study of international regime creation for natural resources and the environment stresses the "pervasive collective-action problems"

among states that "make cooperation problematic at the international level." *See* Oran R. Young, *International Cooperation: Building Regimes for Natural Resources and the Environment* (Ithaca: Cornell University Press, 1989), pp. 5, 84.

51. It is not unusual for international relations theorists to assume away internal differences. For a recent example, *see* Thomas Bernauer, "The Effect of International Environmental Institutions: How We Might Learn More," *International Organization*, Vol. 49, No. 2 (Spring 1995): 351–377.

52. When international relations scholars do offer unit level explanations for environmental cooperation (explanations based on the characteristics of states at home rather than on their position in the international system abroad), for convenience sake they will tend to take a unitary view of state preferences. Countries (and their governments) will be imagined as having "preferences" and "goals" that can change during a negotiation, but which nonetheless give expression to a unified rather than a divided internal political process. *See* Detlef Sprinz and Tapani Vaahtoranta, "The Interest-Based Explanation of International Environmental Policy," *International Organization*, Vol. 48, No. 1 (Winter 1994): 78–79.

53. James K. Sebenius, "Overcoming Obstacles to a Successful Climate Change Convention," in Henry Lee (ed.), *Shaping National Responses to Climate Change: A Post-Rio Guide* (Washington, DC: Island Press, 1995), p. 48.

54. Robert O. Keohane, *After Hegemony: Cooperation and Discord in the World Political Economy* (Princeton: Princeton University Press, 1984).

55. *See* Peter M. Haas, "Introduction: Epistemic Communities and International Policy Coordination," *International Organization*, Vol. 46, No. 1 (Winter 1992): 1–35.

56. Several other distinctive features of the U.S. political system also stand in the path of easy government-to-government cooperation on environmental issues abroad, including the autonomous power of state and local government, and the power of courts open to citizens bringing lawsuits within the U.S. legal system. *See* Robert L. Paarlberg, *Leadership Abroad Begins at Home: U.S. Foreign Economic Policy After the Cold War* (Washington, DC: Brookings Institution, 1995), pp.32–53.

57. Internal objections were also a reason for this downgrade. The United Kingdom (an energy exporter) and several southern European nations (less wealthy) opposed the original carbon tax proposal. Henry Lee, "Introduction," in Lee (ed.), *Shaping National Responses to Climate Change: A Post-Rio Guide*, p. 11.

58. "Revised Commission Proposal on CO_2 Calls for Voluntary Taxation Scheme," *International Environment Reporter*, Current Report, May 31, 1995, p. 357.

59. Jessica Tuchman Mathews, "The Implications for U.S. Policy," in Mathews (ed.), *Preserving the Global Environment: The Challenge of Shared Leadership* (New York: W. W. Norton, 1991), p. 311.

60. After a blistering review of the many scientific and technical uncertainties still standing in the path of a global political consensus that climate change is an imminent and dangerous threat, Gregg Easterbrook notes that the threat does not have to be large or imminent to justify the modest goals that were set in Rio, because there are so many other good ("no regrets") reasons for reducing our wasteful use of fossil fuels:

> Considering that energy is the world's leading pollutant; that energy efficiency saves money; that fossil fuel supplies, while today robust, are nevertheless finite; the sorts of fuel efficiency strictures that would buy greenhouse-effect insurance will soon be seen as a global priority regardless of the thermostat.

Easterbrook, *A Moment on the Earth*, p. 306.

61. For an examination of the distinctiveness of U.S. environmental policymaking institutions, *see* Raymond Vernon, "The Triad as Policymakers," in Lee (ed.), *Shaping National Responses to Climate Change: A Post-Rio Guide* (Washington, DC: Island Press, 1995), pp. 147–175.

62. Robert D. Putnam, "Diplomacy and Domestic Politics: The Logic of Two-Level Games," *International Organization*, Vol. 42, No. 3, 427–460.

63. Putnam's favorite example of how this might work is the agreement on macroeconomic stimulation and energy policy reform reached at the Bonn economic summit in 1978. In this agreement, Chancellor Helmut Schmidt agreed to an added fiscal stimulus in Germany in return for President Jimmy Carter's pledge to decontrol domestic crude oil prices. This public exchange of commitments on the world stage strengthened the hand of each leader in the subsequent policy battles at home, helping each to implement the commitments made. *See* Putnam, pp. 428–429.

64. Edward A. Parson, "Protecting the Ozone Layer," in Peter M. Haas, Robert O. Keohane, and Marc A. Levy (eds.), *Institutions for the Earth: Sources of Effective International Environmental Protection* (Cambridge: MIT Press, 1993), p. 41.

65. Richard E. Benedick, *Ozone Diplomacy: New Directions in Safeguarding the Planet* (Cambridge: Harvard University Press, 1991), p. 206.

66. The imitative transfer of innovative norms and policy institutions across cultures is well known to historians and social geographers. Arnold Toynbee described it as *mimesis*. *See* Peter H. Sand, *Lessons Learned in Global Environmental Governance* (Washington, DC: World Resources Institute, 1990), p. 25.

67. In a number of post–Cold War issue areas, this "inward-first" approach to U.S. policy leadership is likely to be more successful than the "outward-first" alternative. For an extended discussion *see* Robert Paarlberg, *Leadership Abroad Begins at Home: U.S. Foreign Economic Policy After the Cold War* (Washington, DC: Brookings Institution, 1995).

68. For a general presentation of this argument *see* Gregg Easterbrook, *A Moment on the Earth* (New York: Viking, 1995), especially pp. 577–600. For a discussion of the larger environmental problems that developing countries face in the area of agricultural policy specifically, *see* Robert L. Paarlberg, *Countrysides at Risk: The Political Geography of Sustainable Agriculture* (Washington, DC: Overseas Development Council, 1994).

69. If U.S. environmental interests are understood in narrow terms (avoiding direct physical harm), then climate change and ozone depletion may currently be the only global environmental threats that present a direct challenge to U.S. interests. *See* Marc A. Levy, "Is the Environment A National Security Issue?" *International Security*, Vol. 20, No. 2 (Fall 1995): 61.

70. William K. Stevens, "G.O.P. Bills Aim to Delay Ban on Chemical in Ozone Dispute," *New York Times*, September 21, 1995, p. A20. DeLay, a former exterminator, has referred to the EPA as "the Gestapo of government."

Part III

Regional Problems

··

The Collapsing Partnership: Why the United States Has No Russia Policy

Stephen Sestanovich

"The honeymoon is over." Few words have been used more often than these to describe the evolution of Russian-American relations since the end of the Cold War. They refer to the passing of that first post-war interlude, typically called "euphoric" or "romantic," in which leaders showered each other publicly with heartfelt praise, diplomats and bureaucrats began to do their business on a first-name basis, and large cooperative initiatives were not delayed by lawyerly haggling over details.

In late 1991 and 1992, the competitive norms of international politics were, or seemed to be, suspended, as they often are, or seem to be, when great wars end. Many Russians and Americans—politicians and officials, experts and commentators, as well as ordinary citizens—felt that for the foreseeable future a major, intractable disagreement between the two sides was all but out of the question. Certainly there was no sign of partisan division on the issue in the United States. In the presidential election of 1992, candidates Bush and Clinton actually vied to be the first to propose a huge aid package for Russia. And after the presidency changed hands, the newly installed Clinton administration repeatedly made clear its strong commitment (arguably even more enthusiastic than its predecessor's) to Russian-American "partnership."

With the end of the Cold War now half a decade in the past, it is easy to deride these expectations as utopian and unserious. Russian-American relations have been marked by disagreement on one issue after another: on the implementation of previously negotiated arms control agreements; on Russian policy in the so-called "near abroad"; on the scale and conditionality of Western economic assistance (and the pace and content of Russia's reforms); on Russia's sale of sophisticated

Stephen Sestanovich is Vice President for Russian and Eurasian Affairs at the Carnegie Endowment for International Peace in Washington, DC. A former senior staff member of the National Security Council, he has written on Western policy toward the former Soviet Union for Foreign Affairs, The National Interest, The New Republic, *the* New York Times, *and other publications.*

arms and technology to India, China, and Iran; on Western air attacks against Bosnian Serb forces and UN sanctions against Serbia proper; on Russia's Carthaginian treatment of Chechnya; and—by far the most contentious and persistent issue of them all—on the proposed expansion of NATO into Eastern Europe. In December 1994, warning of the damage that could ensue from this Western initiative, President Boris Yeltsin suggested that the Cold War might in the end be replaced by nothing better than a "Cold Peace."

Not surprisingly, the accumulation of such disagreements (and the sharp rhetoric that often accompanied them) gave rise to a revised picture of Russia in American strategic thinking. Far from being a potential ally, it was increasingly viewed by many as, at the very best, a state whose interests would often differ from those of the United States. Attempts to create a truly cooperative relationship were therefore expected to come to grief.

Apart from this presumed clash of interests, the case against seeing Russia as a long-term "partner" of the United States was further strengthened by the nerve-wracking course of Russian politics. With the success of a radical nationalist like Vladimir Zhirinovsky in the elections of December 1993, and then of the Communist Party in the elections of December 1995, American policymakers were on notice not to count on the success of Russian reform. Political extremism, economic dislocation, bureaucratic corruption, institutional paralysis, widespread anti-Americanism—all these seemed reasons to hedge one's bets about the kind of relationship that the United States might be able to create with post-Communist Russia.

In the first years after the end of the Cold-War, American views of Russia grew less "romantic," more hard-boiled, in two separate ways: its reforms were seen to be precarious, and its international agenda was seen to be different from that of the United States. Yet these more "realistic" views do not fully account for the way in which Russian-American "partnership" unraveled. To understand what happened, one has to take note of a third, and in many ways even more consequential, change: Russia has lost the central place that it used to have in U.S. strategy. Both analytically and practically, the full implications of this transformation are only slowly being absorbed.

The fact that Russia preoccupies us less means much more than the opportunity to pull nuclear-armed bombers and missiles safely off alert, or to cease treating bilateral summits as make-or-break moments for world peace. It means that *U.S. policy toward Russia is likely to be derivative of choices and calculations that have nothing directly to do with Russia.* Policy will rarely be based on a straightforward judgment about the kind of relationship with Russia that best serves American interests. Far from having the *wrong* policy toward Russia, the United States may actually cease to have one at all.

During the Cold War, the U.S. relationship with the Soviet Union provided the context for the formulation of policy toward many other countries. Now this link has been reversed. Policy toward Russia is, increasingly, a function of policy toward others. This connection is the starting point for the analysis that follows: we have to see Russia in context. It is impossible to separate U.S. policy toward Russia in the past half-decade from the broader and, as things have turned out, highly frustrating attempt to develop a new, post–Cold War foreign policy.

What disappeared in the mid-1990s was not merely a Russian-American honeymoon, but the strong, positive record of diplomatic achievement with which the United States had come out of the Cold War. As the difficulties of defining and realizing their foreign policy goals grew, American policymakers came under intense pressure—international, domestic, even personal—to show that the United States was in fact still able to lead. It was these pressures, and the way in which U.S. policy responded to them, that put "partnership" with Russia at risk.

The International Environment

Seen historically, the gradual resumption of a more competitive relationship between Russia and the United States might seem completely normal. When postwar honeymoons end, states start thinking about how to preserve and enhance their ability to act effectively against potential adversaries. This is not merely the course of action that academic "realists" predict. It is also the easiest thing for policymakers to do, since it allows them to fall back on old strategic habits and calculations, rather than devise new ones.

For U.S. policymakers, there is no more ingrained habit or calculation than international coalition building. At every major turning point of the Cold War, it was the successful practice of alliance politics that gave the United States an edge in the East-West competition. In the late 1940s and early 1950s, a network of new alliances in Europe and beyond reflected a judgment that Soviet power could not be countered in any other fashion. In the late 1960s and early 1970s, rapprochement with China strengthened Washington's hand in dealing with Moscow (and bolstered China in the face of a strong Soviet military build-up in the Far East). In the late 1970s and early 1980s, NATO decided to counter the growing Soviet force of SS-20 intermediate-range missiles by deploying new missiles of its own in Western Europe, the better to prevent the intimidation of American allies.[1] The West's successful deployment of these missiles—despite a barrage of Soviet threats—proved one of the culminating victories of the Cold War.

If there is a threat to international security, political-military alliances are the answer: this is the received wisdom, and central tradition, of modern American diplomacy. It would hardly be a surprise, then, to find tradition reasserting itself as U.S. policymakers struggled to develop appropriate policies for the post–Cold War era. As Russian-American disagreements mounted up, one would *expect* talk of eternal "partnership" to give way to power politics. As Russia's neighbors began to worry about whether they would be able to stand up to Moscow in the future, one would *expect* the United States to offer them security guarantees in an enlarged Atlantic alliance.

There is only one problem with this reading of how U.S. policy toward Russia developed after the Cold War: it is not what American policymakers thought they were doing. To be sure, if one combs through official pronouncements, it is possible to find a scattered hint or two of a traditional *Realpolitik* approach to dealing with Russia. In a series of speeches in October 1995, for example, Vice President Al Gore announced that the Clinton administration intended to treat Russia as it would "any other great power."[2] And Strobe Talbott, the deputy secretary of state, has written that the West must recognize that Russia may "return to the threatening patterns of international behavior that have sometimes characterized its history, particularly during the Soviet period."[3]

Yet these remarks are rarities. On balance, there have been few signs that U.S. policy is shaped by calculations of any kind about Russian power—present or future, global or regional, nuclear or conventional. After a half-century in which Soviet power was the organizing problem of American strategy, Russia is treated neither as a large potential asset nor as a probable threat. The old habits created by decades of Cold War—above all, a hyper-sensitivity to the military balance—seem not to have survived its end.

This transformation is most striking when one considers what has happened to the old "balance of terror." The competitive logic of nuclear weapons has largely ceased to have any effect on Russian-American relations. And the forces that made the Soviet Union one of the world's two superpowers have been transformed from a strategic problem into a technical one. As a measure of this change, there is Vice President Gore's description of the Clinton administration's top priorities with regard to the former Soviet Union, in which he spoke of the need "to reduce the danger posed by Soviet-era nuclear warheads and reactors."[4]

In this revealing formulation, the policy problem created by Russia's huge nuclear arsenal no longer has anything to do with the possibility that Russia might use it. Russian power is not a worry; what creates real trouble is Russian weakness. In this spirit the Bush administration initiated, and its successor continued, a series of incremental fixes to reduce the risk of nuclear accidents and improve control over fissile materials—lowering the alert status of forces, "detargeting" each other, tightening procedures for handling nuclear weapon stockpiles, and so forth.

In the mid-1990s, in short, the United States no longer has a real strategic nuclear policy toward Russia. As the palest of substitutes, it has the Nunn-Lugar program (so named after its originators in the U.S. Senate), which provides approximately $400 million annually for the dismantling of nuclear weapons systems and other measures to strengthen nuclear safety (including that of nuclear power plants). It is, moreover, hard to imagine a serious resumption of nuclear rivalry between the two sides. Where there are disagreements on nuclear issues, such as over the ratification and implementation of the START II treaty, these have more to do with resource constraints (Russia can ill afford the expensive reshaping of its strategic forces that the treaty demands) than with attempts to gain military advantages.

The nuclear issue most likely to threaten Russian-American relations in the next few years arises (once again) out of U.S. efforts to develop effective ballistic missile defenses (BMD). Yet, far from illustrating continuity, this issue reveals how thoroughly the old Soviet-American rivalry has been transformed. Ten years ago, a similar program, Ronald Reagan's "Star Wars," was designed as a frontal challenge to the Soviet Union, and it became the focus of controversy between Moscow and Washington. Today, the United States insists that its interest in BMD actually has nothing at all to do with Russia, but instead reflects worries about emergent nuclear powers like North Korea or Iraq. To repeat, U.S. policy toward Russia is the by-product of decisions about how to deal with problems other than Russian power itself.

The same pattern is evident if one looks at the seeming resumption of Russian-American competition for influence in Eastern Europe. For both Russians and East Europeans, the idea of enlarging NATO so as to take in the former members of the Warsaw Pact, and possibly even the Baltic states as well, can be easily understood in power terms: after a long, costly struggle, the victor tries to lock in a (possibly temporary) advantage, so as to keep the loser from making a comeback. Poles and Russians may disagree about whether such "neo-containment" is a good idea, but they have no trouble interpreting what is going on.

Seen from Washington, however, the story looks very different. It would be a gross misreading of events to think that the United States embroiled itself in a major dispute with Moscow so as to check the resurgence of Russian power over Eastern Europe. In fact, American policymakers were swayed by a mix of motives, both analytical and practical, that had little to do with Russia. Analytically, U.S. interest in an enlarged NATO was set in motion by, inter alia, anxiety about how to hold the alliance together in the future; the desire to head off any rethinking in Germany about its Western orientation; the hope to prevent "future Bosnias" in the post-Communist states of Eastern Europe; and the nervous recollection that twice in the twentieth century this region was the "seedbed" of wider wars.[5]

Whether these ideas, vague and intellectually dubious as they are, would have carried the day by themselves is of course unknowable. But practical considerations greatly increased their impact. American policymakers came under acute pressure to show that they had an active strategy for addressing the problems of post–Cold War Europe because the record of American policy as a whole was so poor. Above all, the spectacle of Western weakness in the former Yugoslavia put new pressure on the United States to demonstrate American "leadership." The inability of the United States and its allies to stop the fighting in Bosnia seemed to show that, despite its victory in the Cold War, the West had no adequate formula for dealing with the kinds of conflicts that seemed most likely to emerge in its aftermath. As a consequence, the predicament of East European states seemed far less tolerable. They could not be expected to rely on Western verbal assurances, since the Bosnia experience had shown those to be totally empty.

To see how much Western failure in handling this first postwar crisis meant, one has only to imagine the different environment that would have been created by an early and successful assertion of Western power and influence in the Yugoslav drama. An effective intervention would have completely transformed the subsequent debate about NATO expansion. Success would have given the Clinton administration the freedom to move much more carefully in transforming the alliance, making it possible to offer East European states a steadily growing security relationship without an early decision about formal membership.[6] As it was, the United States could not convince these states, or even convince itself, that it took their security seriously. Failure in Bosnia raised the threshold of credibility for other Western policies.

By letting the Bosnian problem fester, then, the United States guaranteed that the far broader issue of NATO expansion was addressed in the context of intense demoralization about the alliance's purposes and effectiveness. Under the impact of its failure in Bosnia, no one disputed the idea that NATO had lost its sense of mission. "Out of area or out of business" was an effective rallying cry for advocates of expansion precisely because the alliance was handling such a serious "out-of-area" problem so miserably.[7]

This was the highly prejudicial context in which U.S. policy toward Russia was formed in the early Clinton administration. An American policy to expand NATO gathered momentum not in relation to fears of Russian power, but against the background of repeated Western failure to deal with a threat to peace on the European continent itself. This record of failure created an atmosphere in which continued passivity was expected to do lasting harm to American influence in European affairs.

The Impact of Domestic Politics

It is persuasively argued elsewhere in this volume that the end of the Cold War has made domestic political considerations much more important in the formulation of American foreign policy.[8] This is true of policy toward Russia as well, but not in the way that is sometimes suggested. The reason that the Clinton administration found itself in a dispute with Russia over NATO expansion was not that some particular interest group had acquired additional leverage over policy, or that congressional pressure forced the president to yield control over his own decision-making. The explanation is a little more complex. The Clinton administration's commitment to NATO expansion grew because, even with the Cold War over, a president's need to show that the United States had an effective foreign policy remained very great.

Policy toward Russia has long had an unusual connection to U.S. domestic politics. Russia is one of the few countries whose emigre populations in the United States are a source not of support for good relations with the old country but of hostility toward it. Emigres from the Tsarist empire and later from the Soviet Union were typically members of ethnic minorities (whether Jews, Poles, Ukrainians, Lithuanians, or others) with, to say the very least, little affinity for Russia itself.[9]

During the Cold War, the sentiments of these groups (and of others with East European backgrounds) coincided with the strategic imperative of opposing the Soviet Union. The collapse of Communism changed this. U.S. policymakers may have wanted, for strategic reasons, to explore and develop a cooperative relationship with the new Russia, but domestic considerations still seemed to argue for a tougher, less conciliatory line. Any politician, after all, who needs to do well in the industrial Midwest has to take the views of Polish-Americans and other ethnic voters seriously. And for Democratic presidential candidates in particular, the support of these constituencies is increasingly a matter of survival. With the South and Rocky Mountain states becoming Republican strongholds, Democrats cannot really hope to be competitive in presidential elections unless they carry New York, Pennsylvania, Illinois, and Michigan.[10]

To explain NATO expansion in this way—as a reflection of the electoral weight of ethnic voters—has the sound of finely tuned political realism, but it is in fact misleading. Although virtually every major government decision is heavily lobbied by one or more interest groups, the intensity of their lobbying (or the intensity of their interest) is not by itself proof of their influence. Even when a president clearly wants and needs the support of a particular bloc of voters, as Clinton did in courting Polish-American and other East European voters, he also considers the broader impact on his presidency of trying to satisfy them. The administration's handling of other issues makes this clear. When, for example, President Clinton decided to push hard in the fall of 1993 for ratification of the North American Free Trade Agreement (NAFTA), he was taking a large risk with some core Democratic constituencies, including Midwest industrial workers. But taking the risk, and winning, strengthened him politically.

A major initiative like NAFTA involves calculations going far beyond the positive or negative reaction of any individual interest group. The same is true of NATO expansion. In defining his position on this issue, the president faced a vastly more serious problem than whether he might please or displease Polish-Americans (and others). He had to take a stand at a time when *his handling of foreign policy had become a glaring—and, some of his advisors were obviously telling him, potentially fatal—political weakness.*

In the presidential election of 1992, with the optimism (complacency, one might say) of the initial post–Cold War period still very high, Bill Clinton had been able to neutralize the Republican Party's long-standing claim that it alone could be trusted with responsibility for national security. Because the vote was relatively close, it can be argued that Clinton's victory *depended* on the irrelevance of foreign policy as a campaign issue. By the same token, his prospects for re-election were closely tied to keeping the Republicans from regaining their traditional advantage in this area.

The Clinton administration's foreign policy difficulties in 1994 were significant in domestic political terms precisely because they seemed to be giving the president's opponents such an opportunity. On one issue after another, from North Korea's nuclear weapons program and the continued influx of Haitian refugees to China's trading status and the war in Bosnia, U.S. policy came under harsh and unceasing criticism. Foreign policy is normally a subject of considerable controversy, but the Clinton administration's record seemed so poor that few in the president's own party defended it.

When a president's foreign policy credibility collapses in this way, the impact is likely to be visible in his handling of almost every major issue. He will ask how even the smallest step will affect his standing. One telling sign of how policy toward Russia would be affected came in a speech by Senator Richard Lugar in early 1994, in which he challenged the basic premises of the administration's approach. The Russians, he said, should not be treated as "partners," but recognized as "tough rivals."[11] Facing a challenge of this kind from Lugar, long regarded as a pillar of Senate reasonableness, the administration could no longer expect to handle Russia policy in the same way it had handled NAFTA—that is, by continuing a Bush policy and expecting moderate Republicans to support the president out of some sense of bipartisan duty. Russia was becoming an issue on which the two parties were sharply divided. Given the weakness of his overall foreign policy record, this was something that Clinton could ill afford.

The issue of NATO expansion, by contrast, offered the administration an opportunity to present itself as the defender of foreign policy bipartisanship in pursuit of traditional American goals. It was perhaps the only initiative available to the president that might actually strengthen his political position. Giving priority to "partnership" with Russia offered him only further vulnerability. Given these choices, it was hardly surprising that the administration began to give greater emphasis to expanding NATO. Doing so put the president's policy toward Russia at risk, but reduced his political risks at home.

Among domestic sources of foreign policy, then, the influence of particular interest groups has been less consequential than the president's need to show effective leadership. For a full explanation of the domestic considerations that pushed U.S. policy away from "partnership" with Russia, bureaucratic politics and policymaking also need to be considered. For under ordinary circumstances, when a president shapes policy to serve his own political interests, there are usually signs of bureaucratic opposition to his initiatives. To exaggerate only a little, the modus operandi of career civil servants—Washington's "permanent government"—is to show outward responsiveness to a president's wishes while subtly blocking him if he tries to move existing policy too far in one direction or another.

With this pattern in mind, one would have expected a major initiative like the expansion of the Atlantic alliance to face considerable bureaucratic resistance. Oddly enough, the Clinton administration appeared to encounter very little internal opposition of any kind. This was a particularly surprising result when one bears in mind the president's famous lack of interest in foreign affairs and the absence of any dominant personality among his principal advisors. This was not a case of a president—a Nixon, for example—managing to get his way by making foreign policy his highest priority or by giving a strong-minded aide—again, a Kissinger—the authority to roll over anyone who stood in the way. In fact, the only significant instance of resistance to the policy of NATO expansion came not from the bureaucracy itself but from the president's close friend, Strobe Talbott, who had overall responsibility for handling policy toward the former Soviet Union.

In the fall of 1993, Talbott wrote a long memorandum to Secretary of State Christopher on NATO expansion, which was widely believed at the time to have persuaded Christopher and other senior officials that moving quickly would unnecessarily damage relations with Russia.[12] The result was the creation of an interim structure, the Partnership for Peace, which all post-Communist states were invited to join. At the time it seemed that a major clash with Russia had been indefinitely postponed. Six months later, however, the push for early expansion of the alliance resumed, and this time Talbott (having been promoted by then to deputy secretary of state) apparently did not try to block it.

This strange policy result—passive bureaucratic acceptance of a major strategic innovation, which only the President's close friend, (briefly) opposes—needs an explanation. One might think, that the answer has to do with the unusual way in which the Clinton administration organized itself to handle policy toward Russia. Within the State Department, the states of the former U.S.S.R. were for the first time separated from the rest of Europe. Where once the same assistant secretary of state developed U.S. policy toward both regions, now different officials divided the work. The original purpose of this separation, ironically, was to signal the high priority of policy toward the former Soviet

Union, and as long as the job of "Russia czar" was held by Talbott, it worked. When he moved up, and a career civil servant took his place, the position lost influence.[13]

Yet the weakened position of those in charge of the Clinton administration's Russia policy offers only a very limited explanation of the lack of any serious resistance to NATO expansion. Much more important was the fact that even narrow bureaucratic interests were being harmed by the overall ineffectiveness of U.S. policy. Members of the "permanent government" typically resist sharp policy departures because these make it harder for them to do their job in the way they have grown accustomed to. But in the first years of the post–Cold War period, it was precisely the passivity and confusion of the Clinton administration's policy that were, for those charged with carrying it out, the more serious threat to the day-to-day effectiveness of American diplomacy. As a result, the usual bureaucratic resistance to new initiatives was reduced.

The most striking case of acceptance of NATO expansion where, for institutional reasons, one would not have expected it was the Defense Department. The Pentagon had every reason to be wary of a major change in the role and composition of the alliance, and senior officials were known to dislike the idea. *Yet they did not oppose it.* Having blocked any involvement in Bosnia, the military could not easily veto a second major initiative, even one that they thought mistaken, without provoking the charge that the Pentagon had become an obstacle to American leadership in the post–Cold War world.

The Personal Factor

For all the force of domestic politics in shaping U.S. policy toward Russia—and it is very great—it cannot be treated as the end of the story. Different people, after all, will understand the same political situation in different ways. How they decide to respond to it will also vary, as will their reasons for doing so. Some may have no guide other than political expediency; others may choose to defy it; still others will be so influenced by their personal preferences and outlook that they are unable even to understand what the politically expedient course is.

Two famous cases of Cold War policymaking, from the late 1960s and early 1970s, show just how important the personal factor can be. President Lyndon Johnson is usually remembered as a supremely cunning practical politician, yet he prosecuted the war in Vietnam far past the point where he could have considered it politically advantageous. In the end, his inflexible policies cost him his job, and the fact that he was unwilling to declare a halt in the bombing of North Vietnam until just days before the 1968 election clearly helped elect Richard Nixon rather than Johnson's own vice-president, Hubert Humphrey. In a case like this, personality—pride, stubbornness, and other individual motives both large and small—accounts for much that purely political explanations do not capture.

It would be equally incomplete to analyze Richard Nixon's rapprochement with the Soviet Union and China in the early 1970s without considering psychological factors. Nixon's opening to China is commonly cited to illustrate the point that a major policy reversal can be most easily accomplished by a president who has long opposed it; he thus confounds predictable partisan alignments. But in Nixon's case personal motives seemed as strong as political ones. Being praised as a great "peacemaker" and visionary surely had a deep-down appeal for someone so relentlessly criticized as a warmonger and dirty-trickster. A lifetime as a hardliner probably also helped to ease any doubts that he himself might have had about the wisdom of what he and Kissinger were doing: could any concession to the other side be too great if he, Richard Nixon, the original Cold Warrior, were prepared to make it?

Trying to understand the interplay between politics and personal psychology is always the hardest kind of analysis. There is usually only very poor evidence to work with, and the interpretations that arise from it are necessarily speculative. Applied to the comparatively colorless figures who made foreign policy in the Bush and Clinton administrations, overly personalized explanations may seem unconvincing. Given these obstacles, a discussion of the personal factor in the formulation of recent U.S. policy has to be very tentative, an attempt to frame questions rather than to set out firm answers.

Consider, for example, the psychological impact of American foreign policy debate over the last 20 years of the Cold War. During this period, for all the continuing rhetoric about bipartisanship, debate about the international purposes and conduct of the United States was extremely polarized. Even a well-established element of policy such as NATO was in fact treated quite differently by opposing sides of the debate. Broadly speaking, the Democratic Party was far less patient than Republicans with the demands placed on American policy by European allies. Europeans were inclined to fret about the need to keep U.S. nuclear strategy strongly "coupled" to the defense of the continent, and about even the smallest signs of a reduced American commitment. Democrats, looking for ways to reduce the international risks and burdens shouldered by the United States, tended to want to look into ideas like no-first-use of nuclear weapons; they were skeptical about the need for INF deployments in the early 1980s, and periodically proposed to draw down the level of troops on NATO's Central Front.

In the entire second half of the Cold War, the principal rallying cries of Democratic foreign policy were opposition to the war in Vietnam and encouragement of the nuclear-freeze movement. Whatever the merits of these positions, they estranged Democrats from the rallying cries of the first half of the Cold War—from Harry Truman and John

F. Kennedy. And they gave Democrats a weak basis for claiming a share of the Cold War "victory."

Looked at in these terms, the central place of NATO in the Clinton administration's European strategy takes on new importance. The cause of NATO expansion represented an opportunity to overcome this legacy of partisan disagreement, to claim once more the mantle of traditionalism, to get squarely back into the mainstream of policy—and to do so for the first time in decades without accepting any large military burdens. For people who had spent the second half of the Cold War largely in opposition to U.S. military policies, the opportunity to become the boosters of an expanding NATO was probably not viewed purely in strategic or political terms. It surely offered personal satisfaction as well.

The Atlantic alliance is the most respected single institution of American foreign policy in the twentieth century. Psychologically, its pull on those who were unsure that they had done their bit to "win the Cold War" may have been very strong. Conversely, the idea of being seen as once more against the expansion of American political-military commitments—and most of all, because it might alarm the Russians—must have seemed a dreary repeat of past debates that had long since been lost.

Richard Nixon obviously derived intense satisfaction from being praised as a statesman in the editorials of the New York Times (which he otherwise loathed), and his personal satisfaction with the result helped to strengthen the new policy toward Beijing and Moscow. No one would consider this a skewed or overly conjectural reading. How different is it to suggest that for Bill Clinton a policy that led Henry Kissinger and Zbigniew Brzezinski to praise him had more than merely political advantages?[14]

Personal psychology may help to explain a further problem that the Clinton administration encountered in its Russia policy: U.S. officials clearly overestimated Moscow's potential flexibility on the issue of NATO expansion and seemed to assume that the problem could be solved by American professions of good faith, frequently repeated. To overcome Russian skepticism, they stressed the nonconfrontational, nonexclusive character of an enlarged alliance, and insisted that, far from isolating Russia, it would offer "benefits for everyone."[15]

This was an interesting miscalculation, suggesting some of the confusion that political leaders can create (not least in their own minds) when they try to balance contradictory lines of policy. Richard Nixon, for example, seemed to believe that he could make any concession he wanted in the name of nurturing detente, without losing his reputation as a tough guy. Clinton administration policymakers seem to have made the opposite assumption: they thought they could expand NATO while at the same time presenting themselves to the Russians as proponents of international understanding. And why not? The people in charge of U.S. policy had in fact spent their careers advocating arms control, multilateral conflict-resolution, and cooperative, non-zero sum diplomacy. But if they thought that their own biographies would make it any easier for Moscow to accept their policies, they were only deceiving themselves.

Conclusion

In the immediate aftermath of the Cold War, it was very common to speak of the United States as the world's only superpower, and to see American policy as decisively shaped by this dominant position in international affairs. Yet in looking at the way in which policy toward Russia has unfolded in the past five years, a rather different conclusion emerges. United States policy was importantly shaped by weaknesses of various kinds: weakness in addressing the first post–Cold War threats to the peace of Europe; weakness in the domestic political position of the president; perhaps even weakness at a personal level. The result, not surprisingly, was to undermine American leadership, and to put the Clinton administration under intense pressure to adopt a more assertive approach in its foreign policy as a whole. That it would do so was hardly in doubt, but its initiatives—above all, a strong commitment to expand NATO—made policy toward Russia increasingly contradictory and incoherent.

Incoherence, it should be said, is not merely an aesthetic or intellectual defect. It means that policymakers are less likely to be able to solve the problems that they themselves are most worried about. In contemporary policy toward Russia, the stand-out example of such incoherence—and its consequences—involved Ukraine. Soon after its term began, the Clinton administration properly identified the future of Ukraine as critical both to Russian-American relations and to the creation of a satisfactory European order. It was U.S. policy to promote accommodation between Moscow and Kiev, and the trilateral agreement signed by the presidents of all three states in January 1994 was a sign of considerable American success. The pursuit of NATO expansion, however, put American leverage over relations between Russia and Ukraine at risk. In particular, friction over this issue made it much less likely that Ukraine would readily expand its own security relations with members of NATO. It would do so, at a minimum, only while looking over its shoulder to gauge Russia's likely reaction.

American policymakers, of course, could decide with perfect reasonableness that this was a risk worth taking. Their policy can be described as incoherent not because they chose wrongly, but because they took the risk without having chosen at all.

There are many ways in which the incoherence of U.S. policy toward Russia might be lessened over the next several years. The most straightforward of these would be the re-emergence of Russia as an obvious security problem. A restored Communist government, making a strong push to re-assemble the old Soviet Union, would immediately give Russia a much higher priority in U.S. policy and simplify calculations about how to deal with it. Under these circumstances, there would be—as there always was in the course of the Cold War—considerable debate about how to proceed. But there would be no doubt that the United States had the resources and the political will to answer Russia's new challenge.

Such a worsening of the European security outlook would surely make U.S. policy toward Russia more coherent. So, oddly enough, would a strongly improved security outlook. Were, for example, the Bosnian settlement negotiated under American leadership, and indeed under the threat of NATO air power, to prove durable, much less would be heard of the once-ubiquitous idea that "NATO has no mission in the post–Cold War world." With the effectiveness of the alliance reconfirmed in this way, East European states would have far more confidence in the credibility of Western security assurances, even if these were made without full NATO membership. An American administration with a more successful foreign policy record would have a better chance of building productive security relationships with all the states of Europe—without choosing one at the expense of another.

If things get either much worse (because Russia becomes more threatening) or much better (because U.S. policy brings peace to the Balkans), America's policy toward Russia will become simpler. More coherent policy will become possible without difficult choices. But if things stay as they are, choice is unavoidable. The United States now has in place one policy, expansion of NATO, that many see as the key to reviving American leadership. It has another policy, partnership with Russia, that represents the most significant new opportunity created by the end of the Cold War. In the next half-decade, American diplomacy is likely to face no task more difficult than reconciling these policies or choosing between them.

Endnotes

1. It is important not to make these policies seem simpler in retrospect than they were at the time. There were always those who believed that Western responses to Soviet power were only making matters worse, but these doubters rarely carried the day. At the beginning of the Cold War, George Kennan worried that the creation of NATO would make German re-unification impossible. A decade before it ended, Cyrus Vance argued that too-close military cooperation with China would set back arms control negotiations with Moscow. With some few exceptions, such disagreements were about how to deal with the security problem created by Soviet policy, not about whether there *was* a problem. As a result of the steady growth of Soviet military power, those who insisted that the West had to answer the challenge firmly and decisively almost always got the better of the argument.
2. Remarks at the Kennan Institute/U.S.-Russia Business Council, Washington, DC, October 19, 1995. The statement was ambiguous, of course, since the United States does not have clearly established policy for dealing with "great powers," whether

Russia or "any other." Are they to be viewed primarily as potential rivals or potential collaborators? Gore's speech continued to lean in the latter direction, referring to Russia and America as "friends and partners."

3. "Why NATO Should Grow," *The New York Review of Books,* August 10, 1995, p. 29.

4. Remarks at the U.S. Military Academy, West Point, New York, October 17, 1995.

5. *See* Richard Holbrooke, "America as a European Power," *Foreign Affairs,* (March/April 1995): 41. That these were the motives of U.S. policy does not mean that they made any real persuasive sense. Uncertainty about how a reunified Germany would react to finding itself at the edge of a possibly unstable region was understandable; the fear that it would write off decades of integration into Atlantic and European institutions was pure fantasy. Similarly, the determination to prevent "future Bosnias" was laudable, but of no real relevance to the issue of expanding NATO into Eastern Europe, since there were and are no plausible Bosnia-like conflicts in or between the states of this region. As a matter of fact, the only part of Europe in which one could sketch plausible scenarios for such conflicts was among the states of the former Soviet Union, but none of these was being treated as a serious candidate for NATO membership in the foreseeable future.

6. Resolving the Bosnian crisis early, before it had thoroughly sapped Western credibility, would have produced a further benefit. An effective policy would almost surely have required some Western use of force, but in 1992 or 1993 the impact on relations with Russia would have been less than it was later, when cooperative expectations were already eroded.

7. For an influential argument along these lines, *see* Ronald D. Asmus, Richard L. Kugler, F. Stephen Larrabee, "Building a New NATO," *Foreign Affairs,* Vol. 72, No. 4 (September/October 1993).

8. *See* Chapter 1 by Robert J. Lieber, Chapter 2 by William Schneider, and Chapter 3 by Bruce W. Jentleson.

9. In this respect, Russia fits the pattern of Cuba: the strongest opponents of improved Cuban-American relations are Cuban-Americans themselves.

10. The importance of domestic interest group calculations is even more important when an Administration has to sell a foreign-aid package, as President Clinton did for Russia by emphasizing the economic payoffs for Americans. Jeremy Rosner, *The New Tug-of-War: Congress, the Executive Branch, and National Security* (Carnegie Endowment, 1995), p. 100.

11. Speech at the American Spectator Dinner Club, Washington, D.C., March 7, 1994.

12. Michael Gordon, "U.S. Opposes Move to Rapidly Expand NATO Membership, the *New York Times,* January 2, 1994, p. 1.

13. Talbott should have had even greater control over Russia policy as a result of his promotion. As deputy secretary, however, he took on a much wider portfolio and had less time for Russia. More importantly, a protracted confirmation had clearly damaged his authority. Making use of his previous writings, Senate critics had portrayed him as naive about Soviet foreign policy—and hence likely to be naive about Russia as well.

14. Michael Mandelbaum has described the president as burdened by widespread public "doubt about whether he measured up to the job of chief executive and commander in chief." It is impossible to say whether this doubt infected Clinton himself, but if so the support that he won from senior statesmen like Brezezinski and Kissinger would have been doubly welcome. *See* "Foreign Policy as Social Work," *Foreign Affairs* (January/February 1996): 32.

15. This ingenuous phrase is from Strobe Talbott's article "Why NATO Should Grow," *The New York Review of Books,* August 10, 1995.

Chapter

8

The United States and Western Europe

Stanley Hoffmann

It is not easy to define the Clinton administration's policy toward Europe. When it came to power, it found a relatively neat situation. The Bush administration had, with great dexterity,[1] managed the historic transition from the Cold War to a seemingly reunified continent. I say seemingly, because there remained a huge disparity between Western Europe, encased in a variety of sturdy institutions and reasonably prosperous despite rising unemployment, and Eastern Europe, fragmented, with economies in various stages of disarray; civil societies that needed to be strengthened; political systems that had to be recreated; and a host of troublesome problems, such as purges at home, and minorities to look after. Eastern Europe was an institutional vacuum, except for the participation of its states in the Conference on Security and Cooperation in Europe. François Mitterrand's idea of a European Confederation, presented in Prague in June 1991, was rejected by the East Europeans, who did not want a half-way house instead of admission as full

Stanley Hoffmann is Douglas Dillon Professor of the Civilization of France at Harvard University, where he has taught since 1955. He has been the Chairman of the Center for European Studies at Harvard from its creation in 1969 until 1995. He has also taught at the Institut d'Etudes Politiques of Paris, from which he graduated, and at the Ecole des Hautes Etudes en Sciences Sociales.

His books include Contemporary Theory in International Relations *(Prentice-Hall, 1960),* The State of War *(Praeger, 1965),* Gulliver's Troubles *(McGraw-Hill, 1968),* Decline or Renewal: France Since the 30s *(Viking, 1974),* Primacy or World Order: American Foreign Policy Since the Cold War *(McGraw-Hill, 1978),* Duties Beyond Borders *(Syracuse U Press, 1981),* Dead Ends *(Ballinger, 1983),* Janus and Minerva *(Westview, 1986) and* The European Sisyphus: Essays on Europe, 1964–1994 *(Westview, 1995). Tanner Lectures on Human Values, Vol. 15 (University of Utah Press, 1994). He is co-author of* In Search of France *(Harvard U Press, 1963),* The Fifth Republic at Twenty *(SUNY Press, 1981),* Living with Nuclear Weapons *(Harvard University, 1983),* The Mitterrand Experiment *(Polity Press, 1987),* The New European Community *(Westview, 1991),* After the Cold War *(Harvard University Press, 1993).*

Professor Hoffmann is currently working, with Professor Michael Smith of the University of Virginia, on a book on ethics and international relations.

partners into the European Community (EC), and resented being treated in the same way as Russia.

The task of the new administration was going to be to deal with states impatient to rejoin the institutions of the West. It also had to re-define North Atlantic Treaty Organization's (NATO) mission, now that its main raison d'être: deterrence of and defense against the Soviet Union and its Warsaw Pact allies, had disappeared. Could it find a new rationale in coping with possible conflicts, inter- and intra- state, in Eastern Europe? That would have meant, following the precedent of the Gulf War, an extension of NATO's role, "out of area"—something the French had always resisted, except in the Gulf War case (and even then, there had been prickly moments). Indeed, when the Clinton ad-ministration took over in Washington, one bloody war was raging in Europe: the Yugoslav tragedy had turned violent in June 1991, and the Bush administration had decided to let the eager EC deal with the con-flict. When the Europeans' effort at a settlement failed in the fall of 1991, it was to the United Nations that they turned, in part because the French objected to any call to NATO.

What happened over the past three-and-a-half years can be exam-ined under three headings: transatlantic economic issues, the NATO conundrum, and the Yugoslav war.

Transatlantic Economic Issues

The GATT negotiations known as the Uruguay Round had been going on for a long time, and although for the most part the Europeans sup-ported U.S. attempts at expanding the range of free trade by including a large variety of services, a number of important issues remained unre-solved. France, which had accepted an EC plan that entailed a reduc-tion of the protection French agriculture had enjoyed, thanks to the in-genious and complex mechanisms of the EC's Common Agricultural Policy, resisted attempts by the United States to force a further cut in domestic subsidies and subsidized exports. There was also a clash over French and EC policies of "cultural protection" that limited access to U.S. films and popular music, and a transatlantic brawl over the Airbus plane, which the United States denounced because it received subsidies from the French and German governments and thus had an "unfair" ad-vantage over comparable American planes.

One of the few areas of foreign policy in which the Clinton admin-istration had a firm agenda was foreign economic policy. A vigorous drive to open foreign markets further to U.S. goods and services was an essential part of Clinton's plan to stimulate the U.S. economy and to "grow it," as he kept saying. It became even more essential when Con-gress rejected the measures for domestic stimulation submitted by the new administration and gave priority instead to a policy of deficit reduction. The new Trade Representative Mickey Kantor made it clear that the administration's drive was not going to spare America's main allies—the EC and Japan—and that the United States was determined to play it rough, to resort to unilateral retaliation if necessary, even though, in the beginning, multilateralism was high on the administration's policy agenda. There followed, in 1993, a remarkable test of wills between the United States and France. At first, the French appeared isolated within the EC, where the United Kingdom (UK) supported American demands, and Germany pressured the French for a compromise. But the skillful new foreign policy team led by Foreign Minister Juppé, in the conservative government that "coexisted" with President Mitterrand after the elections of the spring of 1993, succeeded in obtaining German and EC support (i.e., the support of the European Union's Commission, headed by Jacques Delors) for a program of resistance to U.S. demands. The alternative was splitting the new European Union (EU), at a time of public disenchantment with it. In the end, the U.S. negotiators had to choose between a failure of the Uruguay Round and a deal that preserved the status quo in a number of areas. They chose the latter. As a result, French concessions on agriculture did not go beyond those already consented to in the Brussels' Common Agricultural Policy (CAP) reform plan. On "cultural protectionism" and the Airbus issue, an agreement to continue to disagree and to leave a solution to the next round of GATT was all that the United States could obtain. The French had played a very Gaullist card, the power of obstruction, and with the encouragement of the EC Commission they had also successfully argued that the need for the EC members to stay united exceeded the need to accommodate a rather rough American pressure. Chancellor Kohl, eager to preserve the Franco-German partnership, agreed with the French, and their cause thus became the EC's position. The Clinton administration obtained little beyond what its predecessor had gained in the earlier years of that long Uruguay Round.

The NATO Conundrum

The story of the United States's NATO policy since January 1993 has a minor part and a major one. The minor one is another Franco-American story. The major one deals with NATO's role and membership.

The Franco-American relationship over NATO has been difficult ever since General de Gaulle came to power in 1958. In 1966 the French left the integrated command structure and military institutions of NATO, while remaining members of the North Atlantic Alliance, establishing various procedures of cooperation with NATO, and keeping forces in Germany. In the 1980s, even though Mitterrand encouraged the Bundestag to accept U.S. cruise missiles and Pershing IIs on

West German soil, two bones of contention kept the Franco-American strategic relationship tense. One, already mentioned, was France's reluctance to allow NATO to expand its mission outside of the geographical sphere defined in the 1949 treaty. The other was the quasi-theological battle over what ought to be the predominant security institution in Western Europe: NATO, under U.S. leadership and military domination, or the Western European Union (WEU), which was created in 1955 to provide a (pale) replacement for the defeated European Defense Community. The Western European Union had been a rather dormant organization. All its members were also members of NATO. Only NATO had the infrastructure necessary to support extensive military operations. But in 1984 when Mitterrand began to push greater European integration, the French aimed at turning WEU into the security arm of the "relaunched" EC, and the Maastricht treaty of 1991 had solemnly included foreign and security policy in the functions of the European Union. As James Baker puts it in his memoirs, "this rather theological debate revolved around different conceptions of America's role in Europe," and the United States was hostile to any European defense identity "in which America's role on the Continent was minimized."[2] Not only were Washington officials convinced that even after the Cold War the Europeans still needed "an engaged America," but NATO was the one international institution that the United States dominated and that gave Washington a hold over the Europeans. After all, managing one's allies is one of the main functions of alliances.

One of the achievements of the Clinton years has been a Franco-American rapprochement over this issue. Partly, it results from a U.S. concession: the willingness to accept that, in certain cases, the European members of NATO could accomplish missions without U.S. participation and that combined joint task forces could be set up by them for such purposes. Partly, it results from a considerable French evolution. They agreed that, in an emergency, the Eurocorps created in 1991 could be put at the service of either the WEU or NATO. In Yugoslavia, the French, dissatisfied with UN weakness and its peacekeeping force UNPROFOR's plight, agreed, grudgingly at first, to contribute to NATO's military mission, and in 1995 to put the Quick Reaction Force it created with the British under NATO command. This experience led not only to French participation in NATO's IFOR, deployed in Bosnia at the end of 1995, after the Dayton agreements (see below) but also to two remarkable developments. One was the return of France to the Council of Defense Ministers and the Military Committee of NATO (but not to the Nuclear Planning Group or to the integrated military command); the other was the abandonment of the effort to revitalize the WEU at NATO's expense. Given the opposition of the UK, the coolness of Germany, and the reluctance of the smaller EU powers toward France's attempt, the French recognized, in early 1996, that a European defense identity could only be formed within, not outside of, NATO. This means that the French, disappointed by the lack of a common European foreign and security policy, have temporarily given up the hope that the EU could produce a European defense identity around the WEU.

This does not mean, however, that the Franco-American conflict is over and that the French (under a Gaullist President!) have given up the heart of Gaullist policy. Their aim is clearly to obtain through participation a reform of NATO aimed at establishing this European defense identity, in particular by putting the Military Committee over the Supreme Allied Commander in Europe (SACEUR) and by having a European as Deputy SACEUR. The French policy is a shift of means, not of ends. The French goal remains a modicum of European military independence from the United States. However, now that the "American peril" is no longer, as it was 30 years ago, America's overbearing presence but rather the possibility of America's exit, this independence can be sought—at lesser financial cost—within NATO. But the United States remains hostile to any European military operations without U.S. consent, and it has done little to establish the combined joint task forces (which the French would like to be independent of U.S. command, and the United States would like to keep under its control). The test of wills and goals will continue within NATO. At least, the theological battle over NATO's versus WEU's supremacy is over. The Yugoslav experience has had a great deal to do with it. The French have applied a familiar lesson: "if you can't beat them, join them," so as to influence them from inside. Whether NATO can be reshaped remains to be seen. In 1966 de Gaulle had concluded that it could not. History seems to run in circles.

The major part of the NATO story is much messier. It could be called: What to do with NATO after the Cold War? On the one hand, it remains difficult to find a specific military mission for NATO, except for an eventual return to its Cold War mission of deterrence and defense should Russia turn aggressive again. This residual but important role justifies the continuing presence of 100,000 Americans in Europe and the preservation of the nuclear doctrine as revised (over French objections) in Berlin in 1991. But what is to be done if Russia becomes cooperative, or more likely, incapable of mounting a real threat because of military decay and domestic turbulence? It is hard, especially after the Yugoslav experience, to imagine NATO's military involvement in civil wars in Eastern Europe. The U.S. preventive deployment of a small military contingent in the "former Yugoslav state of Macedonia" may commit NATO to defend it against a Serb invasion (although not a Greek attack!), but other inter-state disputes in that part of the world are either being defused by the Organization for Cooperation and Security in Europe (OSCE) and the network of security treaties sponsored by France, or unlikely to trigger NATO military operations.

What this means is that the main NATO roles, more or less disguised in the jargon (what the French call *langue de bois*) of NATO communiqués, such as the Joint Action Plan of December 3, 1995, are both a traditional role of *encadrement* (containment would be excessive and unfair) of Germany, willingly accepted by Bonn, and important for reassuring Germany's neighbors West and East, and a new role of *reassurance* of the former Soviet satellites of Eastern Europe.[3] But in this respect, the United States has found itself in a delicate position. The countries of Eastern Europe, and particularly the so-called Visegrad states of Poland, Hungary, the Czech Republic, and probably Slovakia, which were left at the EU's door for a variety of economic reasons, have pressed their case for membership in NATO, the one remaining way of obtaining integration in the Western network (as well as a vital security guarantee should Russia try to regain its lost Empire). But such integration via NATO would seriously compromise U.S.-Russian relations (this is discussed at length in Chapter 7) and create an equally delicate problem of relations with Ukraine and the Baltic states. Including them would be unacceptable to Moscow, excluding them would look like leaving them, who are the most likely to be in danger, at the mercy of the Russian bear.

The Clinton administration tried to find a middle course between the Charybdis of immobility—bad for an Alliance that had lost its main mission, and for an Eastern Europe in quest of integration in the West— and the Scylla of recreating a kind of iron curtain, this time between the former Soviet Empire and Russia. And this at a time, as had been the case ever since the last year of the Bush administration, when cooperation with a reforming Russia for arms reduction and nuclear safety, as well as help to Russia for democratization and economic liberalization, were major goals of U.S. foreign policy. The middle course was the Partnership for Peace (PFP), devised by Secretary of Defense Aspin at the end of 1993, and approved by the NATO Brussels Summit in January 1994.[4] It followed the pattern set by the North Atlantic Cooperation Council (NACC), established in December 1991: it was open to East Europeans and to former members of the U.S.S.R. But the NACC, partly because of the "explosion in the number of participants," lacked a clear focus. The PFP was supposed to link NATO to candidate states through bilateral agreements, "outlining particular areas and levels of defense cooperation for an explicit period." Like many compromises, it was met with dismay by both East European leaders (especially Lech Walesa), who thought that this was another half-way house in which they were being lumped with their former oppressors, and by Russian officials, who saw in PFP a form of creeping NATO expansion. And yet Yeltsin was finally persuaded to sign on, and more than 20 states have done so and thereby accepted a variety of commitments concerning military transparency, operational compatibility for joint actions, the democratization of their armed forces, and joint exercises and planning with NATO.

No sooner had the West European partners of the United States become persuaded of the merits of this initiative (not without some French grumbling over the fact that the Partnership Planning Cell was established close to Supreme Headquarters, Allied Powers in Europe (SHAPE) headquarters rather than under the NACC's jurisdiction), than they learned of an abrupt change in the United States's course. At the end of 1994, for reasons that remain somewhat obscure, the United States made it clear that it now favored NATO expansion, that is, the inclusion of states from Eastern and Central Europe into the Alliance itself. There seems to have been little warning given such allies as the United Kingdom, France, and, Germany, and little discussion within the administration itself, which was far from united, although Strobe Talbott, the deputy secretary of state and the chief advocate of good relations with Russia, did his best to defend the new course. The public reasons given for it were extremely vague. The spokespersons for the administration talked about the need for a broader security structure in Europe, "the benefits of common defense and greater integration into Europe and Euro-Atlantic institutions," "help to protect the further democratic development of new members," the objective of an undivided Europe, and so forth.[5] It was said repeatedly that Russia had no reason to feel threatened, and it was hinted that NATO forces would not be deployed in the new member countries (although the NATO enlargement study of September 1995 declared that "it is important for NATO's force structure that Allies' forces can be deployed, when and if appropriate, on the territory of new members").[6]

For an administration whose president had emphasized the need for not introducing a new division between Europe and the former Soviet Union, the change was startling, especially as support for Yeltsin and reform remained vital goals. Moreover, even though the new Republican majority in Congress was in favor of NATO enlargement (largely because of its distrust of Russia) there was no serious discussion of the implications of enlargement, that is, the extension of the U.S. security guarantee to the new members (at a time when Congress was reluctant even to endorse U.S. participation in IFOR), and the possibility of NATO becoming embroiled in disputes among the new members (at a time of renewed tensions between Greeks and Turks).

When questioned, off the record, about the shift in policy, officials mentioned the strong pressure for admission from Poland in particular, and also from Hungary and the Czech Republic. That it is in the interest of these states to join is obvious; that their interest and the United States's coincide—given the potential damage to Russian-U.S. relations, and the contribution of NATO expansion to the sense of humiliation and defeat that Russian nationalists and Communists are busy exploiting—is not obvious at all. Should there be a new Russian threat, NATO could always extend its protection eastward, and plan accordingly, through PFP. (After all, the United States has not gone to its wars in this century because of formal treaty obligations.) Should NATO forces be deployed in the East, a major crisis in relations with Moscow would be inevitable, under any Russian regime. Should they not be deployed there, why would not PFP suffice? That NATO expansion was endorsed by the leading old Cold War warriors was to be expected, but shouldn't one beware of self-fulfilling prophecies?

It seems that what had happened was the seizure of the policy ball by the aggressive and ambitious new Assistant Secretary of State for European Affairs, Richard Holbrooke, who had been appointed in the middle of 1994. He had been ambassador in Germany and was able to enlist what I would call the NATO brigade—the enthusiasts of NATO as the Holy Arch of U.S. policy, in the State Department in particular. In a fragmented administration, the most resolute player often prevails. I suspect that a major part of the drive was provided by the sense that the West Europeans had doubly missed their chance: in Yugoslavia, and in not admitting the former Soviet satellites into the EU. It was now the United States's turn to act, and to expand into Central and Eastern Europe the links that, through NATO, had provided for a U.S. supremacy that its champions considered to be beneficial to all and irreplaceable.

The strong and hostile Russian reactions, and the increasingly skeptical reactions in the West European capitals, including Bonn, where Chancellor Kohl is especially eager to preserve good relations with Yeltsin, as well as the divided response in the policy community in Washington itself have resulted in a semi-retreat.[7] The enlargement study of October 1995, the "new transatlantic agenda," and the ministerial meeting of the North Atlantic Council in December 1995, have made it clear that the enlargement process will be slow, gradual, and begin as a protracted mutual learning process. What the NATO-Russia security relationship will be, what states will be admitted to NATO, and which ones will be left out, all this—which is essential—remains to be figured out. Much will obviously depend on events in Russia. At this point, the shift from PFP to enlargement seems like much ado about very little, except in so far as it has had a negative effect on relations with Moscow and raised excessive hopes in Warsaw and other East and Central European capitals. Precipitation without adequate forethought looks remarkably like improvisation, in an area of crucial importance where long-range designs and thinking ought to be essential.

The Yugoslav War

Improvisation was also one of the marks of U.S. policy in Yugoslavia.[8] The Bush administration, having argued for a long time about the need for the Yugoslav Federation to be preserved, decided to let the eager West Europeans deal with the drama, and did not recognize Croatia and Slovenia before April 1992, several months after the EU. Bosnia was recognized at the same time (along with the Europeans' recognition of its independence). In two respects, it set a pattern for what was to come under Clinton. On the one hand, there was irritation at what was perceived as European pusillanimity, resulting both from "rigid adherence" to the rule of unanimity over foreign policy in the EU, and from the divisions caused by conflicting sympathies and memories, for instance between Britain and France on one side, and Germany on the other.[9] At Lisbon in May 1992, James Baker denounced "European indifference, even inaction" in the face of the horrors of Bosnia, thereby, he suggests, triggering the economic embargo on Serbia imposed by the Security Council the following week.[10] Baker does not mention it, but it appears that he did not give his support to the EU's Cutileiro plan of March 1992 for a division of Bosnia into three constituent nations and for its regional cantonization along ethnic lines—a plan that was rejected (after an initial acceptance) by the Bosnian Moslems and also by the representative of the Croats of Bosnia. On the other hand, while criticizing European efforts for their meekness or excessive concessions to Serbia, the Bush administration also decided that there was no U.S. interest there that justified the use of force. A "game plan" submitted by Baker's aides in June 1992, at a time when humanitarian relief could not reach Sarajevo, recommended a collective use of force to make its delivery possible under UN authority. Baker supported it; Secretary of Defense Cheney and Colin Powell opposed it; a strong UN resolution made it unnecessary at that moment; and Baker's successor, as well as Bush, never raised the issue of force again. (Indeed, in September 1992 Colin Powell objected to the establishment of a no-fly zone over Bosnia.)

This prompted candidate Clinton, on July 26, 1992, to criticize his opponent, to ask for a tighter embargo against Serbia, and to call for a UN authorization of air strikes to protect relief efforts to be conducted with U.S. military support. When he came to power, the main immediate issue was not military action, but whether the United States would support the Vance-Owen Peace plan that provided for a ten-province structure in a decentralized Bosnia and a partial retreat of Bosnian Serb forces, who opposed the plan. The Croats accepted it; the Bosnian Moslems hesitated because of problems they had with the map. In its final days, the Bush administration had appeared divided: James Baker's successor, Secretary of State Eagleburger, favored the plan, but without the backing of the State Department. In the weeks that followed the inauguration of Clinton, David Owen was going to be surprised and angered by the lack of support provided by his partner Vance's former right-hand man, Warren Christopher, the new secretary of state, whom Owen found poorly informed.[11] Clearly, the new administration was also divided. Those who opposed the plan, like Colin Powell and many State Department officials, did so on very different grounds: either because they thought that the United States should not get involved in risky operations to enforce it, or because they thought that the Owen-Vance map ratified too much Serb ethnic cleansing. A statement by

Christopher on February 10, 1993 offered U.S. support and participation in the negotiations that were still going on, reaffirmed the U.S. refusal to help *impose* a solution, but promised U.S. participation in *enforcing* an agreement accepted by the parties.

In the weeks that followed, it became clear that the administration had second thoughts about the plan, and in April Christopher presented a list of conditions for U.S. participation in enforcement that were very close to the famous Weinberger-Powell conditions. "None of these conditions was likely to be met in the early stages of implementation."[12] The administration, under pressure from the Joint Chiefs, then moved to its own preferred policy: a lifting of the arms embargo on Bosnia and limited air strikes only in support of humanitarian operations. This meant not only giving up the Vance-Owen plan, but also proposing nothing to replace it. It also meant incurring the wrath of the European allies whose troops served in UNPROFOR, since air strikes would expose UNPROFOR to Serb retaliation, and a lifting of the embargo might lead to an escalating arms race. Indeed, when Christopher went to Europe to recommend this policy, he was badly received, and the administration quickly backed away from it. "The President had developed cold feet in mid-consultation."[13] He was determined that no U.S. ground troops should be sent to Bosnia while the war was going on, despite European requests for U.S. contingents in UNPROFOR. He did not want to get involved in the enforcement of a plan that the parties had trouble accepting. And he was worried by the escalatory implications of lift and strike. Thus, the United States moved (and stuck for two years) to what Owen calls a policy of containment, which entailed sending forces preventively to Macedonia, but letting ethnic cleansing and Serb advances continue in Bosnia except in designated "safe areas" and, in effect (and in agreement with Russia) shelving the Vance-Owen plan. The Europeans resented the lack of U.S. support for Vance-Owen, the Americans resented the European negative reaction to lift and strike. The Vance-Owen plan died when a referendum called by the Bosnian Serbian Assembly decisively rejected it. This made it possible for the Security Council to call on NATO not only (as in an earlier resolution of March 31) to enforce the no-fly ban, but also to provide air support for UNPROFOR and to threaten and carry out air strikes to protect "safe areas."

This scenario of vacillation and ultimate immobility in a climate of mutual recriminations led to the resignation of several State Department officials who were anguished by Bosnia's plight. Nevertheless, it was repeated a few months later when the Vance-Owen plan was replaced by an Owen-Stoltenberg plan that conceded more ground to the Bosnian Serbs and proposed a "union of three Republics." Once again, the United States provided little support, because of dissatisfaction with the territorial concessions the plan imposed on the Moslems. Clinton's 1993 UN speech listed "stiff terms for sending U.S. troops to

Bosnia" for help in eventual implementation, NATO discussions focused not on the mission it would have but on an "exit strategy," and the Bosnian Moslem government rejected the plan.[14] Later, a new plan presented by Foreign Ministers Juppé and Kinkel received a cool reception in Washington because it suggested linking a lifting of sanctions against Serbia to progress toward peace, that is, to a willingness by Milosevic to force the Bosnian Serbs to retreat. The EU action plan (which conceded 49 percent of Bosnia to the Serbs, 17.5 percent to the Croats, and 33.5 percent to the Moslems) had the same fate as the previous ones, because of the lack of U.S. support and willingness to offer "a NATO guarantee for the boundaries of the Muslim Republic."[15] Paradoxically, U.S. dismay with European "realism," and sympathy for the cause of the Moslems, only resulted in prolonging the agony, given Washington's opposition to the use of force to oblige all parties to accept a settlement, and in prolonging the plight of UNPROFOR, whose mandate did not include the use of force except in self-defense, and whose ability to carry out its humanitarian mission was at the mercy of the Serbs.

After the shelling of the Sarajevo market on February 5, 1994, NATO finally got into action, by threatening air strikes—not, as Juppé would have wished, in order that the blockade of Sarajevo be lifted—but so that Serb heavy weapons be moved farther from the city. Under Russian pressure, the Serbs complied. And the United States began to get a little more involved, obliquely. Clinton did not object when Moslem countries, including militant Iran, shipped weapons to Bosnia through Croatia. Congress moved toward lifting the arms embargo on Bosnia (the Senate voted for it in May 1994, the House in June), but this would have led to a withdrawal of UNPROFOR, which the U.S. government did not desire, because it feared that it would then be under pressure to help the Bosnians with air strikes that could either fail or escalate. The United States decided instead to become more engaged in the search for a settlement: it sent a member to the new five-power Contact Group, and promoted the formation of a Croat-Bosnian federation and a Confederation between it and Croatia. Clinton announced this in Washington on March 18, 1994. In July, the Contact Group proposed its own plan, very close to the previous European one: a 49.51 percent division of Bosnia between a Serb entity and a Croat-Moslem one. Jimmy Carter went to Sarajevo and Pale even though the Serbs had not accepted the new plan. He obtained a temporary ceasefire but made no progress toward a settlement. Serb acquiescence seemed to depend on a lifting of the sanctions. The Europeans were willing and so was the U.S. negotiator sent to Belgrade, Robert Frasure. But Washington torpedoed the deal he negotiated by insisting on the right to reimpose sanctions.

Following this fiasco, the crisis of UNPROFOR became acute. Limited NATO air strikes led the Serbs to capture hundreds of UNPROFOR soldiers and later to invade and "cleanse" with utmost ferocity several "safe areas" that UNPROFOR was powerless to defend, even though numerous UN resolutions had called for their protection. NATO chose not to defend them, except through token raids, because of the risks to UNPROFOR. The United States now faced a dilemma. UNPROFOR's main forces, the British and French components, were threatening to leave if the war continued. President Clinton rashly promised to send U.S. troops to help extricate UNPROFOR if necessary (after having denounced Senator Dole's advocacy of lift and strike, which had once been the Clinton administration's own policy, as bellicose). This would have meant intervening in a war, if only to get disengaged from it.

The alternative was a determined push toward peace, followed by enforcement of an agreement by a force in which the United States, as promised long before, would participate. This time, Clinton moved quickly and decisively (in circumstances not so dissimilar from his intervention in Haiti, which resulted less from a deliberate choice than from the resounding fiasco of the earlier policy aimed at pressuring the military rulers out of power. In both cases, Clinton backed into a success). The credibility of NATO was now at stake, and intervention for extrication of UNPROFOR would have been both a humiliation for NATO (and the UN) and a guarantee of casualties, which, after the Somalia fiasco of October 1993, would have been massively unpopular in Congress and the country. Re-election was only a little over a year away. Success in recapturing Western Slavonia in early May 1995 encouraged Croatia into reconquering the Krajina, and in forcing the Serbs to retreat from parts of Western Bosnia (thus reducing them to 49 percent of that country's land) in early August 1995; the United States looked the other way, but only after having provided arms and advice for the operation; the United States also said little about the ethnic cleansing that resulted from it. The main target was the Bosnian Serb leadership, intransigent until then; it had been clear for a long time that Milosevic was willing to strike a deal along the Contact Group's lines, if he obtained a lifting of the sanctions in exchange. The Bosnian-Serbs received a second blow: after another murderous shelling of Sarajevo on August 28, NATO unleashed a violent campaign of air strikes, made possible by the evacuation of vulnerable enclaves by UNPROFOR, and the absence of UNPROFOR "hostages" in Serb-held parts of Bosnia. After a diplomatic blitz, first in Geneva, then in the region, Assistant Secretary Holbrooke achieved a ceasefire in early October. In Dayton he brokered a settlement that resembled the Contact Group's plan, providing for lifting of the sanctions and the sending of IFOR (including approximately 20,000 Americans) to implement the military provisions of the agreement.

It was necessary to tell this story to extract from it the main points about the United States's policy. First, one of its dominant motifs seemed to have been *both* a reluctance to exert strong leadership to override European objections to any policy that abandoned a (de facto pro-Serb) "impartiality"—not so much to preserve unity among NATO members as out of hesitation at moving toward a use of force with unpredictable effects—*and* a reluctance to support European efforts toward a settlement, judged to be morally flawed, despite the initial decision to leave this conflict to them. It was as if there was a need to demonstrate that the Europeans could not succeed without U.S. help (which was true) and that the only plan the U.S. would accept to risk American lives for was an American one (albeit one borrowed from European drafts). This was a strange combination of moralism and rather devious power politics (tougher on the allies than on the guilty parties in Bosnia), in which power politics ultimately prevailed. On the one hand, the Dayton negotiations reduced the Europeans to the role of observers (the French, of course, grumbled loudly about this, given their role and casualties in UNPROFOR and the absence of Americans on the ground). On the other hand, the Dayton plan ratifies a good deal of ethnic cleansing. It leaves the Bosnian Republic's future unclear and reduces its "integrity" to the dubious co-existence of a Serb Republic that has not given up secession, and a Croat-Moslem Confederation that is extremely fragile. Its provisions concerning the return of refugees as well as the arrest and punishment of indicted war criminals are weak, and the mission of IFOR seems, to paraphrase Michael Mandelbaum's words, above all focused on a quick exit and, in the meantime, on the prevention at all costs of any "mission creep."[16]

This minimalism of the United States's commitment, for all its ultimate decisiveness, resulted less from the lack of domestic support for U.S. involvement (such a lack did not prevent intervention in Haiti at the end, and support could have been mobilized by a determined and forceful presidential effort), than from a constant fluctuation between the belief that this was a civil war resulting from ancient hatreds among savage tribes, as Christopher once suggested, and the conviction that it was a deliberate campaign of aggression carried out with ruthless methods by Serbia (and to a smaller extent Croatia) at the expense of the multi-ethnic society of Bosnia. There was also, accordingly, a fluctuation between the belief that no important U.S. interest was at stake in Bosnia itself (hence "containment" was the best policy) and the conviction, expressed twice by Clinton, after the two murderous shellings of Sarajevo, that there was a national interest in bringing that conflict to an end, both because of the strategic implications of any Balkan war, and because of the precedent which the atrocities perpetrated in this war created for other would-be ethnic cleansers. Some members of the administration were always clearly on one side or the other—UN Ambassador Albright on the side of involvement, the Secretaries of Defense on the other. The president's chief advisors and the president himself, who seemed engaged only at certain moments, vacillated until they had their backs against the wall, and called on Holbrooke, who had quite unreluctantly let it be known that he was disenchanted with past policy, to rescue them.

The saddest aspect of this is not the legacy of mutual exasperation between the United States and its European allies. It is the fact that a firm U.S. commitment to any of the successive plans—to diplomatic support and pressure on the parties, to air strikes against the party that rejected the plan, and to participation in enforcing it—could have brought the war to an end sooner, and in conditions less tragic for the Bosnian Moslems. It is also possible that a limited U.S. military intervention in the early stages of the Yugoslav conflict, during the Bush administration—when the Serbs shelled Dubrovnik, and a few months later when they besieged Sarajevo—might have had a sobering effect on Milosevic, a man who knows both how to exploit the weakness of others, and where to stop when the going gets rough. Also, the longer the United States waited, the greater the Russian resistance to pressure on Serbia grew. And the more discredited the United Nations became (because, in part, of its own flaws, but even more so because of the lack of leadership by the main powers, and their quarrels and tendency to vote for resolutions they had no intention of enforcing) the more the Clinton administration undermined its own brave initial policy of multilateral action and contributed to a national mood of withdrawal that was so evident in the congressional debate on sending U.S. troops to IFOR. It is a pity that the brilliant tactics of the summer and fall of 1995 could not have fitted into a much earlier and coherent strategy.

At this point, the only judgment one can reach about the Clinton administration's European policy is that it is marked by a constant tension between a desire to preserve as much of the United States's primacy as possible under the new international and domestic circumstances, and a conspicuous strategic vacuum insofar as policy is concerned. The former is ultimately impossible to preserve in the absence of well thought out policies; a continuation of oscillations and discordances can only endanger both U.S. leadership (if only by further undermining domestic support) and U.S.-European relations, by fostering doubts in London, Paris, and Bonn about the seriousness of this administration.

Endnotes

1. *See* Philip Zelikow and Condoleezza Rice, *Germany United and Europe Transformed* (Cambridge: Harvard University Press, 1995).
2. James A. Baker III, *The Politics of Diplomacy* (New York: Putnam, 1995), pp. 636–637.
3. *See The New Transatlantic Agenda: Joint US-EUActions Plan* (Washington, DC: State Department Bureau of Public Affairs, Dec 1995).
4. *See* Catherine McArdle Kelleher, *The Future of European Security* (Washington, DC: Brookings Institution, 1996), especially pp. 98ff.
5. *Study on NATO Enlargement*, September 1995.

6. Ibid., p. 3.
7. *See* Michael Mandelbaum, "Preserving the New Peace," *Foreign Affairs*, Vol. 74, No. 3, pp. 9–13, May–June, 1995.
8. For a study of the Europeans' fiasco in Yugoslavia, *see* my essay in Richard Ullman (ed.), The World and Yugoslavia's Wars, Council on Foreign Relations, forthcoming.
9. Baker, *op. cit.*, p. 644.
10. Ibid., p. 647.
11. David Owen, *Balkan Odyssey* (New York: Harcourt Brace, 1996), pp. 100ff.
12. Ibid., p. 146.
13. Ibid., p. 162.
14. Ibid., p. 220.
15. Ibid., p. 254.
16. *See* Michael Mandelbaum, "Foreign policy as social work," *Foreign Affairs*, Vol. 75, No. 1 (January–February 1996): pp. 16–32.

Chapter 9

The "Inverse" Relationship: The United States and Japan at the End of the Century

Steven K. Vogel

The U.S. and Japanese positions within the world economy have fundamentally shifted during the postwar period, and yet the U.S.-Japan relationship remains relatively unchanged. In 1950 the U.S. economy was 26 times greater than the Japanese economy, but by 1994 it was only 1.4 times as large.[1] The United States has been transformed from the world's largest creditor to its number one debtor, while Japan has emerged as the world's top lender. The United States now runs colossal trade deficits, while Japan runs huge surpluses.[2] The United States, once the world's dominant technological leader, has moved to second place behind Japan in many sectors.[3] Although the United States still boasts the world's largest economy, the economic balance of power between the two countries has shifted from total U.S. dominance to near parity.[4]

The United States and Japan at the end of the century find themselves in inverse positions: they both confront an imbalance between international responsibilities and economic capabilities, but their respective imbalances point in opposite directions. The United States continues to play a hegemonic role in the face of relative economic decline, while Japan plays a modest role despite its economic rise.[5] In the

Steven K. Vogel is an assistant professor of government at Harvard University, specializing in Japanese politics and comparative and international political economy. He has recently completed a book entitled Freer Markets, More Rules: Regulatory Reform in the Advanced Industrial Countries *(Cornell University Press, 1996). He has also published articles and monographs on Japanese security issues, and co-authored (with six others)* The Highest Stakes: The Economic Foundations of the Next Security System *(Oxford University Press, 1992).*

The author would like to thank the Institute for Global Conflict and Cooperation (IGCC) for valuable research support; Tami Bainbridge, Alexis Martinez, and Amy Stanley for excellent research assistance; and Ted Alden, Robert Lieber, Robert Paarlberg, Richard Steinberg, and Susan Sherrerd for insightful comments on an earlier draft.

economic sphere, the United States remains the world's most consistent champion of free trade despite huge trade deficits that one would expect would push it further toward protectionism.[6] And Japan maintains a legacy of industrial protection and promotion despite huge trade surpluses that one would expect would push it more decisively toward free trade. In the security sphere, the United States continues to bear the burden of leading collective security efforts despite increasing political and economic constraints on its ability to do so. And Japan still prohibits its own armed forces from participating in these missions despite a substantial capacity to contribute.[7] While the relationship between the two countries has gradually evolved toward one of greater equality, it has not changed nearly as much as the underlying shift in economic power would lead one to expect.[8]

Thus the United States and Japan confront an increasing tension between the ideas and institutions that have shaped their respective economic and security policies throughout most of the postwar era, on one hand, and their changing positions within the international economy, on the other. I do not contend that this situation is necessarily unnatural or undesirable, or that the United States should do less and Japan should do more. I leave this for others to debate.[9] Rather, in this chapter, I merely suggest that the nature of this tension goes a long way toward explaining the peculiarities of the two countries' respective trade and security policies—peculiarities that cannot be explained by the reigning paradigms of neorealism or pluralism. And the interaction of these two sets of policies, in turn, defines the singular U.S.-Japan relationship.

The Economic Dimension

In the case of trade policy, for example, American leaders have remained committed to the ideology of free trade throughout the postwar period. And this ideology has been embedded in the institutions of American trade policy formulation: a strong American president with the ability to make trade agreements that Congress can approve or reject but not amend ("fast-track" authority), an office of the U.S. Trade Representative (USTR) with considerable leeway to negotiate on trade matters, executive branch agencies such as the Council on Economic Advisors dominated by free trade economists, and two major parties which have generally avoided a bipartisan split over trade policy such as that which characterized much of the prewar period.[10] Yet American workers and industry have demanded relief as trade deficits have soared, and their voices have only become more pronounced as the end of the Cold War has shifted attention toward economic problems. The tension between these two forces—the ideology of free trade, on the one hand, and the mounting interests against it, on the other—helps to explain the U.S. government's distinctive approach to its trading relationship with Japan. As Judith Goldstein has demonstrated, the U.S. government has strongly supported a liberal international trade regime despite its own relative economic decline and a deteriorating balance of trade. In the face of increasing pressure from domestic interests suffering from import competition, the U.S. government has opened markets, not closed them. From a neorealist perspective, one would expect the United States to withdraw from its role as the champion of free trade in the face of relative economic decline. And from a pluralist perspective, one would expect the U.S. government to respond more actively to powerful interest groups demanding protection.[11] In this light, therefore, the mystery is not why the United States has occasionally sought to protect its industries, but why it has remained fundamentally committed to free trade despite a shift in global economic power and powerful domestic pressures for protection.

The combination of a deep-seated free trade ideology with powerful pressure for protection has produced a distinct pattern in U.S. policy toward Japan during recent years. First, the U.S. government has focused much more on opening the Japanese market than on protecting the American market. Pushed to "do something" about the trade deficit, successive administrations have focused on those measures that could be seen as consistent with a liberal trade regime, namely measures to liberalize the Japanese market. In fact, American officials have only pushed the Japanese so fervently because they felt they needed Japanese concessions to preserve a fragile coalition in favor of free trade at home.[12] Meanwhile, the government has generally bypassed more interventionist policies such as import restrictions, industrial promotion, or trade adjustment assistance, even though these measures might address the damage to U.S. interests more directly.[13] Second, the U.S. government has made its case to Japan in a strongly ideological and even moralistic tone. American leaders have accused the Japanese not simply of pursuing their own narrow interests but of violating international norms of fair play. They have readily threatened to punish the Japanese for these transgressions, yet they have been reluctant to carry through with their threats. Thus they have "spoken loudly, and carried a small stick." Third, even when American officials have resorted to protection, retaliation, or managed trade, they have been riddled with internal divisions and self-doubts about the merits of these measures. As a result, they have introduced these measures in an ambivalent and tentative manner, failing to articulate a clear rationale for their action. And fourth, the tension between liberal ideology and protectionist politics has played itself out in the arena of domestic politics through role playing among the primary political actors. The president has typically served as the defender of liberalism, while Congress has provided a forum for the voices for protection. Likewise, the Departments of State and Defense have served as guardians of the overall relationship with Japan, whereas the Departments of Commerce and

Agriculture have been more likely to defend the narrower interests of American business.

This contrasts sharply with the Europeans' approach to their trade conflicts with Japan. European countries have been more likely than the United States to adopt pragmatic protectionist measures, industrial policy, or trade adjustment solutions; less likely to engage in rhetorical denunciations of Japanese practices; less likely to push Japan for broad structural changes; and more likely to lobby Japan for specific concessions to improve access for particular European firms or industries.

Japan, as noted above, finds itself in precisely the inverse situation to that of the United States. The postwar tradition of industrial protection and promotion remains firmly embedded in Japanese ideology and institutions despite Japan's increasing stake in the free trade regime.[14] The Ministry of International Trade and Industry (MITI) fuses the functions of industrial sponsor and trade negotiator; the central economic ministries and industry are directly linked through a dense network of relationships; most politicians have won office with a commitment to protect producers and/or workers; and the prime minister rarely even attempts to override the narrower interests of the ministries or of industry. Thus while Japanese exporters recognize their reliance on a liberal trade regime, they have not been able to shift the basic orientation of policy at home. Both government officials and many industry executives remain wedded to a set of institutions that served them well in the era of rapid economic growth but which may no longer be appropriate to Japan's needs.[15]

As in the U.S. case, this combination of embedded ideology and institutions with shifting interests begets a particular pattern of behavior. Japanese officials' instinctive response to the surplus with the United States has been to curtail exports or to promote direct investment rather than to open up the domestic market. That is, they have favored those measures that conflict least with their instinct to protect and promote Japanese industry and to minimize disruptive adjustments at home. Likewise, they have liberalized in form more readily than in substance. They have endorsed the rhetoric of free trade and removed the most overt trade barriers, such as tariffs and quotas, while leaving structural impediments in place. This combination of liberalism at one level combined with residual protectionism at a deeper level has worked in Japan's favor in trade negotiations. Japanese officials have been able to argue that they practice free trade, while still allowing industry some residual protection from imports.

These two patterns of behavior, the American and the Japanese, have combined to aggravate friction and impede real change. American ideological appeals have not resonated with Japanese domestic groups, and have only served to irritate Japanese leaders and sour Japanese public attitudes toward the United States. Meanwhile, the U.S. government's internal divisions and its reluctance to carry through with threats have undermined its credibility. Likewise, the Japanese tendency to advocate free trade in principle but not in practice has enraged U.S. officials and the informed American public. And the Japanese government's reluctance to liberalize without outside pressure has prevented it from getting full credit for those concessions that it has made.[16] Over time, the increasing acrimony has made it harder to achieve results, for leaders on both sides must make sure not to appear to their domestic constituents as if they are giving in.

In the Cold War period, however, the security alliance kept this invidious pattern of interaction from going too far. As Robert Lieber notes in the introduction to this volume, the common military threat provided the United States and its allies with a powerful incentive to prevent trade conflicts from undermining cooperative security relationships. With this factor gone, the United States and Japan are now more willing to push their trade relationship to the brink. Domestically, they face more daunting political constraints on their ability to cooperate on trade issues. In the United States, as Lieber puts it, the "Madisonian" features of the political system have reasserted themselves. Divisions between the executive and Congress, between the two parties, and within the administration have become more pronounced. This situation was then exacerbated in 1992 with the election of a Democratic president who was more likely to be responsive to labor and industry interests demanding protection. In Japan, even more dramatically, 38 years of Liberal Democratic Party (LDP) one-party rule abruptly came to an end in 1993, leaving a period of severe instability in which political leaders were more focused on surviving the political transition than on policy leadership. In the short term, this left policy in the hands of intransigent bureaucrats, who saw little reason to appease the United States. Meanwhile, both countries have faced substantial economic constraints as well. In the United States, a huge federal budget deficit powerfully constrained spending increases, and continuing bilateral trade deficits hardened the U.S. stance toward Japan. And in Japan, a prolonged recession beginning in 1990 made Japanese industry far less willing to accede to U.S. demands.

In the Reagan-Bush era, the Republican president acted both as champion of free-trade principles and guarantor of the overall relationship with Japan, while the Democratic Congress voiced the frustrations of those displaced or injured by trade competition. Members of Congress lambasted Japan with fiery rhetoric and threats, while the president confidently pledged to veto any protectionist measures that actually made it through both houses. The president could then use Congressional furor as a threat with the Japanese, portraying himself as "good cop" to Congress' "bad cop." Open your markets, he would plead, so I do not have to unleash these crazy Congress members. Over time, however, this dynamic undermined the U.S. government's credibility, as it rarely carried through with the Congressional threats. Even as the Cold War ended, President Bush continued to contain Congressional pressures for the sake of preserving free trade and maintaining the overall security relationship with Japan. Bush only diverted from this pattern early in the election year of 1992, when he led a group of auto executives on an ill-fated tour to Japan. He thus undercut his own free trade image, appearing more as a representative of the U.S. auto industry than as a chief executive with an independent agenda.

With the inauguration of a Democratic president in 1993, the dynamics of American trade politics shifted. As a Democrat, Bill Clinton had to be more sensitive to those groups demanding protection, particularly labor unions. As a candidate, he had vowed to defend working Americans and had offered only a qualified endorsement of the North American Free Trade Agreement (NAFTA). Under Clinton, however, the Democratic Congress had less incentive to launch irresponsible rhetorical attacks on Japan and more incentive to cooperate with the president. Clinton won election on a platform focusing on the domestic economy above all else. With respect to trade policy, he stressed that with the end of the Cold War the United States should pursue its economic interests more vigorously, without holding back so as to placate military allies. Once in office, he institutionalized the new emphasis on the economy by creating a National Economic Council (NEC). This transformed the trade policy process by transferring a major locus of debate from the National Security Council (NSC), where security experts were well represented, to the NEC, where they were not. Moreover, Clinton's new trade policy team—including Mickey Kantor, the U.S. Trade Representative; Robert Rubin, the chair of the NEC; W. Bowman Cutter, Rubin's deputy; and Roger Altman, deputy secretary at Treasury—were convinced that the government had to be willing to press Japan without backing down for diplomatic or security reasons.[17] At the extreme, they were willing to "wager" the relationship to achieve meaningful results in trade talks. They hoped that this added leverage could help them break away from a legacy of many agreements but few results.[18]

Thus the Clinton team was determined to incorporate a mechanism for monitoring results into a new framework for bilateral trade negotiations. The Reagan administration had pursued a sectoral approach under the banner of the Market Oriented Sector Specific (MOSS) talks, and the Bush administration had shifted to a broader structural approach with the Structural Impediments Initiative (SII). Clinton and Prime Minister Kiichi Miyazawa agreed to establish a new framework during their first meeting in April 1993, which they would inaugurate as the U.S.-Japan Framework for a New Economic Partnership in a subsequent meeting in July.

The two sides sparred over two central issues from the start. American negotiators insisted on the use of objective criteria to monitor results, whereas the Japanese refused to commit to specific targets. And the Americans reserved the right to impose unilateral sanctions under U.S. trade law, whereas the Japanese objected to negotiating under the threat of punishment. In pushing for objective criteria, the U.S. team had the model of the 1986 Semiconductor Agreement in mind. Under a side letter to this agreement, the Japanese had agreed to aim for a 20 percent foreign market share. Some on the Japanese side denied that such a side letter even existed, and others claimed that it did not represent a commitment. Yet American negotiators felt that this approach was ultimately successful because it did produce results. The Bush administration then used a similar results-oriented approach in persuading Japanese auto makers in January 1992 to agree "voluntarily" to increase their purchases of foreign parts. While Clinton's advisors were committed to the notion of objective criteria, they were less than clear on what this would actually entail. They wavered in their use of language, alternatively using such terms as "benchmarks," which implied only general goals, and "targets," which implied more specific commitments.[19] And while they claimed that they would not insist that the Japanese commit to meeting these goals, they clearly left themselves the option of retaliating under Section 301 of the 1974 Trade Act if they deemed progress to be insufficient.

Meanwhile, Japanese officials were determined to put an end to "managed trade" solutions to bilateral trade issues. They were particularly wary of the new administration, for they had come to associate Republicans with free trade and Democrats with protectionism.[20] Furthermore, they felt that the Clinton administration's "managed trade" rhetoric gave them an opportunity to take the moral high ground, which they seized with a vengeance. They argued that the Clinton administration's approach of employing numerical targets and requiring the Japanese government to regulate private sector behavior blatantly violated the principles of free market competition. In this way, they quickly gained the support of Japanese exporters, who had been more sympathetic with American demands in the past. MITI directly attacked the Clinton administration approach in its 1993 White Paper, arguing that the trade imbalance was not due to closed markets but to macroeconomic factors.[21]

As the July 1993 Clinton-Miyazawa meeting in Tokyo approached, the U.S. side used political back channels to appeal to the prime minister to agree to the use of "objective criteria." Miyazawa, who already appeared to be a lame-duck prime minister (see below), then shocked the bureaucracy by taking matters into his own hands.[22] He wrote directly to Clinton, stating that Japan would accept an "illustrative set of criteria," although it would not agree to numerical targets. In the subsequent agreement, the two sides agreed to use "objective criteria, either qualitative or quantitative or both as appropriate" to monitor progress. The U.S. negotiators sought to focus on areas where the American industry was competitive and could benefit substantially from further market opening. They selected automobiles and auto parts, government procurement of telecommunications and medical equipment, and insurance. By choosing automobiles, of course, they not only targeted the sector responsible for the largest share of the bilateral deficit, but they also appealed to labor, a critical Democratic constituency.[23]

The Framework Agreement was reached on July 10, just as Japanese domestic politics were unraveling. A group of LDP members who were disgruntled with the party's failure to enact electoral reform had joined the opposition in a vote of no confidence in the government on June 18. This group then split from the party, forming two new parties: the Japan Renewal Party (Shinseito) and the Harbinger Party (Sakigake).[24] While those remaining in the LDP actually fared reasonably well in the July 18 Lower House elections, the defectors managed to join with five other parties to form a coalition government.

While the Japanese lamented the political transition in Washington, the Americans welcomed the revolution in Tokyo. The new prime minister, Morihiro Hosokawa, provided just the message that Washington had been waiting to hear. He pledged to reform Japanese politics, decentralize administration, and deregulate the economy. He would promote the political rights of ordinary citizens and the economic interests of household consumers. He also brought a refreshing new style to Japanese politics, speaking clearly, answering questions directly, and dispensing with some of the formality of Japanese political protocol. All of this led the Japanese media, the U.S. media, and even the U.S. government to expect greater change in politics and policy than Hosokawa could possibly deliver.[25]

While the Ministry of Foreign Affairs (MOFA) had taken the lead in preparing the Framework Agreement, the Ministry of International Trade and Industry (MITI) and the Ministry of Finance (MOF) took charge in the subsequent negotiations. The gap in perspective between MITI and MOFA parallels that in the United States between Commerce and Agriculture, on the one hand, and State and DOD, on the other.[26] That is, MITI tends to pursue the narrower interests of Japanese industry, whereas MOFA is more concerned with the overall relationship. But MITI and MOFA usually keep their differences concealed far better than their counterparts in the United States. In a notable exception to this, a MITI official and a MOFA counterpart were caught in a well-publicized late-night brawl over their differences on trade talks at the Hotel Okura.[27] Having stayed in the background during the initial negotiations, MITI and MOF officials felt less committed to the spirit of the agreement than their MOFA counterparts.

Meanwhile, MITI itself was undergoing a gradual generational shift, with a new group of younger officials rising in power. These officials had risen through the ranks with a growing feeling of frustration and resentment as their elders seemed to make endless concessions to the United States. They felt less obligated to the United States for past debts and they judged that Japan had less reason to defer to the United States in the post–Cold War era.[28] In addition, they recognized that they were in a position of greater strength now that they had dismantled many of the formal barriers to imports. They could make the case that they had already opened their markets, and that any affirmative action for U.S. producers would violate the spirit of free trade.

Thus Japanese officials were prepared to take their case to the court of world public opinion. In talks with European and Asian officials, they stressed that market access deals made with the United States would only serve to crowd out imports from other countries. They also suggested to their Asian counterparts that if the U.S. government succeeded with "managed trade" with Japan, it would then apply the same strategy to other Asian countries as well. And in their encounters with the press, both domestic and foreign, they went out of their way to characterize the U.S. position as extreme and unreasonable. American negotiators were thus put in the position of insisting that they had not demanded numerical targets, when most people within Japan were already convinced that they had. Japanese officials borrowed the language and logic of U.S. free trade economists and then used it against the American government, and a number of these economists backed up the Japanese stance.[29] Meanwhile, U.S. officials were divided on how far to take managed trade. Those trained as economists, such as Lawrence Summers at Treasury and Laura Tyson at the Council on Economic Advisors (and later at the NEC), expressed reservations about taking measures that would undermine the spirit of free trade.[30] Those more sensitive to domestic politics, such as Kantor and Cutter, pushed for a hard line.

As the February 1994 meeting between Clinton and Hosokawa approached, both sides publicly declared that they would not give in this time. The Clinton administration had already pushed the free trade cause in passing NAFTA in November 1993 and signing on to the Uruguay Round of trade talks in December, despite considerable resistance from organized labor. In addition, it faced a tough battle for ratification of the Uruguay Round later in the year.[31] Thus presidential advisors were particularly keen to take a tough stand to demonstrate that they were still prepared to fight for the interests of American industry and American workers.[32] While they recognized the intransigence of the MITI bureaucrats, they hoped that they could get Hosokawa and other political leaders to pull out some concessions. For his part, however, Hosokawa was in no position to back down. He had pledged to pass a political reform bill by the end of 1993, yet the bill failed in the Upper House in late January 1994 when Socialists from his own coalition refused to support it. The bill then only passed after the opposition LDP agreed to support the bill in exchange for substantial revisions in the substance of reform. To make matters worse, the Socialists were threatening to abandon the coalition altogether over a MOF proposal for tax reform which would cut income taxes and raise consumption taxes.

At the summit meeting, Clinton abruptly called an end to trade discussions once he realized that Hosokawa was not prepared to make any major concessions. The administration had decided that it was better, both politically and tactically, to fail to agree than to produce an agreement that would not deliver results. Both leaders recognized that a stalemate would not cause them much political damage at home, and that it was far better to disagree than to appear to have caved in at the last minute. As it was, the stalemate played very well with the public and the press, both in Tokyo and in Washington.

Clinton then reinstated the Super 301 clause of the 1988 Trade Act to increase the pressure on Tokyo. Hosokawa announced his own package of deregulation measures, but refused to respond to the U.S. demands. Japanese politics encountered renewed instability as Hosokawa resigned in the face of a scandal in April 1994, and the non-LDP coalition toppled altogether in July. The Socialists defected from the coalition and joined their former archenemies in the LDP in a new coalition. The U.S. negotiators had initially chosen to give Hosokawa some breathing room to work out his problems at home, but as the upheaval continued they decided to move on irrespective of what was going on in Tokyo.

Throughout the Framework process, U.S. officials simultaneously pursued alternative strategies to lower the trade deficit with Japan. Under the Framework agreement, they had pledged to try to reduce the American budget deficit, and Japanese officials had promised to stimulate domestic demand. In any case, the Japanese had their own reasons to stimulate demand, given the prolonged recession. They lowered interest rates to historic lows, announced successive public works spending programs, and even pushed through a major tax reform that substantially reduced income taxes. Ministry of Finance officials refused to push this fiscal stimulus too far, however, because they did not want to increase the national debt more than was absolutely necessary. In a delicate political compromise, the government decided to cut income taxes but to raise consumption taxes at a later date. The Americans also applauded the Japanese government's campaign for deregulation. While Hosokawa and his successors managed to elevate deregulation to a top priority issue, their successive deregulation packages still failed to break the bureaucratic hold over the economy.[33] And to the extent that deregulation measures succeeded, they did not necessarily benefit U.S. producers.[34] The Americans' most powerful weapon of all, however, was the yen-dollar exchange rate. As the yen appreciated, this augmented the pressure for liberalization and structural reform within Japan. And while the exchange rate adjustment did not reduce the trade imbalance in the short run, it did improve the prospects for U.S. producers to sell their goods and services in Japan.

The two sides finally resumed the Framework talks in May 1994 after a three-month hiatus. With the talks still making little headway in

July, Clinton cited the Japanese government under Title VII of the 1988 Trade Act for discriminating against U.S. communications and medical equipment producers. This then left a 60-day consultation period before the U.S. government would decide on retaliation on September 30, the same day when the government would announce whether it was targeting Japan under Super 301. At the last moment, the two sides managed to reach agreements on communications equipment and services, medical technology, insurance, and flat glass. They failed, however, to agree on automobiles and auto parts, and the U.S. side then cited Japan for investigation under Section 301 of the 1974 Trade Act for regulatory barriers in the market for replacement parts.[35]

The American demands in the automobile sector centered on three major areas: manufacturer-dealer relationships that hindered U.S. firms from developing dealer networks, manufacturer-supplier relationships that closed U.S. parts suppliers out of the new car market, and government inspection regulations that impeded U.S. parts suppliers from gaining in the replacement parts market. The two sides had more difficulty in reaching an agreement in the auto sector because the stakes were higher and their differences in approach were more pronounced. That is, the U.S. negotiators came closest to demanding targets in this sector because they wanted Japanese auto makers to agree to increase their purchases of foreign parts. Moreover, MITI was particularly uncomfortable with U.S. demands because they required that the government issue guidelines to the private sector. And while MITI certainly had extensive experience with such "administrative guidance," ministry officials had staked out a position in which they refused to negotiate changes in private sector behavior because this would violate the spirit of free market competition.[36]

Meanwhile, the Republican landslide in the November 1994 midterm elections did nothing to soften the American stance on U.S.-Japan trade. In fact, outspoken Republicans such as Representative Doug Bereuter of Nebraska argued that the Clinton administration should take an even tougher stand with Japan.[37] By May 1995, the U.S. side saw no prospect of Japanese compromise without increased pressure, and thus threatened sanctions that would take effect on June 28. The government tailored the sanctions to maximize the harm to Japanese interests while minimizing the damage to American interests— something that has become more difficult in an increasingly interdependent world economy.[38] Thus it would impose high tariffs on Japanese luxury autos, an important source of Japanese manufacturers' profits. At home, this would only harm wealthy consumers, who could always buy German luxury autos instead, and the relatively small number of American auto dealers who sold these Japanese luxury cars. Nonetheless, the Japanese government and industry launched a public relations campaign to convince Americans that these sanctions would hurt the United States as much as Japan. The Japanese government then raised the ante in the battle for the high ground by declaring that it would protest U.S. sanctions with an appeal to the new World Trade Organization (WTO). The United States threatened its own appeal, arguing that Japanese government toleration and support of anti-competitive practices in the auto sector "nullifies and impairs" past Japanese commitments to international trade treaties. After protracted negotiations, the two governments worked out a compromise just prior to the implementation of the sanctions. The Japanese government pledged to revise vehicle inspection regulations so as to make it easier for U.S. suppliers to sell replacement parts in Japan and to assist American auto manufacturers in finding Japanese dealers to sell their cars. And Japanese automobile manufacturers announced plans to increase their purchases of foreign parts, especially from their transplant production facilities in North America.[39] Both sides declared victory, with the Japanese claiming that they had avoided the peril of numerical targets and the Americans insisting they had never demanded numerical targets but only objective criteria. With this issue resolved, U.S.-Japan relations entered a quieter period as both countries shifted all the more toward domestic priorities in anticipation of upcoming elections.[40]

The Framework episode nicely illustrates the American and Japanese patterns of behavior outlined above, and how they interact in practice. The U.S. administration found itself under increasing pressure to take action against Japan, but focused on opening the Japanese market rather than opting for protection. American negotiators threatened to adopt "managed trade" and to impose severe retaliatory measures. Yet they made very clumsy protectionists at best. They failed to articulate a clear rationale for their policy, they were riddled with doubts and internal dissent, and they lost the public relations battle despite Japan's dubious credentials as a free trade haven. Meanwhile, the Japanese government found itself in a position where its own exporters were pushing for deregulation and trade liberalization, yet it tried to structure a solution that would limit the damage to domestic industry, placing the greatest burden of adjustment on Japanese production facilities in the United States. Moreover, for once the Japanese found themselves in a situation where they could position themselves as the proponents of free trade rather than the defenders of protectionist practices. And they were far more adept at playing free traders than the Americans were at playing protectionists. They had a ready-made handbook in the form of American economic theory, whereas the Americans were groping into new territory without any paradigm to guide them.[41]

The Security Dimension

In the security arena, the United States and Japan also find themselves in inverse positions. The United States remains the preeminent global leader despite increasing economic constraints on its ability to perform this role. Japan, in contrast, retains a supporting role despite its status as the world's number two economic power. From a neorealist perspective, one would expect the two countries to change their behavior more radically with the collapse of the bipolar structure of the international system.[42] From a pluralist perspective, one would expect the U.S. government and the Japanese government to respond more actively to calls from their respective publics for a partial or complete withdrawal of U.S. troops from Japan. But once again, we find that the two countries remain wedded to the ideas and institutions of an earlier period, and thus have not abandoned their traditional postwar roles. American international leadership is reinforced by a strong president with considerable autonomy in the foreign policy arena, a powerful Department of Defense committed to a U.S. military presence abroad, and bipartisan support for U.S.-led intervention given the right conditions.[43] Likewise, Japan's inability to lead in this realm is institutionalized in the form of the peace constitution, codified constraints on military expansion, a weak defense agency, and the legacy of political parties historically opposed to military expansion.[44]

While the end of the Cold War has weakened the American commitment to leadership somewhat, it has not substantially strengthened Japanese resolve to assume a greater leadership role. Thus the United States in recent years has tried to extend its leadership in the face of growing constraints by pushing its allies to share more of the financial and military burden of leadership, and by working more through multilateral organizations such as the United Nations. Meanwhile, Japan has tried to assert itself more diplomatically and to increase its financial contributions to international causes, but has been reluctant to assume the more costly responsibilities of international leadership: stimulating demand and opening its own market, and contributing its own forces to military missions abroad.

In this case, however, the interaction between the two countries' patterns of behavior has been much more benign. They have found it much easier to achieve a mutually agreeable resolution to their respective dilemmas: for Japan can simply help to finance the gap between American goals and capabilities, thus allowing both sides to sustain their positions. In this spirit, Japan has paid an increasing share of the cost of stationing American soldiers on its territory. Likewise, Japan has increased its contribution to development aid, implicitly compensating for American reductions in its own aid programs.[45] This pattern took its most extreme form with the Gulf War, when Japan did not send a single soldier to battle but bankrolled the U.S. effort with a contribution of $13 billion—ironically giving the United States its first quarterly trade surplus in years.[46]

Despite the potential congruence of interests, the security relationship has faced a number of complicating factors in recent years. First, vocal minorities in both countries have threatened to undermine a compromise solution. Many Americans have urged the U.S. government to cut off Japan's free ride and withdraw American troops from

Asia, and Japanese pacifists have argued that Japan should reduce its military and expel American forces. Second, the American government's focus on trade disputes has threatened to destabilize the security relationship. And third, the two sides have faced tough negotiations over some of the substantive issues in the security relationship, including the status of U.S. forces in Japan and military technological cooperation.

In the short run, Japan and the United States responded to the end of the Cold War in very different ways. The Japanese authorities, particularly officials in the Japan Defense Agency (JDA) and MOFA, insisted that the end of the Cold War did not signal any major diminution of the military threat to Japan. They still saw the Russian Republic as a major security threat, especially because they had an outstanding major territorial dispute over the Northern territories (four islands north of Hokkaido). They saw no sign of disarmament in the East Asian region as a whole, and they particularly feared instability on the Korean peninsula.[47] While they refrained from saying so publicly, of course, they were also increasingly wary of Chinese military expansion. Over time, however, many political leaders argued that Japan should slow its own military expansion and MOF bureaucrats seized the opportunity to restrain budget increases.[48]

Meanwhile, the United States responded more quickly with substantial cuts in spending and a thorough reassessment of strategy. With respect to the U.S. military presence in Asia, DOD reports in 1990 and 1992 outlined a plan for a gradual reduction of troop strength through the year 2000. Accordingly, U.S. force levels dropped from 135,000 to 100,000 by 1995, although most of the cuts came from the removal of two U.S. bases in the Philippines after the Philippine government refused to renew the bases' charter. Other Asian leaders generally supported the U.S. military presence in Asia as a stabilizing force in the region and an effective counterpoint to the rising power of Japan and China. With respect to Japan, of course, U.S. forces not only protect Japan, but also serve to contain Japanese military expansion.[49]

As the Clinton administration came to power in 1993, the focus on economic policy threatened to detract from maintenance of a sound security relationship. In fact, as noted above, some Clinton administration officials were prepared to "wager" the security relationship to achieve a breakthrough in trade talks. Meanwhile, DOD and State Department officials were not well positioned to quell the passions of such zealous trade negotiators because they were left out of a deliberation process that was now centered in the NEC. While the president and top cabinet officials continued to stress the overall relationship in their public statements, trade negotiators were determined not to let security matters constrain their leverage.

In the meantime, Defense officials had become all the more convinced that the U.S. presence in East Asia best served American interests as well as East Asia's security needs. A group of officials within DOD, under the leadership of Assistant Secretary for International Security Joseph Nye, then began a dialogue (later referred to as the "Nye initiative") with Asian allies, particularly Japan, to reaffirm bilateral ties. In its February 1995 report on East Asian security, the Pentagon declared that it would halt force reductions and maintain a presence of 100,000 troops in the Asia-Pacific region (based primarily in Japan, South Korea, and Hawaii) for the foreseeable future. It articulated a three-pronged security strategy based on the U.S. forward-based presence, bilateral alliances, and regional cooperation. The report also recommended that the two sides supplement their primary forum for bilateral security consultations, the Security Subcommittee, with more frequent working-level meetings.[50]

The Nye Initiative meshed well with developments in Japan. When the Socialists joined the LDP in a coalition in July 1994, they agreed to recognize the legitimacy of the Self-Defense Forces (SDF). But the LDP also moved toward a more dovish stance to seal this political marriage of convenience. Given this turn of events plus severe MOF budgetary ceilings, JDA strategists were increasingly pessimistic about Japan's ability to sustain defense spending increases. While Japanese strategists had toyed with visions of a more independent strategy in the 1980s, JDA officials concluded that the only way they could maintain security would be to strengthen the U.S.-Japan alliance and continue to rely on American support.[51] Furthermore, they recognized that a more autonomous defense posture would meet with hostility among many of Japan's Asian neighbors, who remember Japan's militarist past only too well. Meanwhile, in August 1994, a Japanese government advisory council chaired by Hirotaro Higuchi recommended that Japan assume more responsibility for defense but remain firmly committed to the framework of the U.S.-Japan alliance.[52]

Thus the Nye initiative articulated a solution to the problem for both sides that was already emerging, namely that Japan use its financial power to help the United States to extend its role of military leadership beyond the Cold War. Yet the two sides continued to spar over the terms of the settlement. Japan was already bearing almost 70 percent of the cost of maintaining U.S. forces in Japan. In fact, the Defense Department stressed that it would cost more for the U.S. government to maintain these forces in the United States than in Japan.[53] Although the U.S. government pushed Japan to increase this support even further, the Japanese government struggled to come up with fairly modest increases under a new five-year host-nation support pact signed in September 1995.[54] Likewise, the DOD had difficulty in persuading the Japanese government to cooperate more fully on war planning, or to commit to more extensive backup of possible U.S. missions in the region. The U.S. side was particularly anxious to elicit more Japanese support in this area in the face of the North Korean crisis in 1994, but the Japanese side insisted that constitutional and political constraints made it difficult to do much more.

More critically, the Japanese public's support for U.S. troops was seriously eroding. In Okinawa, in particular, where the majority of U.S. troops in Japan are stationed, local politicians increasingly demanded that the troops be cut back or withdrawn. This issue came to a head in September 1995 when three American soldiers were accused of raping a Japanese schoolgirl in Okinawa. The Japanese people were outraged because the U.S. forces refused to surrender the three soldiers to the Japanese authorities until they were formally indicted. The controversy prompted apologies from U.S. Ambassador Walter Mondale and the local American commander, and a quick revision of procedural rules with respect to the treatment of U.S. soldiers suspected of crimes. The incident fueled existing anti-base sentiments, and Governor Masahide Ota demanded that the United States drastically reduce its military presence on the island.

On military technology cooperation, the two sides clashed over the terms of their co-development of the FSX, Japan's new fighter support aircraft. They had agreed on co-development as a compromise in 1987. The United States had pressed Japan to buy an American aircraft off the shelf, whereas Japan had pushed for indigenous development. Nonetheless, U.S. Congress members forced President George Bush to renegotiate the agreement in 1989 because they saw it as a giveaway of U.S. technology. This controversy delayed progress for at least one year, and shrouded the project in an atmosphere of acrimony from the outset. Since that point, the two sides have clashed over the terms of their collaborations, especially with regard to their respective shares of production and procedures for sharing technology. For the U.S. side, technology transfers from Japan to the United States represented one more way that Japan could support continued American military leadership. On the Japanese side, however, MITI rather than the JDA was the central player, and MITI's primary concern was to promote the Japanese defense industry rather than to reinforce the bilateral security relationship.[55]

The two governments did manage to produce a plan to enhance bilateral military technology exchange under the American "Technology-for-Technology" initiative, a program initiated by the DOD to encourage U.S. allies to transfer their technology. Japan certainly has considerable dual-use technology that could benefit the United States, but technology sharing programs have been fraught with logistical problems and a mutual lack of trust.[56] DOD officials have also sought Japanese cooperation on the development of a new Theater Missile Defense system, but the Japanese side has avoided making a firm commitment to the program because of its high cost and concerns that participation would violate its constitution.[57]

In the diplomatic sphere, Japanese leaders have gradually taken more initiative. Yet they have still been careful not to venture too far from the U.S. position, particularly in areas where the American government takes a strong stand. While they have been eager to cultivate an economic relationship with Vietnam, for example, they have made sure not to move too far in front of the United States. They have been much less inclined than their American counterparts to criticize China for human rights abuses, yet they did join the United States in imposing sanctions after the Tiananmen incident of 1989.[58] In issues involving a direct military threat, such as the North Korean nuclear threat in 1994, they have been all the more anxious to support the U.S. position. Japanese leaders have also clearly stated their desire to assume a seat on the United Nations Security Council, although they have not resolved whether they will be willing to play the military role in UN missions that may be expected of a Security Council member.

With respect to regional cooperation under the new Asian Pacific Economic Cooperation (APEC) forum, the United States continues to play the hegemonic role, at least with respect to trade liberalization. The U.S. government hosted the first APEC Summit in November 1993 in Seattle, and it pushed forward a plan for trade liberalization within the region by 2020 at the next summit in Bogor, Indonesia in November 1994. While Japan then hosted the 1995 summit in Osaka, it sought more to slow down the liberalization process than to promote it. In particular, the Japanese pressed for differential treatment of economic sectors so as to give Japan and other major Asian food importers the leeway to forestall further agricultural liberalization.[59]

On global problems, the United States and Japan have enjoyed a fairly strong cooperative relationship. Under the rubric of the Framework agreement, the two countries agreed to pursue a Common Agenda for Cooperation in Global Perspective. They focused especially on environmental issues, but also worked on issues ranging from children's health to narcotics use. Nevertheless, the two sides played a tactical game on these issues in which Japan tried to play up its cooperation to stress that the trade relationship was only one facet of a broader relationship, while the United States tried to downplay the program so as to maintain pressure on Japan to make concessions in the trade arena.

Questions for the Future

As the United States and Japan head into the twenty-first century, some fundamental puzzles remain unresolved. At the bilateral level, for example, can the United States and Japan sustain their "inverse" positions? That is, can the United States continue to promote free trade in the face of growing interests that oppose it? And can Japan maintain protected markets despite its substantial stake in a liberal trade regime? Likewise, on the security front, can the United States continue to bear the burden of leading collective security efforts despite severe

economic constraints? And can Japan continue to eschew armed participation in these efforts despite its formidable economic power? While
there is some pressure for change, I would argue that the United States
and Japan will not necessarily move to an "equilibrium" position in the
short to medium term. They remain wedded to their historical roles by
deeply embedded ideas and institutions, and thus underlying power
shifts will only redefine their relationship over the long term, if at all.

Then, at the regional level, how will the United States and Japan fit
into the new Asian order? As bilateral strains have intensified, Japan
has increasingly looked toward Asia. In economic relations, Japan has
already shifted its trading and investment activity increasingly toward
its Asian neighbors.[60] And the appreciation of the yen has only served to
accelerate Japanese direct investment in the region. This shift in turn
gives Japan more leverage in its relationship with the United States. Yet
Japan still shows no signs of replacing the United States as regional
hegemon in the security or diplomatic arena. It remains bound by a historical legacy of militarism compounded by an inability to atone for this
historical role and thereby reorient relations with its Asian neighbors.[61]

And finally, at the global level, will Japan's positions on issues of
diplomacy, security, and economic development begin to diverge further from those of the United States? Throughout the postwar era,
Japan acted as a loyal follower of American diplomacy. And even as
Japanese leaders began to pursue a more assertive foreign policy in the
1980s and 1990s, they rarely articulated positions that directly conflicted with those of the United States. However, there are signs that
Japan may begin to chart a more distinct course. For example, Japanese
officials have begun to articulate their misgivings about the liberal economic philosophy that underlies the development assistance programs
of the United States and U.S.-dominated international organizations.
They advocate a much more interventionist approach to the economy,
for example, than American agencies recommend. In the case of the
World Bank, the clash between American and Japanese views surfaced
in a major dispute over what lessons to glean from the postwar East
Asian miracle.[62] While the U.S. government will welcome a more activist Japan to the world stage, it will be much more wary if Japanese
activism begins to function at cross-purposes with American efforts.

Endnotes

1. International Monetary Fund, *International Financial Statistics*. (IMF, Washington, DC).
2. In 1994, for example, the United States ran a global merchandise trade deficit of
   $166 billion; Japan ran a global surplus of $146 billion; and the United States ran a
   bilateral trade deficit with Japan of $67 billion, *JEI Report* 34A, September 15, 1995.
3. Steven Vogel, "The Power Behind 'Spin-Ons': the Military Implications of Japan's
   Commercial Technology," in Wayne Sandholtz et. al., *The Highest Stakes: The
   Economic Foundations of the Next Security System* (New York: Oxford University
   Press, 1992).

4. Numerous authors have vigorously debated whether or not the United States is in "decline" and what this (potential or real) decline implies. *See, for example,* Susan Strange, "Still an Extraordinary Power," in Ray Lombra and Bill Witte (eds.), *The Political Economy of International and Domestic Monetary Relations* (Ames: Iowa State University Press, 1982); Paul Kennedy, *The Rise and Fall of the Great Powers* (New York: Random House, 1987); and Joseph Nye, *Bound to Lead: the Changing Nature of American Power* (New York: Basic Books, 1990). While the United States may or may not have declined in an *absolute* sense, it certainly has encountered a *relative* decline in economic power.

5. In Benjamin Cohen's terms (*see* Chapter 4 in this volume), the United States has resisted a "return to normalcy." Ichiro Ozawa, the leader of Japan's New Frontier Party (Shinshinto), uses similar language in arguing that Japan should become a "normal" nation, that is, a nation with a security and diplomatic role that befits its economic power. *See* Ozawa, *Nihon kaizo keikaku* (Tokyo: Kodansha, 1993), translated into English as *Blueprint for a New Japan: The Rethinking of a Nation* (Tokyo: Kodansha, 1994).

6. As I. M. Destler notes, growing deficits not only strengthen the demands of labor unions and industries hurt by trade, but also weaken the offsetting demands of industries that benefit from trade: *American Trade Politics*, 3rd ed. (Washington D.C.: Institute for International Economics, 1995), p. 205.

7. Chalmers Johnson addresses the theoretical implications of the Japanese anomaly in "The State and Japanese Grand Strategy," in Richard Rosecrance and Arthur A. Stein (eds.), *The Domestic Bases of Grand Strategy* (Ithaca: Cornell University Press, 1993), pp. 201–223.

8. A 1995 poll (*Wall Street Journal*, April 24, 1995) suggests that people in both countries support some rectification of these imbalances. According to the poll results, 6 percent of Americans respond that the United States should import more, whereas 62 percent say it should import less, and 61 percent of Japanese reply that Japan should import more and 5 percent say it should import less. Likewise, 17 percent of Americans answer that the United States should be more active in world affairs, whereas 34 percent say it should be less active, and 72 percent of Japanese feel Japan should be more active, whereas 2 percent say it should be less active.

9. *See, for example,* the debate between Chalmers Johnson and E. B. Keehn, "The Pentagon's Ossified Strategy," and Joseph Nye, Jr., "The Case for Deep Engagement," in *Foreign Affairs* Vol. 74, No. 4 (July-August 1995): 90–114.

10. *See* Destler, *American Trade Politics*. The president's "fast-track" authority expired in December 1993 after Congress had ratified both the North American Free Trade Agreement (NAFTA) and the Uruguay Round. Democratic and Republican efforts to reinstate this authority broke down in the fall of 1995.

11. Judith Goldstein, *Ideas, Interests, and American Trade Policy* (Ithaca: Cornell University Press, 1993), especially pp. 1–9. For the neorealist perspective on trade policy, *see* Stephen D. Krasner, "State Power and the Structure of International Trade," *World Politics* Vol. 28, No. 3 (1976): 317–347, and Robert Keohane, "The Theory of Hegemonic Stability and Changes in International Economic Regimes, 1967–77," in Ole Holsti et. al. (eds.), *Change in the International System* (Boulder: Westview, 1980): 131–162. For the pluralist perspective, *see* E. E. Schattschneider, *Politics, Pressures and the Tariff: A Study of Free Private Enterprise in Pressure Politics* (Englewood Cliffs, NJ: Prentice-Hall, 1935), and Destler, *American Trade Politics*.

12. Destler (*American Trade Politics*, p. 215) argues that American free traders have used the pursuit of trade liberalization abroad to fight protection at home more broadly, not just with respect to Japan.

13. Likewise, with respect to reducing the bilateral deficit, economists overwhelmingly agree that macroeconomic measures would have a greater impact than Japanese trade liberalization. For an assessment of the potential impact of Japanese liberalization on the trade balance, *see* C. Fred Bergsten and Marcus Noland,

Reconcilable Differences? United States-Japan Economic Conflict (Washington D.C.: Institute for International Economics, 1993), especially pp. 179–197.

14. Prime Minister Morihiro Hosokawa went so far as to declare that "Japan's greatest national interest lies in supporting free trade," *Asahi Shimbun* (August 21, 1993): 1.

15. Steven K. Vogel, *Freer Markets, More Rules: Regulatory Reform in Advanced Industrial Countries* (Ithaca: Cornell University Press, 1996), especially pp. 51–61 and 196–213.

16. On the relationship between foreign pressure and Japanese liberalization *see* Kent Calder, "Japanese Foreign Economic Policy: Explaining the Reactive State," *World Politics* Vol. 40, No. 4 (July 1988): 517–541, and Leonard J. Schoppa, "Two-level Games and Bargaining Outcomes: Why *Gaiatsu* Succeeds in Japan in Some Cases but Not Others," *International Organization* Vol. 47, No. 3 (Summer 1993): 353–386.

17. Clay Chandler, "U.S. Japan Team Has Learned the Hard Way," *Washington Post,* February 22, 1994.

18. This chapter is based in part on a large number of interviews with American and Japanese government officials and business executives conducted in 1994 and 1995. Most of the interviewees requested anonymity.

19. Glen S. Fukushima, "Repairing the U.S.-Japan Relationship," *American Chamber of Commerce in Japan (ACCJ) Journal* (June 1994): 11–13.

20. Historically, of course, precisely the opposite was true: Democrats were free traders and Republicans were protectionists. *See* Goldstein, *Ideas, Interests.*

21. MITI, *Tsusho hakusho* [Trade and Industry White Paper] (Tokyo: Okurasho Insatsukyoku, 1993). Former MITI official Sadao Nagaoka presents MITI's argument in "Shihonshugi-kan tairitsu no jidai no nihon no shucho" [The Japanese Viewpoint in the Era of Competing Capitalisms], *Ekonomisuto* (June 1, 1993): 32–36.

22. *Nihon Keizai Shimbun* (July 9, 1993): 5.

23. Ellis S. Krauss & Simon Reich offer a model to explain variations in U.S. trade policy across sectors in "Ideology, Interests, and the American Executive: Toward a Theory of Foreign Competition and Manufacturing Trade Policy," *International Organization* Vol. 46, No. 4 (Autumn 1992): 868–869. They characterize the auto sector as a non high-tech sector in which U.S. industry is competitive, and suggest that in such sectors the American executive is likely to opt for "managed trade" solutions designed to provide temporary relief.

24. For an analysis of the underlying forces propelling this revolution, *see* Takashi Inoguchi, "Japanese Politics in Transition: A Theoretical Review," *Government and Opposition* Vol. 28, No. 4 (Autumn 1993): 443–455.

25. Steven K. Vogel, "American Press Illusions about Japanese Politics," *Japan Policy Research Institute (JPRI) Critique* Vol. 2, No. 2 (February 1995).

26. The classic work on American bureaucratic politics is Graham Allison, *Essence of Decision: Explaining the Cuban Missile Crisis* (Boston: Little, Brown, 1971). On the Japanese variant, *see* John C. Campbell, "Policy Conflict and Its Resolution within the Governmental System," in Ellis S. Krauss, Thomas P. Rohlen, and Patricia G. Steinhoff (eds.), *Conflict in Japan* (Honolulu: University of Hawaii Press, 1984), pp. 294–334, and Chalmers Johnson, "MITI, MPT, and the Telecom Wars: How Japan Makes Policy for High Technology," in Johnson, Laura D'Andrea Tyson, and John Zysman (eds.), *Politics and Productivity: the Real Story of Why Japan Works* (Cambridge: Ballinger, 1989), pp. 177–240.

27. David Wessel and Jacob M. Schlesinger, "How the U.S., Japan Resolved Differences to Reach a Trade Pact," *Wall Street Journal*, July 12, 1993, p. A1.

28. Interviews. Yukio Okamoto makes the same point in "Tsusho senso ni piriodo o" [Stop the Trade War], *Nihon Keizai Shimbun*, February 11, 1994, p. 27.

29. The *Yomiuri Shimbun*, June 11, 1993, p. 9, reports that Japanese bureaucrats also borrowed heavily from the works of Japanese economist Ryutaro Komiya. A group of American economists signed an open letter to Clinton and Hosokawa on Sep-

tember 26, 1993 urging the leaders to abandon managed trade solutions to trade problems. *Also see* Jagdish Bhagwati, "Samurais No More," *Foreign Affairs* Vol. 73, No. 3 (May-June 1994): 7–12.

30. Arthur J. Alexander, "Sources of America's Asia Policy in the Clinton Administration," *JEI Report* 15A (April 21, 1995): 8. Ironically, Tyson had been criticized by many of her fellow economists for selectively advocating managed trade in her published work: for example, Tyson, *Who's Bashing Whom? Trade Conflicts in High-Technology Industries* (Washington DC: Institute for International Economics, 1993).

31. Congress ultimately ratified the Uruguay Round in December 1994.

32. Roger C. Altman, deputy secretary of the Treasury in the Clinton administration, stresses that the government needed the Japanese to cooperate to preserve its own efforts to liberalize trade through NAFTA and the Uruguay Round: "Why Pressure Tokyo?," *Foreign Affairs* Vol. 73, No. 3 (May-June 1994): 5.

33. Vogel, *Freer Markets*, pp. 196–213.

34. Glen S. Fukushima, "Deregulation is Not Enough," *Tokyo Business Today* (January 1994): 56.

35. Given the progress in other areas, the U.S. government chose not to cite Japan under the Super 301 provision.

36. On administrative guidance, *see* Chalmers Johnson, *MITI and the Japanese Miracle* (Stanford: Stanford University Press, 1982): 242–274.

37. B. Anne Craib, "The Republican Electoral Landslide: Implications for U.S. Foreign Economic Policy," *JEI Report* 3A, January 27, 1995, p. 11. By late 1995, Republican presidential candidate Patrick Buchanan was proposing a 10 percent tariff on all Japanese imports until the bilateral trade deficit disappears. *See* David E. Sanger, "Buchanan's Tough Tariff Talk Rattles G.O.P.," *New York Times*, October 8, 1995, p. 1.

38. The Cohen chapter in this volume analyzes economic interdependence and its impact on U.S. capabilities.

39. The Japanese auto manufacturers had originally sought to increase purchases of foreign parts only in their North American plants, *JEI Report* 24B, June 30, 1995.

40. The dispute re-emerged in October 1995, when a *New York Times* story charged that the Central Intelligence Agency had been spying on Japanese negotiators during the Framework talks. In their story, "Emerging Role for the C.I.A.: Economic Spy," *New York Times*, October 15, 1995, p. 1, David E. Sanger and Tim Weiner stress that these spying efforts did nothing to improve the outcome for the U.S. side. While the allegations were not new, Japanese government officials responded to this particular story with considerable outrage.

41. Some American advocates of managed trade or protectionism have cited strategic trade theory as an intellectual rationale for their position. The theorists themselves, however, have stressed that the theory only justifies protection under very specific circumstances. *See* Paul Krugman (ed.), *Strategic Trade Policy and the New International Economics* (Cambridge: MIT Press, 1986).

42. For the classic work on how the bipolar system structured state behavior, *see* Kenneth N. Waltz, *Theory of International Politics* (New York: Random House, 1979).

43. *See* Jentleson, Chapter 3 in this volume on the politics of U.S. military intervention abroad.

44. These codified constraints include the three non-nuclear principles, a ban on sending forces abroad, a ban on military exports, and a practice of limiting defense expenditures to about 1 percent of GNP.

45. From 1990 to 1994, Japanese official development assistance (ODA) rose from $9.1 to $13.2 billion, whereas U.S. ODA fell from $11.4 to $9.9 billion (*JEI Report* 26B, July 14, 1995, p. 6).

46. *New York Times*, June 12, 1991, p. D8. Takashi Inoguchi analyzes the factors that shaped Japan's response in "Japan's Response to the Gulf Crisis: An Analytic Overview," *Journal of Japanese Studies* Vol. 17, No. 2 (Summer 1991): 257–273.

47. Japan Defense Agency, *Boei hakusho* [Defense White Paper] (Tokyo: Okurasho Insatsukyoku, 1990).

48. Thus defense spending increases remained relatively high at 6.1 percent for fiscal 1990 and 5.45 percent for 1991, and then dropped to 3.8 percent in 1992, 1.95 percent in 1993, 0.9 percent in 1994, and 0.86 percent in 1995, *Boei handobukku* [Defense Handbook] (Tokyo, Asagumo Shimbunsha, 1995), p. 226.

49. As Mike M. Mochizuki puts it, U.S. government policy attempts both to "change" Japan and to "contain" it: "To Change or to Contain: Dilemmas of American Policy Toward Japan," in Kenneth A. Oye, Robert J. Lieber, and Donald Rothchild (eds.), *Eagle in A New World: American Grand Strategy in the Post–Cold War Era* (New York: HarperCollins, 1992).

50. Department of Defense, Office of International Security Affairs, "United States Security Strategy for the East Asia-Pacific Region" (February 1995).

51. On the more hawkish elements within Japan, *see* Mike M. Mochizuki, "Japan's Search for Strategy," *International Security* Vol. 8, No. 3 (Winter 1983–1984), and Steven K. Vogel, "A New Direction in Japanese Defense Policy," University of Maryland School of Law, Occasional Papers / Reprints Series in Contemporary Asian Studies (1984).

52. *Asahi Shimbun*, August 12, 1994, evening edition.

53. Nye, "The Case for Deep Engagement," p. 98.

54. *JEI Report* 37B, October 6, 1995, pp. 3–5.

55. *See* Richard J. Samuels, *"Rich Nation, Strong Army": National Security and the Technological Transformation of Japan* (Ithaca: Cornell, 1994).

56. On Japan's potential for technology "spin-ons" (applications of commercial technology to military uses), *see* Richard J. Samuels and Benjamin C. Whipple, "Defense Production and Industrial Development: The Case of Japanese Aircraft," in *Politics and Productivity*, pp. 241–274, and Vogel, "The Power Behind 'Spin-Ons.'"

57. Barbara Wanner, "Clinton Administration Refocuses Asian Pacific Security Strategy," *JEI Report* 11A, March 24, 1995, pp. 13–14.

58. *See* Friedman, Chapter 10 in this volume.

59. Christopher B. Johnstone, "An Awkward Dance: The Osaka Summit, Japanese Leadership and the Future of APEC," *JEI Report* 39A, October 20, 1995.

60. From 1990 through 1994, Japan's trade with East Asia as a share of its total trade grew from 33 to 41 percent, and its foreign direct investment in East Asia as a share of the total rose from 20 to 27 percent (*JEI Report* 33A, September 1, 1995). Edward J. Lincoln surveys Japan's role in East Asia in *Japan's New Global Role* (Washington DC: Brookings Institution, 1993), especially pp. 160–200; Sandholtz et. al. assess the potential for a Japanese bloc in East Asia in *The Highest Stakes*, especially pp. 39–42 and 167–205; and Eileen M. Doherty et. al. analyze the implications of Japanese investment in Doherty (ed.), *Japanese Investment in Asia* (San Francisco: Asia Foundation and Berkeley Roundtable on the International Economy, 1995).

61. Many LDP Diet members stubbornly refused to endorse a symbolic Diet resolution apologizing for Japan's wartime aggression on the fiftieth anniversary of the end of World War II. The Diet passed a compromise resolution in June 1995 which expressed remorse but offered no apology.

62. *See* Edith Terry, "How Asia Got Rich: World Bank vs. Japanese Industrial Policy," Japan Policy Research Institute (JPRI) Working Paper No. 10 (June 1995). This clash ultimately resulted in a report that straddles a fine line between the two views: The World Bank, *The East Asian Miracle: Economic Growth and Public Policy* (New York: Oxford University Press, 1993).

Chapter 10

The Challenge of a Rising China: Another Germany?

Edward Friedman

The Honeymoon Era

The end of the Cold War combined with the disintegration of the Soviet Union and the military decline of Russia to remove from America-China relations a major basis for close cooperation—strategic entente against a militaristic Soviet Russia.[1] The Nixon-Mao detente of 1972 occurred only after the Soviet Union forcibly crushed the 1967–1968 Czech struggle to build socialism with a human face and Soviet leader Brezhnev insisted that Moscow had the right to act similarly toward any country leaving the "socialist commonwealth," a proclamation understood in Beijing as a direct and immediate threat to China. Mao then sought detente with the United States to deter a Soviet Union that had been considering an attack on China from 1969, and would do so until 1974.[2]

During that tense period, top American officials wanted Mao to restrain Hanoi's Soviet-armed forces in Southern Vietnam from using armed might to wipe out the U.S.-backed government in Saigon. However, Moscow hastily moved military supplies to its friends in Vietnam. China did try—but without success—to restrain Hanoi. Beijing-Hanoi relations had been in flux ever since February 1965 when Russia agreed to arm Hanoi with advanced weapons to use against American bombers, a Vietnamese imperative that China lacked the military hardware to meet. Given China's anxieties over Soviet military actions against China itself, warming Moscow-Hanoi military relations seemed part of a Soviet forward encirclement aimed against Beijing.[3]

Edward Friedman, a professor in the Department of Political Science at the University of Wisconsin, Madison, served as a China specialist on the staff of the U.S. House of Representatives Committee on Foreign Affairs in 1981, 1982, and 1983 and was a contract employee in the Secretary's Office in the U.S. Department of Defense in 1993, 1994, and 1995. He has cowritten Chinese Village, Socialist State *(Yale, 1991) and written* National Identity and Democratic Prospects in Socialist China *(Sharpe, 1995), and was the editor of* The Politics of Democratization: Generalizing East Asian Experiences *(Westview, 1994).*

Much was changed by the rise of Deng Xiaoping as China's paramount leader in the post-Mao era. Deng moved for full normalization of Washington-Beijing relations on January 1, 1979. By then, economic mutual benefit drove the U.S.-China relationship. An exhausted and cynical Chinese people was wooed by promises of rapidly rising standards of living. The new economic priority seemed a matter of life and death to China's rulers. Even the 1979 Soviet Russian invasion of Afghanistan hardly slowed China's normalization of relations with the U.S.S.R., part of a larger effort to build a regional environment in which rulers in Beijing could make the peaceful raising of the populace's standards of living a top policy objective. Expanding the economy became Deng's priority because the old legitimations of anti-imperialist socialism had lost meaning to the people of China.[4] Whereas Mao attacked foreign capital as the source of evil imperialism, Deng welcomed it as a source of growth. Still, China's rulers remained proud patriots. Chauvinist desires for revenge against Vietnam for the pummeling China took when it invaded Vietnam in early 1979 gave an added tang to Beijing's wooing of Moscow away from Hanoi. China's rulers relished being able to impose their will on an isolated Vietnam.

Deng's abandonment of the rhetoric of anti-imperialism for one of economic modernization led to an optimistic belief in the United States that post-Mao Chinese reform was tantamount to *China's Second Revolution*.[5] Mutual U.S.-China benefits would supposedly now happily infuse bilateral relations. American business invested heavily in China. Trade exploded between the United States and China. Whereas an industrializing Britain "took six decades to double living standards," China was "accomplishing the same feat within ten years."[6]

Deng's government seemed a model that other command economies with Leninist dictatorships should follow if they too wished to succeed economically.[7] China's economic success had great power implications. The Deng era seemed in 1988 like "the early stages of Frederick the Great's reign. . . ."[8] Analysts looked at the rise of China remembering the rise of Germany. As the emergence of Germany in the nineteenth century had transformed international politics in Europe, so had the sudden eruption of wealth and power in China shaken up relations in the Asia-Pacific region.

But then, a euphoric vision of mutual U.S.-China gains seemed almost insane after the earth-shaking events of 1989–1990. The great spring democracy movement in China was bloodily crushed on June 4, 1989 in an international television spectacle that made a deep impression on the United States's political psyche. Later in 1989, Communist Party dictatorships began democratizing one after the other, with political freedoms sprouting from Albania to Mongolia. Suddenly good U.S. relations with a repressive Chinese dictatorship seemed an embarrassment in Washington. Rather than a model, China looked like an anomaly as democracy spread and the promotion of human rights became more central to U.S. foreign policy. A re-examination of the interests of ruling groups in both Beijing and Washington led each side to conclude that real, but previously obscured, conflicts of interest would inevitably make for far more complex future relations. The honeymoon was over.[9]

Deteriorating Relations

In Beijing, ruling groups, no longer worried by a Soviet threat, put domestic politics first. They worried about the survival of the dictatorial system that kept them in power. Consequently, the United States no longer was an anti-Soviet friend. Instead, Chinese powerholders saw the United States more as a real and present threat to the system that rewarded these powerholders so richly. They saw the United States promoting forces of peaceful evolution toward political democracy in China. In response, Deng Xiaoping reached out to surviving Communist Party dictatorships. China became Cuba's number one trading partner, adding yet more of an anti-American skewing of perspective to China's worldview. The dictatorship in China also joined rulers in Malaysia and Singapore who touted East Asian developmental authoritarianism to oppose any American effort to promote universally recognized human rights that might weaken less-than-democratic regimes.

Whereas China increasingly touted developmental dictatorship, the United States increasingly promoted human rights. Political prisoners of conscience in China and Chinese democrats in exile grew more salient in U.S. politics, sharpening a U.S. focus on inhumanities committed in China.[10] Beijing and Washington appeared in ever more negative hues to each other.

The heightening of democracy and human rights as a factor in Beijing-Washington relations was intensified by developments in Taiwan.[11] Just when China seemed uniquely repressive, Taiwan democratized. Taiwan is an island about 90 miles off mainland China's southeast coast whose rulers were heirs of the defeated side of the civil war that won state power for Mao in 1949. Democratic Taiwan's friends in the United States, including a sophisticated lobby run by Americans of Taiwanese descent, pressured elected officials in Washington to back the cause of a democratic Taiwan as superior to a dictatorial China which, since the Cold War with the Soviet Union had ended, was no longer a strategic factor for the United States.[12]

The new factor of a democratic Taiwan exacerbated U.S.-China relations. It engendered a feeling among super-patriots in Beijing that democracy was an unpatriotic idea, a slogan invoked to negate the legitimacy of Beijing's claim that Taiwan, despite separation from Chinese governments since 1895, was still a province of China, temporarily, but only very temporarily, detached from the motherland. Tough patriots in China claimed to see through a smokescreen of human rights and democracy to an essential reality, a threat to Chinese national unity, an attempt to prevent a united China from rising to assume again its proper position in the world as one of the few truly great powers. Democrats were portrayed in Beijing as traitors.

In short, the age of U.S. partnership with China against the Soviet Union was dead.[13] China instead challenged U.S. interests because, in China, the United States seemed a direct danger to the dictators in Beijing, who alone supposedly could make China great again. While there were still many important issues on which Beijing and Washington could cooperate, such as trying to prevent the government of North Korea from possessing nuclear weapons, Chinese chauvinists sought to confront America. Only the mutual benefit in expanded economic ties, taken as a top priority by both governments, seemed to keep relations from fraying altogether.

The U.S. business community lobbied Washington to maintain China's most favored nation (MFN) trading status.* Yet the pro-business U.S. Congress was quite upset about what China was doing at home and abroad. Congress fretted about the export to the United States of Chinese goods made with the slave labor of political prisoners, which immorally threatened U.S. jobs. It was outraged by irresponsible Chinese exports of nuclear material and strategic weapons, especially to nations in West Asia. Chinese exports threatened to destabilize a vital and oil-rich region of the planet.

In Washington, the ruling groups in Beijing no longer seemed a desired ally against Moscow. Rather they looked like a worrisome threat to world peace and human decency. The days of U.S.-China entente were ancient history. A Beijing decision in the summer of 1995 to use military means to hasten a resolution of the Taiwan issue even threatened the fragile structure of peace in the entire West Pacific region. Could the rise of China, as the rise of nineteenth century Germany, auger dangers ahead? Could dangers of war be avoided? What if, as a U.S. analyst concluded, "China is neither a normal state nor satisfied with the status quo. It is instead highly nationalistic, seeking primacy as the regional hegemon in the creation of a greater Sinocentric east Asian order."[14]

In the post–Cold War environment, it was not clear what policy Washington should take toward Beijing. Should America practice engagement or containment[15] or something else? Lacking a general inter-

---

*Basically, there are three levels for trading with the United States. Enemies, such as Castro's Cuba, are kept from the American market. Poorest countries are allowed to export to the United States on the best terms, a General System of Preferences. The ordinary level of tariffs given most nations is called MFN. The notion of "most favored" is diplomatic puffery, not economic reality.

national cause, the United States did not seem to act in a coordinated way. Rather it responded in terms of momentary, domestic imperatives.

When President Bush[16] utilized UN resources and auspices to respond to Iraq's invasion of Kuwait, an act that also threatened Saudi Arabia, China's veto power, as one of the five permanent members of the UN Security Council, made it necessary for the United States to conciliate China. But China seemed more an obstacle than a partner in the common global effort. Even Beijing-Washington cooperation came with grudging difficulty. Difficulties, if not a further deterioration of relations, seemed likely if China pursued an expansive empowerment that made it a direct challenge to important American interests, first and foremost, maintaining peace in the Asia-Pacific region, the region of emerging markets most important to the future American economy.

Since only mutual economic benefit weighed heavily on the positive side of the ledger,[17] the movement of those weights to a negative scale badly rent the frayed relationship. President Clinton made economic growth a strategic priority in 1993. But China's extraordinary export success, a matter of joining with capital and technology rich East Asian neighbors and copying the export-aggressive strategies of Japan and the East Asian tigers, brought Washington and Beijing into a frontal clash on economic matters. The United States confronted an exploding trade imbalance with China. The major shared remnant interest that had hitherto led the two governments to subordinate political conflicts turned into a realm of contention.

China exported most aggressively, masking its textiles as those of other places. The United States responded with economic penalties. China also pirated, sold, and even exported throughout Southeast Asia various American information technologies—movies, cassette tapes, CDs and computer software. This loss of control of U.S. intellectual property rights (IPR) weakened the capacity of the United States to earn foreign exchange through entertainment software, the second largest source of American export earnings, second only to jumbo jets. In Washington, China now seemed the enemy of global stability and of regional peace, of American prosperity, and of the cause of democracy. Prognoses for the future of Beijing-Washington relations were dire. With the Chinese propaganda machine turning out anti-American tirades, young urban Chinese reportedly saw the United States as the country they most disliked.[18]

As with Germany and Britain in the first part of the twentieth century, analysts worried that the downturn in Beijing-Washington relations could plummet toward all the horrors that exploded after the Great War, the First World War—fascism, depression, and another war. China and the United States had fought a bloody war in Korea (1950–1953). The possibility of another clash loomed over the horizon.

But dark clouds and cooling relations will not automatically snowball like an avalanche. Germany's early twentieth-century fate was not preordained. Dangerous political possibilities must be confronted. They can be checked by wise politics and policies. Although China is rising now as Germany did a century before, war with China is far from inevitable. In fact, there are important signs that more internationalist political forces could prevail in the ongoing power struggle in China.

The hope is that cooperation can be achieved to prevent worst case disasters in Beijing-Washington relations and to expand mutually beneficial economic and other relations.[19] The waning years of the rule of Deng Xiaoping and the 1993–1997 presidency of Bill Clinton were filled by policies reflective of both tendencies, dangerous clashes and healthy cooperation. But if both parties are mesmerized by life and death matters of internal politics, then it is difficult to be optimistic that the better forces will win out in foreign policy. In the post–Cold War era, the U.S. president's first responsibility seems to be making the American economy productive and fair. But if the United States lacks an overriding international political cause, the Chief Executive may lack the direction, will, and wherewithal to stave off worst case international possibilities until the pile of reactive material is out of control. The U.S.-China relation consequently has become one of continual crisis management.

Delinking Human Rights and Most Favored Nation Status

Candidate Bill Clinton had promised that, if elected president, he would not be indifferent to violations of human rights in China as President George Bush had been. Actually, when China murderously crushed a popular democracy movement on June 4, 1989, Bush had imposed sanctions. But Japan was against sanctions. And Japan was the major economic factor in East Asia. With Japan swiftly resuming normal economic relations with a China that was home to more than one-fifth of the human race and whose economy was growing at the world's fastest pace, U.S. business insisted that it needed to participate in China's economic dynamism. Not to be in the China market seemed tantamount to not being a world-class player. For the United States to exclude itself from China would be to wound the United States economically and to give advantage to a Japanese competitor.

Concerned about the U.S. economy and seeking to promote U.S. trade with China, candidate for re-election George Bush vetoed bills from Congress that made a grant of MFN trade status to China conditional on its meeting a long list of human rights objectives, such as an accounting of the dead of the June 4, 1989 massacre and allowing religious freedom in Tibet.[20] But proud ruling groups in China would not meet conditions they found to be humiliating infringements of a hard-won sovereignty. Bush then sought an expansion of economic involvement with China, justifying this policy of engagement, in part, as also promoting long-term political liberalization in China. Supposedly, rapid economic growth would foster a large middle class and a private economy that in combination would facilitate eventual democratization.[21]

Bush, however, was vulnerable in American politics on the issue of MFN for China. Right after the June 4 Beijing massacre, Bush promised to end high level exchanges with the regime of the murderers, but then immediately sent a secret high level mission to China. Its cover was blown when the Chinese published a picture of Bush's emissaries clinking glasses and toasting with Chinese counterparts whose hands seemed figuratively to be covered in democratic blood. Bush looked like a hypocrite and a friend of mass murderers. The Democrats in Congress then were joined by ideologically anti-Communist Republicans in bills to sanction a despotic China. Granting MFN status to China thereby became an issue within American politics, a stick with which to beat George Bush, a tactic used both by liberal, human rights-oriented Democrats and by Bush's more right-wing Republican competitors. Yet sanctions against China would also hurt U.S. business and isolate the country in Asian politics.

An economic recession increased unemployment in the United States at this time. In addition, disturbing revelations, in which Harry Wu, an American who had been imprisoned in China's Gulag, played a prominent role, produced headline news, revealing that Chinese prison labor exports were bought and sold in America. It therefore seemed that normal economic relations with China meant throwing Americans out of work. It meant supporting China's slave labor system, which included democratic survivors of the televised massacre of June 4, 1989. Members of Congress did not enjoy defending in their home districts normal economic relations with this China. In short, Democratic presidential candidate Clinton had a good stick with which to beat President Bush in insisting that, if elected, a President Clinton would have a very different China policy than the purported Bush policy of coddling China's mass murderers and penalizing American workers.

But, upon election, Clinton found himself confronting a difficult dilemma. If he conditioned MFN status for China on the long series of conditions in Congressional bills, China would not meet those conditions. Sanctions against China would adversely affect U.S.-China economic ties. American investors in China and U.S. exporters to China, from high technology to agriculture, would be hurt. Clinton's commitment to make re-energizing the U.S. economy his number one priority would seem undermined by an unwarranted privileging of human rights. But if Clinton failed to tie human rights to the granting of MFN status to China, then he would seem a hypocrite, "slick Willie," someone who said one thing and did another, someone who, therefore, could not be trusted on anything. Clinton unexpectedly found he needed wiggle room on MFN and China.

The president was persuaded by his Assistant Secretary of State for East Asian Affairs, Winston Lord, to promote a policy of minimum conditionality. If China would merely meet two conditions, allowing emigration (which was in fact limited by receiving nations which allowed few Chinese, fearing a tidal wave) and ending prison labor exports (actually an infinitesimally small part of U.S.-China economic interchange), and the president certified that China had also made some progress on other issues, supposedly an inevitable consequence of economic growth, then MFN would be granted. Democrats in Congress were persuaded to accept the compromise. Meanwhile President Clinton banned weapons imports from China.

American business cheered. The President's team was happy because a removal of China's MFN status was believed to threaten billions of dollars worth of West Coast business with China, a loss that could weaken vital California support for Bill Clinton's re-election.

It should have been easy for the government of China to meet the two simple conditions with no loss of public face, thus preserving the standing of China's rulers at home and improving Beijing-Washington international relations. Unexpectedly, rulers in Beijing refused to meet even minimal conditionality. They were buoyed in 1993 and 1994 by a tremendous economic surge. Investments from Taiwan and Japan poured in. Post-massacre sanctions had failed. International financial institutions projected that China, early in the twenty-first century, would become the world's largest economy. China indeed was rising as Germany had in the nineteenth century.[22] United States business so much wanted, even needed, a piece of the Chinese action, that China's rulers concluded that U.S. business would compel President Clinton to back away from even minimal conditionality on MFN. The United States's economic self-interest would compel it to end all linkage of MFN status to China's human rights performance.

The president, whose campaign slogan had seemed to be "It's the economy, stupid," could not afford to hurt the growth of U.S. exports and investments in China in the new age of globalization. The competitive strength of the U.S. economy had to be a top priority. Few international causes could come before economic imperatives. The U.S. Central Intelligence Agency was tasked to a new, major focus, helping American business in the global economy.

Even were China hurt badly by a loss of MFN access to American markets, as indeed China would be, the United States could not afford to wound itself and fatten its competitors in China. The United States had to find a way to benefit from participation in Asia-Pacific economies, the only rapidly growing region of the world for a quarter of a century. So Chinese rulers, identifying with the strength of a rising Asia, stood firm against even minimal U.S. conditionality. Among Chinese ruling groups, the caning of an American teenager by the mosquito-sized state of Singapore symbolized the rise of China and East Asia and the relative decline of the United States. Chauvinistic pride infused China's defiance of the United States. It seemed delicious to stand up to this country. Chinese nationalism was on the rise.

At the same time, a struggle to succeed China's aging, paramount leader, Deng Xiaoping, made all Chinese competitors for the leadership position feel a need to woo the tough, even chauvinistic Chinese military elite. Anti-Americanism had political pay-offs in the succession struggle in China. Those military super-patriots opposed any human rights concessions to appease the United States. Their view was that any concession would lead to U.S. demands for more concessions, which would encourage Chinese democrats. They insisted on no concessions to the United States to hold MFN status, seeing concessions as a breach in a dike holding back supposedly dangerous popular forces. Democratization would destabilize China, as it supposedly had Russia. A strong and wealthy China meant an authoritarian China. A need for authoritarian development supposedly was the major lesson of East Asia's unique economic dynamism.

To paramount leader Deng, little Singapore had shown that authoritarian development was the Asian way to advance. China's ruling groups suspected that the real purpose of America's human rights policy was not actually human rights. After all, the United States was, for China's Communist rulers, a racist and exploitative society that had never sanctioned murderous allies in anti-Communist Taiwan or anti-Communist South Korea for human right abuses. China's rulers concluded that the real goal of the U.S. human rights policy was to destabilize China, block China's rapid growth, and prevent China from resuming its rightful place as one of the great world powers. China therefore would not concede on human rights to obtain MFN status.

Nonetheless, Beijing needed assured access to the American market, the destination of about 40 percent of all China's exports. In January 1994, China agreed to a memorandum against prison labor exports. In April, it released a handful of political prisoners and made verbal concessions on lesser matters. The U.S. president was convinced that China would go no further. Consequently, there was no American advantage to ending China's MFN status. Besides, the human rights community had no ideas on how to sanction China so as not also to hurt the U.S. economy.

Persuaded that the United States would not be able to play a leading role in the world on human rights, democratization, or any other cause if it did not first restore its economic vitality, President Clinton decided that it was in the United States's interest both to delink China's MFN status from human rights conditionality in particular and to seek a policy of broadly engaging China in a general way that was conducive to U.S. economic well-being and did not incite a chauvinistic anti-American backlash in China. The President announced his delinking decision on May 26, 1994.

What he and his advisors did not fully foresee was how much the political and economic rise of Asia had already unleashed forces on the mainland of China and elsewhere that would, despite the President's desire to the contrary, guarantee that China would continue targeting the United States as its number one, short-run enemy. Despite the intention of the United States to win smooth relations with China by a grant of MFN status and a policy of broad engagement, Beijing-Washington relations continued to sour. Yet the U.S. policy of engagement remained the only way to build mutual interests with healthier forces in China who worried that chauvinists in that country were taking China down a no-win, war-prone course. Much depended on who won the power struggle in China.

The Issue of Taiwan

Political survival in China was not a given for a Communist Party dictatorship starting in late 1989 when Leninist states fell apart. For a while it seemed that the initiatives of Russian leaders most threatened the top goal of regime survival shared by China's powerholders when Gorbachev and Yeltsin dismantled the Leninist system in the U.S.S.R., the original homeland of the socialist dictatorship. That made China's state socialist system seem the odd nation out, an anomaly, perhaps the next dinosaur that might succumb to laws of progressive evolution. Hate in *Zhongnanhai*, the seat of power in Beijing, toward Gorbachev and Yeltsin led to hope for the success of the August 1991 Moscow coup by Stalinist hardliners. But the coup failed. Nonetheless, the Russian parliament that had in 1989 supported China's democracy movement became more nationalistic and open to cooperation with China's dictatorship in the 1990s.

Mesmerization in Beijing by the perils of the Soviet implosion was ended by the victory of U.S. weaponry in the Persian Gulf War. It made the United States seem the world's only superpower. Nationalists in both Moscow and Beijing found a common purpose in opposition to a world in which Washington might be able to dictate. Russia sold advanced weapons to China. Trade flourished between the two; friendship grew.[23] As Russian leader Yeltsin did not want the United States's military reach to incorporate Poland, Latvia, Lithuania, and Estonia, so China's post-Mao rulers led by Deng Xiaoping did not want U.S. power to be capable of unilaterally determining issues of concern to China in Southeast Asia, the South China Sea, the Taiwan region, or Korea. The Chinese preferred situations, such as the United Nations Security Council's voting on how to deal with Iraq's military annihilation of an independent Kuwait, in which Washington could not move without wooing Beijing. China's rulers sought, and believed China merited, a great power position on the stage of world politics worthy of a nuclear-armed nation with veto power in the UN Security Council and almost a quarter of the world's population within its borders. The Chinese tended to believe that a China that had been a world leader for more than a millennium before the rise of Europe should be great again.

China sought the role of a major actor on the world stage, as had nineteenth century Germany.

China's irredentist post-Mao rulers had identified with Iraq's victory over Kuwait, viewing it as an auger of what could happen to Taiwan, which China claimed. Iraq conquered Kuwait using weapons from the Soviet Union, the same kind of weapons China possessed. The subsequent liberation of Kuwait using America's smart, microelectronic weapons, the kind of weapons used to protect Taiwan, was celebrated on Taiwan. Beijing was stunned. America's rise suddenly seemed to guarantee that the last unfulfilled goal of China's original revolutionary generation, the incorporation of the island of Taiwan into a unified People's Republic of China, might be indefinitely postponed. The chauvinistic Chinese military insisted on new initiatives toward Taiwan. The Deng Xiaoping ruling group rethought its Taiwan policy to find new ways to expedite the return of Taiwan to the motherland. At first this brought a policy from China of maximum engagement with Taiwan. That policy inadvertently contributed to a heady feeling on Taiwan that mainland China needed Taiwan's economic inputs of capital, machinery, management, and market know-how to keep China's economic dynamism going.

Euphoric leaders in Taiwan, feeling safer after the Gulf War, missed the import of the new, sharp edge in China's policy toward Taiwan.[24] Taipei* acted as if it could do far more than merely finesse the Taiwan issue, as U.S. policy had done ever since Nixon first went to China in February 1972 and the United States began to move its recognition of China from a nation with Taipei as its capital, to a nation with Beijing as its capital. Since 1972 the United States's goal had been to have differences between Taipei and Beijing decided peacefully in the long run. In effect, this meant delaying a resolution until after the chauvinistic leaders of China's Civil War generation, on both sides of the Taiwan Straits, had left the political scene and angry passions could be replaced by a tranquil search for peaceful and mutually beneficial solutions.

The Gulf War provided an added fillip to a surging sense of confident Taiwanese nationalism that led a newly proud, secure, and powerfully optimistic Taiwan to take diplomatic initiatives that unexpectedly fed the raging fires of an unsatisfied nationalism on China's mainland. On Taiwan, the late 1980s breakthrough to democracy brought a change in political identity.[25] The more than 80 percent of the people on the island who were *not* descendants of the defeated side in China's civil war found a voice. It was in the local language, not the tongue of groups of

---

*In Beijing, the capital of the province of Taiwan is spelled Taibei. To the Republic of China on Taiwan, that "b" should be a "p," Taipei. This chapter uses the preferred spelling of whomever controls the area in question, hence Beijing and not Peking, but Taipei, not Taibei.

the defeated armed force from the mainland who still had pretensions to rule the Chinese mainland. The use of the local language engendered a renaissance of Taiwanese culture and a feeling that Taiwan, a Japanese colony from 1895 to 1945 and a subsequent protectorate of the United States, had a special identity and role, a synthesizer of the best that Japan, China, and the United States had to offer, all infused by domestic particulars. Taiwan had a destiny of its own.

The people on Taiwan happily supported the first Taiwan-born President, Lee Teng-hui, in a flexible diplomatic effort to re-establish international political standing for Taiwan. Most people on the island believed Taiwan merited it. Taiwanese movies were winning international recognition, just as its little league baseball team regularly won the world championship. Taiwan's corporations were globally competitive. Acer was making a name in the computer world. Taiwanese owned Girl Scout Cookies. Only America and Japan exported more computers than Taiwan, which actually was number one in world exports in a whole series of computer peripherals. Only Japan held more foreign exchange reserves than Taiwan.

In the 1990s Taiwan rose to become the top investor in the new economic dragons across Southeast Asia, including Vietnam. Taiwan may well have been number one in China too. By 1993 Taiwanese were infused with a surging self-confidence and wanted to be treated with the dignity their achievement deserved. Taiwan's quest for a more diplomatically institutionalized political status engendered demands on the mainland of China for a more active policy to challenge Taiwan's de facto independence. A rising Asia engendered clashing nationalisms. China's leaders also were concerned about a potentially resurgent India and Japan.

Taiwan's new identity and pride clashed with mainland China's quest for treatment with proper dignity. The clash of rising patriotic ambitions on both sides of the Taiwan Straits reflected the rise of Asia in general.[26] East Asia saw itself as the world's better future. For the last quarter of the twentieth century, it was the world's fastest growing region. American trade with Asia, as European trade with Asia, both outweighed European-American trade. Seeing the West in decline, the leaders of flawed democracies in Singapore and Malaysia (sometimes called soft authoritarian states) blamed western individualism for western decay and instead embraced collectivistic, authoritarian, supposedly Asian values as superior to western human rights preoccupations, said to be merely a selfish individualism that subverted social cohesion and personal discipline.[27] Conservative rulers in Beijing, who identified with the Confucian authoritarianism promoted by Singapore's senior statesman Lee Kuan Yew, insisted that Asian development was the direct consequence of a superior and benevolent authoritarian Asian culture. The United States was seen as a declining nation suffering from social decay. For a rising China to surrender to a declining United

States's human rights demands would mean, in China's cultural authoritarian perspective, abandoning the Asian value basis of economic success that was now making China rich and powerful, that was allowing
China once again to stride the stage of world history.

An ever more confident Chinese leadership even insisted that its
human rights record was superior to the United States's. China seemed
to seek issues on which to confront the United States and strut before
the Chinese people as the defender of Chinese growth, strength, and
dignity. It hurt Chinese national pride, even for Chinese opponents of
the Communist dictatorial system, when the Olympics for the year
2000 were awarded to Sydney, Australia rather than to Beijing, China.
In 1995 Beijing's confrontation with Washington explosively focused on
the future of Taiwan. The priority of domestic politics as a source of
U.S. foreign policy worsened the clash.

In 1992, his last full year as president, George Bush had offered to
sell Taiwan advanced U.S. fighter aircraft to meet the challenge of Chinese military modernization and maintain peace through a balance of
power in the region. Being oriented to domestic politics, the rulers in
Beijing wanted Bush re-elected rather than Clinton who seemed to suggest he would emphasize human rights in dealing with China. Therefore, Beijing let slide the issue of Bush's fighter sale to Taiwan even
though such arms sales probably violated written declarations agreed to
in 1972, 1978, and 1982 by chief executives in Washington and Beijing.

President Bush wanted the arms contract with Taiwan to create jobs
in America and win votes for himself in his campaign for re-election. So
far had China fallen as an American diplomatic priority since the end of
the Cold War, so little was American foreign policy infused by an overriding cause, that Bush's temporary, domestic political interest outweighed concern over breaking three executive agreements with China.

As president, Bill Clinton did far, far less than George Bush to in-
fringe executive declarations between leaders in Washington and Beijing when, in 1995, he allowed Taiwan's President Lee to visit the
United States to speak at an alumni reunion at Cornell University
where Dr. Lee Teng-hui had begun a short but distinguished academic
career as an agricultural economist. Clinton was under pressure from
the Republicans who dominated Congress to treat a leader of a prosperous Asian democracy with proper dignity. Given all his many disagreements with the Republican Congress on economic issues, matters of
highest concern to the president, Clinton decided to conciliate the Republicans on the issue of how to treat Taiwan's president. Like Bush,
Clinton was concerned with domestic American politics. Like Bush,
Clinton had no desire to hurt Beijing-Washington relations.

Taiwan President Lee had previously visited with government leaders in Southeast Asia, calling the trips private tourism. The term
masked real diplomacy. President Lee, to be sure, played golf. But he
also talked for hours with Southeast Asian heads of state, including

China's friends in Singapore. The government in Beijing hardly muttered a protest. Taiwan President Lee's private visit to America, in contrast with his Southeast Asian "tourism," included no meetings with top members of the U.S. executive branch of government and no press conference, not even a visit to the capital city, Washington, DC. The Clinton administration tried not to injure U.S.-China relations.

Yet in late June 1995 Beijing called President Lee's visit to Cornell the cause of a crisis in U.S.-China relations, an act that took the relationship to its worst point since President Nixon had first set foot on Chinese soil 23 years earlier. China called its ambassador home from the United States, turning an alumni reunion into a diplomatic crisis. Clearly, something in Chinese politics led Beijing to make a Mount Everest-sized problem out of what need only have been another bump on a bumpy diplomatic road.

In Beijing, the leadership saw the United States as China's number one enemy. Chinese rulers concluded that Taiwan was the unresolved issue that polluted U.S.-China relations the most and therefore had to be turned around. Here, too, domestic politics produced international dangers. Chinese ruling groups were struggling for power, as paramount leader Deng Xiaoping, who was 91 in 1995, seemed on the verge of meeting his maker. In that struggle, much as in presidential primaries in the United States, a particular constituency, in China's case, the hard line security forces, had more weight than they would have once a new leader was entrenched in power and the ruler had to govern and, consequently, appeal to many other constituencies, especially economic ones. Thus, groups more open to better relations with Washington for reasons of economic self-interest could yet emerge victorious in the long run in Beijing. Therefore the policy of both Bush and Clinton of engaging China on a broad range of issues seeking arenas of cooperation made sense, despite Chinese denunciations of the United States. This analysis seemed borne out by the case of Harry Wu.

Mr. Wu was a courageous fighter on behalf of human rights in China. Although he had suffered in China's Gulag for almost two decades in the Mao era, Wu subsequently secretly returned three times to China at great risk, with hidden cameras to capture proof that Beijing violated internationally recognized human rights and also ignored agreements with the United States. In the spring of 1995, Wu was arrested upon his fourth return to China. The military hardliners in China wanted him treated as a spy, an enemy of the people who besmirched China's good name.

Wu, an American citizen of Chinese heritage, could have been turned back at the border by Chinese Customs, thereby avoiding a conflict with the United States. If Wu were punished as a spy, then Hillary Clinton, the wife of the U.S. president, could not go to Beijing to head an America delegation at an international women's conference scheduled for Beijing for September 1995. China sought status from hosting that conference. Economically oriented ruling groups wanted China to seem a safe place for tourists to spend billions of dollars and for investors to place billions more.

Chinese reformers argued that treating Wu harshly would poison the investment climate in China. It might even scare off many people of Chinese ancestry from Taiwan and Southeast Asia who were major investors in China. Such people might feel as vulnerable as Wu. A spate of investors and reporters of Chinese cultural heritage had recently been arrested, apparently victims of arbitrary local Chinese power. In a rare moment of lucidity, paramount leader Deng Xiaoping, supposedly unconscious and deathly ill, is rumored to have also weighed in on the Wu case on the side of reasonableness, not obduracy.

President Clinton also took initiatives to reverse the crisis of deteriorating relations with China. His administration reiterated America's commitment to the executive declarations with China of 1972, 1978, and 1982. The Chinese side responded positively. The views of China's reform coalition, committed to openness with the world as a source of growth won out. Wu was merely expelled. Hillary Clinton then went to the conference in Beijing. A temporarily withdrawn Chinese ambassador could return to Washington. A U.S. ambassador was approved. Quiet talks continued on arranging one-on-one meetings between senior leaders and on trying to avoid future misunderstandings.* Reformers and internationalists seemed positioned for victory in China's power struggle.

Nonetheless, while military-minded chauvinists and economically oriented internationalists struggled, China acted as an armed bully and pressed Taiwan militarily, carrying out missile tests and war exercises that interfered with Taiwan shipping and communications. This caused the Taiwan stock market to plummet. China pressed the ruling party on Taiwan, the Nationalists, to dump President Lee and replace him with an individual free of the new Taiwanese nationalism, someone more accommodating to Beijing's wishes for rapid steps toward reunification.

The pressure backfired. A candidate for president of Taiwan who conceded to Beijing would have no future with the nationalistic Taiwan electorate. But mainland China seemed committed to a policy of armed pressure tactics. In fact, further armed initiatives by the rulers of mainland China against Taiwan seem likely as long as Beijing is entangled in a succession crisis that gives veto power to military hardliners, and expansive notions of patriotism are the main means the Communist Party

---

*It is said that President Clinton was not in a hurry to meet again with China's head of government, Jiang Zemin, because of the futility of their meeting at an APEC meeting in Seattle two years earlier when Jiang kept reading a long, prepared statement and brushed off all of Clinton's overtures aimed at real discussions.

dictatorship in Beijing has to entice the people of China, a people who have no love for parasitic state-owned enterprises or a corrupt and privileged Communist Party caste.

Throughout the Asia-Pacific region analysts saw China on the verge of becoming an enemy of peace in Asia. Arms spending by China's southern neighbors skyrocketed. Washington, too, worried that China might destabilize Asia as a rising Germany a century or so earlier had destabilized Europe.

This perception of a militarily dangerous China was shared by leaders in Japan and the Association of Southeast Asian Nations (ASEAN). Yet, for them, little could be done to stop China. Containment was a nonstarter. Neither Japan nor the nations of ASEAN (Brunei, Indonesia, Malaysia, the Philippines, Singapore, Thailand, and Vietnam) would confront an expansive China with force. While ASEAN was a great economic success (Vietnam joined in the summer of 1995) and Japan was an economic giant, neither ASEAN nor Japan had a political constituency at home that would support standing up to a militaristic China. Could the United States contain China on its own, that is, in isolation from other Asian actors? Rulers in Beijing believed not. Therefore China could succeed at territorial bullying. The gains strengthened the views of Chinese chauvinists that a rising China could not be stopped. Analysts tried to derive lessons from the rise of Germany that helped spark two global wars.

Asia's future seemed fraught with high risk. The U.S. policy of engagement seemed incapable of defusing a situation defined by China's quest for world power status. The initiative was with Beijing. As was the case earlier in the twentieth century with Germany, dangerous possibilities lay on the horizon as the United States, Japan, and ASEAN grappled with a chauvinistic and revanchist China that insisted it was merely reincorporating territory that was indisputably Chinese from the South China Sea to China's northern border with Russia.

The Economic Clash Between the United States and China

China spent heavily on its military. After the sobering defeat of Iraq's Soviet-style weaponry in Kuwait, Chinese leaders were more convinced than ever that national strength required economic modernization to provide the wealth and technology suited to a first-rank military power in the age of microelectronic information technology. Increasingly, China's military got what it wanted. Ever since the use of armed might on June 4, 1989 to crush China's democracy movement, China's military enjoyed more weight in the highest councils of power. The military budget expanded at what may have been the fastest rate on the planet in the post–Cold War era. Considering that it cost China one-twentieth of what it cost America to put a soldier in the field, the real purchasing power of the defense budgets of Beijing and Washington for the Asian theater was comparable, a fact denied in Chinese official propaganda. An advancing China paraded as a victim.

The Chinese military leadership, however, was also a business leadership, wed by family ties to a set of companies that exported Chinese weapons to the world. The sales made great wealth for military families. But in the wake of U.S. success in the Gulf War, nations no longer sought to buy Soviet-style weapons such as China purveyed. China's foreign currency earnings from weaponry plummeted to near zero, while the United States weapons sales soared. The United States was indeed the number one threat to China, that is, if China were equated with the luxurious life of China's families of military-connected arms merchants. Those families resisted and resented U.S. efforts to destroy the little business that remained in such items as land mines. Military hardliners in China had plenty of reasons for strong antagonism toward the United States.

In Beijing, the United States's evils seemed endless. Angry at the United States for supposedly causing China not to be selected as a venue for the Olympics and fuming at many other U.S. actions that seemed to hurt the narrowest interests of China's leaders, Beijing powerholders got even with the United States by selling missiles to West Asian nations that the Clinton administration believed would use the weaponry to destabilize that region, an oil-rich powder keg. China's ruling groups enjoyed both the earnings and the idea of sticking a thumb in one of Uncle Sam's eyes. China would stand up to the United States.

China provided technology to Pakistan that furthered Pakistan's nuclear weapons programs. The Clinton administration had few real options to deter China because U.S. law was not calibrated to serve an executive branch facing a nation like China. While America threatened China with sanctions, Washington did not want a hostile relation with Beijing. The United States ended up usually engaging China in a dialogue, trying to persuade China's rulers that peace and stability were also in China's self-interest. Washington sought Beijing's cooperation. It could not compel Beijing's compliance to limits on strategic weapons transfers. No one could. Clinton truly did want to engage China in cooperative efforts. But China regularly demurred.

In Washington, Beijing seemed on the side of dangerously destabilizing policies. The United States in 1993 tracked a Chinese ship heading to the Persian Gulf with chemical weapon components for Iran. China denied the charge. When non-Chinese boarded the ship, they did not find what U.S. intelligence said had been there. Quietly, the U.S. intelligence community let the word spread that hard evidence showed that China had dumped the material into the sea and that, in embarrassing China, the United States had gotten its message through to China's leaders on not transferring destabilizing weapons systems.

That was not the message heard by the Chinese people. China's top military brass, humiliated that they had to permit a foreign boarding of a Chinese ship, put out propaganda at home that, while China actually had clean hands, America was playing a dirty imperialist game of ignoring the sovereign rights of independent nations. China's rulers depicted the United States as China's greatest enemy, the nation most committed to preventing China's rise to a proper position of dignity on the world scene.

China's ever greater self-confidence led national leaders to believe that China was now so important to world economic growth that it would be allowed rapid entry into the World Trade Organization (WTO), which was the successor to the GATT (the General Agreement on Trade and Tariffs), and that a globally weighty China would be allowed not to adhere to many of the general rules of the WTO economic regime. In particular, China's economic laws would not be transparent; China would continue import substitution protection to promote industrialization in sectors such as automobiles; and China would not permit an independent judiciary to rule in disputed cases. When Beijing stood firm for these and other concessions and exceptions to WTO membership rules, Washington unexpectedly blocked China's entry into the WTO.

Ruling groups in China were shocked. They became irate. They had guaranteed their people that negotiations would definitely result in China's entry into the WTO. This was a major issue for ruling groups in Beijing. Increasingly their limited legitimacy rested on international prestige, at times won by Beijing's brazenness and bullying. The rulers' legitimacy also rested on a rapid rise in living standards. Both might be weakened or threatened by exclusion from the WTO. The United States was blamed.

Several studies showed that China would be a major beneficiary from WTO membership. China's exports would continue to zoom. Its domestic industries would move competitively into higher, value-added, manufacturing sectors. By keeping Chinese currency at as low a price as possible to make its exports globally competitive, in imitation of Japan's great success at export-oriented industrialization (EOI), Chinese leaders saw EOI combining with protectionist-based import substitution industrialization (ISI) to make China a world class power that could compete with Japan in Asia. Instead, it seemed in *Zhongnanhai* that a United States that had earlier facilitated Japan's rise during the Cold War was now unilaterally blocking China's rise. Chinese leaders had no intention of passively accepting a world of Japanese economic superiority.

Whatever they said for short-run diplomatic purposes, ruling groups in Beijing and Tokyo saw each other as long-term adversaries. The relationship was infused with passion. The Japanese had been cruel and aggressive occupiers of China during the Asian-Pacific war and much of Chinese patriotism was based on anti-Japan passions. When Beijing damned Washington to the people of China as the major obstacle to Chinese greatness, the patriotic message received in China was that America was the cause of continued Japanese dominance in Asia. To Chinese rulers, that dominance was an injustice.[28]

In fact, the Clinton administration had no animus against China. Rather, Washington was pursuing policies to keep the Asia-Pacific region at peace and to permit the continued expansion of international economic exchanges so that the U.S. economy could benefit from winning its fair share of that growth, and jobs and wealth would be created in the United States. This meant putting an end to the special privileges long permitted to Japan and to others in East Asia who emulated Japan. Effective post–World War II U.S. concessionary policies had permitted Japan to recover rapidly and then climb to the pinnacle of the world economy in an age of U.S. economic predominance. But the Chinese saw the United States changing the rules just as China got into the game.

The Clinton administration challenged Japan, Korea, and Taiwan for economic policies that did not play by the rules of fair trade and openness to financial services and foreign investment. As part of this self-interested policy switch to do right by the weakened U.S. economy, the United States also opposed a China that copied earlier East Asian techniques of EOI and ISI. In Beijing, this U.S. shift looked like Washington had singled out China after facilitating the rise of Tokyo, Seoul, and Taipei. Once again China felt the victim of palpable U.S. unfairness.

In reality, American leaders felt they could not afford to promote the rise of another Japan. China's trade surplus with the United States was soaring astronomically toward Japanese levels in the 1990s. Clinton could not deliver on his promise to the American people to make the U.S. economy his top priority if he conceded to a China of 1.2 billion people that was about to emulate a Taiwan EOI model. While Taiwan was home only to 20 million people, less than the population of California, China was home to four times as many people as the total U.S. population. There had to be different rules toward a mosquito and a mammoth. A relatively weakened United States could not afford unrestrained economic aggression by China at its expense. The 1990s were not the 1960s. America could not afford to treat a huge China in the 1990s as it had a tiny Taiwan in the 1960s.

In addition, in the post–Cold War era, international economic policy was high politics in Washington, a major focus of diplomacy. It also was a key electoral concern for Clinton, since voters in the automobile industry and other industries felt that the major issue for them was protecting their jobs. It was not easy to justify transferring American jobs to people in a China whose government seemed bloody and nefarious. China's undiplomatic tirades at the United States made it more difficult for Washington to accommodate Beijing.

Beijing and Washington also clashed over the protection of intellectual property rights (IPR). Software exports tied to the U.S. entertainment and information industries had special salience in California. China intended to master microelectronic technologies quickly and not squander precious foreign exchange on purchasing low-end products that China already had the technology to copy, such as CDs of rock stars. During Taiwan's 1960s rise, Taipei had been a master at getting away with information pirating. My bookshelves are lined with cheap classics pirated in Taiwan. This IPR pirating, a form of ISI, was little talked about in the 1960s. But the U.S. economy had so weakened that East Asian pirating of IPR in the 1990s, in contrast to the booming 1960s golden age of U.S. growth, could no longer be overlooked in Washington as a petty problem.

American companies such as Microsoft wanted to be in the expanding China market. High-tech Silicon Valley companies in California and other software firms that supported Clinton's election campaign with money and business endorsements were not happy about a loss of some $2 billion a year in potential U.S. sales in Asia because China pirated and exported American IPR.

To be sure, U.S. policy toward developing countries that pirated technology merely to save foreign exchange was often permissive. China, however, did not only pirate for home use. It also exported to the emerging markets of the new tigers of Southeast Asia, ignoring IPR and costing U.S. wealth and jobs. Following Japan's practice, the Chinese government, when confronted by America with proof of violations of international rules, promised only meaningless concessions in response to U.S. requests for abiding by IPR rules. After many months of fruitless talks, the Special Trade Representative of the U.S. president received permission from Clinton to put punitive tariffs on potential Chinese imports to the United States equal to the potential loss to American firms from IPR violations. The United States would not be a patsy for China.

Beijing again was stunned. China's rulers apparently expected the United States to back down and accept merely cosmetic changes. Instead, Washington stuck to its guns. To avoid punitive sanctions, China was forced—at least temporarily—to close down pirating factories so as not to lose uniquely valuable export access to the United States, China's most important market and most important source of the foreign exchange required to import advanced technology used to upgrade Chinese industries. China needed good economic relations with the United States if China were to rise quickly. In fact, U.S. openness was, in general, central to the economic success of developing nations, with the United States importing far more manufactured products from the developing world than all of the European Union and Japan combined. China actually had especially favorable access to the U.S. market because of privileges granted by Washington during the entente against the Soviet Union.

The United States had to adjust to a new era brought on by the end of the Bretton Woods system that it had made work for a generation after the end of World War II. Under Bretton-Woods an open trading system had strongly benefitted all parties by permitting governments to manage national economies using macroeconomic policy levers to facilitate the expansion of a mass middle class that stabilized societies. In the post–Bretton Woods era, in contrast, internationally mobile private capital made government macro-management of a national economy in the interest of growth plus equity virtually impossible. Instead, the uncontrolled movement of private capital was wagered against policies of social equity, engendering economically polarizing forces.

Exploding inequality was destabilizing China. In contrast to most East Asian development states, polarization accompanied growth in China and threatened to splinter the national society. Therefore, one major economic area on which the United States, China, and many other nations might well cooperate was fostering international organs that could help governments reverse polarizing forces.[29]

Solutions to post–Bretton Woods conundrums required large initiatives and bold, creative thinking. Mutual benefit seemed hard to achieve in a world where foreign policy served narrow domestic political needs in various countries. Consequently, the clash of interests between the United States and China also reflected the inevitable impact of each side merely looking out for its own priority interests in the new, post–Bretton Woods, post–Cold War era that threatened mutually beneficial international economic cooperation, as described in this volume in Chapter 4 by Benjamin Cohen and Chapter 9 by Steven Vogel.

Yet China wanted the United States to act as it had in the Bretton Woods era so that China too could grow as most of East Asia had in that prior period. At first, after Nixon's 1972 visit, that seemed possible. In contrast to Soviet Russia, China was given MFN access to the U.S. market. In addition, the United States granted China the largest import quota to the U.S. market in the Multi Fiber Agreement (MFA), which had previously been granted to Hong Kong. With labor costs in Taiwan, Korea, and Hong Kong increasing by the mid-1980s, their businesses moved machines and capital to China to use cheap Chinese labor and thus hold historic U.S. market shares. China raged at America in the 1990s for not welcoming the growing of China's economy by applying the rules used in the Bretton Woods era, super-generous rules that the United States no longer could afford in an age of relative decline and intensifying polarization.

Leaders in Beijing scapegoated Washington for no longer being able to shoulder impossible burdens. United States domestic politics in the 1990s, however, precluded a president, any president, from the broad concessions of the kind that marked American policy in the 1940s, 1950s, and 1960s. Thus large changes in the United States and the world virtually guaranteed that Chinese rulers trying to repeat the East

Asian economic miracle in the 1990s by aggressive exporting to the United States would be a bit frustrated in achieving their goals. Given the great power preoccupations and nationalistic preconceptions of China's rulers, the first casualty of this inevitable change and clash was good China-America relations.

America as China's Number One Enemy

When international economic sanctions against the perpetrators of the June 4, 1989 Beijing massacre of democracy movement demonstrators failed, when there was no response in China subsequent to democratization in East Europe, when Chinese growth resumed in 1992 at a record pace, and when international agencies projected that in a quarter of a century China could well be the world's largest economy, the self-confidence of China's rulers soared. As Germany had at the end of the nineteenth century in Europe, so was China fundamentally changing the world dynamics of power politics by its rise in the Asia-Pacific region at the turn of the twenty-first century. China was an ever weightier political actor. The new feeling of national pride was exploited in an attempt to legitimate ruling groups in Beijing who the populace blamed for an alarming inflation, skyrocketing unemployment, violent social disorder, pervasive corruption, merit-denying nepotism, and destabilizing income polarization. China's combination of economic strength, great power ambitions, and social fragility could prove an explosive mixture.

As with other reforming Leninist command economies, rulers in Beijing were beset by almost intractable and divisive forces. Power seemed to shift from the center to the regions where local governmental entities sought to maximize the interests of their communities whose cultural identities were passionately embraced and deeply appreciated in ways that had brought disintegration to Czechoslovakia, Ethiopia, Yugoslavia, and the Soviet Union. To the Chinese, China seemed both a rising economic giant and a splintering polity.[30] America had to respond to a Chinese foreign policy that reflected this bifurcation, which simultaneously promised both best-case and worst-case possibilities. The hope was that the promise of mutual benefit was so strong that the worst case forces in Chinese politics would always be forced to pull back from the brink of disaster. That is what seemed to happen in mid-1995 after the crisis over Taiwan. The U.S. Government consequently stuck with a policy of across-the-board engagement with China, while maintaining close and quiet consultations with its anxious neighbors.

Military-minded, old-fashioned hardliners in China, however, sought to contain the splintering forces there by introducing tough policies at home and abroad. They offered 110 percent support to an expansive Chinese nationalism. China's people supposedly would welcome a foreign policy in which China's new might was used to compel neighbors to respect its territorial rights. National strength would legitimate the old guard dictatorship as true Chinese patriotism. This hardline approach seemed supported by old peasants and young urban workers, both of whom feared that economic reforms threatened their interests. Any mention by non-Chinese of anxieties over Chinese military expansiveness was immediately denounced by Chinese chauvinists as ignorant and unfriendly, a continuation of imperialist attitudes that no longer would be tolerated.

In contrast, more open-minded Chinese reformers sought more federalist ways to conciliate regional discontent at home. These more internationally minded reformers sought more mutually beneficial ways to resolve differences with foreign neighbors. The clash between the two groups and the two policies was vivid on the issue of South China Sea oil.[31] Whose oil was it? How should China obtain that oil? Hardliners and reformers seemed to offer fundamentally different answers.

The hardliners would press with military force to monopolize the wealth and territory for China even if it alienated ASEAN neighbors, worried Japan, and prevented cooperation. According to a Chinese Naval spokesman:

> Since 1970, over 30 islands in China's Spratley archipelago have been occupied by other countries who have stolen marine resources. China's rights and interests are now under challenge. . . . only with a strong naval force can the ocean protect the mainland and ocean resources become a treasure trove to enrich the nation. . . . the role of the navy will grow as the importance of the wealth of the oceans rises. A global struggle for the seas will intensify and armed conflicts and regional wars on the seas will occur more frequently.[32]

Keeping the South Sea issue unresolved also kept the petroleum from being pumped out and put to productive use. Reformers, in contrast, would seek mutually beneficial international agreements to share the wealth, build friendly relations, and make China a partner in the general prosperity of East and Southeast Asia. The chauvinist's policy could long delay exploitation of the rich resource, said to be among the largest untapped oil fields in the world. Chauvinists held back China's economic rise.

The reform policy, however, could be portrayed by the hardliners as a surrender of Chinese sovereignty, a failure to stand up to foreign challenges, something that Chinese patriots should not tolerate. China's rise had fostered a vengeful nationalism that made it feel in China like it was finally time to stand up. Therefore, numerous outside observers predicted that the internationalists would be bested by the chauvinists.

The political clash in China over the nation's future course also reminded numerous observers of the contrasting possibilities that existed in the rise of nineteenth century Germany. Historians still debate when the rivalry between Britain and France, on the one hand, and a rising Germany, on the other, passed a point of no return and made war inevitable. A similar debate pervades the high politics of both Japan and the members of ASEAN vis-à-vis China. United States policy is to engage China so as to make the worst case outcome less likely. But the clashes are real and explosive.

While China insists that the South China Sea, even 800 miles from its mainland, is Chinese, Japan wants the South China Sea ocean route to West Asian oil open. Tankers for oil for Japan pass through every half hour. The nations of ASEAN want a fair share of the wealth in the sea. Taiwan agrees with the perspectives of Japan and ASEAN. While the United States sympathizes with the concerns of Taiwan, Japan, and ASEAN, Washington certainly is not looking for a fight with the Chinese military, which regularly overpowers the navies of ASEAN in the disputed South China Seas far more frequently than is publicly reported. China's strategy has been to give vague and empty reassurances to neighbors and then push further with its military. Adjacent countries have not been reassured. Consequently, anxieties in ASEAN and Japan keep growing.

China's expansion in the South China Seas and its flaunting of Japanese public opinion in continuing to test nuclear weapons in 1995 led, for the first time, to a Tokyo policy of explicit opposition to Beijing's policies.[33] Japan froze its concessional aid to China, the largest bloc of such funds available to Beijing. In addition, Tokyo refused to renegotiate the terms of yen-denominated loans to Beijing, which cost the recipient much more when the yen increased in international value. Finally, Japan publicly sided with ASEAN on South China Sea issues. Chinese rulers were shocked and appalled by Japan's retaliation.

Policy toward Japan is a most sensitive issue in China. Seeking to drum up popular support in 1995, Chinese rulers for the first time allowed public demonstrations demanding reparations for Japanese atrocities committed during World War II. Day after day China commemorated the fiftieth anniversary of the end of the war by focusing on Japanese savagery. Never before had China celebrated the end of the war this way. Japanese evils of more than half a century ago had been swept under the rug in the Mao era when Tokyo and Beijing normalized relations in 1972. Tokyo apparently saw its generous concessional aid to China as reparations under a face-saving name. Hence, in Tokyo it seemed that China in 1995 had taken an uncalled-for anti-Japanese tack. China seemed to have launched a crusade against its neighbors and benefactors. In response, attitudes toward China were changing throughout the region.

American responses to the challenge of China's rise were restrained. The U.S. Navy patrolled the South China Seas. The Navy saw continual evidence of China's gunboat diplomacy. That Chinese policy actually began in 1974, on the heels of the first OPEC oil crisis, when China seized islands in the South China Sea held by the nearly extinct Saigon government. The Communist Party regime in Hanoi experienced the Chinese conquest as, in fact, an attack on it, since Hanoi would soon topple Saigon and unite all of Vietnam. Hanoi claimed those islands as integral to its Vietnam. Indeed, Vietnam had the largest oil claim in the South China Sea that conflicted with China's insistence that the sea and all its oil, was, and always had been, sacred Chinese territory.

China argued that a weak navy had long made China vulnerable to imperialist aggression. China now demanded the return of lost territories, including the oil-rich South China Sea, seen as the energy source for the economic growth of China in the twenty-first century. The government-run media insisted that anything less than everything for China was national betrayal, no matter what the conflicting claims.

By the mid-1990s, China's policy seemed one of bait and switch. In response to complaints by aggrieved neighboring states, Beijing regularly said it would observe international law both toward Japanese shipping and ASEAN seabed claims; but, in practice, China quietly kept moving south, insisting it was acting on unquestionable, age-old sovereign rights. In addition, China would soon obtain an aircraft carrier to assure itself the military strength to hold the disputed region.

By 1996, China's diplomatic sweet-talk and military hard ball had set off alarms in Japan, Vietnam, Singapore, Taiwan, the Philippines, and Indonesia. Yet no government contemplated military action against China. Their internal political realities made a policy of containment taboo. ASEAN's economic unity was premised on not confronting sensitive political issues. Japan's democratic government was restrained by cruel memories of Japan's military aggression in Asia in World War II. ASEAN and Japan therefore merely appealed to Chinese reason, to mutual benefit, and to international law. China saw a window of opportunity and kept moving south.

As in the United States, China's Asian neighbors hoped that reform forces would win out in China and that a policy of maximum positive engagement with China would strengthen internationalist political forces that sought a policy of peace, prosperity, and mutual benefit. The United States continued its policy of engagement toward China, promoting cooperation on numerous important issues of mutual concern: AIDS research, nuclear power plant safeguards, drug interdiction, nuclear testing computer simulation, international corporate alliances, science and technology exchanges.[34]

No nation directly confronted Beijing. None embraced a policy of containment. None specifically asked for U.S. backing. Military chauvinists in Beijing took this lack of a military response to Chinese expansionism as evidence that there was a short time slot for China before ASEAN, Japan, and the United States could act in a coordinated way to preclude Chinese irredentism. The oil-rich South China Seas became a potential flash point for war. Whether some little spark might ignite a conflagration or some blitzkreig action by newly formed Chinese rapid action forces would do it, China seemed capable of following the path that Germany had taken earlier in the twentieth century.

In response, the United States chose only to keep monitoring the region with the U.S. Navy and making explicit the strong U.S. interest in a peaceful and negotiated resolution of outstanding issues. But in China that formula sounded like a threat, more a provocation than a restraint, a paper tiger United States's way of bluffing to keep China from using its newly acquired military strength to take back what was rightfully China's. Giving in to the United States's merely verbal insistence that China act peacefully would keep Taiwan separate from the mainland of China. Hence, America was portrayed in China as a direct threat to Chinese sovereign rights.

To hardliners in Beijing, America seemed the number one enemy of a rising, strong and united China. Hardliners called for a halt to reform and a recentralization of power in Beijing. Given the regionalist tendencies inherent in reform economics that moved away from a centralized command economy, Chinese chauvinists could imagine a world where, as a result of reform and central government weakness, China's west and north, areas popularly known as East Turkestan, Tibet, and Inner Mongolia, half the territory of China, would seize the opportunity of Beijing concessions on claims of territorial sovereignty to split off. Consequently, centralization of all power and using it to back an active military was presented as the only way to achieve the promise of a united and powerful China.

Washington kept assuring China that it did not threaten Chinese nationalism, that the United States in no way challenged the notion of one China, that America accepted the rise of a strong and united China. But nativists in Beijing insisted that U.S. actions contradicted U.S. reassurances. They pointed to U.S. policies toward Taiwan, the U.S. Navy in the South China Sea, and the U.S. promotion of human rights, seen as a major incitement to splittist forces in China. The United States therefore seemed the enemy. To be sure, China's economy needed the U.S. market and backing in international financial institutions, but the superpatriots insisted that national dignity should not be sacrificed for mere material gains. Even Chinese reformers dared not publicly contradict chauvinistic rhetoric during a succession crisis.

Yet the United States was not the source of China's problems. The partial loss of central control over Chinese regions was inherent in China's reform project. The assertiveness of Turkic Muslims, of the nations of ASEAN, Taiwan nationalism, and Japan all had indigenous causes. The United States served as a scapegoat. Unless Chinese reformers defeated hardliners in the power struggle in Beijing, the United States would continue to be cast in the role of China's number one enemy.

The harsh truth for Washington was that the United States's power and influence were quite limited. Washington could do little beyond maintaining good relations with Japan and ASEAN, cautioning Taiwan, and continuing a policy of broad engagement with China. In the post–Cold War era of no over-riding political purpose to restrain narrow nationalisms, Washington had little impact on whether China would spark the kind of tragic denouement that Germany significantly contributed to earlier in the twentieth century.

Conclusion

Diplomats and area specialists in the United States tend to resist the conclusion that China's expansionist nationalism is mainly a reflection of internal changes in China, including a power struggle in which nativist elements in the military have momentarily joined with enemies of deeper reform in China. These analysts have so long earned their keep by insisting that the place they study is misunderstood by nonspecialists that many have overlooked the new and rising Chinese challenge that cries out for understanding and analysis. Analysts continually overstate the influence of the United States and other foreign forces, as if more sweetness from Washington could reverse Beijing's chauvinistic actions. Perhaps containment could do that, but containment is politically impossible just now.

Still, reformers in China remain optimistic that, if America is not provocative, then, after the succession struggle to paramount leader Deng Xiaoping is settled by their triumph, it will be easy to remove irritants to mutually beneficial relations in the Asia-Pacific region by sharing the oil wealth of the South China Seas with ASEAN; by offering Taiwan a fair deal, perhaps including the benefits of a common Chinese market; by adhering to the terms of the agreement for China to resume sovereign authority over Hong Kong at the end of June 1997 in ways that will guarantee Hong Kong's social system and prosperity; and by devolving more power within China.[35]

But this happy outcome is far from guaranteed. The United States, and all others, therefore, should act to make more likely a peaceful and mutually beneficial resolution of Beijing-Washington tensions. This has been well understood in the White House. It has led to a policy of broad engagement in which promoting APEC is the heart of U.S. China policy. The goal is to make it palpable to contending groups in Beijing that what is best for the people of China is mutually beneficial economic cooperation.

Reformers and internationalists in China may be winning out on just such a platform. After all, victory for the chauvinists means a loss of the international ties and access needed to raise living standards, a primary concern of the long-suffering people of China. Consequently, many analysts see a consensus developing in China to reign in chauvinists who would take China down a less peaceful path. Yet "irrational atavisms" cannot absolutely be ruled out. It is uncertain whether this rising China will pull back from direct confrontations with Japan, Taiwan, ASEAN, and the United States to avoid aborting its extraordinarily promising rise to great power status.[36] Mutually beneficial, long run economic relations can still infuse the relationship. But real differences cannot be willed away.

Economic policy has become high politics in an era in which there is no overarching political cause to rally Americans or to unite with friends and allies. Washington wants to make Beijing's membership in APEC the heart of a positive-sum game that all sides can win, expanding their economies and raising the standards of living of all parties. Unfortunately, the U.S. vision for APEC has not meshed with Beijing's ideas on how to rise in the world economy. Washington seeks market-openness. In contrast, China seeks to emulate Japan's post–World War II combination of ISI and EOI, of import protectionism and export aggressiveness. But America can no longer allow a China of 1.2 billion people to one-sidedly benefit from the U.S. economy as Japan, South Korea, and Taiwan could a generation ago. As with economic dislocations before World Wars I and II, which facilitated hate-filled, narrow nationalisms, a particularly dangerous moment in the world economy can be fraught with uncontrollable war-prone forces.

There is no nation in Asia or anywhere in the rest of the world capable of the generosity of a hegemon, capable of the openness and beneficence which can guarantee that nasty economic tensions do not deteriorate into misunderstanding, scapegoating, and political warfare. Many believe that it was the decline of a hegemonic Britain that turned English-German adversarial cooperation into the all-out hostilities that made war more likely in the era before the First World War. If so, this suggests that the U.S. focus on engaging China in forms of economic cooperation has actually not been strong enough. To preclude worst case outcomes, China and the United States have to do more. They have to join with others to build new and mutually beneficial international economic organs. The imperative for cooperation is truly international. More energetic action is needed to end the financial disorder of the last quarter of the twentieth century that makes it so difficult for countries to manage their own currencies and to use macroeconomic levers at home to facilitate growth with equity. Newly expanded and mobile private capital in the trillions of dollars moves rapidly to punish governments committed to social equity.[37] Both China and the United States, indeed virtually all countries on the planet, consequently suffer the destabilizing pains of income polarization. If reformers cannot deliver on promises of growth with equity, chauvinistic demagogues may win support by scapegoating foreigners and promoting expansive strength. Can governments legitimate a call to action to reverse the polarizing forces of the international economy?

At a time in the United States when there is a consensus in favor of neo-liberal assumptions that the best government action to help the economy is no government intervention, however, it is not likely that a U.S. president could easily lead the world to create new institutions of international governance that would mitigate or reverse out-of-control international financial forces that promote destabilizing polarization. Instead each nation is on its own. One scapegoats the other. Mistrust grows across borders. The habit of scapegoating the foreigners grows at home. When Washington and Beijing have economic clashes, it is therefore far more likely to add fuel to the fires than to prod cool thinking toward building useful new international institutions.

This means that, if the United States wishes not to go down the path with China that led to British-German hostilities and the First World War, then it may have to embrace a new economic cause as a high priority and to persuade all major nations that reining in the power of speculative private capital is a shared interest. What is needed for an era of peace and prosperity with China, as with others, is a joining together to build international economic institutions that will provide for the information age what the Bretton Woods system did for the age of mass production and mass consumption, that is, make it easier for governments to deliver the goods to their people so that militaristic and nativistic demagogues do not meet with a popular response to their hate-filled appeals that blame the foreign. If Washington can not help lead the world in that better direction, if reformers do not continue to win the power struggle in China, then its rise to power could indeed lead to disasters similar to those associated with the rise of Germany in the first half of the twentieth century.

Endnotes

1. For an up-to-date overview of U.S. policy to China, see Michael Mandelbaum, *The Strategic Quadrangle* (New York: Council on Foreign Relations Books, 1995).
2. On Chinese relations with the Soviet Union, see Lowell Dittmer, *Sino-Soviet Normalization and Its International Implications, 1945–1990* (Seattle: University of Washington Press, 1991).
3. *See* William Duiker, *China and Vietnam* (Berkeley, Calif.: Institute of East Asian Studies, 1986).
4. Edward Friedman, *National Identity and Democratic Prospects in Socialist China* (Armonk, N.Y.: M. E. Sharpe, 1995).
5. Harry Harding, *China's Second Revolution* (Washington, DC: Brookings Institution, 1987).
6. The Commission on Global Governance, *Our Global Neighborhood* (New York: Oxford University Press, 1995), p. 139.

7. Marshall Goldman, *Lost Opportunity* (New York: Norton, 1994).

8. Paul Kennedy, *The Rise and Fall of the Great Powers* (New York: Lexington Books, 1987), p. 448.

9. Gerald Curtis (ed.), *The United States, Japan and Asia* (New York: Norton, 1994).

10. Ann Kent, *Between Freedom and Subsistence: China and Human Rights* (Hong Kong: Oxford University Press, 1993).

11. Tun-jen Cheng, et al. (eds.), *Inherited Rivalry: Conflict Across the Taiwan Straits* (Boulder, Colo.: Lynne Rienner, 1995).

12. Nancy Bernkopf Tucker, *Taiwan, Hong Kong and the United States, 1945–1992* (New York: Twayne, 1994).

13. Harry Harding, *A Fragile Friendship: The United States and China Since 1972* (Washington, DC: Brookings Institution, 1992).

14. Samuel Kim, "China's Pacific Policy," *International Journal* I (Summer 1995): 471.

15. Zhiling Lin and Thomas Robinson (eds.), *The Chinese and Their Future* (Washington, DC: AEI, 1994) defends a policy of containment.

16. On Bush era U.S. policies toward China, *see* Steven Levine, "Sino-American Relations: Testing the Limits of Discord," in Samuel Kim (ed.), *China and the World* (Boulder, Colo.: Westview, 1994), pp. 77–93.

17. William Overholt, *The Rise of China* (New York: Norton, 1993).

18. *China Youth Daily* (in Chinese), January 9, 1995, p. A4. Chinese friends suggest that the survey reporting negative attitudes toward the United States was concocted and is not credible.

19. Yoichi Funibashi, et al., *An Emerging China in a World of Interdependence* (New York: The Trilateral Commission, 1994).

20. David Lampton, "America's China Policy in the Age of the Finance Minister: Clinton Ends Linkage," *The China Quarterly*, No. 139 (September 1994): 599–621.

21. For a refutation of the notion that democratization is the direct result of socio-economic development, *see* Edward Friedman (ed.), *The Politics of Democratization* (Boulder, Colo.: Westview, 1994).

22. Nicholas Kristoff and Sheryl Wudunn, *China Wakes* (New York: Random House, 1994).

23. Russia also had worries about China. Hundreds of thousands of Chinese poured in to Russia. Beijing wooed newly independent Central Asian republics. Resurgent, expansionist Chinese nationalism kept on its agenda large sections of Russia in Asia that Chinese super-patriots claimed had been stolen from, and should be returned to, China.

24. Hsin-hsing Wu, *Bridging the Strait: Taiwan, China, and the Prospects for Reunification* (Hong Kong: Oxford University Press, 1994).

25. Jaushieh Joseph Wu, *Taiwan's Democratization* (Hong Kong: Oxford University Press, 1995).

26. James Fallows, *Looking at The Sun* (New York: Pantheon, 1994).

27. Robert Bartley, et al., *Democracy and Capitalism: Asian and American Perspectives* (Singapore: Institute of Southeast Asian Studies, 1993).

28. Allen Whiting, *China Eyes Japan* (Berkeley, Calif.: University of California Press, 1989); Akira Iriye, *China and Japan in the Global Setting* (Cambridge: Harvard University Press, 1992).

29. *See Our Global Neighborhood.*

30. David Goodman and Gerald Segal (eds.), *China Deconstructs: Politics, Trade and Regionalism* (London: Routledge, 1994).

31. Eric Heyer (ed.), "The South China Sea Territorial Disputes," *The American Asian Review*, Vol. 12, No. 4 (Fall 1994): 1–209.

32. An interview with the Director of the Department of Naval Equipment Technology, Warship Division, *Jianchuan Zhishi*, July 8, 1995, translated in FBIS-CHI-95-169 (August 31, 1995), p. 30.

33. Satoshi Ista, "On China Policy, Japan Takes Off the Kid Gloves," *Nikkei Weekly*, August 14, 1995.

34. Richard Suttmeier, "Does 'Globalization' Matter?" *In Depth*, Vol. 4, No. 3 (Fall 1994): 65–84.
35. Frank Ching, "A New China-Taiwan Scenario: An Accord to End the Current Stalemate is Still Possible," *Far Eastern Economic Review* (September 21, 1995): 42.
36. Paul Monk, *China: An Emerging Superpower* (Taipei: Chinese Council of Advanced Policy Study, 1995), pp. 18, 22, 26, 30.
37. Eric Heilleiner, *States and the Emergence of Global Finance* (Ithaca, N.Y.: Cornell University Press, 1994).

The Clinton Administration and the Americas: Moving to the Rhythm of the Postwar World

Robert A. Pastor

For 40 years, Americans were so fearful of a thermonuclear bang that they barely noticed the whimper when the Cold War ended. They could not even agree on the date of the war's end. Still, the American people sensed its eagle had completed a great adventure and was returning to its nest, and that's where they wanted it.

President George Bush was more sensitive to the shift in the balance of power in the Persian Gulf than to the swing in the American mood. His quick success in the Persian Gulf lifted his popularity to a zenith, making his re-election defeat the next year all the more painful and seemingly inexplicable.

But Bush's 1992 defeat was not hard to explain. Forty years before, Frank Klingberg wrote about the swings in American policy between periods of "extroversion," when the United States turned its attention and energies abroad, to "introversion," when it concentrated on internal problems.[1] The pendulum tended to swing toward home after wars. Like Bush, Woodrow Wilson and Harry Truman also expected tributes from the American people for their triumphs in war; all were stunned

---

Robert A. Pastor is professor of political science at Emory University and a Fellow at The Carter Center where he has organized 14 election-monitoring missions to 10 countries in the Americas and the Middle East. The author of ten books on U.S. foreign policy and on Latin America, he was Director of Latin American Affairs on the National Security Council from 1977–1981. In September 1994, he advised the Carter-Nunn-Powell team that negotiated the peaceful restoration of constitutional government to Haiti.

I would like to thank Robert Lieber, Richard Feinberg, Michael Shifter, Abraham Lowenthal, and David Carroll for superb comments on previous drafts of this chapter.

246

by the severity of the rejection. Wilson and Truman were fortunate, comparatively, that the next election—in 1918 and 1946, respectively—was for Congress; only Bush faced a presidential election right after a war. But the verdict was the same in all three cases: the American people voted for the opposition and "a return to normalcy" and domestic concerns.

Bill Clinton read the shift in the national mood. Foreign policy experience was no longer Bush's asset or his liability; Americans wanted their leaders to focus on domestic issues.[2] Communism was defeated and could no longer serve to justify U.S. involvement abroad. In the post–Cold War era, foreign policy needed new justifications as well as criteria to judge when to engage. The Clinton administration chose to justify its internationalism by reference to domestic political concerns like drugs, crime, or jobs, and it employed a domestic political calculus to judge when and how to respond to a foreign crisis. This heightened the influence of interest groups, whether ethnic or business, in foreign policy decisions on a par to their effect on domestic policy. The guidance for President Clinton's foreign policy advisors was to limit the President's time and the nation's commitments in the international arena and to avoid mistakes that could reduce the political capital needed to achieve the administration's domestic goals.

Bill Clinton's foreign policy challenge was similar to the one faced by Franklin D. Roosevelt (FDR) and Harry Truman in 1945: how to define a mission in which the United States would play a leading role in the world despite the popular mood to stay at home. FDR's answer to this challenge was to lock the United States into an international role by creating new international institutions—the UN, the International Monetary Fund (IMF), the World Bank. Clinton's formula was to blur the line separating foreign and domestic issues, addressing international issues as if they were domestic. Instead of relating U.S. interests to changes in the world, as had been done in the past, he approached the challenge from the opposite direction: trying to cope with the internal causes and consequences of international crises.

The Clinton administration's hemispheric policy can be divided roughly in half. For the first two years, the administration focused on the two issues inherited from George Bush—the North American Free Trade Agreement (NAFTA) and Haiti. After awkward beginnings, President Clinton succeeded in fashioning solutions to both problems. Clinton faced a second challenge after the November 1994 election: how to lead a divided government in which the Republican Congress was even less internationally minded than the president and even more political in the sense of viewing foreign policy as a vehicle for wooing or winning constituent support. At a time of unrivaled U.S. power, the president and his opposition competed to demonstrate their disinterest in international affairs, except at those moments when a foreign policy or posture could yield a domestic political benefit.

The Inherited Agenda: Two Problems and an Opportunity

President George Bush completed and signed NAFTA in December 1992. Upon taking office, President Clinton needed to decide *how* to modify it, *when* to send it to Congress, and *how much* political capital to invest in getting it approved. Beyond that, NAFTA posed central issues for the United States in terms of how it should relate regional and global trade strategies to new geopolitical realities. The problem of Haiti was twofold: what to do about the thousands of refugees fleeing to our shores, and how much effort should be made to restore President Jean-Bertrand Aristide?

Both Haiti and NAFTA were discrete issues, but both sat in the intersection of two roads—democratization and free trade—that were reshaping the Americas and providing the United States with a "regionalist option" to compete against the two other great pan-regions—the European Union (EU) and East Asia.[3]

Latin America had felt the swing of the pendulum between democracy and dictatorship three times since World War II, but the most majestic swing toward democracy began in the mid-1970s and continued to the point that almost every government in the Americas in 1992 had conducted a free, competitive election. Still, most of these democracies were fragile, and even those like Venezuela and Colombia that had decades of experience found themselves threatened by military coups and drug-traffickers. The issue for the nations of the hemisphere was whether and, if so, how to reinforce each other against coups, and specifically, whether to take forceful steps to reverse the 1991 coup in Haiti.

Of equal significance for the region was its economic transformation since the mid-1980s. To overcome the adverse effects of the debt crisis, Latin American governments replaced an old import-substitution model with a more modern, export-oriented one. Virtually all the governments reduced trade and investment barriers as well as their fiscal and trade deficits. Governments became smaller, and many state corporations were privatized.

In the spring of 1990, Mexican President Carlos Salinas proposed a free trade agreement with the United States. This was a revolutionary proposal from a country that had spent 150 years building walls to keep out U.S. goods, investment, and influence.[4]

Canada judged that the best way to prevent dilution of its own trade agreement with the United States was to make the U.S.-Mexican talks three-sided. So all three countries approached the pact defensively, unaware of the degree to which they were already integrated or of their pan-region's potential to compete with the EU or Asia. Trade among the three North American countries had increased ten-fold in 20 years, from roughly $120 billion in 1970 to $1.2 trillion in 1990.[5] Intra-regional trade as a percentage of the total trade of the three North American countries was 42 percent—smaller than the 62 percent of the highly integrated EU, but larger than the 30 percent for Asia. The gross product of North America was $6.2 trillion in 1990—more than the EU ($5.9 trillion) or Asia (Japan, ASEAN, the Four Tigers = $3.8 trillion).

With the end of the Cold War, trade within each of the three pan-regions began to grow far more rapidly than between them.[6] The United States and Latin America increasingly turned to each other economically. From 1986, U.S. exports to the hemisphere grew three times as fast as U.S. exports to the entire world, making the region the fastest growing market for U.S. goods. Canada's growing involvement in the Organization of American States (OAS) and throughout the region provided the United States the opportunity to expand its focus from Latin America to the entire hemisphere.

Regrettably, NAFTA and Haiti were initially treated by the Clinton administration as specific problems not as opportunities to construct a wider, trade-based democratic community. Indeed, the administration tried to postpone decisions on both since they were viewed as no-win issues politically. During the presidential campaign, Clinton tried to avoid NAFTA because unions and environmentalists—two key constituencies in the Democratic Party—were vehemently opposed, believing that it would induce U.S. companies to invest in Mexico where labor was cheap and environmental laws were weak. Clinton did not want to antagonize these groups by supporting NAFTA, but he also knew that opposing NAFTA would make him vulnerable to Republican charges of being a "protectionist." Bush wanted to force Clinton to take a stand, and on October 4, 1992, Clinton did so in North Carolina.

Clinton explained that he would support NAFTA and improve on it by negotiating side agreements on the environment and labor and by placing the agreement within the context of a national economic strategy that created more and better jobs. Clinton concluded his remarks by bringing the issue home: "In the end, whether the North American Free Trade Agreement is a good thing for America, is not a question of foreign policy. It is a question of domestic policy."[7] Bush signed the agreement after the election, leaving the hard part—gaining Congress's approval—for Clinton.

The second inherited issue was Haiti. In December 1990, Haiti conducted the first free and fair election in its history with the substantial assistance of the UN and the OAS, and the mediation by the Council of Freely Elected Heads of Government, a group of 25 presidents of the Americas, chaired by Jimmy Carter. Jean-Bertrand Aristide, a young priest, was elected with two-thirds of the vote. His election turned Haiti's traditional power pyramid upside down, putting the champion of the masses on top in the Presidential Palace and pushing down the elite. It was a delicate transition, and it did not last. On September 30, 1991, barely seven months after his inauguration, the military overthrew Aristide with the consent of the oligarchy and perhaps at their invitation. When he later reflected on what had gone wrong, Aristide acknowledged that perhaps he had won the election by too much. He had little incentive to compromise, and he showed too little respect for the independence of the Parliament.[8]

Three months before the coup, the OAS General Assembly had met in Santiago, Chile and approved a resolution of solidarity for democracies. In the case of an interruption of constitutional rule, the foreign ministers all agreed to convene an emergency meeting of the OAS to consider specific steps to permit the restoration of democracy. Haiti provided the first test. Within days of the coup, the OAS foreign ministers met in Washington, quickly condemned the coup, and sent a delegation to Haiti to demand the return of Aristide. Paramilitary thugs threatened the ministers, and the military treated them shabbily. The OAS responded by imposing an economic embargo on the regime.

Secretary of State James Baker said the coup would not stand, but the Bush administration was divided on whether Aristide's return was desirable. The principal concern was stopping the flow of Haitian refugees, and in the spring of 1992, after Bush ordered the U.S. Coast Guard to return Haitians, the pressure on him to restore Aristide diminished. During the campaign, Bill Clinton criticized Bush's "cruel policy of returning Haitian refugees to a brutal dictatorship without an asylum hearing, but Bush maintained the policy."

Promises and Their Implications

Shortly after Clinton's election, the news media reported thousands of Haitians building boats to flee to the United States. Bush administration sources explained that this was due to Haitian expectations of a more lenient policy by Clinton because of his comments during the campaign. Through confidential briefings and selected leaks to the press, Bush administration officials conveyed their fear that if the president-elect postponed a decision on Haitian refugees, he would face a massive boatlift in his first week in office.

On January 14, 1993, Clinton rejected a host of intermediate options and announced that he would continue Bush's policy of using the Coast Guard to return the Haitian refugees. He pledged that the policy would be temporary and that it's purpose was to prevent loss of life by Haitians fleeing in unsound boats. To gain President Aristide's support, Clinton promised that he would restore him to power. The president-elect was criticized severely for reversing his campaign position, but his decision was a signal of the importance that the refugee problem would play in the new administration's foreign policy calculations.

Encouraged by Bush, Clinton also acted on NAFTA before his inauguration. He met with Salinas, reaffirmed his commitment to NAFTA, and promised he would expedite the completion of side agreements on labor and the environment.[9] But on taking office, the administration decided to give highest priority to reducing the budget-deficit and gaining approval of a domestic agenda, and so the talks on NAFTA were put on a slow-track.

In mid-August, after the Senate approved Clinton's economic plan, the administration reopened the debate on the timing of NAFTA. The secretaries of treasury and state strongly recommended moving quickly, and the Mexican and Canadian governments urged the completion of the side agreements right away so as to permit NAFTA to be implemented by its deadline of January 1, 1994.[10] On the other hand, the president's signature program on health care could be jeopardized if the Democratic coalition fragmented over NAFTA. Many House Democrats led by Majority Leader Richard Gephardt and Whip David Bonior strongly opposed NAFTA.[11]

The president compromised. He decided to complete NAFTA and send it to Congress but to save his major address to Congress for his proposal on health care. Because of the "fast-track" procedure, Congress could not delay action on NAFTA after the president submitted the agreement.[12] In the meantime, the administration could begin to build support for the health plan.

Getting NAFTA approved was no easy matter. A bipartisan group led by five former U.S. presidents was organized by the Center for Strategic and International Studies and The Carter Center to bring the broader issues related to NAFTA to the public's attention. Clinton invited Carter, Ford, and Bush to the White House on September 14, 1993 for the signing of the side-agreements, and he recruited Bill Daley, the brother of the Chicago Mayor and Clinton's Illinois campaign chairman, to manage the NAFTA campaign in Congress, which proved quite difficult.[13] In the end, the president devoted a much larger share of his time to getting NAFTA approved than he had wanted, but in trying to persuade the Congress and the country of NAFTA's benefits, he also seemed to convince himself and to evolve a broader strategic approach to the issue and the hemisphere.

The political problem was that the debate within the Democratic Party was more divisive than between the Democrats and the Republicans. The side agreements bought some support from moderate environmental groups, but none from the unions. The toughest battle was in the House of Representatives, but on November 17, the president won, 234–200. One hundred and thirty-two Republicans voted with the Democratic president, and only 102 Democrats. Three days later, the Senate approved NAFTA by a vote of 61 to 38. The president had his second victory, and his first foreign/domestic policy accomplishment.

It was far more difficult to realize Clinton's promise to restore Aristide in Haiti. The president reiterated his commitment to Aristide in a White House meeting on March 16, 1993 and threw his support behind a UN diplomatic mission. After the United Nations imposed sanctions, UN envoy Dante Caputo brokered an agreement on Governor's Island on July 3, 1993. The agreement involved the lifting of sanctions; appointment of a new prime minister; amnesty for the military; the arrival of 1,300 U.S. and UN peacekeeping officers; and finally, the return of Aristide in late October 1993.

On October 11, Haitian paramilitary thugs blocked the landing of U.S. and UN troops aboard the *Harlan County*, humiliating the United States, and undermining the credibility of its diplomatic efforts. The Clinton administration briefly considered military intervention but rejected it. It took another year of failures before the administration recognized that no diplomatic effort would succeed unless backed by a credible threat, and that would require both a decision to intervene and someone who could convince the military that the threat was serious.

The president remained committed in principle to restoring Aristide, but the difficulty of accomplishing that goal tempted some of his advisors to put the issue aside. However, Randall Robinson, the director of TransAfrica, and the Congressional Black Caucus compelled the administration to keep Haiti on its radar screen and to replace the chief U.S. negotiator with Bill Gray, a former member of the Congressional Black Caucus. When negotiations stalled, Robinson began a hunger strike, which induced the administration to take a giant step forward.

In July 1994, the U.S. persuaded the UN Security Council to pass a resolution calling on member states to use force to compel the Haitian military to accept Aristide's return. This was a watershed event in international relations—the first time that the UN Security Council had authorized the use of force for the purpose of restoring democracy to a member state. In August, President Clinton decided that the United States would take the lead in an invasion, and preparations got underway.

On September 15, in a national address, President Clinton declared that all diplomatic efforts had been exhausted, and he publicly warned the Haitian military leaders to leave power immediately. In fact, the U.S. government had stopped talking to the Haitian military six months before. Nonetheless, General Raoul Cedras, the commander of the Haitian military, had opened a dialogue during the previous week with former President Jimmy Carter, who he had met during the 1990 elections. Carter informed President Clinton of the talks, and the President decided on Friday, September 16, to send Carter with Senator Sam Nunn and General Colin Powell to try one last time to negotiate the departure of Haiti's military leaders.[14]

Within one hour of their first meeting with the Haitian military high command, the three statesmen convinced the generals, for the first time, that an invasion would occur if the talks failed. But the Haitian military leaders were not interested in negotiating *their* exit or wealth. Representing the traditional elites', the military wanted to preserve their institution and prevent Aristide from unleashing the masses against them.

By 1 P.M. on Sunday, September 18, the Carter-Nunn-Powell team succeeded in gaining an agreement to allow the peaceful entry of U.S. forces into Haiti and the restoration of President Aristide. But there were details that remained to be negotiated, and President Clinton's deadline had passed. Suddenly, Haitian General Philippe Biamby burst into the room with news that the 82nd Airborne was being readied for attack, a fact not known to all the members of the Carter team. Biamby accused the Americans of deception and informed them he was taking Cedras to a secure area where they would prepare for the invasion.

It is hard to find a better example of the difference between a credible threat, which was essential to reach an agreement, and the actual movement of troops, which in this case and at this moment, was counterproductive. Because the Carter team had conveyed a threat with credibility but without brandishing it, Cedras was ready to sign the agreement. After learning the attack was underway, he refused to sign or even to negotiate further.

Carter could not persuade the generals to complete the agreement, and so he tried a different tactic. He changed the venue of the negotiations from the Military Headquarters to the Presidential Palace, and he asked Cedras to accompany him. There, the de facto President Emile Jonnaissant agreed to sign the agreement. This then created problems for President Aristide, who was in Washington, and was reluctant to accept any agreement with people he viewed as illegitimate usurpers. With the U.S. Air Force half way to Haiti, President Clinton finally ordered them recalled, and authorized Carter to sign the agreement on his behalf.

The president asked Carter, Nunn, and Powell to return to the White House immediately, and they asked me, who had accompanied them as an advisor, to remain to brief the U.S. Ambassador and Pentagon officials, who had not participated in the negotiations, and to arrange meetings between Haitian and U.S. military officers. This proved to be extremely difficult because the Haitian Generals went into hiding, and U.S. government officials in Port-au-Prince distrusted the Haitian generals so much they feared a double-cross such as had occurred with the *Harlan County* incident.

With less than two hours before touchdown by the U.S. military, I finally reached Cedras and arranged the crucial meetings that permitted U.S. forces to arrive without having to fire one shot. Twenty thousand U.S. troops disembarked without a single casualty or even one civilian hurt. There was no question that U.S. forces would have prevailed in an invasion, but because of the *Harlan County*, the Somalia experience, and the need to minimize U.S. casualties, the U.S. military plan called for a ferocious assault that would have involved hundreds, perhaps thousands, of Haitian casualties, and inevitably, some Americans. General Hugh Shelton, the commanding officer, said that such an invasion would have engendered long-term bitterness among some Haitians, making it more difficult for the United Nations to secure order and for the country to build democracy. General Cedras stepped down from power on October 12, and three days later, Aristide returned.

Like NAFTA, Haiti was transformed from an unwelcome problem into a success story, at least for the moment, but the process by which the administration made that journey was so messy and, at times, so accommodating to demands of pressure groups that the president was robbed of much of the credit that he deserved.

The Summit and Other Pieces of the Hemispheric Agenda

NAFTA and Haiti were the main issues in inter-American relations but hardly the only ones. Much of Latin America hoped NAFTA would be the first step toward a hemispheric free trade area. Chile, with the most advanced trade policy, asked to be next in line, and while NAFTA's leaders agreed in principle, the United States had not yet decided how it would expand NAFTA—whether by adding individual countries or by a broader negotiation.

Haiti's was the first democratic government in the Americas overthrown in the 1990s, but it was not the only one threatened. Peru's President Alberto Fujimori closed his Congress in 1992. The Venezuelan military attempted two coups. In Central America, every government except Costa Rica faced an embittered but strong military, and in the Andean countries, drug-traffickers corrupted and terrorized weak democracies.

The administration was slow in making appointments and erratic in coordinating policy, and one result was that the rest of the U.S.-Latin American agenda was addressed at the middle levels of the bureaucracy in a highly compartmentalized way. This evoked complaints from some Latin leaders that the administration was ignoring the region,[15] and it led Senator Christopher Dodd, the chairman of the Subcommittee on Western Hemisphere Affairs, to call the administration's performance "amateur hour."[16]

In December 1993, still floundering on Haiti, the administration decided to build on its success with NAFTA. Vice President Al Gore visited Mexico and proposed a Summit of all "democratically elected heads of state" of the Americas. It was a bold idea, but the administration was slow to follow up. It took four months and a heavy lobbying campaign by Florida's politicians before the site and date of the Summit was announced—Miami in December. The administration had still not decided on its goals,[17] and so it could not tie together the other issues of the hemispheric agenda.

To some Americans, the drug war replaced the Cold War. It sat at the intersection between domestic fears and foreign threats. Democrats and Republicans accused each other of not doing enough to keep drugs from America's children. The result was that while the overall government budget contracted, expenditures to fight drugs soared from the time President Bush declared war in 1990 to a cumulative total of more than $70 billion. Most of those funds were spent in the United States, but an increasing proportion of aid to Latin America was devoted to counter drug trafficking.

The Clinton administration initially shifted its strategy from attacking the supply-side of the drug problem toward addressing the consumption side, but in September 1993, when Andean governments complained of reduced aid, the administration announced that it would spend less on interdiction and more on drug eradication and cartel-busting. Six months later, the administration re-emphasized the need for treating drug addicts, but in its 1996 drug-war budget of $14.6 billion, it requested that 65 percent be devoted to supply-side efforts, only 5 percent less than the average during the Bush administration.[18]

The drug program appropriated an increasing share of a much reduced aid program to Latin America. From 1992 to fiscal year 1995, U.S. aid to Latin America had shrunk by almost half to about $760 million of a total $12.7 billion aid program. The drug program in Peru, Colombia, and Bolivia surpassed the aid program to all of Central America.

By the 1990s, most Latin American governments had come to realize that drug-trafficking was a more serious menace to their political and territorial integrity than it was to the United States. However, instead of the shared threat being a stimulus to a cooperative approach to the problem, Congress used the aid to mandate a new paternalism. The State Department was required by law to either certify that individual governments were working diligently on the problem or suspend aid. This created a demeaning process. Instead of building more mature relationships, the United States was compelled to grade Latin American governments, and they naturally resented it.[19]

Who was winning the drug war? Since 1990, there was no reduction in the number of hard-core drug users in the United States. Coca and poppy production increased, and the street prices of illicit drugs in the United States dropped precipitously.[20] The war had no discernible effect on the real problem or on government funding; its only effect was to inject a paternalistic, unhealthy element into U.S. relations with Mexico and the Andean governments. After a report issued by the National Institute of Drug Abuse in November 1995 showed a significant increase in the use of drugs by youth, the White House Drug Czar Lee Brown resigned and was replaced by General Barry McCaffrey, the head of the Southern Command. A military hero, McCaffery ironically could be the best person to demilitarize and depoliticize the issue and reorient drug policy toward prevention.

The Clinton administration's policy toward Central America was also shaped to a great degree by members of Congress, but unlike the widespread concern about drugs in Congress, Central America attracted fewer individuals, some of whom were still fighting the Cold War. This was particularly tragic because the governments in the region were desperate to escape the Cold War demons that had ravaged their countries in the 1980s. Each needed help from the United States to bring longstanding rivals together and complete the awkward transition to democracy. That is not what they received from the United States.

In Nicaragua, instead of encouraging national reconciliation, the State Department withheld aid in a manner that exacerbated divisions within the country and made resolution of problems, like property, more difficult. In a reception at the U.S. Embassy in Managua in June 1993, in a statement more attuned to the views of the Bush administration than its Democratic critics, the deputy secretary of state praised several conservative opponents of President Chamorro without recognizing her; Nicaraguans interpreted the message as meaning that the United States was more interested in pressuring her than in supporting her policy of reconciliation. A visit several months later by the new assistant secretary of state reinforced this message.[21] Pushed by conservatives in Congress, the State Department used aid to compel the Nicaraguan government to change some government personnel and to give priority to settling at full value the property problems of Nicaraguans who had emigrated to the United States. Instead of encouraging a solution to the problem, U.S. efforts encouraged Nicaraguan property holders to become more rigid in their talks. Costa Rican President Rafael Angel Calderon denounced U.S. policy, saying it "helped worsen the situation in Nicaragua," and his foreign minister said the overall policy made the region feel "punished and abandoned."[22]

In El Salvador and Guatemala, the Clinton State Department seemed to prefer to conceal or downplay mistakes or bad policies made by its Republican predecessors in Central America than to send clear signals on human rights. For example, in 1993, in response to newspaper reports of atrocities in El Salvador that had occurred at the beginning of the Reagan administration, Secretary of State Warrren Christopher appointed a review panel, whose report was criticized by *The Miami Herald* as "disturbingly evasive," and it urged Christopher to reject it: "The report covers up the truth rather than confronting it."[23] Christopher accepted the report.

Administration officials repeatedly denied information to Jennifer Harbury, an American lawyer, about her husband, a Guatemalan guerrilla, who had been captured by the Guatemalan military. In 1995, a Democratic Congressman disclosed what the administration had not: a Guatemalan Colonel was a paid agent of the Central Intelligence Agency (C.I.A.) when he was alleged to have been involved in the torture and death of Harbury's husband and in the obstruction of an investigation into the murder of an American citizen in Guatemala in 1990. Clinton administration officials criticized the Congressman. Only a change in the leadership of the C.I.A. led to the dismissal of some of the responsible officers.

The administration did handle an attempted auto-golpe (self-coup) by Guatemalan President Jorge Diaz Serrano in May 1993 very effectively. Its strong condemnation and suspension of aid caused the military to abandon Serrano and permit a transition to another civilian president. The administration also supported the UN-sponsored peace making efforts with the guerrillas, but the problem in Guatemala remained the military's control of the political system, and the U.S. government seemed reluctant to confront that difficult problem, as was evident in the Harbury case.

With the end of the Cold War, Cuba's principal trading partner and source of aid, the Soviet Union, self-destructed. During the next four years, the Cuban economy plummeted. Conservative leaders from the Cuban-American community led by the Cuban American National Foundation (CANF) urged Congress to bring down the regime by forcing our trading partners to stop trading with Cuba. This idea was introduced by Representative Robert Torricelli in a bill that also included a "Track II" approach to encourage more communication with Cuban civil society. President Bush opposed the bill because of its adverse effect on Canada among others, but when Clinton endorsed it in the spring of 1992, Bush reversed course and signed it. Torricelli said the law would cause Castro to fall "within weeks."[24] That didn't happen, of course, but his law defined U.S. policy to Cuba during the Clinton administration.

Faced with signs of unrest in August 1994, the Castro government allowed people to flee the country on rafts, and more than 30,000 left. The Clinton administration feared a repetition of the Mariel boatlift of 1980, in which more than 120,000 Cubans fled to Florida. That event had disastrous political effects for both President Jimmy Carter and Governor Bill Clinton of Arkansas, in whose State thousands of Mariel refugees were housed until they rioted.

In August 1994, Florida Governor Lawton Chiles was running for re-election, and he and CANF leaders went to the White House to recommend a policy to prevent another Mariel. First, they proposed a new migration agreement with Cuba that included increased legal Cuban emigration to the United States and the interception by the U.S. Coast Guard of Cuban rafters, who would be sent to another country or to the U.S. base at Guantanamo, Cuba. To win support in the Cuban-American community, which was furious that the United States would consider sending Cubans home, the president tightened sanctions by restricting travel and reducing remittances. The CANF was criticized, but the immigration agreement worked to deter the flood of rafters.

On the issues of Central America and Cuba, U.S. policy seemed driven by the most determined interest group—whether in Congress or in Miami. These issues were not priorities, and administration officials tried to keep them separate from the Miami Summit.

The administration delayed in making a decision on its goals for the Summit until a few months before it occurred because it wanted first to

secure Congressional approval of three trade-related goals: fast-track negotiating authority to extend NAFTA, an interim trade program that
would permit quasi-parity to NAFTA for the small Caribbean Basin
countries, and the GATT agreement. By October, the administration
had given up on its first two goals, and the vote on GATT was postponed until after the November 1994 Congressional election. In the
meantime, the Latin Americans were waiting for a message from the
administration.

The election demoralized the Clinton administration. Even in his
worst nightmare, the president would not have predicted that the Republicans would win control of both Houses of Congress. It was a victory for a Republican agenda, but it was also viewed as a loss for the
president. With a month to the Summit, however, the administration
needed to pull itself out of its funk and negotiate a plan of action with
the Latin Americans that would make the Summit not just an entertainment extravaganza but also a meeting of real substance. It proved
to be both.

The Summit occurred at an historic moment. Canada was viewed
by Latin Americans as an important interlocutor with the United
States. An expanded NAFTA, which included Canada, permitted Latin
Americans an opportunity to retain their identity and autonomy while
being part of a larger unit that could compete with Europe and Asia. Far
more significant, the Summit was a reflection of the convergence of two
phenomena—democracy and freer trade—that transformed the region
and provided a shared perspective and a common set of problems.[25] In
Miami, the 34 heads of state were all civilians, the winners of competitive elections, all trying to improve the lives of their electorate.

Of course, NAFTA and the Summit were born in original sin in the
sense that a founding member of the democratic community—Mexico—was not democratic. Its elections had long been manipulated by
the ruling party, the PRI. Salinas had deliberately opened the Mexican
political system more slowly than the economy. By the August 1994
presidential elections, Salinas had dispensed with the crude methods for
rigging the election, but numerous problems remained—most due to
the PRI's use of state resources for its candidates. Regrettably, the
United States downplayed these electoral problems and mistakenly left
the impression that it endorsed the PRI candidate.[26] The U.S. ambassador described the election as "a major advance for democracy in Mexico." A *New York Times* editorial was less enthusiastic but closer to the
mark, by calling it "the least tainted election in decades."[27]

Salinas's real leadership was in freeing trade. Mexico had long vetoed Latin American initiatives to move closer to the United States.
Suddenly, Latin America awoke to find that Mexico had opened the
door of the U.S. market and walked in. Everyone wanted to follow. Bush
and, subsequently, Clinton promised they could, but Congress made it
difficult for the Presidents to fulfill their promises.

In the meantime, Latin American governments decided to look to their neighbors to either refurbish existing subregional trade regimes or establish new ones. Brazil and Argentina had been rivals almost since their independence, but the civilian presidents realized that only the military would benefit if they failed to cooperate. These two South American giants ended their nuclear weapons programs, reduced their defense expenditures, and joined with Uruguay and Paraguay to establish Mercosur in 1991. On January 1, 1995, Mercosur made 90 percent of their trade duty-free. On the same date, the Andean Pact countries established common external tariffs, ranging from 5 to 20 percent, and the Group of Three—Mexico, Venezuela, and Colombia—pledged to eliminate all tariffs and quotas within a decade. From 1991 to the Summit, the region reduced its trade barriers by 80 percent.[28]

In just four years—from 1990-1994—Latin American exports grew 10 percent per year (three times faster than its gross product), but its trade within the region grew at a rate of 16 percent.[29] Trade within each of the subregions—Mercosur, Andean, Central America, Caribbean Community (CARICOM), NAFTA—grew faster than their world trade, meaning that regional integration was proceeding at a fast pace. Each country had learned the benefits of freer trade and was prepared to accelerate the process and widen it.

At the Summit in Miami, the presidents agreed to a "Declaration of Principles" and "A Plan of Action"—fulsome statements of solidarity on behalf of democracy, prosperity through economic integration and free trade, and sustainable development through environmental protection. Besides the rhetoric and the many committees established to discuss a wide agenda, one goal stood out: the presidents agreed to conclude negotiations on a "Free Trade Area of the Americas" no later than 2005. That was the single goal that, by itself, made the Summit a success.

The Rise of the Republicans and the Fall of the Peso

For the Clinton administration and much of Latin America, the Miami Summit was a moment of sunshine between two ominous clouds—the Republican takeover of Congress, which jeopardized Clinton's program, and the collapse of the Mexican peso, which called into question the premise of the Summit, that Latin America was on a high-speed trajectory to the first world. The significance of the two events was not fully grasped at the time, but within one year the events had eclipsed the Summit.

A Republican Congressman from Georgia, Newt Gingrich, brazenly proposed a national agenda—the Contract with America—which captured the American mood and both Houses of Congress in the 1994 Congressional elections. The Contract had nothing to say about the world or about Latin America. If Clinton's international agenda seemed meager in 1992, it was ample as compared to the Republican agenda.

The Congressional revolution fast-forwarded the campaign for the 1996 presidential election. The Republicans viewed Clinton as a lame duck, and several started running to replace him even before the 104th Congress was sworn in. The Senate became a campaign arena with four Republicans competing against each other even as they tried to position themselves vis-à-vis the president. Senate Majority Leader Robert Dole had to continually watch his right flank as Phil Gramm, the conservative Senator from Texas, sought to out-maneuver him for the nomination.

Jesse Helms, the Senator who took perverse pride in blocking or killing laws and treaties and holding up nominations, became the chairman of the august Foreign Relations Committee. When the Republicans had won the Senate in 1980, the leadership encouraged Helms to step aside to allow Senator Richard Lugar to chair. In 1992, Helms asserted his seniority, and with the Republican Party tilting to the right, Dole was compelled to accept him even though some of Helms's comments after the election were so embarrassing that even Helms was moved to apologize.

Helms opposed NAFTA, GATT, and financial support to Mexico; he viewed the Cold War as a continuing struggle, and although he opposed foreign aid, he often used it as a lever to manipulate poor countries. Another item on his agenda was to reorganize the State Department by having it absorb three other agencies that would be reduced in size: the Agency for International Development, the U.S. Information Agency, and the Arms Control and Disarmament Agency. While an argument could be made for folding these agencies into a reorganized State Department at the beginning of an administration, his insistence on doing it in the middle of the president's term was a mischievous prank to sow bureaucratic discord.

The Republican leadership reduced foreign aid by 20 percent in the 1996 budget cycle, but aid to Latin America was cut even more substantially. The Republicans were also distrustful of international organizations, being fearful that U.S. sovereignty could be jeopardized. Most of the world believed that these international organizations existed largely to serve the interests of the United States; the irony apparently escaped the Republicans. Although the issue of abortion seemed tangential to U.S. interests in the developing world, this was the reason Republicans impeded the aid bill.

Most Republicans strongly opposed President Clinton's strategy to restore President Aristide to Haiti, largely because they viewed Aristide as an unstable, anti-American leftist. After Aristide's return, the Republicans were averse to supporting him or keeping U.S. troops there longer than their mandate of February 1996.

The elections for Haiti's Parliament and municipalities on June 25, 1995 and the subsequent reruns and runoffs suffered serious administrative flaws. Legitimate complaints did not elicit satisfactory responses from the Provisional Elections Council (CEP) or the government, and as a result, 22 of 27 political parties boycotted the subsequent elections. The Clinton administration and the international organizations chose to downplay the electoral problems and celebrate the elections as "an important milestone in [Haiti's] progress toward sustainable democracy."[30] Instead of using its influence to correct the elections, the administration gave higher priority to economic development by suspending some aid until President Aristide privatized state companies.

Aristide made the popular decision to dismantle the Haitian military, although he had accepted it as part of the Carter agreement. With U.S. aid, he established a Police Academy to train a 5,000-person police force. In the interim, UN forces kept law and order and an artificial lid on Haiti's inequitable social equation. With most parties boycotting the presidential election on December 17, 1995, and a campaign that was compressed because Aristide hinted he would remain in office until a few weeks before the election, the voter turnout was very low—28 percent. Aristide's hand-picked successor Rene Preval won 88 percent of the vote.

Power was transferred peacefully on February 7, 1996, but the new president faced tough problems with less legitimacy and independence than his predecessor. United States troops began to leave, but Preval asked the United Nations to keep about 2,000 peacekeepers for at least six months. With a disputed electoral process, and intense fears between the masses and the elite, the administration's claims of success seemed, at best, premature.

The other Caribbean country whose destiny was shaped by a partisan struggle in the United States was Cuba. Helms introduced a bill with Congressman Dan Burton of Indiana to try to topple Fidel Castro by tightening the embargo, discouraging foreign investment, and precluding meaningful negotiations until Fidel and Raul Castro were removed from power. The bill would permit Cubans, who had become U.S. citizens, to sue in U.S. courts anyone who had purchased their property. This procedure angered U.S. allies and was contrary to international law, but it was one that Helms had already applied to Nicaragua.

One of the reasons that the Clinton administration and the CANF were on different sides of the Helms-Burton bill was because they had a falling out as a result of a secret agreement reached on May 6, 1995 between Cuba and the Clinton administration on returning Cuban migrants to the island. The September agreement had proven unsustainable. Only one country—Panama—had come forward to accept Cuban refugees, and six months later, after the Cubans rioted, and the United States failed to demonstrate its gratitude, the Panamanians decided to return the 15,000 refugees to Guantanamo. The U.S. military in Guantanamo feared major riots unless a permanent solution were devised.

The problem was that if the Cubans in Guantanamo were sent to the United States, that would violate the September accord with Cuba and stimulate a new flow of refugees. Therefore, the United States proposed to Cuba that the Guantanamo-based refugees be sent to the United States, but to prevent a new exodus, the United States would intercept at sea and return to Cuba any future migrants. In other words, Cubans fleeing the island were no longer automatically considered refugees; they would be returned to Cuba if they failed to prove they had a well-founded fear of persecution. To most Cuban-Americans, the mere suggestion that a Cuban fleeing Castro's Cuba might not be a refugee was blasphemous. The fact that CANF had not been consulted gave them an opportunity to condemn and split from the Clinton administration.

For some reason, the Clinton administration had not expected the intensity of the criticism from Miami, but they were saved by a public opinion survey published in the *Miami Herald* on May 15 that showed the majority of Florida residents supportive of the president's decision restricting immigration. The Clinton administration had stumbled upon a Democratic answer to California's anti-immigrant Proposition 187 that passed in November 1994 by a 3 to 2 margin.[31]

The president remained cautious about dealing with Cuba largely because he viewed the state of Florida as critical to his re-election, but also because of the potency of the anti-Castro movement in Congress. Nonetheless, the administration began to consider small steps to permit greater exchanges and communications with Cuba. As the administration justified these steps as ways to undermine Castro, the Cuban government was naturally reluctant to approve them. Any prospect for easing tensions was discarded in February 1996 when the Cuban Air Force shot down two small planes piloted by members of a Cuban-American group that had repeatedly violated Cuban airspace. The Clinton administration responded firmly by seeking a condemnation in the United Nations and reversing its opposition to the Helms-Burton bill, which the president signed on March 12, the day of the Florida Presidential primary.

The Republicans also constrained the president on the central promise of the Summit of the Americas: free trade. In 1993, as a minority party, Republicans reluctantly accepted the environmental and labor side agreements of NAFTA. As the majority party, however, they insisted on excluding the side agreements as a condition for approving fast-track. The Clinton administration declared that was unacceptable to them and also to our trading partners and so negotiations stalled. Despite periodic consultations and a useful trade ministerial in Denver in the spring of 1995, the momentum toward an Americas Free Trade Area ebbed, and Brazil and several other Latin American governments decided to build closer ties to the EU and to each other.

The most immediate danger to the promise implicit in the Summit of the Americas was the collapse of the Mexican peso, just ten days after Mexico's model was praised at the Miami Summit. On December 20,

1994, Mexico devalued the peso by about 13 percent and then let it float. It sunk, as capital fled the country. Mexican President Ernesto Zedillo had taken office just three weeks before, and his team fumbled trying to put together an economic plan to reattract confidence and capital.

There were many warnings throughout the year that the peso was grossly over-valued. Among them was the massive withdrawal of billions of dollars by U.S. investors. Subsequent investigations by Congress showed that the Clinton administration was aware of the problem but had not approached the Mexicans with ideas on how to address it and thus minimize the damage to both countries of a huge devaluation.[32]

Mexico assembled an economic plan, and by January 12, the Clinton administration announced a $40 billion package of loan guarantees. In a politically astute maneuver, President Clinton coaxed the new Speaker Newt Gingrich and the new Majority Leader Bob Dole to endorse the package. Their colleagues pummelled them for that. Gingrich and Dole had read the mood of the country so well in November, but two months later, they had already forgotten two of the election's messages, that of suspicion of government and distrust of foreigners. The two suspicions connected in Mexico.

Many asked whether the peso crisis was a sign that NAFTA had failed. In fact, it was a sign that it succeeded; trade had expanded by more than 20 percent in both directions during 1994. The problem was that NAFTA was only a trade agreement; it was inadequate to the challenge of integrating three such divergent economies. NAFTA had attracted large movements of short-term capital, but there was no coordinating mechanism to cope with the fast exit of such capital. Incredibly, the U.S. National Economic Council, which had been charged with coordinating U.S. economic policy, had not forseen the magnitude of the financial crisis and, indeed, its director acknowledged that his first reaction was to let the markets handle it.[33]

During 1994, Carlos Salinas had tried to steer his government through two tragic assassinations, an uprising in the southern state of Chiapas, and an anxiety-ridden presidential election. With each crisis, capital fled, but Salinas and his Minister of Finance, Pedro Aspe, reacted by lifting interest rates and tying the bonds (tesobonos) to the dollar. Domestic savings continued to fall, and so they were just buying time.

Salinas's second choice, Ernesto Zedillo, won the presidential election in August. Salinas should have devalued the peso shortly after the election, but he feared that could jeopardize his chance to be the first head of the World Trade Organization. His Finance Minister, Pedro Aspe, wanted to keep his reputation unsoiled, so when Zedillo tried to persuade Salinas to devalue, Aspe threatened to resign. That alone would have caused a run on the peso so the hard decision was postponed.

Zedillo was prepared to discuss the peso issue in a meeting with President Clinton on November 23, 1994, but neither he nor Clinton administration officials mentioned it. In a press conference afterward, President Clinton "expressed confidence in Mexico's economic prospects," and he repeated that point at the Summit of the Americas two weeks later.[34]

While the Republican leadership looked for support for President Clinton's rescue package, the peso sank still further. Finally, on January 31, President Clinton announced a $53 billion package that included $20 billion from the U.S. Exchange Stabilization Fund. The Republican leaders were content for the president to use that fund by Executive Order rather than try to get congressional approval. Unfortunately, another month would pass before the agreement was signed, and by that time, Mexican reserves had declined so much that the government had to accept an unusually austere economic program that would create massive unemployment, a catastrophic number of bankruptcies, and a 7 percent decline in Mexico's GDP for 1995, the worst drop since 1932. Sixty-five percent of Mexicans blamed Salinas for the economic crisis, but Ernesto Zedillo did not escape; only 16 percent rated his overall job performance as good.[35]

The Mexican crisis rippled through Latin America as American capital fled the region. Decisive actions by Argentina's finance minister prevented a major devaluation, but the economy declined 3 percent. Fernando Henrique Cardoso, Brazil's brilliant new president, not only kept inflation under control but he also restructured the economy, generated new growth and reserves, and helped his country to change places with Mexico as the most dynamic and hopeful economic model in Latin America.

The Postwar Political Template and the Clinton Paradox

Bill Clinton was the first U.S. president to take office after the Cold War, and he moved to the rhythm of a postwar era. The anti-communist landmarks that had guided his predecessors across a treacherous international political landscape were no longer of use. The compass bequeathed to him by the American electorate compelled him to look inward, and he needed time and political capital to address the fiscal deficit, crime, drugs, and health care. Secretary of State Warren Christopher's role was to counsel the president on how to avoid mistakes or foreign commitments. Latin America was among the Secretary's lowest priorities. His first visit to South America occurred in February 1996 after being criticized for visiting Syria 17 times and the region not once.[36]

In the hemisphere, the Clinton administration inherited two problems—Haiti and NAFTA. At the end of agonizing journeys, the president made the tough and correct decisions—to restore constitutional government in Haiti and to secure the approval of NAFTA. He followed up both initiatives with a Summit of the Americas, which set a hemispheric goal of free trade by the year 2005. These were three significant achievements.

Yet the administration's overall policy to the Americas seemed less, not more, than the sum of these three parts. The president made wise and politically courageous decisions, but he received little credit for these achievements. Indeed, he was frequently criticized for being excessively responsive to interest groups and captive to public opinion surveys. What accounts for this paradox?

The answer lies not in the president's achievements but in the journey—the process—for reaching the decisions. The administration initially treated NAFTA and Haiti as specific and distinct problems rather than as opportunities to grasp a "regionalist option" or construct a democratic community. Similarly, separate mid-level groups in the administration addressed the rest of the hemispheric agenda, namely, drugs, immigration, Central America, and Cuba without relating each issue to one another or to a hemispheric strategy.

Ironically, the mistake-avoidance strategy that typified the State Department's approach may have sapped more of the president's time and capital than would have been the case had he either moved decisively at the beginning, or fashioned a longer-term strategy, as Franklin D. Roosevelt had done. Within one year of America's entry into World War II, FDR began to prepare for the shift in the public mood that he expected when the war would end. He designed international institutions and forged a bipartisan consensus to keep the United States engaged globally despite the desire to avoid entangling alliances.

Instead of formulating a similar foreign policy to counter the swing in mood in the post–Cold War era, Clinton administration officials argued that "containment" was not discovered in a day; it was a product of trial and error. There is some truth to that, but FDR's vision and strategy locked the United States into the post–World War II world before the Cold War started.

In the post–Cold War world, the president tended to be drawn into crises. There was no design or strategy beyond "engagement and enlargement"—two succinct principles for aiming the United States toward the world. The hard questions related to setting priorities and making trade offs—should the U.S. use force and, if so, where and how? Which crisis should engage the secretary of state and/or the president? To answer these questions, the administration used a political template—a composite of public opinion, media exposure, and pressure from interest groups. If a crisis did not engage the public or attract the media or an interest group, it was ignored. The administration, however, could not afford to ignore intense objections from a core constituency group, such as the Congressional Black Caucus on Haiti. It was wary of antagonizing a Florida ethnic group, like the Cuban-Americans, unless a broader national domestic interest, for example, on stopping refugees, compelled a recalculation.

What was missing in these political judgments was some picture of what the world should look like and how U.S. policy should try to influence its shape. In the Americas, the United States faced not a problem, but an unprecedented opportunity—to create a community of democratic, market-oriented neighbors. This community could have been assembled from governments that were ready to address either NAFTA or Haiti. In 1993, Latin America wanted an expanded NAFTA, and the United States and the Caribbean wanted cooperation from Latin America to restore a constitutional government to Haiti.

A strategic approach would have mobilized prestigious U.S. statesmen to try to persuade Latin leaders, who wanted NAFTA extended but did not much care for Haiti, of the need to address the two sides of the Americas challenge. With Latin American support for Haiti acting as a kind of down-payment for NAFTA's extension, such an approach could have been mutually reinforcing: if Congress saw Latin America as cooperative on Haiti, it might have been more sympathetic to extending NAFTA. Assembling such a package would not have been easy and could not have been accomplished by sending cautious mid-level officials to the region. It would have required detailed plans on economic integration and democratic reinforcement.

The State Department was on the margins of both negotiations. If one were to believe the rhetoric about the centrality of NAFTA to its policy, then the Department of State should have redesigned itself not to preempt Jesse Helms, but to ensure that each interest would be woven into a thick fabric representing the entire nation. One place to start would have been to combine the offices dealing with Canada and those with Mexico into the same bureau rather than two different ones. While the Special Trade Representative has authority to negotiate trade agreements, the State Department could certainly have played a larger role in pursuit of the United States's regional trade policy. Indeed, the State Department even relinquished its responsibility for dealing with diplomatic issues—Haiti, Cuba, Central America—to interested groups in Congress or outside that approached the issues from a specific rather than a general national interest. The administration did not pursue a strategic approach because the motives driving the policy were domestic—interests and interest groups, the fear of refugees, drugs, and terrorism, and the desire to please groups of hyphenated Americans.

The geo-politics were never more propitious. The democratic transformation of Argentina and Brazil provided the avenue for a new cooperative relationship between the traditional South American rivals. Both governments also sought a constructive relationship with the United States and, despite the administration's disproportionate attention to single issues in each country—intellectual property rights in Argentina and the drug issue in Brazil (!)—both South American governments saw the larger picture. Argentina undertook UN peacekeeping missions—an opportunity to employ their military constructively and build new bonds with the United States. Brazil began to assume its mantle as a leader in human rights and democracy and international economics.

The Summit provided the vehicle to pursue an Americas strategy that was broader than these two relationships and as expansive as the inter-American agenda. Unfortunately, the administration wasted the better part of a year before it began to consult with Latin America. The best that could be said of this delay was that it lowered the region's expectations. But by the time the Summit was held in December 1994, the attention of the American people had shifted, the Republicans had captured Congress, and the regional effect of the peso crisis was about to spoil the party. The decision to hold the Summit in Miami made political sense given the intensity of the community's interest and commerce in the region, but it invited a public focus on the one head of state, who was not there, Fidel Castro, rather than the 34, who were. Moreover, the press did not fathom the significance of the event.

President Clinton did recognize the importance of the Summit, and in the course of discovering that his domestic agenda was shared by his colleagues, he began to articulate the overarching concept of an Americas policy. He also committed himself to the consensual goal of completing a free trade area of the Americas by the year 2005. One year later, however, the administration had not yet obtained fast-track negotiating authority—the first step to 2005—and the prospect of taking that step faded as the presidential election campaign moved to center stage. The momentum was gone. The opportunity to fill in the outline of a democratic community drawn so graphically by the president passed.

In a second term Clinton could begin to construct a community that could resemble Europe's, but one that reflected different economic structures in the Americas and the need for a Latin American difference. The mechanism connecting the states of the Americas ought to be less bureaucratic and more respectful of each nation's autonomy.

In 1909, Herbert Croly wrote: "The American habit is to proclaim doctrines and policies, without considering either the implications, the machinery necessary to carry them out, or the weight of the resulting responsibilities."[37] The insight seems as penetrating as the century closes as when the century opened, but there remains time to change that habit.

In the aftermath of the Cold War and in the absence of a compelling threat, the U.S. president had to choose among a plethora of international crises. The Clinton administration seemed to make these decisions by weighing the different pressures from domestic constituencies. The views of the U.S. electorate seemed fluid, and thus public opinion surveys seemed as good a compass for locating priorities as any other. The flaw in such an approach was that it actually invited political pressure to build to the point that the president was compelled to respond.

But when he did, he looked as if he was pushed into doing it. This perception was reinforced by the new power of the Republicans, who constrained the president's trade policy, goaded his Cuban and Central American policy in an old Cold War direction, and incited a more belligerent approach to drugs and immigration.

In the end, however, President Clinton's choices on NAFTA, Haiti, and the Miami Summit were the defining ones of his policy toward the Americas. NAFTA is a revolutionary event that will not only reshape North America and if the Miami goal is implemented, extend the model to the hemisphere. But if used properly, the hemisphere's trade initiative could compel Europe and Asia to play by similar and fair rules. The UN and OAS decisions, under U.S. leadership, to restore Aristide to power was also pivotal, perhaps even more as a collective statement by the Americas than for Haiti. If the region builds on the twin models, then freer trade and democracy might have a durable future, and Bill Clinton's legacy will be a memorable one.

Endnotes

1. Frank L. Klingberg, *Cyclical Trends in American Foreign Policy Moods: The Unfolding of America's World Role* (Lanham, Md.: University Press of America, 1983). His first essay on the subject was published in 1952 in *World Politics*.
2. A *Times Mirror* poll in October 1992 found that Americans wanted the president to give highest priority to the budget deficit, jobs, health care, education, and the environment. Foreign policy issues were far down the list. *See National Journal* (November 21, 1992): 2697. Two years later, a poll done by the Chicago Council on Foreign Relations found crime and jobs the biggest problems and foreign policy "now constitute the smallest number of overall problems since 1978 for the public and the smallest ever among leaders. The preferred goals of foreign policy address matters directly related to local concerns: controlling and reducing illegal immigration and stopping the flow of illegal drugs into the country." Chicago Council on Foreign Relations, *American Public Opinion and U.S. Foreign Policy, 1995* (Chicago, 1995), p. 6.
3. For a description of this option and its rationale, *see* Robert A. Pastor, "The Latin American Option," *Foreign Policy*, Vol. 88 (Fall 1992): 107–125.
4. *See* Robert Pastor and Jorge Castañeda, *Limits to Friendship: The United States and Mexico* (New York: Alfred A. Knopf, 1988).
5. *See* my "The North American Free Trade Agreement: Hemispheric and Geopolitical Implications," *The International Executive*, Vol. 36, No. 1 (January/February 1994): 19.
6. An analysis of trade and investment after the two World Wars suggests a similar pattern explained by the same reason: the United States and Latin America drew closer economically because Europe was self-preoccupied and Asia was distant and closed. (Ibid.)
7. Governor Bill Clinton, "Expanding Trade and Creating American Jobs," remarks at North Carolina State University, October 4, 1992, p. 18.
8. President Aristide offered these reflections at two conferences held at the Carter Center of Emory University in January 1992 and September 1993.
9. Thomas L. Friedman, "Clinton Says U.S. Will Act Fast on Trade Pact If . . . ," *New York Times*, January 9, 1993, p. 8.

10. Bob Woodward, *The Agenda: Inside the Clinton White House* (New York: Simon and Schuster, 1994), pp. 55, 314–319.

11. Keith Bradsher, "Democratic Rifts May Hurt Clinton on Foreign Trade," *New York Times*, December 27, 1992, pp. 1, 13.

12. Under the "fast-track" negotiating authority, first approved in the 1974 Trade Act, a trade agreement would be submitted to Congress, which had to approve it in 60 to 90 days without amendments.

13. Gwen Ifill, "Ex-Presidents Asked to Help Push North American Trade Agreement," *New York Times*, September 1, 1993, p. C18.

14. The author was an advisor to the Carter team and has described parts of the negotiations in the following two articles, "With Carter in Haiti," *Worldview*, Vol. 8, No. 2 (February–April 1995): 5–10; and "A Short History of Haiti," *Foreign Service Journal* (November 1995): 20–25.

15. The Venezuelan president said: "What troubles me is that there doesn't seem to be a Clinton administration policy toward Latin America. We obviously maintain a friendly, favorable expectation that President Clinton will maintain the tradition [of support for Latin America] of other Democratic presidents such as Kennedy and Carter. But we're not seeing an interest in Latin America." Cited in Andres Oppenheimer, "Latins Fear Region Will Be Ignored," *Miami Herald*, April 26, 1993, p. 10.

16. Dodd was upset at the slow pace of appointments and the "mixed messages" on NAFTA, with the budget director calling it "dead" and the treasury secretary saying it remained high priority. See Christopher Marquis, "Latin Policy: 'Less of the Same,'" *Miami Herald*, May 10, 1993, pp. 1, 7.

17. For a good analysis of the weakness, delay, and strengths of the Summit process and outcome, *see* Peter Hakim and Michael Shifter, "U.S.-Latin American Relations: To the Summit and Beyond," *Current History*, Vol. 94, No. 589 (February 1995): 49–53.

18. Coletta Youngers, "Fueling Failure: U.S. Drug Control Efforts in the Andes," *Issues in International Drug Policy* (Washington, DC: Washington Office on Latin America, April 1995), p. 2.

19. To take just one example, on February 1, 1996, the Mexican Foreign Ministry issued a statement that it "does not accept the certification," and it rejected the patrolling of the border by the National Guard. "Mexico Does Not Accept U.S. Certification in the Drug War," *La Jornada*, republished in *Foreign Broadcasting Information Service*, 5 February 1996, p. 15.

20. See Mathea Falco, "U.S. Drug Policy: Addicted to Failure," *Foreign Policy* 102 (Spring 1996), p. 124; and Coletta Youngers, "Fueling Failure."

21. "Lacayo, Politicians Said 'Visibly Annoyed' by Wharton Speech," *Foreign Broadcasting Information Service*, 10 June 1993, p. 14; Christopher Marquis, "U.S. Demands Nicaraguan Reforms as Condition to Aid," *Miami Herald*, August 13, 1993, p. 14.

22. "Calderon Assails U.S. Policy on Nicaragua," *Foreign Broadcasting Information Service (FBIS)*, 31 August 1993, p. 8; and "Central American Presidents' Meeting with Clinton Previewed," *FBIS*, 27 November 1993, p. 1.

23. *Report of the Secretary of State's Panel on El Salvador*, July 1983, pp. 3, 10. "Half Truths of Whole Cloth: U.S.'s Salvador Report," *The Miami Herald*, July 17, 1993.

24. Cited in Wayne S. Smith, "Shackled to the Past: The United States and Cuba," *Current History*, Vol. 95, No. 598 (February 1996): 51.

25. For the development of the idea of a convergence of democratic and market values in the context of a "hemispheric democratic community," *see* Robert A. Pastor, *Whirlpool: U.S. Foreign Policy Toward Latin America and the Caribbean* (Princeton, N.J.: Princeton University Press, 1992), especially, Chapter 15, "Crossing the Sovereign Divide: The Path Toward a Hemispheric Community"; and *Convergence and Community: The Americas in 1993*, A Report of the Inter-American Dialogue (Washington, DC: Aspen Institute, 1992).

26. This was due to an ill-advised congratulatory statement by the White House spokesperson on the nomination of the PRI candidate. It was strongly criticized by leaders from the main opposition parties. *See* "PAN, PRD Protest U.S. Spokesperson Remarks," *FBIS*, 3 December 1993, p. 15.

27. The Ambassador's comment was in the *New York Times*, August 25, 1994; the editorial was "Mexico's Political Crisis," *New York Times*, October 11, 1995. For a detailed analysis of the election, *see* Council of Freely Elected Heads of Government, Carter Center of Emory University, *The August 21, 1994 Mexican National Elections: Fourth Report*, January 1995.

28. James Brooke, "On Eve of Miami Summit Talks, U.S. Comes Under Fire," *New York Times*, December 9, 1995, p. A4.

29. The Inter-American Development Bank, *Economic Integration in the Americas* (Washington, DC, July 1995), p. 2.

30. Testimony by Ambassador James F. Dobbins, Special Haiti Coordinator, before the Senate Foreign Relations Committee, July 12, 1995, p. 6.

31. John Lantigua and Stephen Doig, "Limit Cuban Immigration: Yes, Most in Survey Agree," *Miami Herald*, May 15, 1995, pp. 1, 16. For a good analysis of why Clinton risked a little by alienating the Republican Cuban-American vote, but gained a lot by "sending a big message on immigration to other important states such as California," *see* William Schneider, "Immigration Politics Strikes Again," *National Journal*, May 13, 1995, p. 1206.

32. The Senate Banking Committee compiled numerous documents from the Treasury Department and prepared a detailed and authoritative chronology based on those documents. *See* "Report on the Mexican Economic Crisis," presented by Senator Alfonse D'Amato, June 28, 1995, *see especially* Appendix E.

33. *See, for example,* David Sanger, "The Education of Robert Rubin," *New York Times*, February 5, 1995, p. III, 1, 5.

34. Cited in "White House Statement," *Foreign Policy Bulletin* (January/April 1995), p. 26.

35. "Poll Records Mixed Results for Zedillo," *Reforma*, republished in *FBIS*, 21 November 1995, pp. 10–12.

36. Thomas L. Friedman, "Three Little Words," *New York Times*, February 11, 1996, p. E15.

37. Cited in Arthur M. Schlesinger, Jr., *The Cycles of American History* (Boston: Houghton, Mifflin, 1986), p. 54.

Chapter 12

U.S.-Africa Policy:
Promoting Conflict Management in
Uncertain Times

Donald Rothchild and Timothy Sisk

With the ending of the Cold War, and following a bitter experience with humanitarian intervention in Somalia and the difficulties of complex emergencies such as Rwanda, American policymakers have retreated further than before from an involvement in the continent's affairs. Whereas the Cold War mobilized the United States for a global struggle to contain the expansion of Soviet influence in the region—leading to the subordination of African issues to an all-encompassing East-West confrontation—the post–Cold War environment has been marked by a broadened agenda and by lower U.S. stakes in the continent's future.[1] As Africa becomes increasingly marginalized in the global economy, the incentives for U.S. engagement continue to diminish.

Donald Rothchild is professor of political science at the University of California, Davis. He has been a member of the faculty at universities in Uganda, Kenya, Zambia, and Ghana. His books include Racial Bargaining in Independent Kenya *(Oxford University Press, 1973),* Scarcity, Choice, and Public Policy in Middle Africa, *co-authored with Robert L. Curry, Jr. (University of California Press, 1978), and* Politics and Society in Contemporary Africa, *co-authored with Naomi Chazan, Robert Mortimer, and John Ravenhill (Lynne Rienner and Macmillan, 1992). His most recent edited works are* Africa in World Politics, *co-edited with John W. Harbeson (Westview, 1995), and* Africa in the New International Order: Rethinking State Sovereignty and Regional Security, *co-edited with Edmond J. Keller (Lynne Rienner, 1996), and he has been co-editor and contributing author of the four previous* Eagle *volumes. He is now completing a book entitled* Pressures and Incentives for Cooperation: The Management of Ethnic and Regional Conflicts in Africa.*

Timothy D. Sisk is program officer in the Grant Program at the U.S. Institute of Peace (USIP), a quasi-governmental institution that conducts research and activities to promote international conflict resolution. The author of Democratization in South Africa: The Elusive Social Contract *(Princeton University Press, 1995), he has also written articles for scholarly journals on ethnic conflict and its mitigation. From 1990–1991, Sisk was a Fulbright Scholar in South Africa, where he conducted field research on the negotiated transition from apartheid to majority rule, and he has also been a visiting fellow at the Norwegian Nobel Institute in Oslo, Norway.*

Given Republican control of Congress following the 1994 mid-term elections, domestic constraints on spending have combined with greater reluctance to become militarily engaged abroad. This has resulted in changing United States relations with the African countries, changes symbolized by caution, pragmatism, and inaction. "In countries such as the United States," National Security Adviser Anthony Lake warned Organization of African Unity (OAU) officials in late 1994, "those of us who recognize the importance of continued active engagement and support for Africa are confronting the reality of shrinking resources and an honest skepticism about the return on our investments in peacekeeping and development."[2] A spirit of "Afro-pessimism," the belief that little can be done by the United States to alter perceived deteriorating political and economic conditions in Africa, seems undeniable at this juncture.[3]

United States Interests in Africa

This perception of "Afro-pessimism," however, undermines joint U.S.-African problem-solving initiatives that are desperately needed at this time. Realism, which is grounded on national self-interest, nonetheless justifies a continued U.S. concern with Africa's fate. Africa's leaders recognize that they must shoulder the primary responsibility for building Africa's stability, liberty, and development; however, given the dimensions of the challenge, it is only natural that they look to the international community for encouragement and support and to the United States as the unrivaled global power in the post–Cold War order.[4] What American national interests exist in Africa? What course can African leaders expect U.S. policymakers to follow in pursuit of these interests?

The Clinton administration, emphasizing the need for American engagement and leadership in the post–Cold War world, stresses that U.S. involvement in global affairs "must be carefully tailored to serve our interests and priorities."[5] The three components of this national strategy include enhancing U.S. security, promoting prosperity at home, and facilitating democracy. With respect to Africa, American national interests on the continent are often overlooked. The United States has real, albeit limited, interests on the continent. High on the list are such objectives as promoting global stability, encouraging trade and investment, securing a continuing supply of raw materials, and encouraging Africa's economic development; other important U.S. objectives in Africa include facilitating an end to civil wars and regional conflicts, backing experiments with more open and accountable political systems, furthering human rights as well as racial and ethnic justice, containing population increase at reasonable levels, ending the destruction of forests, coping with famine and refugees, and dealing with such health-related issues as the spread of diseases (among others, AIDS).

These interests are interrelated: sustained stability depends on Africa's economic development, which requires attention to the processes of conflict management and effective governance. As a 1994 Clinton administration strategy statement maintained: "All of America's strategic interests—from promoting prosperity at home to checking global threats abroad before they threaten our territory—are served by enlarging the community of democratic and free market nations."[6] In this regard, democracy is viewed as a conflict management strategy that reconciles a responsive and effective state with a vibrant civil society, thereby providing a political foundation upon which economic development and improved trade and investment ties can be built.[7] The essential premise behind a strategy that promotes conflict management as a prerequisite for other foreign policy objectives was articulated in a 1991 U.S. Agency for International Development policy document: "When political systems falter, and there is violent civil conflict, military usurpation of political power, and arbitrary and unresponsive government, economic and social development cannot be sustained."[8]

Moreover, in terms of creating new opportunities for promoting American trade and investment in the future, the United States cannot expect to gain access for its exports in markets abroad unless it heeds the current economic and social development needs of the African continent. The administration, pressed by congressional opponents to make the case for continued assistance to Africa on the basis of U.S. interests—not on African needs or on U.S. values—has attempted to respond. J. Brian Atwood, the administrator of the Agency for International Development, has argued:

> Is a continent of half a billion people worth one-half of one-tenth of one percent of the federal budget, which is what we now spend on it? Is the three dollars and change that each American family pays each year to help several dozen sub-Saharan nations a burden worth the price? Of course it is. It's a good deal for Americans. Our aid to Africa is not welfare, nor is it charity. It is an investment we make in our people for our own self-interest. How do we build markets? The answer is simple: we do it by making investments for the future.[9]

Clearly, the thrust of such commitments is contrary to any new cycle of isolationism. As William Schneider has maintained, a sentiment of "populist isolationism" has never really died in the United States, for a strong current of domestic opinion views many American initiatives abroad as wasteful and unappreciated.[10] Such isolationist sentiments seem likely to grow as the twenty-first century approaches, accompanied by hard times for many at home and an increasingly complex and uncertain political, economic, and social environment abroad.

In these circumstances, it is critically important that any administration with a policy of global engagement build a domestic constituency that will enable it to offer vigorous leadership on three important and interrelated issues currently affecting Africa—the diplomacy of conflict management, promotion of democratization and respect for human rights, and economic development—which, taken together, is the main focus of this chapter. Pointing eloquently to the shared fates that unites Africa with the United States, President Clinton asked all Americans at the White House Conference on Africa of June 1994 "to help us to develop an American constituency for Africa that creates lasting links between our people and their peoples and that will not only help to drive the continent ahead but will help to drive a meaningful, sustained agenda here at home."[11] Clinton's realism lies in recognizing global interdependence and promoting an active commitment to deal with Africa's main political, social, and economic challenges in the years ahead. Certainly, as Thomas Callaghy and John Ravenhill write, "Africa remains distinctly 'hemmed in' by its problems of decline."[12] Rather than adopt a stance of false despair over what are admittedly difficult problems, the Clinton administration urges the construction of a supporting coalition for a determined assault on Africa's adversities over time.

The Transition from Cold War to Post–Cold War Regimes in Africa

The new African political and economic realities pose major challenges to U.S. policymakers. Although the diminution of Soviet influence did bring an end to the costly and destructive rivalry between the superpowers, there has been little in the way of a peace dividend and little urgency among Western policymakers to reinforce their African interests following the Soviet disengagement. As a result, Africa remains, in Thomas Callaghy's words, "marginalized from the world economy" yet "highly dependent on it."[13] Its aid levels are declining while the demand for its primary products, and consequently the prices for these exports, is falling. John Ravenhill calculates that Africa's share of extra-European Union imports to the European Union in 1992 was 3.2 percent, less than half of the 1980s' level.[14] Of course, interdependence goes beyond economic ties and includes the environmental, humanitarian, and political (stability) connections discussed above; in this regard, the neglect of Africa's economic development overlooks important U.S. interests on the continent, especially the interrelated nature of social and political interests.

Unless the West in general and the United States in particular respond constructively and generously to the current challenges, they may face a backlash in the form of severe political and economic instability, leading to the collapse and fragmentation of states as well as the movement of substantial numbers of refugees across borders. Not only would such a breakdown cause considerable damage to long-term Western interests on the continent, but it would result in a grim and unacceptable world for all to live in. The tragedies in Somalia and Rwanda, which have prompted unprecedented military interventions to relieve suffering and to rescue "failed states," could be a sign of things to come if Africa is forgotten or neglected.[15]

In substantive terms, one cannot help but be struck by the similarity of the two post–Cold War U.S. administrations. Both were committed to an activist global U.S. leadership that sought to promote a stable world in which capitalism could flourish.[16] The outgoing Bush administration differed from the Reagan administration in tending to make African policy more on the basis of pragmatic evaluation than conservative ideology. Not only did Bush seek to develop a bipartisan approach to African issues, but he sought from the outset to pressure the South African government to institute political reforms and thereby to avoid a new battle with Congress on the issue of stiffer economic sanctions to help end apartheid.[17] But Bush's ability to build coalitions and to respond to international crises, which is the hallmark of an effective foreign policy pragmatist, is no substitute for a design for world peace and development (that is, other than maintaining a world safe for capitalist enterprise). The upshot was an administration that could boast of "significant achievements" in Africa (in such areas as conflict resolution, support for democracy and human rights, and assistance in humanitarian crises) but one lacking a coherent plan for structuring the post–Cold War order.[18]

Although more articulate and more prepared to set out policy guidelines on dealing with Africa, President Clinton nonetheless resembles Bush in emphasizing global U.S. leadership in the post–Cold War era. He sought early on in his campaign to set out an activist agenda on democratization, multilateral (especially UN) peacekeeping, and economic advancement in Africa. In an address at Georgetown University on December 12, 1991, Clinton maintained that the United States must align itself "with the rising tide of democracy"; then, after taking office, he expanded on this, describing the fostering of democracy as "our top priority."[19] In contrast to Bush, he regarded an easing of sanctions against South Africa to be premature in mid-1991 and, while praising his predecessors for providing record amounts of aid to Africa, nonetheless criticized the use of that aid to support some corrupt and dictatorial regimes there. Soon after taking office, Clinton called for a reform of aid programs "to ensure that the assistance we provide truly benefits Africans and encourages the development of democratic institutions and free market economies."[20]

Through his first two years in office, Clinton continued to stress the setting of a new agenda, emphasizing the enlargement of democracy, cooperation with the United Nations and the Organization of African Unity in managing conflict, and the reorganization of programs of economic assistance. His approach seemed stronger on policy guidelines than achievement, however. As Richard Joseph, then at the Carter Center, remarked: "Today, the Clinton administration can 'talk the talk' on African democracy as well as anyone. Will it also 'walk the walk' as African regimes back away from their democratic commitments . . . ?"[21] Others have also raised questions about the Clinton team's competence in handling foreign policy matters, even contending that he did not wish to be bothered with foreign policy concerns until they reached crisis proportions.[22]

In an effort to respond to the call at home and abroad for a more effective U.S. leadership on African questions, the Clinton administration invited some 160 political leaders, businessmen, administrators, and academics to a White House Conference on Africa in June 1994. Although nearly postponed because members of the Congressional Black Caucus threatened to boycott the conference in an effort to exert greater influence, it did finally get underway and received reports from its six working groups. These reports dealt with the challenge of global issues, the promotion of sustainable development, Africa's internal conflicts, human rights and democracy, bilateral trade and investment, and the development of an American constituency for Africa. With new crises then building in Nigeria, Zaire, Rwanda, and elsewhere, the conference was a timely effort to promote new American thinking on difficult issues.

Before this Clinton agenda could receive a fair testing, however, his administration was jolted by the Republican party victory in the November 1994 midterm elections. Republicans, advocating extensive disengagement from global commitments, gained a majority in both houses for the first time in 40 years. The signs of retreat on Africa policies were at hand. Only a strenuous effort by the Congressional Black Caucus and other African sympathizers prevented a merger of the House Africa Subcommittee with the Asian and Pacific Subcommittees as the Republican majority implemented its pledge to restructure and streamline Congress. Moreover, in an effort to reduce the costs of government, there was an effort by the newly empowered Republicans to cut the Development Fund for Africa and place curbs on U.S. involvement in international peacekeeping efforts. In such a restrictive environment, a gap between Clinton's plans for Africa and their implementation seem wider than ever. This gap reinforces the conclusion that the United States does not always act as a single unitary actor with regard to foreign policymaking toward Africa.

The remainder of this chapter reviews U.S. policies toward Africa in terms of broadly conceived objectives on conflict management. Toward that end, it focuses on three broad categories: diplomacy, democratization and human rights, and economic development. The prism of conflict management is chosen because it is rightly perceived as a prerequisite for the achievement of other goals such as democratization and economic development. In the first section, attention is given to the management of conflicts in Angola, Namibia, South Africa, Mozambique, Liberia, Rwanda, Burundi, and Sudan, all countries where the United States has been active in a direct mediatory role or is working under the auspices of another government or international organization. The second section examines various dimensions of governance, especially the critically important issues of human rights and democracy. Finally, the section on economic development focuses on foreign aid trends and the relationship between humanitarian assistance, long-term economic development, and conflict management.

Diplomacy and Conflict Management

The Clinton administration's commitment to conflict management has been a relatively consistent one. When Deputy Secretary of State Strobe Talbott toured Africa in October 1994, his main theme was the need for active American engagement in regional peacekeeping efforts on the continent.[23] The following year, National Security Adviser Anthony Lake pointed to "the drain of civil war and ethnic conflict" in Africa and commented on the role that the United States has played in helping to resolve such terrible civil wars.[24] Not only did such internal wars result in frightful suffering and destruction, they also retarded Africa's political and economic development. Scarce resources were misallocated to military activities rather than to the building of a social and economic infrastructure. And, as Lake warned, "the slightest possibility that conflict or civil war will erupt again causes foreign investors to pull out and to stay away."[25] For Americans, the effective management of conflict was a key to preventing the breakdown of Africa's states and to facilitating a return to normality in the event that civil wars occur.

However, the nature of conflict changes where the effort to structure normal rules of relations prove unsuccessful and intermittent fighting and civil war emerges. In such cases, the intervention of a third party often becomes indispensable. A third party has the ability to offer new options and to attempt to alter the preferences of the actors; in addition, it can use its resources to help guarantee the outcome. In this, the United States, with its enormous resource base, is at a favorable vantage point to influence the processes of conflict management. It has done so on numerous occasions. Sometimes it has worked directly with the rival parties (as in Assistant Secretary of State for African Affairs Chester A. Crocker's mediation of the international conflict in Angola and Namibia in the 1980s). More commonly, it has worked indirectly in support of another power (Britain in Zimbabwe, Portugal in the internal negotiations over Angola, or the Italian government and the Catholic Community of Sant'Egidio in the Mozambican negotiations). The United States has also been a major backer of UN monitoring and international mediation in South Africa and UN peacekeeping operations in Angola and Namibia, and has given important encouragement to the unofficial mediation efforts of the Carter Center (for example, in its efforts to end the war between Ethiopia and Eritrea).

International mediation is at best a risky undertaking. The data on civil wars in this century indicate that most wars have ended through military victory or capitulation, not through mediation.[26] Hence, it comes as no surprise that mediated agreements are difficult to hammer out and more likely than settlements based on military victory to break down.[27] Yet despite these odds, U.S. diplomats have been buoyed by their successes in promoting the negotiation and mediation of settlements in southern Africa in the 1980s and 1990s.

The successful mediation of what had been assumed to be a non-negotiable international conflict in Angola and Namibia by Assistant Secretary Crocker in 1988 raised hopes about peaceful transitions to a high point. By 1987, a stalemate had developed on the ground, with the Popular Movement for the Liberation of Angola (MPLA) and its international backers, the Soviet Union and Cuba, pitted against those of the National Union for the Total Independence of Angola (UNITA) and South Africa, with the United States providing UNITA with limited but critically important military equipment (including anti-aircraft and anti-tank missiles). Still hoping for a military victory, Angolan government forces launched a major offensive against the strategically important town of Mavinga, where they encountered stiff resistance from UNITA and South African forces. After further unsuccessful (and very costly) probes, the Angolan army pulled back to its support base at Cuito Cuanavale, where a punishing six-month siege ensued. Although the South Africans could no longer maintain control in the air, their ground units were able to subject the Angolan-Cuban defenders at Cuito Cuanavale to heavy artillery bombardment.[28]

In an effort to overcome the stalemate, Cuba's Fidel Castro responded to Angolan government appeals and enlarged his combat forces there. The Cuban contingents, greatly strengthened, thereupon launched a new offensive in southern Angola, inflicting substantial damage on South African positions in the area. This represented an important turning point in a war that came to seem increasingly costly and unwinnable. When these events converged with increasing superpower pragmatism regarding cooperation in settling regional conflicts, the stage was set for new initiatives at peacemaking.

In this situation, Assistant Secretary Crocker, who had long pursued the goals of Namibia's independence and regional stability, stepped up his efforts to mediate among the combatants. After a series of informal contacts with all the rivals, Crocker began the formal process of exploratory talks with the representatives of the Angolan, Cuban, and South African governments in London in May 1988. In these and subsequent negotiations the parties focused on the specifics of the settlement: a cease-fire, Namibia's independence, the redeployment and withdrawal of Cuban and South African troops from Angola, and the machinery for implementation and verification.[29] After months of hard bargaining and quiet, behind-the-scenes pressure by U.S. and Soviet diplomats, the conferees narrowed the gaps between them on many of the major issues. What stood in the way of a settlement was agreement on the timing of the Cuban withdrawal and verification. Eventually the parties reached a compromise on timing, but agreement on verification required the intervention of the UN Secretary General. Crocker had successfully mediated the *international* (but not the internal) conflict in Angola, preventing any slide down the slippery slope to heightened global tensions.

Other efforts at direct U.S. mediation were to follow. For example, former Assistant Secretary of State for African Affairs Herman Cohen successfully presided over a conference between Ethiopia's caretaker government and the various insurgent movements in London in May 1991 that smoothed the transition to a new regime. This initiative saved the city of Addis Ababa from extensive destruction. Cohen also took an initiative in March 1990 to encourage a cessation of the savage civil war in the Sudan, proposing a cease-fire and disengagement of forces and the convening of a national constitutional conference. Sudanese military authorities were not receptive to the U.S. plan, however. Consequently, with direct mediation efforts encountering resistance, U.S. diplomats turned increasingly to indirect forms of mediatory activity—that is, working behind-the-scenes under the auspices of other state or international organization actors. Such a low profile approach may prove effective in some cases in achieving the larger peacemaking objectives of U.S. policymakers, for it combines the political legitimacy of the private mediator (Carter Center, World Council of Churches); a middle range power; or regional (Economic Community of West African States Ceasefire Monitoring Group), continental (OAU), or global (UN) organizations backed by the economic and strategic resources of the United States. With African sensitivities about Western intervention into the continent's internal affairs still evident, indirect diplomatic efforts are a means of achieving U.S. purposes in collaboration with other politically acceptable lead mediators.

In recent years, indirect mediation has increasingly become the norm. In Angola, for example, with the signing of the 1988 accords and the implementation of the disengagement process, U.S. diplomats focused next on the unresolved internal war between the MPLA-led Angolan government and the UNITA insurgents. Although the great powers' incentives for becoming involved in the internal peace process were less compelling than in the case of the international conflict (with its potential for serious escalation), they nonetheless remained an integral part of the domestic equation. A summit at Gbadolite, Zaire organized by Zairean President, Mobutu Sese Seko, on June 22, 1989 brought about an agreement between the adversaries on a ceasefire and movement toward national reconciliation. This agreement soon collapsed as the parties disagreed over the terms and were generally distrustful about the peace process. Then, a Portuguese-mediated effort, actively supported by the United States and the Soviet Union, resulted in the Bicesse accords of May 1991. General elections were set for late 1992 and provisions on a ceasefire, unified army, and the implementation process were agreed upon. The agreement proved difficult to implement, however, because UNITA's Jonas Savimbi refused to accept the validity of the 1992 election process, and Angola was thrown again into a highly destructive civil war situation.

Although UNITA seized over 70 percent of Angola's territory during the resumed fighting of 1993, the tide turned late in the year as Angolan government forces, resupplied through heavy arms purchases from abroad and by the addition of South African mercenaries, launched a major offensive. UNITA forces retreated into their heartland strongholds and, fearful of a decisive defeat, displayed a new urgency about negotiating peace. As a consequence, UN Special Representative Alioune Blondin Beye, assisted by a U.S. special envoy and others, was able to hammer out the details of the Lusaka Protocol of November 1994. In reaffirming the Bicesse Accords, the Lusaka Protocol set out details on a ceasefire, a second round of presidential elections, demilitarization, and the formation of a unified army and police force. With high levels of distrust evident on both sides, the agreement is inevitably a fragile one. Even so, the pressures of regional actors combined with UN determination to supervise the implementation process and to deploy 7,000 peace observers throughout the country's contested areas raises hopes that the protocol will provide a foundation for normal relations. The Clinton administration, seeking to avoid another "orphaned settlement" like the Bicesse Accords, strongly supported the early 1995 Security Council decision to deploy a much larger peacekeeping force than before to consolidate peace in Angola, despite the mood in Congress for a reduction in U.S. commitments to the United Nations.

Indirect mediatory action also succeeded in Mozambique, where U.S. diplomats worked with private and public Italian mediators to bring an end to the highly destructive war between government forces and the Mozambique National Resistance Movement (Renamo) insurgents. Following an abortive effort by Kenyan and Zimbabwean leaders to mediate the conflict, the rival parties agreed in 1990 to hold talks in Rome under the joint mediation of the Italian government, the Roman Catholic lay organization Sant'Egidio, and the Roman Catholic Archbishop of Beira. The United States played a facilitative role throughout—meeting regularly with the delegations, helping to advance the agenda of the talks, drafting the texts for possible agreement, and sending legal and military experts to Rome to assist in working out the details.[30] The U.S. also agreed to play an active role in the critically important UN-administered implementation process—providing aid in the verifying of the ceasefire and demobilization processes, overseeing the formation of unified military forces, and guiding the economic and social reintegration of refugees and former combatants. This complex and financially costly effort proved rewarding, for in October 1994 millions of Mozambicans turned out and voted peacefully to give the ruling government of President Joaquim Chissano a solid endorsement. Other examples of indirect U.S. mediation can be cited—support for the negotiation process in South Africa, encouragement of the OAU and UN initiatives in Rwanda, assistance to The Economic Community of West African States Monitoring Group (ECOMOG) efforts in Liberia, and backing for Nigerian and the Inter-Governmental Authority on Drought and Desertification (IGADD) mediation of the Sudan conflict.[31] The point seems clear that in the present context the United States can often be more effective in advancing its peace objectives by working under the auspices of other actors than by assuming the lead role. United States leadership remains important, but with its economic interests and "staying power" in decline in Africa, the leverage of U.S. diplomats is not as apparent as in Haiti or Bosnia. Consequently, to achieve results in negotiating settlements in such conflicts as Liberia and Mozambique, it is important for the United States to catalyze the efforts of others. As former Assistant Secretary of State for African Affairs Chester A. Crocker asserts,

> The bottom line remains an American leadership imperative in African peacemaking. Even the invisible kind can make a crucial difference. Compare the unconscionable delays in fielding an upgraded United Nations Mission in Rwanda (MINUAR) peacekeeping operation in Rwanda after the 1994 massacre began with the fielding in a matter of days of the ONUC operation in the Congo (now Zaire) in 1960![32]

Despite substantial achievements in helping to resolve long-running conflicts in southern Africa, U.S. policymakers have encountered increasing domestic opposition to peacekeeping activities. This resistance can be explained by four main factors: (1) the end of Cold War competition, (2) the efforts to reduce the costs of government, (3) uneasiness over major new commitments that might involve substantial U.S. casualties, and (4) a sense of public frustration over the change of attitude among Somalis regarding the U.S. role in protecting food deliveries and maintaining peace in the country. Public opinion polls in October 1993 indicated that 43 percent of Americans wanted a withdrawal of U.S. troops from Somalia in six months.[33]

Reflecting the changing attitudes on peacekeeping, in May 1994 the Clinton administration published Presidential Decision Directive (PDD) 25 calling for a more selective and effective approach toward peacekeeping on the part of the United States and the United Nations. While observing that "UN and other multilateral peace operations will at times offer the best way to prevent, contain or resolve conflicts that could otherwise be more costly and deadly," PDD 25 noted the need to take into consideration such factors as American interests, the existence of a significant threat to international peace and security, the specific objectives of an intervention, and the means to carrying out the mission before supporting a UN undertaking.[34] In 1995, some members of the Republican-controlled Congress introduced the National Security Revitalization Act which cut U.S. contributions to peacekeeping operations significantly and barred U.S. soldiers from serving under foreign commanders except in specific circumstances. The bill, declared Secretary of State Warren Christopher and Secretary of Defense William J. Perry, "would effectively abrogate our treaty obligation to pay our share of the cost of U.N. peacekeeping operations that we have supported in the Security Council."[35]

The cumulative effect of these policy shifts on peacekeeping could be seen in U.S. reticence to support a more active UN and regional organization involvement in crises ranging from Burundi to Liberia. The United States stands largely on the sidelines while many thousands of Sudanese are killed each year. Moreover, in Rwanda, the Clinton administration seemed powerless to stop the waves of genocidal destruction in 1994, unwilling to silence the inflammatory radio broadcasts or to intercede militarily while the frenzied killing was at its peak and over 500,000 lives were lost.[36] Legislation was enacted designating $1.5 million in the fiscal years 1995 through 1998 to provide assistance for strengthening the conflict management capability of the OAU; such support is important, but when a crisis of major importance seems probable, more direct U.S. involvement may become essential.[37]

Promoting Conflict Management Through Democratization

The limitations of peacekeeping in Africa, borne out by the experiences of Somalia and Rwanda, bolster the view that the answer to conflict management on the troubled continent is to promote stable state institutions that can mediate conflicts over the long term. Under the wrong circumstances (for example, applying a winner-take-all electoral system in a deeply divided society), democracy can exacerbate latent conflicts; potentially adverse effects can be avoided, however, by making use of inclusive, power-sharing formulas where appropriate.

The Clinton administration's emphasis on democracy was in part a recognition that, when operating effectively, such a system of governance had great potential for regularizing relations among competing groups in society.[38] Democratic systems bring together strong states and strong societies and encourage the dominant state elite to abide by formal or informal rules on responding to societal claims, accepting the outcome of elections, and being accountable for its actions. Even if such systems do not end conflict, they may make it manageable. In part, the administration has been guided by theories of the "democratic peace," that is, the belief that democracies rarely, if ever, go to war against other democracies. Moreover, democratic elections have been the culminating event in peace processes that emanate from civil wars, as the elections in Namibia, Angola, Mozambique, South Africa, and Ethiopia attest.

Democratic governance has worked smoothly over the years in a number of African countries, for example, Botswana, Senegal, Mauritius and, more recently, Namibia. Yet with the end of the Cold War, external pressures on the lion's share of nondemocratic African states to democratize—or at least adopt more open, transparent forms of "good governance"—have combined with an internal upswell of popular support for more democratic political systems.[39] Beginning in 1989, Western governments and multilateral lending institutions began to impose more stringent forms of conditionality on the disbursement of aid to African states, warning that one reason for economic decline in Africa was poor governance—the personalized nature of rule, human rights violations, overcentralization, a lack of popular participation, and in many cases control of the state by the military.[40] In response to both external and internal pressures, more than 20 African countries held multiparty elections between 1991 and 1994.

Seeking to develop a comprehensive framework for reinforcing internal pressures for democratization, the Agency for International Development (AID) created a new initiative in December 1990 to help promote and consolidate democracy globally. The initiative seeks to strengthen democratic representation and bolster civil society and the free flow of information, support respect for human rights, improve the rule of law and promote better civil-military relations. With regard to Africa, AID's programs have been limited to "picking the winners," that is choosing to assist countries whose combined political and economic reforms are thought likely to succeed, notwithstanding the potential problems that economic reform can have for promoting democracy.[41] Although the United States maintains bilateral aid programs to some 30 African states, most assistance has been channeled to those states in which officials believe it will yield the best returns: Ghana, Uganda, Malawi, Tanzania, South Africa, Mali, Benin, Zambia, Zimbabwe, Madagascar, Mozambique, and Ethiopia.[42] In each of these cases, aid was targeted to support democratic reforms and to bolster moves to more free market-oriented economies. Countries that fail to make substantial progress toward democracy have seen aid levels drop, and in some cases even erstwhile Cold War allies have experienced a decline in aid, such as Kenya, or termination of all assistance programs, such as Zaire.

United States assistance aims at promoting democratic conflict management both at the level of changing state institutions and practices, such as direct assistance for parliamentary or electoral reform, but also at the grassroots level, where assistance has been targeted for shoring up organizations in civil society that can serve to protect newly won liberties over the long term. Specifically, aid programs seek to: strengthen democratic representation through programs to back multiparty elections, improve parliamentary institutions and political parties, educate voters, and support civil society organizations and the press; encourage respect for human rights, including bolstering the status of historically disadvantaged groups such as women and minorities; promote the rule of law through improved judicial procedures; and foster democratic values through public education and leadership training programs. An example of an aid program seeking to encourage political reform is found in Uganda, where after some 25 years of civil war or dictatorship, the country held elections to a constituent assembly in March 1994 that will be responsible for writing a new constitution. Through the Africa Regional Electoral Assistance Fund, AID supported programs to educate voters, train poll watchers and candidates, and provide technical assistance to the Ugandan Election Commission.

The most significant case of backing for a democratic transition, however, was in South Africa, where the United States spent some $35 million on the April 1994 election that brought apartheid to an end and ushered in a nascent democracy. United States assistance was targeted at direct and indirect support of anti-apartheid political movements that had never before participated in elections, as well as voter education programs and election monitoring. The South Africa program also illustrates a broader trend in assistance programs in Africa: the increasing use of nongovernmental organizations (NGOs), both domestic, U.S.-based organizations, and those in the recipient country. Through U.S. bodies such as the National Democratic Institute for International Affairs and the International Republican Institute, as well as some 40 others, U.S. election specialists worked to curtail the potential effects of violence and intimidation on voters, particularly in strife-torn and rural areas. Because earlier assistance to South Africa, beginning in 1984, was not channeled through the white minority government there, but was provided directly to South African organizations, a precedent was set that would also apply to other situations.[43] Throughout Africa, aid will be increasingly provided to fund organizations in civil society, particularly operational NGOs, circumventing normal state-to-state relations regarding development assistance.

South Africa also holds other lessons for U.S. encouragement of democracy in Africa. In some African countries where ethnic differences are especially acute, problems have arisen in the pursuit of democracy because the majoritarian principle can exacerbate tensions between potential winners and losers. With resources scarce and control of the state perceived as critical (because of its ability to distribute revenues), elections can emerge as highly stressful for those who conclude they might be excluded from the centers of political power. Recognizing the potential for insecurity that such exclusion can cause, U.S. diplomats and observers have sometimes urged modifications in the majoritarian principle. These adjustments in the democratic thrust may involve such confidence-building measures as executive power-sharing, constitutional guidelines on proportional budgetary allocations, and decentralization and federalism. Thus in Angola, following the breakdown of the Bicesse accords and the resumption of the civil war in 1992, U.S. State Department officials appeared to reconsider their unwavering support for majoritarian democracy in all contexts. In an effort to back Angola's negotiation process and to prompt the adoption of measures to allay the fears of such politically vulnerable leaders as Jonas Savimbi, U.S. officials voiced quiet support for the use of wide ranging national coalitions.[44] Also, in South Africa, U.S. facilitation of the negotiating process led over time to the backing of proposals for cabinet power-sharing and features of federalism in the new, transitional constitution.[45] United States diplomats also successfully worked behind-the-scenes to pressure recalcitrant political parties, who had threatened to boycott the 1994 election and the post-election power-sharing government, to participate, thereby broadening the base of the coalition and enhancing the stability of the negotiated settlement.

United States efforts to promote political reform in Africa have not always had the apparent success of countries like Uganda or South Africa, however. The United States was active in supporting moves toward free and fair elections in Rwanda and Burundi, where the minority Tutsi ethnic group has long dominated the Hutu majority. When the 1993 election in Burundi produced a victory for the Hutu presidential candidate, members of the Tutsi-dominated military subsequently deposed the president in a coup d'etat in early 1994. Because Burundi has a similar ethnic mix as its neighbor Rwanda, there was and continues to be a tremendous fear that the genocidal instability that erupted in Rwanda would spill over to Burundi. The lesson learned is that democratization, if it fails to take local circumstances adequately into account, may lead to disastrous consequences. Thus the Angolan ambassador to Zimbabwe, by implication, placed some of the responsibility for events in Rwanda on Western countries, for they exerted considerable pressure on Rwandan authorities to adopt democratic forms of governance:

> They wanted to get the Hutu into the power structure, to move them up in the army. All that upset the established order, which had Tutsi at the top. Democracies can work in our countries only if the internal forces are allowed to work without outside manipulation.[46]

Despite a strong preference for democratization, then, U.S. policymakers are likely hereafter to move cautiously toward this objective, displaying a new awareness of the potential dangers of "premature" elections. For this reason, U.S. policymakers seem increasingly inclined to emphasize the broader concept of governance to that of democracy and especially the promotion of elections. In showing a greater sensitivity to local political environments, U.S. officials will be placing primary emphasis on conflict management and power sharing in societies such as Burundi with potentially explosive ethnic relations.

U.S. Development Assistance and Conflict Management

With the linkages between conflict management, political reform, and economic development in mind, U.S. direct bilateral development assistance to Africa has fundamentally changed since the end of the Cold War. During the Cold War, aid was channeled to states that were in a position to support U.S. efforts to contain Soviet influence. Zaire, for example, was a critical factor in the U.S. effort to back the UNITA guerrillas in Angola, and was not surprisingly a primary recipient of aid in the 1970s and 1980s. But times have changed. Likely returns on U.S. investments and the pursuit of long-term stability through democratization have become the critical criteria, and governments like Zaire that have stifled political and economic reform have seen aid programs halted. Countries in which conflict appears to be intractable, or where political instability has made economic development dubious, are unlikely to see significant aid until the situation changes.

A second significant shift in the allocation of economic aid to Africa during the Clinton administration has been the monumental increase in food aid and foreign disaster assistance and rehabilitation. These have been described as "complex emergencies," and Somalia and Rwanda stand as notable examples of such predicaments. As Table 12.1 indicates, while long-term aid has been relatively steady since fiscal

Table 12.1

U.S. Economic Assistance to Africa
FY 1987–1996 (in million dollars)

FY	Development Assistance*	Economic Support Funds	Food Aid†	Foreign Disaster Assistance and Rehabilitation‡	Total
1987	396.2	164.8	400.3	16.6	977.9
1988	572.0	39.7	525.5	37.4	1,174.6
1989	587.5	99.3	385.8	32.3	1,104.9
1990	612.5	28.9	447.6	30.9	1,119.9
1991	826.3	59.3	613.0	40.3	1,538.9
1992	872.4	37.8	935.6	87.6	1,933.4
1993	821.6	22.4	674.3	168.9	1,687.2
1994	826.7	16.1	635.1	139.6	1,617.5
1995 Est.	862.0§	7.5	276.5	31.8	1,177.8
1996 Est.	858.8§	24.5	128.8	TBD	1,010.5

*Includes DFA, DA, Sahel, other OYB transfers.
†Includes Title I, although administered by USDA after 1991. Includes Section 416 and emergency food aid. Includes transport costs for Title II and Section 416, beginning in FY 1985.
‡FY 93 includes $100 million from the African Disaster Assistance account.
§FY 95 and 96 include G Bureau Field Support Attributions.

year 1991, the amount of emergency assistance ballooned in fiscal year 1993 and fiscal year 1994 when the Somalia and Rwanda relief operations reached their peak. For every dollar spent on long-term aid in fiscal year 1993, an additional dollar was spent on short-term relief. It is important to emphasize that the response of the United States to such humanitarian crises is strongly supported by domestic public opinion, propelled by graphic scenes of suffering prominently depicted in the U.S. media. This has led some analysts to express concern that policy priorities toward Africa are "CNN-driven," as opposed to those that are more thoughtfully pursued. Many analysts of Africa decry the perception that policy affecting that continent lurches from crisis to crisis, with little attentiveness to long-term objectives and policy goals.[47]

Equally important is the fact that the emergency food and material aid in "complex emergencies" can sometimes serve to perpetuate conflict conditions. In these "multi-mandate" missions—which involve peacemaking, peacekeeping, disaster assistance, and long-term rehabilitation and reconstruction efforts—the provision of humanitarian assistance has proven to be a dilemma for the United States and the international community as a whole. Sometimes the provision of relief supplies ends up in the hands of combatants, interaction with whom provides a political legitimacy they may not deserve; moreover, the protection of refugees can confer strategic protection from enemy fire on a combatant force. Humanitarian NGOs, with financial and sometimes operational support from the United States (such as logistics) as well as other Western donor states, have become increasingly aware of the possible conflict-prolonging effects of relief. As critics of current practice in multi-mandate relief operations have argued, "Something is terribly wrong in the provision of humanitarian aid, especially to Africa. There is little in the last fifteen years that relief agencies can look back upon with pride. There have been some successes, and some real progress in some areas, but these successes are overshadowed by the failures."[48] Moreover, aid creates dependency, inhibiting Africa's capacity for self-help.

Although total U.S. aid to Africa, at just under $1.2 billion in FY 1995, is only 12 percent of all U.S. foreign assistance, it is often critically important to recipient states. Long-term, or non-disaster assistance, accounts for about half of the total aid package and this assistance, provided through the Development Fund for Africa since 1988, has achieved some success in alleviating poverty. Programs aimed at child survival and health, HIV/AIDS control, population and family planning, basic education, improving agricultural production, and natural resources management have seen some success, particularly in those countries where aid has been linked to opening markets and encouraging competitiveness.[49] United States officials point to Uganda, Mali, Zambia, Malawi, Kenya, Botswana, Ghana, Senegal, and Niger as instances in which U.S. assistance has received demonstrably positive results in these fields.[50] In late May 1994, the United States launched a special initiative for the greater Horn of Africa region (Ethiopia, Somalia, Sudan, Chad, Djibouti, and Eritrea). The purpose of the initiative is to promote conflict management in the region and to encourage agricultural production in the belief that an effort is needed to move away from short-term food assistance and disaster relief programs to sustainable economic development. Indeed, alleviating the underlying causes of violent conflict, such as poverty and its consequences, is the most effective long-term strategy available to U.S. policymakers in this volatile and historically conflict-prone subregion. In this context, the Clinton administration's April 1995 decision to nearly halve food assistance globally—in response to strong domestic pressure to cut foreign aid—will hinder promotion of this strategy.[51]

Increasingly, U.S. economic aid to Africa will be more specifically targeted toward those countries in which the United States has direct trade and investment interests, such as South Africa (identified by the Department of Commerce as one of the ten most promising emerging market economies) and those which have displayed demonstrable progress toward conflict management and democratization.[52] Nothing demonstrates this emerging trend more than the U.S. response to the April 1994 election in South Africa. To show U.S. support for efforts to consolidate democratic conflict management, President Clinton announced a three-year, $600 million aid, trade, and investment package for South Africa on May 5, 1994, more than doubling the previous annual allocation. In fiscal year 1994 (October 1993–September 1994), the U.S. provided $206 million in aid; in subsequent years, a similar level is pledged. The South Africa aid program is controversial as a result of AID's decision to set aside a significant portion of funds—both those to South African and U.S. organizations—for historically disadvantaged groups in the respective countries. Although conceived by AID administrators as part of constituency building among the African-American community in the United States for African development assistance, the aid program's race-preference policies run counter to growing pressure by Republican leaders in Congress to scrap most race-based affirmative action programs in the United States.[53] Annual assistance to South Africa will now be more than all other African countries combined. Interestingly, when U.S. policymakers were searching for budget-neutral ways to finance the fiscal year 1994 aid to South Africa, they reprogrammed funds from other African countries, notably Nigeria, which had witnessed a reversal of the democratization process when its military annulled the results of the June 1993 election.[54]

Conclusions

The end of the Cold War's bipolar era and the successful multilateral intervention to oust Iraq from Kuwait in 1991 led to an initial optimism that a new world order would emerge. This belief lay behind the Bush adminstration's late 1992 decision to unilaterally intervene in Somalia to relieve famine and rebuild the failed Somali state. The passing of the baton to a UN peacekeeping force in early 1993 portended a new pattern of international security and U.S. foreign policy in which initial interventions could be "contracted" to powerful states such as the United States, with the United Nations following to constitute a democratic political order. When, in October 1993, 18 U.S. servicemen deployed in Somalia as part of the UN peacekeeping force died in a fire fight with local combatants—and an American soldier's body was dragged through the streets of the capital Mogadishu, an event covered graphically on television and in the print media—public and policymaker support for U.S. engagement abroad dissipated as quickly as it had earlier emerged.

The Clinton administration recoiled from its activist agenda, pledging that U.S. troops would withdraw from Somalia and adopting new policies, such as PDD 25, that signaled a reduced U.S. commitment to multilateral peacekeeping. The impact of this shift of preferences soon became evident, as America stood on the sidelines while hundreds of thousands of Rwandans (many Tutsi and some moderate Hutu) were massacred by Hutu extremists in the presidential guard and army. By early 1995, with the United Nations unable to forge a new regime in Somalia, the U.S. military played a starkly different role—protecting the rear flank of the UN peacekeepers as they withdrew from Somalia, leaving the Somalis to their own devices.

The Somalia experience illustrates the essential shift of Clinton administration policy toward Africa in the wake of the Cold War: though initially buoyed by the promise of multilateral security and the expectation that democracy could be implanted in even the most unlikely places, the U.S. public now views Africa through the lens of skepticism, caution, and an unwillingness to become actively engaged. Rather than the optimistic outlook of the 1980s, today's fault lines within the U.S. body politic lie between cautious, selective engagement in Africa—with the expectation that the United States can achieve at best mixed results in pursuit of its interests—and complete disengagement from the continent's affairs. Moreover, the uncertainty that characterizes the global order is especially acute with regard to Africa, where events in Rwanda and South Africa send starkly mixed messages about the continent's trajectory.

In this chapter, we have sought to illustrate that conflict management in these times of uncertainty is a prerequisite for the pursuit of U.S. interests in Africa. Where conflict management has been successful, U.S. diplomats have been engaged as mediators and backers of settlements orchestrated largely by others; where conflict management has faltered, it has been a result of enmities that are too deep (e.g., Sudan), diplomatic miscalculations (e.g., Somalia), or disengagement and the neglect of emerging tensions (e.g., Rwanda). Moreover, the thrust of U.S. involvement will be on a more limited scale: seeking to prevent conflicts from escalating into encounters requiring regional or global military responses. The enormity of U.S. official and unofficial efforts to prevent Burundi from becoming "another Rwanda" is reflective of this new emphasis. In this regard, U.S. Ambassador and Permanent Representative for the United Nations Madeleine Albright's trip in early 1996 to Burundi, Rwanda, Angola and Liberia reinforced local perceptions regarding America's continuing commitment to the conflict management processes in these countries and, in the case of Burundi, its support for the UN Secretary General's plan.

In the coming years, U.S. engagement, both diplomatic and in terms of foreign aid, will be tied to promoting stability in areas where the United States has direct trade and investment interests. Neither Cold War concerns, humanitarian impulses, nor the furthering of U.S. values such as democracy will drive U.S. policy toward the continent. New relations will emphasize the importance of trade rather than aid, as Senator Nancy Kassebaum, chair of the Senate Africa Subcommittee, told an assembly of African ambassadors to the United States in early 1995. She said "I [will] work more closely with the American business community to increase awareness and understanding of Africa . . . and [to] review the investment climate in Africa and the effectiveness of federal programs designed to promote the private economic ties of American countries abroad."[55]

The success of this "enlightened interest engagement" approach, of course, is dependent on the ability of domestic constituencies that support ties with Africa—principally business interests, the African-American community, religious organizations, the mainstream media, and development-oriented NGOs—to make the case that U.S. engagement in Africa is in the national interest.[56] This is true irrespective of which party controls the executive branch. As Kassebaum's Senate colleague Mitch McConnell, Foreign Operations Appropriations Subcommittee chairman, asserts, those who control the federal purse do so with an eye on the voters. When explaining his sponsorship of measures to provide aid to the newly independent states of the former U.S.S.R., while at the same time questioning the utility of aid to Africa, McConnell said of ethnic American constituencies that support such aid: "You're talking about real votes in states like Pennsylvania, New Jersey, and New York."[57]

The extent to which the U.S. will continue to be engaged in African affairs in this era of global uncertainty will hinge on the ability of those favoring the enlightened interest position to articulate the clear and unambiguous U.S. interests on the continent, to identify effective policy instruments through which they can be advanced, and to muster the resources required to advance them. Given the constraints under which Africa labors at this time, what is needed is a realistic outlook combined with long-term resolution about clearing away the obstructions to democracy, political stability, and economic development. Although the 1995 Chicago Council of Relations survey found Americans to be increasingly reluctant to shoulder the burdens of international leadership alone and less committed to helping to improve the standard of living of the developing countries, it nonetheless emphasized that Americans have not become isolationist. Despite the recent setback in Somalia, for example, some 51 percent of the public still felt that the United States should be part of a UN peacekeeping force in a troubled part of the world when asked.[58] Hence, there is still scope for an informed, determined, and well-organized effort by Americans concerned with Africa's future to exert an influence on many undecided members of the public; however, in influencing American perceptions at this juncture, they must show that such international involvements manifestly serve U.S. interests at home and abroad.

Endnotes

1. For a discussion of the Cold War agenda, *see* Donald Rothchild and John Ravenhill, "Retreat from Globalism: U.S. Policy Toward Africa in the 1990s," in Kenneth A. Oye, Robert J. Lieber, and Donald Rothchild (eds.), *Eagle in a New World: U.S. Grand Strategy in the Post–Cold War Era* (New York: HarperCollins, 1992), pp. 389–415.

2. Anthony Lake, speech at OAU Headquarters, Addis Ababa, December 15, 1994, as reprinted in "Afro-realism vs. Afro-pessimism," *CSIS Africa Notes*, No. 168 (January 1995): 3.

3. This perception is supported by media reports. *See* the three-part series by John Darton, "Survival Test: Can Africa Rebound?," *New York Times*, June 19, 20, 21, 1994. June 19: "'Lost Decade' Drains Africa's Vitality," p. A2, June 20: "In Poor, Decolonized Africa, Bankers are New Overlords," p. A1, June 21: "Africa Tries Democracy, Finding Hope and Peril," p. A1.

4. *See, for example,* the Kampala Document in Olusegun Obasanjo and Felix G. N. Mosha (eds.), *Africa: Rise to Challenge* (New York: Africa Leadership Forum, 1993), pp. 309–332.

5. President William J. Clinton, "Preface," *A National Security Strategy of Engagement and Enlargement* (Washington, DC: The White House, 1994), p. i.

6. Clinton, *A National Security Strategy*, p. 19.

7. Donald Rothchild, "Structuring State-Society Relations in Africa: Toward an Enabling Political Environment," in Jennifer A. Widner (ed.), *Economic Change and Political Liberalization in Sub-Saharan Africa* (Baltimore: Johns Hopkins University Press, 1994), pp. 201–229.

8. U.S. Agency for International Development, *Democracy and Governance* (Washington, DC: U.S. Agency for International Development, November 1991).

9. Remarks at the "Summit on Africa Aid," Washington, DC, February 3, 1995.

10. William Schneider, "The Old Politics and the New World Order," in Oye, Lieber, and Rothchild (eds.), *Eagle in a New World*, p. 63.

11. President William J. Clinton, address at the White House Conference on Africa, as reprinted in *CSIS Africa Notes*, No. 162 (July 1994): 2.

12. Thomas M. Callaghy and John Ravenhill, "Vision, Politics, and Structure: Afro-Optimism, Afro-Pessimism or Realism?" in Callaghy and Ravenhill (eds.), *Hemmed In: Responses to Africa's Economic Decline* (New York: Columbia University Press, 1993), p. 1.

13. Thomas M. Callaghy, "Africa and the World Political Economy: Still Caught Between a Rock and a Hard Place," in John W. Harbeson and Donald Rothchild (eds.),

Africa in World Politics: Post–Cold War Challenges, 2nd ed. (Boulder, Colo.: Westview Press, 1995), p. 41.

14. John Ravenhill, "Dependent by Default: Africa's Relations with the European Union," in Harbeson and Rothchild (eds.), *Africa in World Politics,* p. 96.

15. *See* I.W. Zartman (ed.), *Collapsed States: The Disintegration and Restoration of Legitimate Authority* (Boulder, Colo.: Lynne Rienner Publishers, 1995).

16. Benjamin Schwarz, "The Vision Thing: Sustaining the Unsustainable," *World Policy Journal,* Vol. 11, No. 4 (Winter 1994/95): 101–121.

17. *Africa Confidential,* Vol. 30, No. 21 (October 20, 1989): 1.

18. George Bush, "The U.S. and Africa: The Republican Record," *Africa Report,* Vol. 37, No. 5 (September/October, 1992): 14.

19. Bill Clinton, "The Democratic Agenda," *Africa Report,* Vol. 37, No. 5 (September/October, 1992): 19.

20. Clinton, "The Democratic Agenda," p. 20.

21. Richard Joseph, "The Clinton Administration and Africa: The Democratic Imperative," *Africa Demos,* Vol. 3, No. 3 (September 1994): 15.

22. Elizabeth Drew, *On the Edge: The Clinton Presidency* (New York: Simon and Schuster, 1994), p. 326.

23. Howard W. French, "In Africa, the U.S. Takes a Back Seat," *New York Times,* October 28, 1994, p. A6.

24. Lake, speeches at OAU Headquarters, Addis Ababa, December 15, 1994 and Lusaka, Zambia, December 19, 1994, as reprinted in "Afro-realism vs. Afro-pessimism," pp. 2 and 5. On this, also *see* Donald Rothchild, "The United States and Conflict Management in Africa," in Harbeson and Rothchild (eds.), *Africa and World Politics,* 2nd ed., pp. 209–233.

25. Lake, speech in Lusaka, "Afro-realism vs. Afro-pessimism," p. 5.

26. Stephen John Stedman, *Peacemaking in Civil War: International Mediation in Zimbabwe, 1974–1980* (Boulder, Colo.: Lynne Rienner Publishers, 1991), p. 15.

27. Roy Licklider, "The Consequences of Negotiated Settlements in Civil Wars, 1945–1993," *American Political Science Review,* Vol. 89, No. 3 (September 1995): 684–685.

28. On the changing balance of military forces, *see* Gillian Gunn, "A Guide to the Intricacies of the Angola-Namibia Negotiations," *CSIS Africa Notes,* No. 90 (September 8, 1988); and Jeffrey Herbst, "The Angola-Namibia Accords: An Early Assessment," in Sergio Diaz-Briquets (ed.), *Cuban Internationalism in Sub-Saharan Africa* (Pittsburgh: Duquesne University Press, 1989), pp. 144–153.

29. For a detailed analysis of the negotiating process, *see* Chester A. Crocker, *High Noon in Southern Africa: Making Peace in a Rough Neighborhood* (New York: W. W. Norton, 1992), Chapters 17 and 18.

30. Cameron Hume, *Ending Mozambique's War* (Washington, DC: U.S. Institute of Peace Press, 1994), pp. 42–44, 87.

31. Francis M. Deng, "Mediating the Sudanese Conflict: A Challenge for the IGADD," *CSIS Africa Notes,* No. 169 (February 1995): 6.

32. Chester A. Crocker, "What Kind of U.S. Role in African Conflict Resolution?" in David R. Smock and Chester A. Crocker (eds.), *African Conflict Resolution: The U.S. Role in Peacemaking* (Washington, DC: U.S. Institute of Peace Press, 1995), p. 126.

33. Steven Kull and Clay Ramsay, *U.S. Public Attitudes on Involvement in Somalia* (College Park, Md.: Program on International Policy Studies, Center for International and Security Studies, University of Maryland, October 26, 1993), p. 3.

34. *The Clinton Administration's Policy on Reforming Multilateral Peace Operations* (May 1994), p. 4. (Typescript copy.)

35. Warren Christopher and William J. Perry, "Foreign Policy, Hamstrung," *New York Times,* February 13, 1995, p. A19.

36. Holly J. Burkhalter, "The Question of Genocide: The Clinton Administration and Rwanda," *World Policy Journal,* Vol. 11, No. 4 (Winter 1994/95): 44–54.

37. *Africa Conflict Resolution Act*, P.L. 103–381.

38. On Clinton administration policies, *see* Larry Diamond, "Promoting Democracy in Africa: U.S. and International Policies in Transition," in Harbeson and Rothchild (eds.), *Africa in World Politics*, pp. 259–261. *See also* Thomas Carothers, "Democracy Promotion Under Clinton," *Washington Quarterly*, Vol. 18, No. 4 (Autumn 1995):13–25.

39. *See* Michael Bratton and Nicholas van de Walle, "Neopatrimonial Regimes and Political Transitions in Africa," *World Politics*, Vol. 46, No. 4 (July 1994): 453–489.

40. *See, for example,* the seminal study by the World Bank, *Sub-Saharan Africa: From Crisis to Sustainable Growth* (Washington, DC: World Bank, 1989), which specifically linked stronger economic performance to democratic decision-making.

41. *See* Jeffrey Herbst, "The Structural Adjustment of Politics in Africa," *World Development*, Vol. 18, No. 7 (1990): 949–958.

42. Specific information on the by-country and by-category allocation of U.S. aid to Africa, *see* the annual "redbook" produced by the U.S. Agency for International Development, "Bureau for Africa: Program and Budget Allocation," most recently published in June 1994.

43. The prohibition on direct state-to-state aid was contained in the Comprehensive Anti-Apartheid Act of 1986, P.L. 98. For further information on the U.S. role in the South African election, *see* Timothy D. Sisk, "A U.S. Perspective of South Africa's 1994 Election," in Andrew Reynolds (ed.), *Election '94 South Africa: The Campaign, Results, and Future Prospects* (New York: St. Martin's Press, 1994), Chapter 9.

44. On the civil war and negotiations in Angola, *see* Donald Rothchild and Caroline Hartzell, "Interstate and Intrastate Negotiations in Angola," in I. William Zartman (ed.), *Elusive Peace: Negotiating an End to Civil Wars* (Washington, DC: Brookings Institution, 1995), pp. 175–203.

45. On the negotiations in South Africa, *see* Timothy D. Sisk, *Democratization in South Africa: The Elusive Social Contract* (Princeton, N.J.: Princeton University Press, 1995); and Thomas Ohlson and Stephen John Stedman with Robert Davies, *The New Is Not Yet Born: Conflict Resolution in Southern Africa* (Washington, DC: Brookings Institution, 1994), pp. 131–188.

46. Quoted in John Darton, "Africa Tries Democracy, Finding Hope and Peril," *New York Times*, June 21, 1994, p. A1.

47. For further information on the issue of "CNN-driven" policy and the need for a longer-term perspective on policy goals, *see* Timothy D. Sisk, "Institutional Capacity-Building for African Conflict Management," in David R. Smock and Chester A. Crocker (eds.), *African Conflict Resolution: The U.S. Role* (Washington, DC: U.S. Institute of Peace Press, 1995), p. 117.

48. Rakiya Omaar and Alex de Waal, "Humanitarianism Unbound? Current Dilemmas Facing Multi-Mandate Relief Operations in Political Emergencies," African Rights Discussion Paper No. 5 (London: African Rights, November 1994), p. 36.

49. *See Africa: Growth Renewed, Hope Rekindled: A Report on the Performance of the Development Fund for Africa, 1988–1992,* (Washington, DC: U.S. Agency for International Development, 1993).

50. *See* the Statement of John F. Hicks, Assistant Administrator of the Bureau for Africa, Agency for International Development, before the Subcommittee on Africa, U.S. House of Representatives, Washington, DC, September 27, 1994.

51. *New York Times*, April 2, 1995, p. 15.

52. As a result of a congressional earmark, outlined in the Africa Conflict Resolution Act of 1994, P.L. 103–381, a portion of U.S. aid will be directly channeled to the conflict management mechanisms of the Organization of African Unity and subregional organizations.

53. Paul Taylor, "Aid to S. Africa Assailed as Tilted Toward Blacks," *Washington Post*, March 27, 1995, pp. A1 and A15.

54. The United States has not taken further steps against Nigeria's military rulers, however, such as freezing the junta's assets in the United States, limiting travel to the

United States, or imposing economic sanctions. With the U.S. economy making extensive use of imports of Nigeria's light sweet crude oil, policymakers are reluctant to make decisions that could result in retaliatory actions by Nigeria.

55. *West Africa*, February 13–19, 1995 p. 231.
56. Regarding the media's views, *see* the *Washington Post* editorial on January 13, 1995, A23.
57. *Congressional Quarterly*, Vol. 52, No. 1, August 6, 1994, p. 2267.
58. John E. Rielly (ed.), *U.S. Public Opinion and U.S. Foreign Policy 1955* (Chicago: Chicago Council on Foreign Relations, 1995), pp. 8 and 18.

Chapter

13

Eagle in the Middle East

Steven L. Spiegel

One of the oddities of the post–Cold War era is that it has reversed many of the tension centers of the Cold War. Thus, areas of former conflict as disparate as South Africa, Central America (especially Nicaragua and El Salvador), the Chinese-Russian frontier, South East Asia, Northern Ireland, and the Arab-Israeli arena have become less conflictual. On the other hand, areas of relative Cold War stability such as the Balkans and the former Soviet Union have deteriorated politically and economically. Seemingly buried ethnic conflicts have resurfaced and sometimes exploded in hostilities and bloodshed. In other regions, including Africa and the Persian Gulf, conflicts that emerged during the Cold War have only intensified.

For U.S. foreign policy, every tension area during the Cold War was a potential arena of confrontation with the U.S.S.R., leading possibly to conflagration. Yet for all the global adversity, during most periods the U.S. focus was hierarchical, beginning with Europe, extending to Asia, and concluding with the Middle East. Not surprisingly, these are the three areas that border upon the massive Soviet Union. Meanwhile U.S. policy-makers sought to maintain the U.S. hegemony over Latin America and to contain Cuba while similarly attempting to prevent sub-Saharan Africa from emerging as a major locus of superpower confrontation. These interests were largely strategic. They involved a global conception of the U.S. place in the world and its role as the primary balance to the Soviet threat.

Steven L. Spiegel is professor of political science at the University of California, Los Angeles. His books include, The Other Arab-Israeli Conflict: Making America's Middle East Policy, from Truman to Reagan *(University of Chicago Press, 1985),* World Politics in a New Era *(Harcourt Brace Publishers, 1995),* Dominance and Diversity: The International Hierarchy *(Little, Brown and Company, 1992),* The International Politics of Regions *(Prentice-Hall, Inc., 1970), written with Louis Cantori. His most recent edited volumes are* Conflict Management in the Middle East *(Westview Press, 1992),* The Arab-Israeli Search for Peace *(L. Rienner Publishers, 1992), and two volumes of* Practical Peacekeeping in the Middle East *(Garland Publishing, 1995), with David Pervin. He is now working on a volume about the Middle East in the post–Cold War era.*

In the new era, the central reliance on deterrence and strategic interests has been reversed by a functional concentration on commerce
and the ability of the United States to compete in a new and more complex international economy. Therefore, the distinction between domestic and foreign policy has been blurred. As President Clinton mused in
late 1995, "The more I stay here and the more time I spend on foreign
policy . . . , the more I become convinced that there is no longer a clear
distinction between what is foreign and domestic . . . because they are
tending to flow together in the global economy."[1]

In terms of regions, this changes the concentration of U.S. interests
toward the North American Free Trade Area (NAFTA), the European
Union (EU), and the emerging Asian economies from Japan to China
and from Vietnam to Singapore. The orientation is toward countries
that can trade, whether as potential competitors or partners. Yet ironically, the Middle East retains its central position as an area of vital U.S.
concern. First, it is an important source of oil, critical to all industrial
economies. The world may currently be awash in oil, but the petrol
peril is ever present—related to a problem of future roots of instability
or scarcity, rather than imminent danger. Ironically, unlike the Cold
War, the region now contains one arena of reducing tensions (encompassing the Arabs and Israel). But it is the center of oil wells, the Persian
Gulf, where hostilities have intensified (focused on Iran and Iraq).

Second, the region is a focal point of the most serious worldwide
danger in the post–Cold War era, the proliferation of weapons of mass
destruction and the means of their delivery. The United States cannot
afford to ignore this peril, especially as it is epitomized by the policies
and the visions of Iran and Iraq.

Finally, there are potential threats to American allies such as Saudi
Arabia, Jordan, Egypt, and Israel from the spread of mass destruction
weaponry or the internal or regional convulsions caused by Islamic fundamentalism and/or domestic extremism.

These interests are reflected in the presence of U.S. troops in the
Gulf, the major U.S. role in the Arab-Israeli peace process, and the huge
attention to ceremonies concluding peace agreements, the Rabin assassination and funeral, and regional meetings such as the anti-terrorism
conference in March 1996. But these engagements mask a confused focus, for Americans are frequently distracted. In the new era, American
preeminence in the region has deepened, but its attention is frequently
diverted elsewhere to such issues as Bosnia and budgets, China and
Chechniya, welfare and medicare, yens and pesos. Without the Cold
War, there is no central theme to organize these disparate problems.

Domestic conflicts, which have traditionally accompanied U.S. policy in the Middle East, have continued, but they have changed. They
now revolve around how active, generous, and passionate the United
States should be, not over whether it should support anti-Communist
Israel or those Arabs who were anti-Soviet. As in so many other con-

texts in the post–Cold War era, U.S. policy is more passive, is certainly in transition, and is heavily influenced by domestic concerns.

We cannot begin to understand the U.S. role in the Middle East today without comparing the Cold War arena in terms of how Americans defined their interests and debated their policies with how the situation is now evolving in a new and more uncertain environment. In both periods, U.S. policies toward the region have been unique in important respects, but the directions and the manifestations of this uniqueness tell us a great deal about U.S. foreign policy in the region and the globe, at home and abroad.

The Old System: The Arab-Israeli Theater

During the Cold War, American policy toward the Middle East was peculiarly consistent from the late 1940s onward.[2] A consensus emerged that U.S. interests were fourfold: First, there was a clearly perceived necessity to contain Soviet expansionism in the area and in particular to prevent Soviet inroads which might have both geo-political and economic implications. Many specialists believed that were the Soviets to gain an expanded foothold in the region, it would have serious implications for Africa and Asia and for possible future control of all or part of the oil fields. Indeed, in the 1960s, when the Soviets had major influence in both Egypt and India, it sometimes seemed as if they were trying to recreate the British Empire.

Second, the United States generally recognized that the oil of the Middle East was critical to the prosperity of the Western world, particularly because of European and Japanese dependence. It was not only oil supplies themselves that were critical but the routes for providing them through waterways and pipelines across the area. Eventually, the United States itself became more dependent on the region's petroleum resources as it began to confront its own depleting supplies, reflected in the energy crisis of the 1970s. The perception of the importance of the area's supplies did not diminish when a worldwide oil glut emerged in the 1980s, although the sense of immediate peril certainly declined.

Third, the United States sought to expand relations with as many Arab states as possible to promote the containment of the Soviet Union and to protect its interest in regional oil supplies and the means of conveying them to the West. It was generally believed that the more Arab states were aligned with the United States through diplomatic and economic ties, the stronger the U.S. position in the region would be.

Finally, the United States developed an interest in protecting Israel's security. This interest had evolved in the 1940s with the establishment of the Jewish state. It found its early origins in the belief that the Jews deserved a country of their own in the wake of their incalculable suffering in the Holocaust, and flourished as a consequence of the shared democratic values between the two countries. The relationship was solidified as a consequence of American-Jewish identification with the fate of their fellow Jews and with the re-establishment of a Jewish state in Palestine. It was also reinforced by the identification of many American Christians with the Holy Land and the possible fulfillment of Old Testament prophecies through the Jewish return to sovereignty.[3] After 1967, when Israeli military success was clearly demonstrated, many began to see Israel as not only a source of humanitarian, democratic, and religious concerns, but also as a strategic asset in the attempt to contain the Soviet Union.

Most engaged Americans agreed that these were America's basic interests in the area, but they often differed bitterly among themselves about the specific policies the United States should pursue to implement those interests. Most of these differences can be summarized as follows: if the Soviets were to be contained and the oil fields protected, how could the United States maintain close relations with both Israel and the Arabs? Yet embracing only Israel was seen as inadequate for promoting the other U.S. interests in the area, and to most Americans, befriending only the Arabs was perceived as unacceptable. Given the hostile and abiding conflict between the Arabs and Israelis who fought seven wars between 1948–1990,[4] mistakes by U.S. policymakers could result in gains by the Kremlin in the area. How to maintain U.S. relations with both the Israelis and Arabs while also protecting U.S. political, diplomatic, and economic interests became the great dilemma of the Cold War in U.S. Mideast policy.

Thus, U.S. Mideast policy was epitomized by a consensus on objectives (i.e., the identity of U.S. interests) and severe differences over tactics. Changes often occurred when new personnel assumed office, especially when new administrations came to power. A range of choice favoring various parties (e.g., conservative Arabs, radical Arab states, and Israelis) were available, and almost every possible combination was tried at some point by one administration or another (e.g., shuttle diplomacy between Arabs and Israelis, a comprehensive accord between them, appointment of UN mediators, and international conferences).[5]

There were general agreements among Americans that resolving the Arab-Israeli conflict would end the dilemmas of U.S. policy in the area. Once the bitter dispute was settled, the U.S. could befriend both sides. Given the extreme tensions between the two, that goal often seemed hopeless. Indeed the quest was made more difficult by Soviet policy. The Kremlin's entrée into the area was based on the shipment of arms. A settlement of the conflict would likely reduce its influence (as indeed happened in Egypt when Sadat decided to move toward a deal with Israel after the October 1973 war). Therefore, the Soviets maintained an extreme diplomatic stance, supporting only the lowest common denominator pro-Arab position, lest their influence in the region be compromised.

Confronted by a deep, bitter dispute and a rarely cooperative super-power opponent, U.S. analysts and policymakers debated endlessly about which alternative directions the United States should take. In an article entitled "Breaking All the Rules: American Debate Over the Middle East," in the journal *International Security*,[6] Daniel Pipes de-scribed the unique dissension over the Middle East that existed in the American polity at the time. He distinguished between liberal and con-servative pro-Arab partisans and liberal and conservative pro-Israeli par-ties. Pro-Arab liberals were primarily concerned with Palestinian refugees after 1948, with so-called Israeli violations of human rights in the territories they occupied after 1967, and with Israeli disputes with the United Nations. They were generally critical of Israel for not mak-ing further concessions and in favor of a Palestinian state. Pro-Arab con-servatives believed that millions of Arabs were more important than the small country of Israel because of the importance of containing the U.S.S.R. in the region and of protecting the oil supplies. Liberal pro-Is-raeli participants in the American political process celebrated Israel's liberal democratic values and government and argued that the main problem in the Middle East was Arab refusal to recognize Israel's right to exist. Conservative pro-Israeli partisans either stressed the signifi-cance of Israel as a strategic asset to the United States or emphasized ties to the Holy Land from a Christian perspective. Of course, the pro-Israeli camp (liberal and conservative) was often—though not always—led by members of the American Jewish community.

All parties tended to cloak their arguments in favor of closer align-ment with the Arabs or the Israelis in terms of justice—who was right in this dispute and which tactics were best for American interests. For example, many bureaucrats argued that U.S. concerns in the area were too important to overemphasize the significance of Israel at the expense of the majority Arabs. Many of Israel's supporters maintained that the United States could have its cake and eat it too, in that conservative Arab regimes had no choice but to align with the United States, no matter how close the special relationship with Israel developed. Emo-tion could mix with analysis because of the lack of clarity in how the United States should resolve its problems. Congress generally pressed in a pro-Israeli direction, especially regarding foreign aid. But on many issues, such as the peace process and diplomacy in general, the State Department often moved on a path more favorable to closer ties to Arab states.

Given these divisions, U.S. policy was often colored by the particu-lar preferences and philosophies of individual presidents and their clos-est aides. Those presidents who had a tough, calculating definition of American interests, stressing oil and/or Soviet containment, tended to be more skeptical of closer ties with Israel and less permissive of its ac-tions, whereas their policies tended to underscore the importance of friendships with the Arabs (Eisenhower, Ford, Bush). Those chief executives who took a more religious or romantic view of the area were more inclined to develop closer ties with Israel (Truman, Johnson, Reagan). Among the presidents who were influenced by a religious perspective, only Carter, who had a grand vision of solving the Arab-Israeli dispute, especially resolving the Palestinian plight, took a more harsh perspective toward the Israelis. Two presidents, Kennedy and Nixon, assumed a more pragmatic attitude, wavering between developing a stronger relationship with Israel and emphasizing the importance of Arab states to U.S. interests. Often during these administrations two policies were pursued simultaneously with confusing signals conveyed to all involved parties, domestic and foreign.[7]

Despite enormous efforts, no administration resolved the dilemmas of U.S. policy because during the Cold War no one could settle the Arab-Israeli dispute except for the separate Egyptian-Israeli agreement. The United States did ultimately win the confrontation with the Soviet Union in the area, however, in large measure because of its willingness to live with the uncertainties of parallel relations with both sides. Even before the U.S.S.R.'s collapse, the U.S. had emerged as the region's preeminent outside power. Since the United States had positive relations with Israel and the major Arab states, both needed Washington's assistance or at least acquiescence if they were to succeed in their objectives toward the other side. In particular, after 1967 the Arab states sought the return of the territory that Israel had captured in that war, but they could not rely solely on the Soviet Union, which had no influence on Israel and had broken diplomatic relations with it as a result of that conflict. The United States's efforts to become engaged with the two sides made it a more valuable ally for both because Washington could serve as an intermediary with the other party in the Arab-Israeli dispute, whereas the Soviets were merely partisans. Indeed, the Egyptian-Israeli peace treaty, signed on the White House lawn in March 1979, served to confirm the advantage of America's ability to deal with both sides and the benefits for the United States of an Arab-Israeli settlement.

The advantages of seeking positive relations with as many countries as possible in the area are only clear in hindsight, however. During the Cold War, many U.S. analysts believed that from any strict calculus of material interests the Arabs clearly had the advantage: oil, population, connections to the wider Moslem world. Many thought the Soviets were pursuing the wiser policy in supporting only the Arab side. Those who held these types of views were always arguing that Israel should make more concessions so that the United States's difficulties in the area would be eased. Yet U.S. values and domestic politics would not allow the United States to move in this direction, though at times some leaders did put pressure on Israel. In general, forced to improvise in producing viable policies to deal with both of the feuding parties,

U.S. officials persevered. The result was a series of hard-won successes, and ultimately the U.S. victory in the Cold War was reflected in its dominance in the pursuit of Arab-Israeli peace.

The Old System: The Persian Gulf Subplot

During a good part of the Cold War, both the Persian Gulf and the Arab-Israeli arena were seen as critical to U.S. interests vis à vis the U.S.S.R. The consequence was intense U.S. activity, especially in the mid-1950s and after 1967. In both periods the Persian Gulf generated acute U.S. involvement, because of the uncertain fate of local regimes and the abiding concern for U.S. oil interests. The Gulf never engendered the kind of fervent public dispute that the Arab-Israeli problem raised. United States policy concentrated on containing the Soviet Union and its clients and protecting its own allies in the area. Because the Gulf was the locus of oil reserves in the region, no administration thought it could afford to allow a Soviet victory there. Until 1971 a British military presence helped stabilize the region,[8] although the United States had already become involved to prevent a Soviet threat to Iran in 1946 and to restore the pro-American Shah to power in 1953. It also supported the Baghdad Pact, formed in 1955, a "mini-NATO" sponsored by Britain and including at its height Iraq, Iran, Turkey, and Pakistan. Until 1958, when a coup by radical army officers overthrew the pro-Western regime in Baghdad, both Persian Iran and Arab Iraq were pro-American. In the 1970s, Saudi Arabia and Iran (until the overthrow of the Shah) were treated generously because they were seen as the "twin pillars" of U.S. policy in the area. Indeed, there were some who saw the rise in oil prices after 1973 as a prudent way to aid the Iranians and Saudis in the protection of U.S. interests in the Gulf.

This policy faltered with the Iranian Revolution. After a series of defeats in the area: the accession to power of Ayatollah Khomeini (1979), the Iran hostage crisis (1979–1981), and the Soviet invasion of nearby Afghanistan (1979), President Carter issued a statement (now known as the "Carter Doctrine") that declared that the U.S. guarantee of protection would extend to the Persian Gulf oil sheikdoms.

However, the crisis Americans anticipated in the area did not evolve as had been predicted. Instead of expanding its influence, the Soviet Union soon became bogged down in Afghanistan. Then Iraq attacked Iran in September 1980 in an effort to thwart the spread of the revolution and to grab territory while Iran was engrossed in the aftermath of its internal convulsion. The result was an eight-year war in which the United States gradually and hesitantly "tilted" toward Baghdad, capped by a naval intervention in 1987–1988, ostensibly to protect shipping in the Gulf during the war, but actually intended to thwart a similar Soviet move. The practical impact was to aid Iraq, since the

United States's presence brought it into direct confrontation with Iranian forces and installations in the area.

After the Ayatollah bitterly sued for a ceasefire, U.S. relations with Iraq did not improve as might have been anticipated given the assistance that Saddam Hussein had received. Despite its assistance, Baghdad deeply resented the Reagan administration's willingness to trade arms to Iran in return for its aid in freeing selected U.S. hostages in Lebanon. Tensions also arose over Saddam's use of chemical weapons against his own Kurdish citizens, his increasing bellicosity toward Israel, and his attempt to pressure his Arab benefactors to continue the aid they had bestowed upon him during the war. As the Cold War was ending in 1990, Saddam became ever more aggressive, culminating in his conquering of Kuwait at the beginning of August, the coalition to counter the aggression organized by President Bush, and the defeat of Saddam in the Persian Gulf War of early 1991.

Even without Soviet interference, the United States had for the first time been confronted by a power, Saddam's Iraq, which seemed to seriously threaten the key oil fields in Saudi Arabia. Washington had demonstrated that it would act forcefully to counter any such peril, but at the end of the Cold War only militarily weak Saudi Arabia and its even weaker Gulf partners were left as indigenous counterpoints to possible threats. As the Soviet Union collapsed, the two-decade search for a local gendarme in the Persian Gulf had seemingly failed.

The New System: The Arab-Israeli Arena and the Gulf

During the Cold War, then, Americans agreed on their interests and the broad direction of policy in the Middle East (settle the Arab-Israeli dispute and find effective local partners in the Persian Gulf). Enormous disagreement over how to achieve these policies, especially toward the Arabs and Israelis, continued, however.In the post–Cold War era, by contrast, there is less of a consensus on U.S. Middle East interests, a more disparate choice of problems on which to concentrate, less dissension among Americans about what U.S. policy should be, and a larger number of distractions to divert U.S. leaders from the Middle East, especially in the domestic arena.

United States moves no longer have to be calculated in the light of the competition with the U.S.S.R., because the United States is paramount. Arab radicals and potential challengers to the United States have no superpower to which they can turn for aid or for arms assistance and support in case they begin to lose a war. From the mid-1950s onward, the Soviet Union facilitated Arab resistance to Israel's existence and made it possible for Arab states to continually fight wars in the hope of one day conquering the Jewish state. They could operate with the confidence that despite repeated setbacks they would be resupplied with weaponry and provided diplomatic clout by Moscow. This support no longer exists, and therefore new pressure is provided on Arab regimes for possible agreement with Israel.

The Arab states are also weakened because with the end of the Cold War, Israel has been able to break out of its former isolation. For example, in late January 1992 almost 40 percent of the world's population established diplomatic relations with Israel when both China and India formalized diplomatic links with Jerusalem. Israel today is a country whose representatives are welcomed in countries from Latin America to Asia, from East Europe to Africa. The Arab attempt to isolate and boycott Israel failed, creating another Arab incentive to peace. The repeal of the infamous "Zionism is racism" resolution in the UN General Assembly in 1991 is further testimony to the end of that isolation.

During the Cold War there were, oddly enough, limits imposed on both Arabs and Israelis. In any war, the Arab states knew they could be saved by the U.S.S.R., either by diplomatic pressure on Israel, by a Soviet threat to intervene, or by Soviet pressure on the United States to pressure Israel. Therefore, Israel could never totally win any conflict. At the same time, the Arab states knew that if they threatened to destroy the Jewish state, the United States might intervene or take dramatic action. Thus, no war could end definitively because the superpowers might allow defeat of one or more of their clients; they would not permit complete surrender.

Simultaneously, no peace was possible because the Soviet Union insisted on backing the lowest common denominator, anti-Israel, Arab position, strengthening those who would resist peace and frightening those who would accept it. Thus, during the Cold War there could be no total war and no total peace, creating a prevailing situation of constant tension punctuated by occasional wars. The chief exception was the Egyptian-Israeli peace treaty which was accompanied by a switch of alliances by Cairo from Moscow to Washington. Egypt was the only Arab state able to make a separate peace because of its strength, prestige, and size. Countries like Lebanon, Jordan, and Morocco might have been tempted at times to make peace with Israel, but they could not even follow Egypt for fear of retaliation by other Arab states backed by Moscow.

In the post–Cold War period, these limits are gone, which means that there are no restraints on a peace process resulting in complete agreement. In parallel terms, a future Arab-Israeli war might not engage outside powers and could lead to more widespread destruction as the Arabs and Israelis could witness a conflict without referees and without constraints. Such crises, as in Bosnia, Rwanda, and Somalia, demonstrate to both Arabs and Israelis that in the post–Cold War era the great power incentive to save local people is limited indeed.[9]

While oil remains a major factor in American calculations, there is no longer a fear that the Soviet Union will capture the oil fields. Yet Washington retains a persisting concern with the Persian Gulf. The fear of radicalism, epitomized by Iraq and Islamic fundamentalism, led by

Iran, suggest that there are continuing dangers for U.S. interests in the area. Whether the United States can maintain the means to balance both powers in the region in a period of its own declining international commitment may be open to question.[10]

The United States's problem is that after the Persian Gulf War it no longer believes that it can trust either Iraq or Iran. The Saudis, having expended huge sums on both the Iran-Iraq War and the Persian Gulf War, are hardly in a political or military position to become Washington's surrogate. Nor are other Arab countries such as Egypt or Syria either prepared or willing to play the role of regional gendarme. Therefore, in the Persian Gulf, the United States finds itself in the unpleasant position of having to maintain a considerable presence (20,000 troops in late-1995) for which there is little enthusiasm at home.[11] It also faces the possibility of having to increase these troops each time Saddam threatens to re-invade Kuwait, as occurred in 1994. The unpleasant alternative is for the United States to reduce dramatically its military engagement and see both Iran and Iraq (after the lifting of the UN embargo) again re-emerge as local powers. The fear of Soviet control over the area has been replaced by the more likely, but less lethal threat of local domination by regional bullies antagonistic to the United States.

As part of its effort to devise a new post–Cold War policy toward the region, the Clinton administration invented a novel strategy toward the Persian Gulf, dubbed "dual containment."[12] This meant an attempt to constrain both Iran and Iraq, to limit their ability to develop mass destruction weaponry, to constrict their avenues of trade with other countries, and to restrict their influence in the region. The United States had thus come full circle from the early days of the Cold War when both the Iranian and Iraqi governments had been pro-Western. In the 1960s and 1970s a pro-American Iranian government was used to balance off pro-Soviet Iraq. In the 1980s Washington tried with unfortunate results to tilt toward Iraq against Iran. Now the Clinton team tried to oppose both governments, in a policy that demanded U.S. dynamism in a period of reduced U.S. activity.

Dual containment therefore was only partially successful. UN sanctions were maintained against Iraq. United States opposition to Iranian support for terrorism, to Teheran's antagonism to the Arab-Israeli peace process, and to development of nuclear weapons were articulate and unambiguous so that no countries, friend or foe, could misunderstand U.S. policy. Yet the Western industrial powers, China, and Russia all chafed under U.S. restrictions, especially toward Iran, and often ignored them. The policy left no opening for dialogue where it might have made a difference, especially toward Teheran. The containment policy toward the U.S.S.R. always included a negotiation as well as a confrontation component. Toward Iraq the United States had no choice, but toward Iran Washington constricted itself. In large measure, the cautious policy was a consequence of the Iranian hostage crisis and the Iran-Contra affair.

While Americans were not sharply focused on the Persian Gulf during the Clinton era, Iran and Iraq were two of the most unpopular regimes in the world for most Americans. Dual containment may not have been a flexible or innovative strategy diplomatically, but it was certainly a safe, even popular policy at home.

As in so many regions of the world, U.S. interests throughout the Middle East have become more diffuse. The United States seeks to secure oil supplies even in a period of oil glut and even when lower prices prevail. It is also anxious to prevent the spread of Islamic fundamentalism, which encourages terrorism in the area and globally, now including the United States more prominently, as demonstrated in the bombing of the New York Trade Center in February 1993. (Ironically, at the time of the Oklahoma City bombing in 1995, the first inclination of the media was to falsely blame Middle Eastern terrorists for the attack). Islamic fundamentalism also threatens to overthrow regimes friendly to the United States, as has already happened in Iran and the Sudan and could occur in Algeria. In the latter case, however, Washington has attempted to maintain contacts with potential fundamentalist rulers. Yet, the possibility of Egypt, Jordan, or a Palestinian entity being taken over by Islamic fundamentalists fills most American policymakers with dread. Even more than in the effort to contain communism, many see little that the United States can do to prevent these groups from coming to power because the fate of these communities will largely be determined by local conditions. In the one area where the United States could make a difference, the provision of aid that might alleviate the conditions on which Islamic fundamentalism thrives, the American people and its elected representatives seem increasingly reluctant to shoulder the comparatively small burden that this task requires.

In the post–Cold War era the United States confronts an even more frightening peril than the expansion of Islamic fundamentalism: the proliferation of weapons of mass destruction: nuclear, chemical, and biological weapons, as well as the long-range missiles to deliver them.[13] The use of SCUDS by Iraq against Saudi Arabia and Israel during the Persian Gulf War demonstrated this peril in the most dramatic terms. Not only was Iraq acknowledged at the time to possess chemical weapons and SCUDS, upgraded to intermediate range, but it was subsequently discovered to have been much closer to a nuclear option than had been realized by Western intelligence agencies.[14] It was then revealed that Iraq was in the process of developing its own long-range ballistic missile program. Belatedly, when Saddam's son-in-law defected in 1995, Iraq admitted it had possessed biological weapons.[15] Despite the destruction of many of its facilities during the war and the limitations imposed by UN inspectors afterward, Iraq is still suspected to be attempting to revive its mass destruction force. Once the embargo is lifted, a rejuvenated effort is likely. Meanwhile, Iran is also known to be developing a nuclear option.

The possibility of either program succeeding is enhanced by the willingness of many Western companies and both Russia and China to export equipment and technology useful in a mass destruction weaponry program. In particular, Iraq, Iran, Libya, or even a terrorist force could conceivably gain access by illegal means to nuclear material or weaponry that continue to exist in the former Soviet Union. They could be aided by Russian criminal elements or scientists or technicians willing to take funds from radical or unsavory sources. The impact of a fundamentalist, radical, or terrorist acquisition of nuclear wherewithal on Middle East stability would likely be devastating.

It can be argued that the proliferation problem is the most serious issue facing U.S. interests worldwide. It is certainly critical in the Middle East because of the region's proximity to the former U.S.S.R., the instability of the area's politics, and the wealth acquired by many of its players due to the oil trade. Thus, the relatively controlled conflicts during the Cold War have been replaced, especially in the Persian Gulf, by a more apocalyptic peril, the possibility of mass destruction weaponry possessed by radicals, fundamentalists, or terrorists, capable of hitting any country in the area, including Israel, Egypt, Saudi Arabia, or Jordan. Eventually, these revolutionary states could possess missiles capable of reaching Europe as well.

Thus, U.S. interests could now be loosely identified in five parts: oil, Islamic fundamentalism, proliferation, and traditional ties to Israel and friendly Arab states. In 1993 Bill Clinton became the first president to address the changed post–Cold War environment upon entering office. Clinton altered U.S. policy toward the Middle East in subtle ways.[16] First, he transformed American priorities, stressing domestic issues. With the preeminence of all foreign policy issues reduced, the Middle East automatically declined as the focus of attention for key policymakers. Second, Clinton came to office when several new conditions in the area were occurring: the absence of the Soviet threat, the aftermath of the Persian Gulf War and the intensified American military engagement there, and the ongoing Arab-Israeli talks initiated at Madrid in October 1991. Although he still regarded an Arab-Israeli peace settlement as of major importance to U.S. foreign policy, he was prepared to be more passive than his predecessors in promoting that goal. Greater passivity was convenient: it fit the new emphasis on domestic policy and it also might well lead the Arabs and Israelis to intensify their new direct contacts without relying on Washington. As the President stated in March 1994, ". . . my position is . . . that the United States should refrain from intervening in these peace talks between the parties themselves."[17]

Third, Clinton was the first president prepared to coordinate U.S. policy with Israel. Despite the special relationship with the Jewish state, even the most friendly presidents, such as Johnson and Reagan, had kept the United States aloof from Israel in moments of crisis (1967,

1982). Until Clinton, the option of pressuring Israel had always remained on the table. Since the Arabs could not turn to the U.S.S.R. any longer and the world was floating in oil supplies, this president seemed to see no reason why the United States could not celebrate the relationship with Israel without any fear of retaliation. Quite the contrary, the argument could be made that by parading U.S.-Israeli amity, the Arab states would be encouraged to deal directly with Israel without the alternative of U.S. intervention.

These positions promoting direct Arab-Israeli negotiations and a special partnership with Israel were facilitated by the election in June 1992 of an exceptionally flexible Israeli government, led by Yitzhak Rabin. By maintaining a particularly close relationship with Prime Minister Rabin, Clinton telegraphed to the area that the Arab parties could no longer hold out any hope that the United States would force Israel to make major concessions if talks failed. Encouraging pressure on Israel had always been a central tenet of Arab diplomacy. When U.S. governments implicitly (sometimes explicitly) held out the option of pressure on Jerusalem, Arab diplomats were motivated to maneuver the United States into a confrontation with the Jewish state. Now key Arab figures had not only lost the U.S.S.R. as a lever against the United States, but in addition the Clinton administration had cut off the option of coaxing Washington into pressuring Israel.

Clinton's approach was facilitated by several other developments. The lessons of the Persian Gulf War had begun to sink in for both sides. For the Arabs, it demonstrated the fantasy of Arab unity and the reality that an Arab state could threaten the very existence of another sovereign Arab government even though such an attack had hitherto been regarded as impossible. For many regimes, the danger of Islamic fundamentalist takeover is the most difficult challenge they now face. The previously perceived threat from Israel was thereby reduced in seriousness.

At the same time, Israel was forced to confront its inability to counter Iraqi SCUDS falling on its territory. The potential danger to the survival of the Jewish state from Palestinian terrorism was placed in perspective, highlighting the greater perils to be faced from long-range mass destruction weaponry, especially from Iraq or Iran. Damascus also possessed missiles and chemical weapons, but it did not have a serious nuclear weapons program. Its greater proximity by comparison with Iraq and Iran also meant that the destruction Israel could inflict on Syria was far greater, and therefore Israel's deterrent was inherently more powerful. Thus, the Persian Gulf War made the dangers of persisting in the familiar Arab-Israeli confrontation clear to many participants on both sides.

Reinforcing these attitudes, the new Rabin government's diplomatic flexibility enhanced the prospects for some kind of breakthrough in the negotiations that the Madrid conference had spawned. Moreover, some Arab leaders could see that their primary hope of success with Israel lay in taking advantage of the new administration. Several key Arab parties had demonstrated considerable stability. Jordan's King Hussein became king in 1952, Yasser Arafat took over the PLO in 1969, and Hafez Assad became president of Syria in 1971. These three aging veterans had the experience and the prestige to make peace with Israel and the incentive, given changing world conditions and their longevity in power.

All of these factors contributed to the new post–Cold War environment: Clinton's emphasis on domestic problems, his willingness to pursue a new partnership with Israel, the impact of the collapse of the Soviet Union and the lessons of the Persian Gulf War, and the peculiar combination of a new Israeli government and old Arab regimes. Yet in explaining the post–Cold War revolution in the Arab-Israeli theater of the Middle East one other dimension must be addressed: the influence of a new global economic order on the region and the behavior patterns with which it is accompanied.

Clinton's strategy reiterated that a new world order replacing the Cold War would be oriented toward economic means of competition and interchange. This process is epitomized by the North American Free Trade Agreement, the European Union, and the newly industrialized countries of Asia. An emphasis on economic advancement is the lingua franca of this new system. The dollar, the yen, and the mark have understandably replaced the tank, the jet, and the aircraft carrier as the primary means of international influence. Fluctuations in exchange rates justifiably attract more attention than changes in great power arsenals.[18]

These new trends emphasized by Clinton have important implications for the Middle East. States mired in internal or international conflict find themselves further behind the economic leaders of international affairs. Unless the Arabs and the Israelis are able to adjust their economies from a military orientation and find a niche in the new global economy, they risk being left behind. Israel's growing economy is testimony to the advantages of reorientation. The peace process has helped to create dynamic growth, aided by an influx of Jews from the Soviet Union and foreign investment encouraged by the peace process and the dissipation of the Arab boycott of Israel.

In the light of these overlapping influences, it should not be surprising that the new post–Cold War U.S. foreign policy pursued by the Clinton administration had rapid effects upon Arab-Israeli negotiations. The bilateral talks left by Bush and Baker continued in early 1993, but with little sign of major progress. Instead, one Arab party decided to move positively by pursuing secret talks with the Israelis toward a possible agreement. The identity of the party, the PLO, was astonishing. Since 1967, the Israelis and the Palestine Liberation Organization had been the bitterest of enemies, the PLO's terrorist attacks against Israelis inflaming public opinion and the Israeli occupation of the West Bank and Gaza causing constant strain for Palestinian residents. The two sides did not even recognize each other's right to exist. Yet, in Oslo, Norway a declaration was prepared in mid-1993, which did just that. And in September, Rabin and Arafat shook hands in an emotional ceremony on the White House lawn, signing a Declaration of Principles (DOP), which confirmed their mutual recognition and setting out a five-year program that was designed to lead eventually to settlement of a 100-year-long conflict.

The plan envisioned in Oslo soon suffered from severe delays and unexpected crises. By mid-1994, however, Israel withdrew from the Gaza Strip and from the small town of Jericho on the West Bank. Yasser Arafat was installed as the head of a "Palestinian National Authority" (PNA) in Gaza and Jericho, and the world no longer marveled at regular talks between Arafat and Israeli leaders. Yet, the process had been delayed in no small measure by early disorganization in the PNA, its initial lagging behind on efforts to control extremists and terrorists in its midst, and its early inability to set up procedures that would facilitate foreign assistance for economic reconstruction.

The Palestinians continued to be divided between those who supported Arafat and the peace process and those opposed, including secular radicals and Islamic fundamentalist groups, particularly Hamas and Islamic Jihad. Most of the opponents remained committed to the destruction of Israel. Hence, in an attempt to disrupt the process Moslem extremists perpetrated a series of devastating terrorist attacks, especially suicide bombings against Israeli bus riders. A particularly lethal series of attacks occurred in Jerusalem and Tel Aviv in early 1996. The assaults had several predictable effects: they increased opposition inside Israel to peace efforts, frequently led to Israeli-Palestinian talks in progress being temporarily suspended, almost always convinced the Israeli government to bar Palestinian workers temporarily from entering Israel, and led to intensified Israeli calls for Arafat to crack down harder on suspected terrorists within the territories he controlled.

Although the Israeli Labor government believed it had no choice given an outraged public opinion, closing the border to Palestinians worsened their economic conditions, thereby making it harder for Arafat to gain support for his policies. Labor, however, was also facing severe opposition, especially from settlers on the West Bank who sought to stop the process by vociferous protest and demonstrations, civil disobedience, and even violence. Although acts of terrorism by Jews were rare, in one case in February 1994 one settler massacred 29 Muslims praying in the mosque of the Tomb of the Patriarchs in Hebron.

While the number of terrorist attacks against Israel declined after the signing of the Declaration of Principles between Israel and the PLO, the number of casualties increased because suicide bombings proved so devastating.[19] Extremists on both sides recognized that derailing the peace process would allow them to continue with their goals of destroying Israel or retaining Israeli control of the West Bank. Thus, one result of the DOP was a new conflict within the internal polities of both the Palestinians and the Israelis, in which those who supported the peace process were in constant conflict with those opposed.

Despite this concerted opposition on both sides, Israel and the PLO did manage to move to a next round in a 400-page accord reached in September 1995 and again signed in Washington by Rabin and Arafat. Under this pact, Israel agreed to withdraw from the major towns of the West Bank, 450-odd villages gained Palestinian management, and Israel retained control over the settlements and unpopulated areas. Successfully conducted Palestinian elections for a governing council and a leader of the Palestinian National Authority were held in January 1996 after Israel withdrew from six major towns. These elections, which proved to be a major victory for Yasser Arafat, were the first ever in Palestinian history, producing a legitimately agreed Palestinian leadership for the first time. After the Palestine National Council voted to delete from its covenant clauses which denied Israel's right to exist, the two sides began final status negotiations in May 1996 to conclude a permanent settlement three years later, which would decide such immensely controversial issues as whether or not an independent Palestinian state would be created, what the borders would be, and the future disposition of Jerusalem. In the Middle East, however, deadlines are almost never met, so the negotiations could well continue into the next century.

The agreements between Israel and the Palestinians did allow a cover for other Arab states to move toward peace with Israel. Despite bitter Syrian opposition, several North African and Gulf states began to establish diplomatic contacts with Israelis. Public meetings occurred with leaders in several of these countries, and Israelis were acknowledged to have visited them. Some countries, including Oman, Bahrain, Qatar, Tunisia and Morocco, even hosted meetings in a series of multilateral conferences held after the October 1991 Madrid conference on the subjects of arms control, environment, water, economic development, and refugees. Morocco, Mauritania and Tunisia established interest sections with Israel, a step just short of formal diplomatic relations. Qatar and Oman made moves toward ties with the Jewish state. The terrorist attacks against Israel in early 1996 caused several Arab governments, especially Saudi Arabia, to step up their public dealings with Israel at an anti-terrorist, pro-peace process conference in Egypt. Beginning in Casablanca in 1994, an annual economic conference was established for business people and diplomats to meet, exchange ideas, and make deals. A second meeting was held in Oman in 1995; a third was scheduled for Cairo in 1996, and a fourth in Qatar in 1997. This proliferation of meetings and willingness to schedule them two years in advance suggest a degree of confidence and routinization in the process.

An even more consequential development for Israel as a result of the DOP, however, occurred in relations with Jordan. A peace treaty was signed between Amman and Jerusalem in October 1994 and particularly warm relations between Jordan and Israel ensued. Closer ties emerged than had ever existed between Cairo and Jerusalem, perhaps because the peace treaty had evolved from years of direct interchanges between officials of the two sides.

In all of the new contacts between Israel and Arab states, the United States was surprisingly in the background. Negotiations were concluded in high level, largely secret negotiations between the two parties themselves. The actual ceremonial events were witnessed by President Clinton, either at the White House, or in the case of the Jordan peace treaty, in an event on the border between the two countries. Thus, the American role had been transformed from mediator and partner, as had been the case in earlier years, to sponsor and supervisor in the Clinton era. In this capacity, the President co-chaired with Egypt's President Mubarak the March 1996 anti-terrorism conference.

Only in the negotiations between Israel and Syria, where President Assad refused to accept direct negotiations with Israel, were Americans present and playing their traditional role. Even here, the president and secretary of state were less involved personally than had been the case in previous shuttle negotiations, especially during the 1970s. Assad's discomfort with the less intense U.S. high-level involvement exacerbated the tense negotiations between the two sides. Since he effectively controlled Lebanon, these two countries remained uncomfortably on the sidelines of the new positive bilateral and multilateral processes that had begun in the region. A series of incidents in April 1996 demonstrated the detrimental impact of Syria and Lebanon's outsider status. After the Iranian-backed Hezbollah (Party of God) stepped up attacks in Israel's self-declared security zone in Southern Lebanon and began shelling northern Israeli civilian targets with *Katyusha* rockets, Israel retaliated massively by air to stop the intensified violence. The outcome included a cease-fire brokered by Secretary of State Warren Christopher but only after much Arab bitterness at the destruction caused by the Israeli raids, in particluar an accidental attack which killed approximately 100 civilians who had taken refuge at a UN compound.

Another negative development marring the new post–Cold War atmosphere in the region occurred surprisingly between Cairo and Jerusalem. Egyptian-Israeli relations cooled as the Egyptians raised the profile of Israel's presumed nuclear force and Israel's refusal to sign the Nuclear Nonproliferation Treaty. They also escalated criticism of the Jewish state's negotiating tactics with other Arab parties. Typical of the reduced U.S. role, Washington did not undertake a high-level or concerted effort to reconcile Cairo and Jerusalem. The Clinton administration was active, however, in gaining reluctant Egyptian acquiescence to a renewal of the Nuclear Nonproliferation Treaty in mid-1995, despite Cairo's qualms about continuing Israeli reluctance to sign. Israel maintained that it could not forswear nuclear weapons as long as potential threats from such countries as Iran and Iraq continued.

The most negative development in the process occurred, however, when one of the leaders of the peace efforts, Israeli Prime Minister Yitzhak Rabin, was assassinated in early November 1995. Nothing could perhaps have delineated the new era more poignantly than the killing, perpetuated at point blank range at a peace rally in Tel Aviv, by a religious Jewish law student convinced he was doing God's work and that his action would prevent Israeli withdrawal from the West Bank. Throughout the Cold War, Israelis had united behind the threat to their survival from surrounding Arab states who refused to recognize Israel's right to exist. But this hostility had gradually eroded, epitomized by the peace treaties with Egypt and Jordan and the agreements with the PLO. The post–Cold War world had become more complex, and some Israelis either refused to accept the fact of new Arab policies, the practical wisdom of Rabin's particular deals with the PLO, or his right to relinquish territory some believed had been promised to the Jews by God. The result was the escalation of bitter rhetoric in the Israeli debate, leading ultimately to the Prime Minister's assassination.

President Clinton himself and two former presidents led the largest U.S. delegation to the funeral of a foreign leader in history. It almost seemed as if the emotion, the tension, the drama, the passion and the pathos of the Middle East conflict were telescoped into one moving ceremony also attended by King Hussein of Jordan, President Hosni Mubarak of Egypt, and foreign dignitaries from about eighty other countries. Arafat, barred from the proceedings by security precautions, sent six ministers and later paid a sympathy call on Rabin's widow, Leah. By contrast, President Assad of Syria refused U.S. entreaties that he send her a letter of condolence.

The Israeli tragedy symbolized the new era because it demonstrated that without a grand global conflict, many states could now permit themselves internal domestic confrontations. The increase in range of choice in options was accompanied by bitter disputes, the emergence of extremists, and a resulting political unpredictability that had largely not been experienced during the Cold War. With Rabin's assassination, Americans were left to ponder whether greater U.S. passivity could work in a region like the Middle East and whether the United States's own domestic turmoil any longer permitted the type of diplomatic activism engaging top leaders that could help seal a delicate peace process such as the one that was taking place in the Middle East.

The New System and U.S. Domestic Politics

During the Cold War, there was consensus both globally and toward the Middle East in terms of the aims of U.S. policy, but considerable controversy over U.S. tactics in the region. In the post–Cold War era, by contrast, there are severe differences over what global U.S. foreign policy should be, but consensus on the Middle East in terms of opposition to

Iran and Iraq and support for the peace process and for Israel. Ironically, the U.S. role has been reduced just when or perhaps because there is greater unity of purpose and agreement on tactics in U.S. policy toward the region.

There are several reasons for these changes, certainly at home. Without the communist threat to unify U.S. foreign policy, Americans have turned inward. In the Middle East, the basic dilemmas of choosing between Arabs and Israelis have been replaced by a series of problems: (1) oil, (2) the Arab-Israeli peace process, (3) Islamic fundamentalism, (4) Iran and Iraq, (5) proliferation and how to prevent it. Indeed, this last element of U.S. policy is tied to the United States's relations with the former Soviet Union and efforts to prevent the seepage of Soviet technology and know-how to potential proliferators in the region.

There also remains one other subtle interest for U.S. foreign policy in the Middle East, but it is difficult to recognize and even harder to sell. Instead of containment, the United States seeks subtly to prevent other great powers from emerging who will contest U.S. leadership and possibly threaten stability in the region. Certainly, the enthusiasm of the Chinese, Russians, French, Germans, and Japanese for increased trade with Iran and Iraq is indicative of these possible challenges. The attempt of the French and Russians to supplant the U.S. as mediator in the Lebanon crisis of April 1996 is another.

If a new great power were to emerge in the region, then the danger of increased regional tensions analogous to the Cold War would be reinforced. Radical Arab parties might be tempted to confront Israel, the United States, or other Arab parties by gaining arms and support from the challenger to U.S. dominance, the way they aligned with the Soviet Union during the Cold War. Thus, it is in U.S. interest to promote the current situation, encouraging a peace process in the area among Arabs and Israelis before another major power can materialize in the region. In the Persian Gulf, major support for Iran or Iraq from a new outside power could lead to serious hostilities, even worse than any conflict seen in the region during the Cold War. This policy opposing potential challengers is so subtle that it is extremely difficult to sell in the public domain, especially because discussing it publicly could lead to serious diplomatic problems with one or more of the United States's potential challengers. Instead, as acute crises in the region seem to fade, many Americans are tempted to retreat to an ideological emphasis on support for Israel, which seems in Washington more widespread than ever.

In domestic politics, one of the most astonishing developments of the post–Cold War era is a unique split within the pro-Israeli camp, even as support for that country's relationship with the United States and its promise for U.S. foreign policy has become greater than ever. Most backed the policies of the Labor Party under both the Rabin and Peres administrations. Others were persuaded that the Labor government may have made too many concessions, especially to the PLO, and possibly even endangered Israel's security. This position, of course, was similar to the opposition Likud Party's arguments. It is attractive to many in Congress, especially Republicans, who have taken a tough stance toward Iran and Islamic fundamentalism, as well as a skeptical attitude toward aid for the PLO. For the first time, a significant coalition in Washington composed of conservatives, Likud supporters, as well as some American Jewish political activists has argued that Israel has become too conciliatory toward the Arab states.[20] During the Cold War, this position would have been inconceivable, but now the Arab side is divided, weaker, and seemingly less influential. Jordan has just begun to recover from its support of Saddam Hussein during the Persian Gulf war. Egypt has differed with the United States on such issues as the Nuclear Nonproliferation Treaty and enhancing relations with Israel. The PLO has difficulty overcoming its terrorist past; Syria remains on the State Department list of state sponsors of international terrorism. Saudi Arabia actually has a budget deficit.

Thus, significant moves were developed in the 1990s on Capitol Hill to take one or more of the following steps: (1) recognize Jerusalem as the capital of Israel, instead of waiting until the peace process between Israel and the PLO is completed, (2) end aid to the PLO for not taking sufficient steps required by the Declaration of Principles, (3) limit support for an Israeli-Syrian agreement should one occur. Although Congress did pass additional aid to the PLO after the signing of Oslo II, it also approved legislation by huge margins in both Houses that recognized a united Jerusalem as Israel's capital and required that the U.S. Embassy in Tel Aviv be moved to Jerusalem by May 31, 1999, the end of the three-year PLO-Israeli negotiating period on a permanent settlement. To gain Clinton's acceptance, it provided the president with the means of suspending the action in 1999 but he has to justify it in national security terms.[21]

Even when Jordan concluded a peace treaty, some in Congress were reluctant to forgive the Jordanian debt to the United States. Ironically, many of the conservatives supporting the Likud position in Israel are not prepared to provide foreign aid for those Arab states that support the peace process. By keeping Israel as the major foreign aid recipient along with Egypt, they leave the Israelis dangerously exposed politically in a budget-cutting Washington environment. Thus, many of Israel's friends who were elected in the 1994 Republican revolution are not willing to fund completely all assistance measures that are favored by Israel's supporters, but are enthusiastic over largely ideological positions such as those on Jerusalem and limiting aid to the PLO.

It is reflective of the post–Cold War era that the issues are less clear and more intricate. A symbiotic relationship between Israeli and American politics has developed, which is unique in the history of U.S. policy toward the Arab-Israeli dispute. Congress, especially representatives of the party out of the White House, traditionally criticized all administrations for being insufficiently supportive of Israel. Now, a subtle alliance has arisen after the Gingrich revolution between Likud and the Republicans on the one hand and Labor and the Democrats on the other, leading to a division among Jewish and pro-Israel partisans. At the same time, the State Department has now emerged as a more sympathetic agency on Israel issues, and key players have pursued a more supportive policy.

One factor in Washington politics remains consistent. As in the Cold War, so in the Clinton era, the president sets the tone. Clinton's insistence on a close relationship with Israel clearly permeates his administration. It will take a longer period to determine if past trends will be altered in the post–Cold War era. Yet some changes are already materializing. During the Cold War presidents primarily determined tactics, but now they can help delineate the United States's definition of its interests in the region. They now decide priorities and even issues (proliferation versus oil versus opposition to Islamic fundamentalism and terrorism versus American involvement in the peace process). Which issues are to emerge and how U.S. interests are defined are now up for grabs. Hence the president today has more latitude than during the Cold War because the consensus on support for Israel and the peace process is broader and less clear. The president can thus play an even greater role in defining the direction of U.S. policy than earlier. If even Israel's supporters are divided among themselves, the president has increased leverage.

Changes in domestic politics also make a greater difference than in the previous period. The election of a new Likud government under Benjamin Netanyahu in May 1996, despite obvious support for Shimon Peres by the Clinton administration is a dramatic example. If the new Likund administration is perceived as impeding the peace process, or one or more key Arab states becomes fundamentalist, or a different president were to occupy the oval office, previous patterns in the U.S. relationship toward the region could reappear. In relations with Israel, the subtle tensions sometimes present during the Cold War could resume. In relations with Arabs, U.S. leaders could again begin to fear their oil leverage or their relations with other great powers. Concern over the possible spread of fundamentalism could lead to preoccupation with the political preferences of particular nonfundamentalist Arab states.

The assassination of Prime Minister Rabin also demonstrates that in the post–Cold War era domestic politics in different countries are intricately intertwined. All of Israel's Arab neighbors were forced to adjust to the event. In the United States, symbolically, Senate Majority Leader Robert Dole and Speaker Newt Gingrich both accompanied Clinton to the Rabin funeral. The temporary political decline of the Likud in the wake of the assassination made moves in Congress skeptical of the Peres government more difficult for several weeks. But, eventually, differences between those who advocated views closer to Likud or Labor resumed. Whether or not a new pattern had been established epitomized by conflicts among Israel's previously unified supporters would be determined by the domestic debate on peace in both countries and the results of the 1996 elections in the United States and Israel for both a legislature and an executive.

Domestic politics dominate U.S. Mideast policy as never before, because the direction of policy is less clear and less urgent. Even more than during the Cold War, then, the identity of the president and his chief advisors, the priorities of his administration, and how he defines U.S. foreign policy will determine the nature of that policy in the Middle East. Approaching the twenty-first century, the United States confronts a peculiar combination of old and new problems in the Middle East. Washington's flexibility has increased after the Cold War; the gravity of the issues is still profound.

Endnotes

1. Jim Mann, *Clinton Struggling to Shape Foreign Policy and America's Place in World* (Los Angeles Times, October2, 1995); p. A5.
2. *See* Steven L. Spiegel, *The Other Arab-Israeli Conflict* (Chicago: Chicago Press, 1985); William Quandt, *Peace Process* (Washington, DC: Brookings Institute, 1993); and David Schoenbaum, *The United States and the State of Israel* (New York: Oxford University Press, 1993).
3. For discussion of these issues, *see* Peter Grose, *Israel in the Mind of America* (New York: Alfred A. Knopf, 1983).
4. The number is seven because the *intifada*, the Palestinian uprising against the Israeli occupation, which began in December 1987, is included.
5. This background is covered in: Spiegel, *The Other Arab-Israeli Conflict*; Quandt, *Peace Process*; and Schoenbaum, *The United States and the State of Israel*.
6. Daniel Pipes, "Breaking all the Rules: American Debate over the Middle East," *International Security* Vol. 9, No. 2 (Fall 1984): 124–150.
7. Spiegel, *The Other Arab-Israeli Conflict*;Quandt, *Peace Process*; and Schoenbaum, *The United States and the State of Israel*.
8. J.B. Kelly, *Arabia, the Gulf and the West: A Critical View of the Arabs and their Oil Policy* (New York: Basic Books, 1980), pp. 47–103.
9. For more information on U.S. intervention in outside crises, *see*: Mary H. Cooper, "Foreign Policy Burden: Should the US Police the World in the post–Cold War era," *Congressional Quarterly Researcher* Vol. 31, No. 3 (August 20, 1993): 723–743; Richard N. Haass, *Intervention: the Use of American Military Force in the post–Cold War World* (Washington DC: Carnegie Endowment for International Peace, 1994); Arnold Kanter and Linton F. Brooks (eds.), *US Intervention Policy for the post–Cold War World: New Challenges and New Responses* (New York: Norton, 1994); Michael Mandelbaum, "The Reluctance to Intervene," *Foreign Policy*, No. 95 (Summer 1994): 3–18.
10. For further discussion of U.S. interest in the region, *see*: David J. Myers (ed.), *Regional Hegemons: Threat Perception and Strategic Response* (Boulder, Colo.: Westview Press, 1995).
11. Douglas Jehl, "U.S. Ships steam to Persian Gulf in Response to Iraqis," *The New York Times*, January 30, 1996, p. A5; Caryle Murphy, "Engulfed in a War that Won't End . . . ," *Washington Post*, July 30, 1995, p. C2; Norman Kempster, "U.S. Troops Likely to Linger in Gulf as Pressure for a Pullout Eases," *Los Angeles Times*, May

31, 1991; David Lauter, "No Cold War, Bush Free to Move Troops," November 9, 1990, p. A10.)

12. For further discussion of "dual containment," *see* F.G. Gause, "The Illogic of Dual Containment," *Foreign Affairs*, Vol. 73, No. 2 (March–April 1994): 56–66; Martin Indyk, Graham Fuller, Anthony Cordesman, and Phebe Marr, "Symposium on Dual Containment: U.S. Policy Toward Iran and Iraq," *Middle East Policy*, Winter 1994, Vol. 3, No. 1, p. 1; Edward G. Shirley, "The Iran Policy Trap," *Foreign Policy*, Fall, 1994, No. 96, p. 75.

13. For further discussion on proliferation issues, *see*: Ronald J. Bee, *Nuclear Proliferation: The Post–Cold War Challenge* (New York: Foreign Policy Association, 1995); Kenneth W. Waltz and Scott D. Sagan, *The Spread of Nuclear Weapons: A Debate* (New York: W. W. Norton and Company, 1995).

14. Kathleen Bailey, *Doomsday Weapons in the Hands of Many* (Chicago: University of Illinois Press, 1991), pp. 100–111; Frank Barnaby, *How Nuclear Weapons Spread: Nuclear-Weapon Proliferation in the 1990s* (London, New York: Routledge, 1993), pp. 86–93.

15. "Steps Taken Towards Establishing Ongoing Verification System," *UN Chronicle*, Vol. 31, No. 4 (December 1994): 32; Robin Wright and Stanley Meisler, "Baghdad Admits to Larger Program of Deadly Weapons," (*Los Angeles Times*, August 23, 1995), p. 1; Caryle Murphy, "Iraq Provides 'Good Information'," *Washington Post*, August 19, 1992, p. A14.

16. For further discussion on Clinton's foreign policy, *see*: Linda B. Miller, "The Clinton Years: Reinventing US Foreign Policy?" *International Affairs*, Vol. 70, No. 4 (October 1994): 621–634; Richard H. Ullmann, "A Late Recovery." *Foreign Policy*, No. 101 (Winter 1995): 76–79.

17. The United States President, *Public Papers of the President* (Washington, DC: Office of the Federal Register National Archives and Records Administration, 1994), p. 542.

18. Steven L. Spiegel, *World Politics in a New Era* (Fort Worth, Texas: Harcourt Brace College Publishers, 1995). Chapters 7 and 8.

19. Steven L. Spiegel, "Continue the Peace Process? Yes, It's Leading to a New Era," *Middle East Quarterly*, Vol. 2, No. 3 (September 1995): 29–35.

20. For further discussion of Likud and Labor opinions on the peace process, *see*: Ze'ew B. Begin, "The Likud Vision for Israel at Peace," *Foreign Affairs*, Vol. 70 (Fall 1991): 21–35; Avi Shlaim, "Prelude to the Accord: Likud, Labor, and the Palestinians," *Journal of Palestine Studies*, Vol. 23, No. 2 (Winter 1994): 5–19.

21. Jerusalem Embassy Relocation Implementation Act of 1995.

APPENDIX
THE PRECURSOR EAGLES

Eagle Entangled: U.S. Foreign Policy in a Complex World
Edited by Kenneth A. Oye, Donald Rothchild,
Robert J. Lieber (New York: Longman, 1979)

Eagle Defiant: United States Foreign Policy in the 1980s
Edited by Kenneth A. Oye, Robert J. Lieber, Donald Rothchild
(Boston: Little, Brown & Company, 1983)

Eagle Resurgent? The Reagan Era in American Foreign Policy

Edited by Kenneth A. Oye, Robert J. Lieber, Donald Rothchild
(Boston: Little, Brown & Company, 1987)

Eagle in a New World: American Grand Strategy in the Post–Cold War Era
Edited by Kenneth A. Oye, Robert J. Lieber, Donald Rothchild
(New York: HarperCollins, 1992)

14 Retreat From Globalism: U.S. Policy Toward Africa in the 1990s
    Donald Rothchild and John Ravenhill
15 America and the Middle East in the Post–Cold War World
    Barry Rubin

INDEX